TRAVELING TO UNKNOWN PLACES

TRAVELING TO UNKNOWN PLACES

Nineteenth-Century Journeys toward French and American Selfhood

Lloyd Kramer

THE UNIVERSITY OF NORTH CAROLINA PRESS
CHAPEL HILL

This book was published
with the assistance of the
H. Eugene and Lillian Lehman Fund
of the University of North Carolina Press.

Manufactured in the United States of America

Designed by April Leidig
Set in Garamond Premier Pro by Copperline Book Services, Inc.

Cover art © RMN–Grand Palais/Art Resource, NY.

Library of Congress Cataloging-in-Publication Data
Names: Kramer, Lloyd S., author.
Title: Traveling to unknown places : nineteenth-century journeys
toward French and American selfhood / Lloyd Kramer.
Description: Chapel Hill : The University of North Carolina Press, 2024. |
Includes bibliographical references and index.
Identifiers: LCCN 2024020849 | ISBN 9781469682389 (cloth ; alk. paper) |
ISBN 9781469682396 (pbk. ; alk paper) | ISBN 9781469682402 (epub) |
ISBN 9781469682419 (pdf)
Subjects: LCSH: Authors, American—Travel—History—19th century. | Authors,
French—Travel—History—19th century. | Identity (Psychology) | Cultural awareness. |
Influence (Literary, artistic, etc.)—History—19th century. | BISAC: HISTORY /
Modern / 19th Century | TRAVEL / General
Classification: LCC PN760.5 .K73 2024 | DDC 910.4092/313—dc23/eng/20240602
LC record available at https://lccn.loc.gov/2024020849

For Gwynne Pomeroy

CONTENTS

ILLUSTRATIONS

PREFACE

THIS HISTORICAL STUDY of nineteenth-century travelers has emerged from reflections on my own transnational journeys and from conversations with friends who have described the ways in which long journeys affected their lives and identities. These personal and dialogical influences, however, have intersected with my longtime interest in the creative scholarship of cultural and intellectual historians who analyze how human beings use language and ideas to interpret both the everyday experiences of social life and the most abstract philosophical ideals or components of individual self-consciousness.

Among the many subjects within this broad field of historical analysis, I have often focused (as in this book) on questions about how human beings develop and redefine their conceptions of individual selfhood and their connections with wider, collective identities. Such questions carried me into earlier historical research on intellectual exiles in Paris, transnational political cultures during the "Age of the Atlantic Revolutions," and modern European or American nationalisms. This book draws on all these historical themes, but it focuses on eight people whose lives show *how* and *why* travel into previously unknown places can reshape personal or collective identities and the meaning of selfhood.

This book therefore examines multiple, intersecting historical questions. How has the long-enduring process of constructing personal/collective identities and individual selfhood evolved in modern times? And how (more specifically) did these identity-shaping processes change in the century after the American and French Revolutions—when modern American and French identities became increasingly linked to the shaping power of nationalist cultures? In other words, how were nineteenth-century conceptions of identity and selfhood influenced and reshaped through new beliefs in individual human rights, new struggles to abolish slavery and gender hierarchies, new nationalist political ideologies, new Romantic literary cultures, new opportunities for social mobility, new forms of scientific research, and new conceptions of professional or social status after the decline of aristocratic systems of family privilege?

All of these *how* questions lead to *why* and *what* questions about the historical significance of nineteenth-century traveling writers. Historical study often becomes most engaging when it connects the ideas and actions of past people with questions about what people are thinking or doing in our own time. When we ask why people traveled in past eras, for example, or examine human aspirations or fears in other historical periods, we can better recognize how all human lives generate complex, unexpected stories. Travel is one of the experiences we share with people who lived in other eras and cultures, even though we are all making different trips and heading toward our own destinations. Analyzing and thinking with nineteenth-century writers open new perspectives on why we are pursuing our current journeys and what we are doing to construct our twenty-first-century selves. Other people in all past and present cultures give us new knowledge about ourselves whenever we ask new questions about their different lives and experiences.

Each part of this book focuses on specific French and American travelers who lived through the cultural transitions, political conflicts, and economic changes that followed the eighteenth-century transatlantic revolutions and continued to reshape the Atlantic world after 1800. A growing interest in other cultures and in cross-cultural experiences pushed ambitious people in postrevolutionary France and America to set off on long journeys that would redefine the meaning of their collective and personal identities. New descriptions of selfhood thus evolved in a historical context that encouraged or forced thoughtful travelers to rethink their ideas about nationality, language, race, gender, religion, science, professional ambitions, and political "isms" that ranged from conservatism to liberalism and early socialism.

Historians have examined Atlantic world affirmations of national identity and selfhood in all kinds of nineteenth-century institutions, social groups, and personal experiences: political parties and political movements, schools and universities, churches, armies, economic systems, worker associations, and sports, to name only a few examples. This book contributes to the ongoing analysis of how and why that era's political and industrial revolutions reshaped modern identities, but it also asserts that travel experiences and travel writing provide specific examples of how individual lives intersected with these wider historical transitions. Both the common and distinctive expressions of modern selfhood can be seen in the personal experiences of French and American writers who traveled across and beyond the Atlantic world between the 1820s and the 1860s.

Travel was of course only one of the identity-shaping experiences of the nineteenth century (or of any other century), but it offers a microcosm of how nationalism and cross-cultural encounters have continually influenced the creation and meaning of modern selfhood. In most general terms, this book argues that traveling to previously unknown places in other cultures also carries you to previously unknown places within yourself.

The introduction explores broad themes in the history of travel and the construction of human identities, which are then examined through the stories of eight specific travelers in the following sections of the book. Readers who have little or no interest in theories or debates about selfhood, travel literature, and the historical meaning of cross-cultural exchanges may want to skip the middle sections of the introduction and move on to the overview of the eight chapters, the discussion of the travelers' postrevolutionary historical context, and the summary of my own autobiographical context. The more conceptual themes of the introduction, however, connect the book's specific life stories to wider questions about the dialogical construction of modern selfhood and the literary genre of modern travel writing.

ACKNOWLEDGMENTS

THIS BOOK carries the influence and reflects the support of generous people who have provided friendship, insights, and assistance over many years. It began in long-ago personal journeys that took me across Asia and Europe and included later opportunities to live and work in France. Its historical themes have developed in recent years, however, with the help of innumerable conversations at the University of North Carolina at Chapel Hill, with the insights of colleagues in the Triangle Seminars on Intellectual History and French Studies, and with the institutional assistance of fellowships at the National Humanities Center and at UNC's Institute for the Arts and Humanities (IAH). Research support and travel grants from UNC's College of Arts and Sciences, from the UNC history department, and from the George Johnson Award at the IAH have helped me work in Paris, collect research materials in multiple libraries, and discuss various parts of this book at academic conferences in both France and the United States. I have also received outstanding assistance from UNC library staff members who have responded efficiently to every request for help in my search for obscure books and journals.

It would be impossible to list all the individuals who have listened to my ideas, pushed me to expand my historical perspectives, or offered helpful critiques of my evolving narrative, but I want to acknowledge some specific colleagues in the Triangle Intellectual History Seminar and the French Studies seminar, both of which have been meeting for over twenty-five years. These seminars include participants from UNC, Duke University, North Carolina State University, Appalachian State University, Wake Forest University, the National Humanities Center, and other institutions, and I would like to thank these "seminar friends" for their diverse ideas and perspectives: Michael Behrent, James Chappel, Malachai Hacohen, Anthony LaVopa, Emily Levine, Terrence McIntosh, Linda Orr, Susan Pennybacker, Don Reid, Dan Sherman, Jay Smith, Noah Strote, Steven Vincent, David Weinstein, Ellen Welch, and James Winders. These colleagues and many others have joined the conversations in these Triangle seminars during the last two decades and helped me explore innovative recent approaches to historical analysis and research.

This ongoing exchange with well-informed academic experts has thus continually expanded my knowledge of contemporary historical methods, but I have also learned enormously from my long-term involvement with Carolina Public Humanities (CPH). Serving as director of this public outreach program at UNC between 2014 and 2024, I became deeply engaged with people outside the university who are eager to discuss history, literature, philosophy, or other humanistic traditions and to draw on the humanities as they respond to the public conflicts and personal struggles in our diverse modern cultures and social lives. CPH programs connect university faculty with public school teachers, community college partners, lifelong learners, and others throughout North Carolina (and beyond) who are using humanistic knowledge to strengthen public education and to build the civic foundations that sustain a democratic society.

My experiences in working with people who support and promote the "public humanities" have helped me broaden my academic scholarship and rethink how I can affirm the value or meaning of historical knowledge through dialogical conversations. The numerous talented people who have enhanced and supported my engagement with this expanding sphere of public intellectual life include my CPH colleagues Max Owre, Christie Norris, Paul Bonnici, Rachel Schaevitz, Joanna Flynn, Kylie Selzer, Susan Landstrom, Vicki Breeden, Brian Entzminger, and Joe Ritok. They have all made vital contributions to an outward-looking community that believes in the public university's commitment to serving people far beyond campus classrooms and centers of academic research.

The UNC history department faculty and graduate students have long fostered lively discussions that constantly pushed me to participate in new cultural and historical debates. I want to particularly thank my departmental colleagues Lisa Lindsay and John Wood Sweet, however, for inviting me to participate in a valuable conference at the National Humanities Center on biographical approaches to the study of Africans and African Americans who lived in the era of the transatlantic slave system. This conference provided well-researched historical work on the brutal constraints of enslavement as well as expansive conceptual frameworks for analyzing the life experiences of African American travelers, and it led to publication of an earlier version of chapter 6 in an edited volume titled *Biography and the Black Atlantic*. I also appreciated early opportunities to publish portions of chapters 1 and 2 in the journal, *History of European Ideas,* and in a collection edited by Steven Vincent and Alison Klairmont-Lingo, *The Human Tradition in Modern France*. No earlier versions of other chapters or sections of this book have been published elsewhere.

Don Reid contributed his perceptive insights to wide-ranging conversations about my overall argument, and I thank Sally Barbour for her personal and professional perspectives on both the experiential and thematic aspects of specific sections in the narrative. The acquisitions editor with whom I worked at UNC Press, Andrew Winters, offered excellent advice and assistance as the manuscript passed through editorial reviews and as the anonymous readers challenged me to clarify my themes and my rationale for writing about nineteenth-century French and American travelers; and I received other kinds of valuable editorial guidance from Mary Carley Caviness, Julie Bush, and Lindsay Starr. I also thank staff members at the following archives, libraries, and art collections for their assistance in finding images that appear in the book: Alamy Ltd., Art Resource (New York), the Houghton Library at Harvard University, the Jesuit Archives and Research Center (St. Louis), the Mariners' Museum (Newport News, Virginia), the Terra Foundation for American Art (Chicago), the Utah State Historical Society, and the Rare Book Collection in the Wilson Library at UNC.

I have received much-appreciated support and encouragement from generous friends in Paris and Montpellier, including Michelle Fracheboud Bailey, Marie-Carole de Groc, Bernard de Groc, Nancy Green, Eric Penso, and Pascal Surville—all of whom have helped me better understand the diverse meanings of French national identity and the evolving history of French culture. I have continually learned from the insights that each of these friends has shared during countless French meals and conversations. My knowledge of enduring friendships has been enriched in other ways through decades of laughter and travel with a group of musical friends (and their spouses) who are called "The Seersucker Singers." We have shared stories from our experiential and intellectual journeys since our long-ago days at an Indiana high school—and they are still singing, while I can only talk or write about our countless life-changing encounters with people and places that were completely unknown to our teenage selves. I also appreciate the supportive interest of my brother, Wayne Kramer; my sister-in-law, Linda Germany Kramer; and my sister, Alice Kramer Hood; and I thank my imaginative, energetic children, Kyle Pomeroy Kramer and Renee Pomeroy Kramer, for bringing new experiences and people into my life during every phase of my research and writing. Finally, I emphasize my deepest gratitude, respect, and love for Gwynne Pomeroy, whose wisdom, companionship, and adventurous spirit have constantly expanded my own life journey and knowledge in more ways than I could ever explain.

TRAVELING TO UNKNOWN PLACES

INTRODUCTION

Travel, Writing, and Modern Selfhood

Everyone in the modern world travels to unknown places. You understand this experience from your own life because you have gone to new schools, visited previously unfamiliar cities, moved to take new jobs, met family members in distant towns, spent holidays in beautiful natural environments, or crossed borders into foreign countries. Modern people live mobile lives, and almost nobody stays forever in the same location. Travel is therefore one of the most common experiences of modern life, but like every aspect of human culture it has a long history and changes over time.

This book examines the meaning of travel in the life histories of nineteenth-century French and American writers, and it draws on their specific experiences to argue more generally that long journeys have often influenced modern ideas about individual selfhood and national cultures. Travel leads people into disorienting social and cultural encounters that reshape personal and collective identities. New interactions with unfamiliar people, customs, and languages force travelers to become more aware of the ways in which their home culture has deeply influenced their self-understanding and their differences from people in other parts of the world. Voyages into unknown places and languages typically generate anxieties, fears, and frustrations as well as unexpected insights, creative tensions, and personal transformations. "Journeys are the midwives of thought," as Alain de Botton has noted in an interesting reflection on the creative influence of travel. People need a home, of course, but Botton rightly emphasizes that "it is not necessarily at home that we best encounter our true selves," because home "finds us more settled in our expectations."[1]

Botton's broad claim about how travel contributes to new knowledge of "true selves" provides a starting point for a historical journey with travelers who left their homelands for long nineteenth-century voyages. These trips helped ambitious people redefine past identities, recognize identities they could not attain, and reimagine future identities in the home countries from which they had begun their journeys. Although some people can pass through unfamiliar places with no more reflection than they bring to their daily lives at home, historians have become increasingly interested in self-conscious travelers whose cross-cultural stories show why both voluntary and involuntary travel into foreign countries has frequently become a transformative personal and cultural experience. "Travel broadens the mind," the literary scholars Peter Hulme and Tim Youngs argue in the introduction to an important volume on travel writing, "and knowledge of distant places and people often confers status, but travelers sometimes return as different people or do not come back at all."[2]

You may well understand these effects of travel from your own journeys and returns, but I want to expand the historical framework for thinking about travel by opening a dialogue with traveling writers who went back to their nineteenth-century nations as "different people" or finally did "not come back at all." Dialogical engagement with long-deceased writers needs a historian (or a "discussion leader"), but intellectually productive dialogues also require an enduring respect for the otherness of people who lived in the past as well as a self-conscious recognition of the social contexts and personal experiences that shaped the historian's own entry into the dialogue.

Travelers leave home with very different resources and motives. They might be refugees who are fleeing wars or political repression, workers who are enslaved or forced to migrate, soldiers or sailors who are sent to foreign wars and military bases, or children or spouses whose families force them to go where they do not want to live. Travel, in short, can be a very unfree social or personal transition, and it can become part of traumatic, life-changing events that go far beyond the disorientations of a long foreign trip: battlefield violence, prolonged imprisonments, or a health-shattering car accident.

Narratives about such unwanted travel experiences thus differ from most of the texts that constitute the genre of "travel literature," though forced or unwanted journeys also lead to unexpected transformations and new personal identities. The influences or effects of involuntary and voluntary travel evolve through a spectrum of experiences rather than through a stark dichotomy of "compelled" versus "freely chosen" social actions. The travelers whose stories appear in the following chapters, however, mostly embody or describe the desires and freedom of "voluntary" travel choices, even when they were struggling to escape from precarious home-country positions within the reigning racial and gender hierarchies.

Most modern writers have viewed self-willed travel as an experience and symbol of freedom and escape. Journeys suggest a departure from family constraints and hometown mores, or a break from obstacles to professional and social advancement, or a flight from the emotional pains of a broken relationship, or a pathway to status-enhancing expertise in science, literature, or religion. Nineteenth-century French and American travelers—like voluntary travelers in other eras and cultures—made long journeys for all of these reasons, and they found even more goals or ambitions as they wrote about what they had learned in other cultures.

The social motives for travel expanded as the cultural meanings of the experience evolved from the "Grand Tour" of eighteenth-century European male aristocrats into the journeys of bourgeois men and women during the early nineteenth century. "Tourist" and "tourism" emerged as new English words around this time, denoting a new kind of traveler whose interests focused on pleasures or personal adventures that bypassed the search for cultural enrichment. Where "cultural travelers" visited cathedrals, museums, and edifying historical sites, "recreational tourists" liked to visit the best restaurants, casinos, health spas, or mountain trails. New guidebooks provided the requisite information for the (mostly male) travelers who preferred contemporary pleasures over self-improving tours of classical art collections. There were also numerous "reform" travelers who crossed the Atlantic in both directions to learn about schools, asylums, prisons, hospitals, or labor practices that might become models for home-country social reforms.[3] Travelers seeking all kinds of cultural education, personal pleasure, and social reform nevertheless shared a belief that modern travel was the self-chosen activity of free persons.

This emphasis on personal freedom gave a distinctive social and political meaning to nineteenth-century journeys. Traveling across oceans became one of the ways that individuals could affirm their newly defined rights and freedom in the decades after the American and French Revolutions. This political context suggests why American and French travelers are the specific subjects of this book: people set off from the United States and France during this era with an acute desire to explore personal freedoms and to assert new ideas about postrevolutionary selfhood.[4] Their conceptions of "free" or "independent" selfhood thus linked nineteenth-century travel to cultural beliefs that differed from ancient or medieval ideas about the tribulations of long voyages. These differences actually coexisted within the linguistic history of the English word "travel," which came from the older French word "travail" and originally evoked the hard labor of painful work or troubled lives.[5]

The historian Eric Leed has discussed the contrasting cultural interpretations of travel in a perceptive analysis of ancient narratives that portrayed human journeys as arduous struggles to return home from exile rather than as opportunities to exercise the traveler's free will. "The ancients valued travel as an explication of human fate and necessity," Leed explains in his summary of long-term cultural

Gallery of the Louvre. Oil on canvas by Samuel F. B. Morse, ca. 1831–33. Morse exemplified the aspirations of "cultural travelers" as he developed his artistic skills in Paris by painting scenes such as this view of visitors in the Louvre Museum. Morse later invented a valuable and famous code for telegraph communications, but his early interests and travels led him to European art museums. Terra Foundation for American Art, Daniel J. Terra Collection, 1992.51.

changes; "for moderns, it is an expression of freedom and escape from necessity and purpose. Ancients saw travel as a suffering, even a penance; for moderns, it is a pleasure and a means to pleasure." The ten-year journey that finally brought Odysseus back to Ithaca after the Trojan War (as described by Homer) exemplified the ordeals of an ancient man struggling with fates beyond his control. Modern journeys, by contrast, acquired the different meanings of autonomous activity, which Leed describes as the "freely chosen opportunity to demonstrate an identity—as freedom, self-display, and self-discovery."[6]

The free person's travel could therefore resemble other forms of freedom that white men increasingly exercised in early nineteenth-century political cultures. The well-to-do white men who participated most widely in national political institutions also moved most freely across national landscapes and political borders. The rights and meaning of "free travel" thus became increasingly important for excluded persons who sought to claim their own right to participate in public life, including Black sailors who worked on merchant ships and Black or white women who could write about their international journeys during an era when they could not join other activities in the expanding public sphere. Travel became a personal action that enabled some politically excluded travelers to assert an autonomous selfhood as writers and cultural experts (who also wanted to gain other public rights). These claims for personal freedom, as James Clifford argues in an influential book, suggest why "travel" has become a broad "inclusive term embracing a range of more or less voluntarist practices of leaving 'home' to go to some 'other' place," where people find new knowledge through "edifying, pleasurable, [and] estranging" experiences.[7]

Historians can use Clifford's voluntarist definition of travel to examine how conceptions of individual freedom helped to shape political, cultural, and social ambitions for a new public status among nineteenth-century travelers. Aspirations for more personal or cultural freedom reappear often among the postrevolutionary American and French authors whom I discuss in this book, and the history of travel writing shows how modern accounts of personal journeys expressed distinctive modern beliefs about the creation of autonomous selfhood.

Travel Experiences and the Meaning of Selfhood

Long trips make people more aware of both their physical and cultural identities because they explore new places through their bodily senses as well as their minds. The senses provide an experiential meaning that can never emerge simply from books or films or images on a modern cell phone. Unfamiliar foreign cities plunge travelers into all the sensory levels of otherness: the visual diversity of new people, streets, buildings, and colors; the audible differences of unfamiliar languages, street noises, and local music; the olfactory stimulation of markets, restaurants, and backstreet odors; the distinctive tastes of vegetables, meats, sauces, and drinks at meals and festivals; and (sometimes) the disorienting touches with which people greet friends or dance or say goodbye.

Unexpected sights, sounds, and smells thus give traveling outsiders a new physical awareness of different daily lives in other cultures, but the bodily dimensions of these experiences also provoke new self-recognitions as travelers become more aware of their own race, language, voice, gender, clothing, and physical appearance. Local people who have long lived in the "foreign" social space perceive the visitor's conspicuous physical presence and body as different, thereby ascribing identities to the outsider that often go beyond the differences that the traveler has already recognized ("How did they know I was American when I did not say a word?"). Meanwhile, travel experiences affect sensory self-awareness in other ways

Les Halles and the rue de la Tonnelerie. Oil on board by Giuseppe Canella, ca. 1828. The Italian painter Canella (1788–1847) traveled extensively in France, Spain, and the Netherlands during the early nineteenth century. His vivid landscape paintings and portrayals of urban scenes conveyed the intensity of a traveler's sensory encounters with new places, as in this image of the people, products, and nearby buildings at a lively Parisian marketplace. RMN–Grand Palais/Art Resource, NY.

whenever people feel the exceptional fatigue or illness that can come from sleeping in bad beds, digesting strange foods, drinking different water, and struggling to comprehend unknown languages.

The immersion in unfamiliar physical environments that brings intense sensory awareness to transnational travelers can gradually transform both the experiential and cultural layers of selfhood that are entangled in human identities. The precise meaning of "experience" is a subject for endless philosophical debate, but cultural historians have rightly argued that human experiences are always enmeshed in linguistic and symbolic systems that create expectations, interpretations, and memories. These overlapping components of physical and cultural experience therefore shape the meaning of travel and connect with broader ideas about history and culture. "Travel is the paradigmatic 'experience,'" Eric Leed notes in his previously cited analysis of long journeys. It is "the model of a direct and genuine experience, which transforms the person having it." The familiar, repetitive trips of a daily commuter rarely alter beliefs or provoke personal transformations, but travel experiences in other cultures become significant whenever they challenge or change the person who encounters and remembers them. "This conception of 'experience' as an ordeal, as a passage through a frame of action that gauges the true nature of the person . . . passing through it," Leed writes, "also describes the most general and ancient conception of the effects of travel upon the traveler."[8] A long journey, in other words, might be pleasurable, but it only becomes an important "travel experience" when unexpected obstacles or disorientations produce physical and cultural consequences that reshape the traveler's identity and sense of selfhood.

These changes become most evident in the traveler's cultural self-perception (though the physical appearances of long-term travelers may change too), so this book focuses on how extended travel experiences influenced the personal, cultural, and political identities of wandering writers. The physical realities of long trips should nevertheless be emphasized at the beginning of this narrative journey, in part because travelers often refer to the discomforts as well as the pleasures of their experiences. This bodily realm of cross-cultural interactions receives detailed attention in John Urry's book *The Tourist Gaze,* which analyzes how travelers and local people inevitably view each other as different nationalities, races, genders, or social beings. Writing with the perspectives of a sociologist, Urry reminds historians that "tourism always involves *corporeal* movement and forms of pleasure" and that the "tourist gaze always involves relations between bodies that are themselves in at least intermittent movement." The traveler's body is thus only one of the moving objects in the interactive social spaces where local people also bring their mobility, senses, and gazes into all cultural and economic exchanges. "Co-presence," as Urry explains, "then involves seeing or touching or hearing or smelling or tasting a particular place."[9] These sensory aspects of transnational encounters are present for even the most rarefied "cultural" traveler, and they suggest why travel was long deemed to be more appropriate for men than for women. If the senses were to be stimulated—as they surely were—then most moralistic people assumed that male bodies could best withstand the physical threats and temptations that flowed through every journey to faraway places.

Voluntary travel was thus viewed throughout the nineteenth century as one of the gateways to physical freedom and exceptional sensory experiences, but my main argument in the following chapters stresses that it also opened experiential doors toward new cultural identities and perceptions of selfhood. The meanings of "identity" and "selfhood," like the meanings of freedom and experience, are never finally settled, yet these meanings almost always refer to both the physical and intellectual layers of human lives. Specific personal dimensions of identity and selfhood intersect with broader cultural inheritances that become especially apparent to people who travel or who live in other cultures. Identity and selfhood are always connected, but identities may differ somewhat from selfhood in that identities can be ascribed to other persons, whereas the sense of selfhood is constructed within an individual's own mind. It is also true, however, that nobody has just one identity or one layer of selfhood.

Although the various dichotomies of ascribed identities (physical/intellectual, personal/cultural) may have greater or lesser influence within each person's interior selfhood, all identities and conceptions of selfhood develop through the relationships with other people that contribute to a person's interior reflections and consciousness. These levels of selfhood are clearly and persuasively summarized in Jerrold Seigel's excellent, wide-ranging book *The Idea of the Self.* Seigel identifies the always-interacting physical, relational, and reflective components of selfhood that shape every individual's (and traveler's) evolving life experiences and that form what he calls the "three dimensions" of a recognizable self:

> We will call them the bodily or material, the relational, and the reflective dimensions of the self. The first involves the physical, corporeal existence of individuals. . . . Our selves on this level . . . are housed in our bodies, and are shaped by the body's needs. The second, relational, dimension arises from social and cultural interaction, the common connections and involvements that give us collective identities and shared orientations and values. . . . In this perspective our selves are what our relations with society and with others shape or allow us to be. The third dimension, that of reflectivity . . . derives from the human capacity to make both the world and our own existence objects of our active regard, to turn a kind of mirror not only on phenomena in the world, including our own bodies and our social relations, but on our consciousness too, putting ourselves at a distance from our own being so as to examine, judge, and sometimes regulate or revise it.[10]

Seigel notes that numerous modern and postmodern accounts of selfhood focus on a "one-dimensional" self that is reduced mainly to *one* of these connected human attributes, but he strongly prefers a "multidimensional" view that recognizes how all three layers continually overlap in all human lives. Reflectivity is the most difficult level of selfhood to recognize and analyze in other people because it exists in the complex, interior "self-awareness" of another mind. Seigel nevertheless argues convincingly that reflectivity is "an essential element of selfhood," though it "cannot stand apart from biology or social existence" and inevitably "exists in a relationship of interdependence with them."[11]

My discussion of traveling writers examines the multiple, intersecting dimensions of identity and selfhood as I explore the entanglement of these "historical categories" and as I describe diverse physical, social, and reflective responses to transnational experiences. These intersecting layers of social identities and interior selfhood often became the most salient themes in nineteenth-century travel narratives, even when authors wrote about public events or transient social encounters. Journeys through unfamiliar countries, in short, made people more aware of the home-country relationships that had shaped their evolving social and cultural selfhood.

The social interactions in each person's lifeworld connect individuals within every culture to a linguistic community in which they find the words to describe their exterior identities and to reflect on their individuated self-consciousness. The relations and languages that construct exterior identities thus continually influence the language of interior reflection; and both the cultural construction and the personal construction of selfhood always require dynamic relations with others who are also constantly changing over time. As the philosopher Charles Taylor argues in another influential analysis of the relational aspects of identity, the self is inescapably involved with "conversation partners" who create the "webs of interlocution" in which selfhood emerges.[12]

This interactive, fluid development of identities and selfhood has received much attention from contemporary historians, anthropologists, literary critics, social theorists, philosophers, and psychologists. My own descriptions of identity therefore draw on a well-known cultural paradigm whose main themes emphasize that the meaning of selfhood emerges from ongoing reflections about social, cultural, and personal differences rather than from a personal or spiritual essence. As Florian Coulmas notes in a concise book on this complex subject, "A vital part of identity—of a person, a group, a corporation—is that it is different from other identities. It does not exist naturally but must be marked off, exhibited, enacted."[13]

We might thus describe the structures of personal identity by comparing selfhood to the structures of social institutions and national identities that are never permanently fixed and that also evolve in changing historical contexts. A recognizable structure of identity and personal selfhood endures across the "*long durée*" of an individual's lifetime and carries a specific name, but this structure resembles other historical structures in that it mixes continuities with changes, memory with forgetting, and conscious with unconscious social practices. Individual identities or conceptions of selfhood, in other words, are microcosms of larger historical processes and social institutions because the structures of identity and selfhood continue to exist while they also change in response to unexpected events, conflicts, or interactions with different people and national cultures. Long, disorienting travel experiences therefore become historical events that disrupt and change the earlier meaning of exterior, relational identities and the internal, reflective structures of selfhood, though the name-carrying self is still physically present in the world.

The history of personal journeys shows how both changes and continuities influence the identities of specific travelers. We can turn again to Eric Leed's helpful historical work for insights on the ways in which the life-changing mobility of travelers contributes to broader ideas about personal and social transformations. "Travel has long been a means of changing selves," Leed argues, "a method of altering social status, of acquiring fame, fortune, and honor. . . . The transformation of social being in travel, becoming someone else through territorial passage, is . . . so common in experience that territorial mobility supplies our chief metaphor of social transformation: that is, *social mobility*."[14] Social mobility gradually became one of the key cultural themes in modern societies (like freedom, experience, identity, and selfhood), and Leed's imaginative account of the mobile, changing "self" suggests why the study of traveling writers adds an important subject to the analysis of wider changes in social and cultural history.

The traveling self, however, always carries the baggage of a previous personal and cultural life, so new insights into identity and selfhood remain connected to the cultural system and language in which the traveler was raised and educated. "Travel is about seeking otherness," the historian Nancy Green has written in a perceptive analysis of early modern foreign travelers in France. Yet this engagement with another culture also requires comparisons with the traveler's previous cultural knowledge, and the new place can be understood only through references to what travelers already know. Long-existing elements of home-country identities thus sustain the cultural continuities of selfhood, even while travelers fervently pursue new cross-cultural encounters. "What the observers 'find,'" Green notes, "is as much a function of prior knowledge as it is of true discovery. It is informed by those who have trod before."[15]

Both the changes and continuities in traveling writers point to the internal dialogues between new and previous identities that developed whenever nineteenth-century travelers used their earlier cultural knowledge to interpret unfamiliar cultures and to affirm their aspirations for a freer, upwardly mobile self. The dual emphasis on how travel changes self-perceptions or reconfirms inescapable cultural origins may also explain the contrasting "identity reactions" that travel often evokes. Some travelers (embracing change) feel profoundly separated from their former lives and increasingly identify with the perspectives and social values of the culture in which they are living as outsiders. Others (embracing continuities) feel a deepening connection with their own national culture and identify more fervently with the values of the culture in which they grew up.[16] Both of these reactions can be seen in nineteenth-century French and American travelers who became more critical of their home nations or prouder of their home nations as they met unfamiliar people and lived in unfamiliar places.

Travelers from France remained highly aware of their "French" identities in the same way that American travelers carried their "Americanness" into every place they visited. French visitors to the United States, for example, frequently criticized the American obsession with money by reaffirming what the historian Jean-Philippe Mathy has called "a humanistic and aristocratic ethos derived from models of intellectual excellence" that emerged during the Renaissance and remained influential throughout "the age of French classicism." French intellectuals who traveled in the Americas often criticized France's political institutions or social hierarchies, but they almost all shared a strong disdain for America's materialism, tasteless food, and boorish table manners; and no French traveler could ever abandon the confident belief that France embodied a universal intellectual significance.[17]

Americans also carried a remarkable national confidence in their own exceptional national achievements, and even the most critical writers (including Black travelers who vehemently condemned slavery) strongly identified with American political ideals or religious traditions. Dialogical comparisons between earlier cultural identities and the unfamiliar ideas or customs of foreign people provoked different personal memories in each traveling writer, of course, yet nineteenth-century travelers from both the United States and France constantly expressed the deepening national identities that spread rapidly after the American and French Revolutions. Nationalism became a pervasive political and cultural ideology throughout America and Europe after 1800, so traveling writers continually drew on public narratives about *collective* national identities to define their *personal* national identities and the differences of other nations.[18] The nineteenth-century process of constructing national identities thus evolved on both macro and micro levels in texts and in personal lives that connected the belief in distinctive national traditions with the belief in a distinctive national selfhood.

The construction of modern national identities was therefore well-advanced within both public institutions and private lives by the middle of the nineteenth century, but the identity-defining government documents of modern nation-states were still rare. Travelers generally did not need a passport to move across national borders or to cross the Atlantic Ocean. White American travelers tended to use travel "passports" that were more like letters of introduction from state officials or overseas consuls than like the carefully documented passports that would become required for international travel after the First World War. Although between 7,000 and 9,000 Americans were crossing the Atlantic each year by the 1840s, the still-informal "passports" were issued to only about 1,000 white citizens and non-citizens in the United States in each year of this decade. The US Congress eventually declared in 1856 that passports would henceforth be granted only by agents of the State Department and only to US citizens, which effectively meant that most white Americans could readily qualify. Black sailors could acquire a "seaman's protection certificate" to work on merchant ships during this era, but enslaved persons were excluded from all citizenship rights, and many free Black Americans were unable to get a passport until after the Civil War.[19] Most nineteenth-century American travelers only had to use some kind of "passport paper," however, if they visited Russia or Turkey; and French travelers usually entered the United States without passports except during the American Civil War.

Despite the lagging development of national travel documents, French and American writers regularly emphasized the social, political, and cultural differences that shaped various national identities. Their narratives showed consciously or unconsciously how nationalism had become a powerful influence in all modern societies, but the era's burgeoning travel literature also expressed personal ambitions and anxieties that went well beyond the new nationalist political cultures and linked travel writing to broader themes in Western literary cultures.

Travel Narratives as a Genre of Literary Culture

Western writers have used travel experiences to affirm their cultural knowledge and social status since the time in which the ancient Greek historian Herodotus (c. 485–c. 425 BCE) described his journeys around the Middle East. There were also numerous travel stories during the era of medieval commercial exchanges and religious pilgrimages, when Marco Polo (1254–1323?) visited China and devout persons visited sacred sites across Europe and Palestine.[20] Travel narratives gradually became a more distinctive literary genre among early modern European explorers, geographers, and missionaries who wrote about their encounters with unfamiliar people, cultures, and landscapes in Asia and the Americas.[21] By the seventeenth century, the literary conventions of travel books and journals were well-established in the texts of itinerant merchants, government envoys, and creative writers, as Michèle Longino has shown in her outstanding analysis of French travelers who visited the Ottoman Empire during the decades before 1700. Although Longino discusses a specific pre-Enlightenment literary culture, she examines the "process of travel and writing about it" in a perceptive summary of how narratives about long trips could also redefine identity and selfhood in later centuries and other places. In their travel journals and published accounts of the Ottoman Empire, Longino explains, French male writers constructed "themselves as subjects, . . . as authors and as characters, in keeping with the central human project of individuation in the early modern era." Pursuing a project of literary self-fashioning, "each of these writers . . . has a distinctive voice, particular preoccupations, and interests, which can only be discovered . . . through the process of their writing."[22]

This evolving desire to connect writing with the rediscovery or reconstruction of selfhood appears often in the texts of nineteenth-century travelers (including women) who contributed to the rapid expansion of travel literature in America and Europe. Bibliographers have compiled comprehensive summaries of the published travel literature that list about 1,825 travel books in the United States before the end of the nineteenth century and roughly 1,800 French books on journeys in North America between 1765 and 1932. The writers came from a wide range of professions and social groups whose motives for travel reflected diverging goals and ambitions. Careful research on pre-1900 American authors, for example, confirms that they almost always wrote about Europe and shows that they included 179 clergy, 117 journalists, 195 soldiers and sailors, 66 missionaries, 54 physicians, 44 lawyers, 36 educators, 34 artists, 32 businessmen, 23 diplomats, and numerous travelers with other professions or social identities. The French authors in America have not been identified with the same social categories, but French travel books regularly described the voyages of political refugees, missionaries, commercial traders, curious aristocrats, and others who wanted to see how American society resembled or differed from the social and political systems in Europe.[23] The bibliographies for both American and French travel literature focus on books rather than on the countless other travel reports in newspapers and periodicals, so the actual dissemination of travel writing far exceeded the helpful statistical summaries that historians have compiled. Yet this vast literature ultimately became influential because of its themes rather than simply because of its ubiquity.

Travel writing typically took the form of a nonfiction memoir or autobiographical narrative that also used the literary conventions of fictional texts to portray a sympathetic character (traveler/narrator) moving through new places, facing unexpected challenges, and gaining new wisdom. The nonfiction travel book could therefore resemble the popular fictional genre of the nineteenth-century bildungsroman, which portrayed the gradual education of a young protagonist (usually male) who gained knowledge and insights by meeting new people and overcoming complex obstacles. The main character's "education" in such novels led toward a better understanding both of selfhood and of the struggle to survive in a threatening social world. Although the meaning and popularity of the bildungsroman developed in German culture, this kind of nonacademic education was also portrayed in notable nineteenth-century French novels such as Stendhal's *The Red and the Black* (1830) and Balzac's *Père Goriot* (1835). Novels about youthful education might be compared to travel stories insofar as the fictional learning process took place over the course of a personal "journey" from youth to adulthood that changed the identity of the main character; and the best travel books—like the best novels—told the story of a long transitional voyage. "The travel narrative is a compelling and seductive form of storytelling," Casey Blanton has noted in a well-informed survey of the genre. "Its reader is swept along on the surface of the text by the pure motion of the journey." Narrators of travel experiences often sought to engage their readers by portraying conflicts or miscomprehensions that could emerge in cross-cultural encounters, but the tensions were eventually transcended when the storyteller returned home or reached new kinds of knowledge. Good travel writing, as Blanton describes the genre, has long used a style "that borrows from fiction in its use of rising and falling action, character, and setting," and successful travel writers have always known how to "represent the strange and exotic in ways that both familiarize and distance the foreign."[24]

The writers of nineteenth-century travel books thus introduced specific information in the way that novelists and historians narrated carefully chosen details in fictional and historical stories. They mostly excluded the tedium of typical travel days as they reported on famous places or dramatic events and explained how they had overcome unexpected setbacks. Their descriptions of "observed realities" also borrowed from the narrative style of modern scientific writing by claiming to provide the empirical, evidence-based information of scientific knowledge—though scientists usually wrote for more specialized scholars and experts. Travel literature and scientific literature could therefore overlap. Historians have frequently stressed, for example, that Charles Darwin's early ideas about the diversity and evolution of animal species came from his experiences on a five-year trip around the globe (1831–36), which he described in a popular book and which he continued to remember in his later scientific work.[25] Darwin became the most famous traveling scientist of his era, but his creative use of a long journey was by no means unique among the many nineteenth-century botanists, geologists, and zoologists who traveled into distant, unfamiliar lands to observe and describe different aspects of the natural world.

Both scientific writing and the literary styles of imaginative novelists gave travelers an intellectual strategy for differentiating themselves from the mere "tourists" who were already viewed as the most superficial visitors to foreign countries. Distinctions between "travelers" and "tourists" began to appear among writers who wanted to show how their knowledge of history, culture, and politics came

The Hiker above Sea Fog. Oil on canvas by Caspar David Friedrich, ca. 1817. Nineteenth-century travelers often interpreted their experiences by drawing on both fictional accounts of journeys toward self-knowledge and scientific accounts of journeys toward knowledge of the natural world. Friedrich (1774–1840) evoked both these themes in this famous German painting of a lonely wanderer contemplating the mystery of cloud-shrouded mountains. Hamburger Kunsthalle, Hamburg/Art Resource, NY.

from authentic experiences rather than from unselfconscious tourism. This literary desire to sustain a traveler/tourist dichotomy is often noted in the scholarship on modern travel, most notably in the influential work of Dean MacCannell. Summarizing the common critiques of tourism, MacCannell has emphasized the widespread "intellectual attitude" that condemns tourist experiences as culturally inferior to the experiences of more thoughtful travelers. "The touristic experience that comes out of the tourist setting," MacCannell explains in his account of the intellectual hostility to tourism, "is based on inauthenticity and as such it is superficial when compared with careful study."[26]

The nineteenth-century search for authentic travel experiences therefore rejected tourism and looked instead for cultural models in Romantic literature, which stressed that writers should separate themselves from the routine activities of daily work to pursue personal quests for more intense emotional experiences and higher spiritual knowledge. Romantic writers such as William Wordsworth and Lord Byron famously shaped the belief that authentic travel would require a deep engagement with natural beauty and a self-conscious flight from the most visited tourist sites.[27] Images of the Byronic wanderer became especially important for traveling men who wanted to escape from what James Buzard has called the "beaten track" of conventional journeys. Byron showed that "anti-touristic gestures" could be performed "*within* tourism" and could place travelers in "an aristocracy of inner feeling" by affirming "an ideology of originality and difference" and by portraying the self as "a lone male wanderer, unfettered by the familial and female influences of home."[28]

Romantic ideas also suggested that travel should ultimately lead to a new self-knowledge that emerged from disorienting encounters with unknown people and places. To quote the twentieth-century neo-Romantic poet Jim Morrison, travelers needed to find new experiential doors to "break on through to the other side" of both tourism and homeland routines. The centrality of this "quest" imagery has been emphasized by the literary historian Tim Youngs, who argues persuasively that travel writers have long described their quests as "outward into the world or inward into the self." Romantic authors wanted to show how they had overcome obstacles during their travel through unfamiliar places, but the quest itself gave a structure to the whole experience and became "central to the travel narrative. . . . Most journeys involve a quest of some kind and there can be no quest without a journey."[29] The writers discussed in this book traveled with diverging beliefs and personal aspirations that went far beyond the aesthetic concerns of Romantic poets, but they all pursued an "outward" quest for new knowledge about other cultures and an "inward" quest for new knowledge about themselves.

Lord Byron in Albanian Dress. Engraving by William Finden, after Thomas Phillips, ca. 1830s. The English Romantic poet Lord Byron (1788–1824) became a model for "antitouristic" male travelers who viewed their journeys as an escape from home-country constraints and as a quest for personal freedom or "authentic" selfhood. This engraving of a well-known portrait exemplified the exotic themes that nineteenth-century men imagined when they set off on "Byronic travel." National Portrait Gallery, London/Art Resource, NY.

This overview of key cultural influences on modern travel writing has stressed its connections with the genres of autobiography, memoir, and scientific writing as well as its convergence with themes in nineteenth-century novels and Romanticism, but I want to conclude this brief summary of travel narratives as a "genre of literary culture" by noting how travel books can also be compared to modern historical writing. Travelers' accounts of foreign countries exemplify what historians like to examine when they study the "transnational history" of cross-cultural exchanges, migrations across national borders, and immigrant influences on modern national cultures. As Nancy Green notes in an insightful account of how historians are now analyzing these historical processes, transnational history interrogates and complicates "the impact of . . . [social] circulation, mobility, and interactions on all individuals, parties, and things involved."[30] The history of traveling writers is particularly relevant for this search to understand transnational circulations and interactions because travelers and their texts are forever moving across cultural borders.

Transnational themes also shape the more specific subfield of global intellectual history, which discusses how people adapt foreign ideas for use in their own societies and how translators, journalists, travelers, and migrants reinterpret transnational ideologies as they carry ideas into different languages and national cultures.[31] Travelers thus become some of the ideas-carrying people whom historians need to examine when they write about how intellectual currents flow across national boundaries. I would also argue more generally, however, that travel writing intersects with historical writing because both kinds of writers translate the ideas and events of unfamiliar societies into languages and ideas that people can understand within the writer's home culture. Good travel writers and good historians want to make mostly unknown societies comprehensible to readers who will never go to these other places or speak the languages of the people who live there.

One of the most concise explanations for such "translation" projects can be found in a single, well-known phrase: "The past is a foreign country; they do things differently there."[32] A deep engagement with distant historical eras, in other words, can defamiliarize the historian's (or reader's) present-day ideas, institutions, or languages in the way that long journeys to distant countries can defamiliarize the traveler's increasingly remote cultural homeland. Placed in this comparative framework of time and space, immersive historical study may resemble a disorienting trip into alien contemporary cultures, while travel writing might resemble historical research that leads into the unexpected, unknown social customs or religious beliefs of alien past societies. In both kinds of intellectual and physical journeys to where "they do things differently," a prolonged encounter with otherness generates new insights into the cultural identity of the historically situated self. This complex linguistic, social, and psychological experience connects travel writing with historical writing and provokes ongoing theoretical debates about how travel affects the meaning of selfhood.

Theoretical Perspectives on Travel, Cross-Cultural Experiences, and Identity

Historians have long used travelers' reports to gather information about past societies, but new cultural theories have continually transformed historical interpretations of travel writing since the 1970s. The influential themes of structural anthropology and poststructuralist literary criticism helped historians recognize how identities evolve through interactions between opposing binary categories and explore how the "other" is always already within the self—even when narrators explicitly separate themselves from foreign people and cultures. Drawing on theorists such as Ferdinand de Saussure, Claude Lévi-Strauss, Jacques Derrida, and Michel Foucault, the analysts of travel writing came to view the genre as more culturally significant than most historians had previously assumed. The growing field of "travel studies" also evolved under the influence of Edward Said's paradigm-shifting work, *Orientalism* (1978), which used the ideas of Foucault and other theorists to argue persuasively that European racism, imperial power, and knowledge-producing experts have long shaped biased, cross-cultural interpretations of non-European people and cultures.[33] Although the study of Western travel literature continues to evolve, it still refers often to anti-colonial and postcolonial themes that emerged from this new critical paradigm of the 1970s.

This book focuses on specific nineteenth-century travelers rather than on the debates of theorists who have shaped contemporary cultural studies and postcolonial literary criticism, but it draws on three salient theoretical themes that emphasize (1) the influence of language and symbols in every traveler's interpretations of other cultures; (2) the influence of gender and racial identities in every traveler's experiences and descriptions of other cultures; and (3) the influence of psychological desires and fears in every traveler's responses to other cultures and to the "other" that also exists within the self.

The linguistic and semiotic interpretations of travel and tourism stress that widely known cultural symbols always guide the traveler's quest for authentic experiences. Travelers arrive in new cities or visit famous monuments with expectations that come from narratives and pictures that have prepared them to "see" the place, so they typically compare their first impressions to descriptions and images they have read or seen before their trip. As Dean MacCannell argues in his influential account of travel experiences, "Usually, the first contact a sightseer has with a sight is not the sight itself but with some representation thereof," and this prior representation of well-known places gives the traveler a symbolic code that enables the new visitor to connect with "a sight already marked by others."[34]

Viewing a sight that symbolizes the history or meaning of Paris (for example, Notre Dame Cathedral) thus confirms that travelers are having an authentic experience in the actual place they expected to see. The authentic sight, however, is always already mediated by languages and images that define its experiential significance for the critical-minded travel writer as well as the most naive tourist. The literary theorist Jonathan Culler has explained the importance of these pre-visit expectations in an interesting essay that notes how pictures, postcards, and travel books prepare travelers to look for the "must-see" sights in each famous city. "Not only do they create sights," Culler explains in his description of influential pre-trip images, but "when the tourist encounters the sight the [previous] markers remain surprisingly important; one may continually refer to the marker to discover what features of the sight are indeed significant."[35] Literary travelers, as noted earlier, want to differentiate themselves from tourists by publishing self-conscious, cultural comparisons and providing new kinds of knowledge, but anti-touristic writers inevitably enter new places (like tourists do) with textual guidance that points them toward subjects they should discuss in a credible travel book.

The linguistic systems that shape a traveler's expectations also carry gender and racial codes that influence both the conscious and unconscious themes in most travel narratives. Historians have often emphasized that travel and travel writing were traditionally viewed as male activities, though women increasingly claimed the right to travel in both Europe and the United States during the nineteenth century.[36] More specifically, gender theorists have shown that most American and European travel books expressed white, masculine perspectives that are now challenged or "decentered" in postcolonial critiques of racist narratives and in critical revisions of earlier scholarship that overlooked the biases of traveling white writers. The feminist critic Caren Kaplan, for example, argues that literary historians such as Paul Fussell gave travel writers a transcendent cultural status by mostly ignoring their specific historical contexts and privileged social positions. "The 'traveler' who occupies primary place in this formation," Kaplan writes in her critique of idealized past writers, "can be characterized as a Western individual, usually male, 'white,' of independent means, an introspective observer, literate, acquainted with ideas of the arts and culture, and, above all, a humanist." Kaplan wants to historicize this kind of "mythic figure" and to emphasize that the works of such writers should "be linked to the histories of the production of colonial discourses."[37]

Although only three of the eight travelers who are the main subjects of this book can be described as white men, it is true (as Kaplan suggests) that gendered and racialized ideas about travel and travel writing influenced everyone who wrote about their nineteenth-century journeys. The white male travel writer embodied the authoritative position of a cultural expert, which meant that authors who wanted to gain the status of a knowledgeable cross-cultural interpreter had to use a "voice" that somehow echoed the style of respected male narratives. Both white men and white women travelers, however, shared many of the same social advantages because, as Mary Louise Pratt has noted in a comparison of gendered travel experiences, "women travelers occupy a world . . . where their class and race privilege is presupposed."[38] Kaplan, Pratt, and other critics have therefore developed valuable perspectives for understanding how social hierarchies and pervasive cultural assumptions about gender and race shaped the experiences of every traveler, even when the psychological effects of different journeys transcended the social categories of male/female or white/Black.

The insights of semiotic literary analysts and feminist critics can be linked to a third theoretical theme that focuses on psychological interactions within the complex layers of selfhood. Individuals construct their sense of self by consciously or unconsciously defining how they differ from other people, yet modern psychological theorists have stressed that these "outsiders" also remain inside each person's self-identity. This theme can be found, for example, in the writings of both Friedrich Nietzsche and Sigmund Freud, but it reappears in later French theorists such as Victor Segalen and Jacques Derrida. The somewhat fragmented theoretical work of Segalen (1878–1919) has recently attracted attention as an imaginative attempt to explain how other people are truly different and also present within oneself. Describing this psychological interaction in his *Essay on Exoticism: An Aesthetics of Diversity* (written between 1904 and 1918), Segalen insisted that people in other cultures must always be understood as truly "foreign, strange, unexpected, surprising, mysterious, amorous, superhuman, heroic, and even divine, everything that is *Other*." Travelers to distant places—as Segalen argued after living for seven years in Polynesia and China—should thus never assume they have fully comprehended the differences they encounter, yet the differences of others also push people toward a new awareness of their own multilayered selfhood. "Only those who have a strong individuality can sense Difference," Segalen wrote. "Only those with a strong individuality can fully appreciate the wonderful sensation of feeling both what they are and what they are not."[39]

Anyone who engages with the differences of other people and cultures eventually struggles with psychological tensions because an honest confrontation with "otherness" also reveals an *internal* diversity that defies full comprehension. Nobody has simply one identity. Later theorists have thus gone beyond Segalen in analyzing how long trips lead to new explorations of unconscious desires and challenge confident beliefs in a coherent selfhood. Dennis Porter calls attention to the psychological provocations of travel, for example, in his claim that an unsettling experience outside one's home culture "invites a form of self-disclosure that is only partially conscious."[40] The traveler's self-disclosure is never finally completed because internal conflicts block the creation of a fully unified self. The psychological significance of this encounter with external and internal differences might therefore be summarized with a theme that Dominick LaCapra draws from his reading of Freud: "the idea that in every other (as in oneself), there . . . [are] unconscious processes that limit the fulfillment of the classical dictum 'Know thyself.'" This always-present (but only partially recognized) "other" can be accepted, feared, or rejected, but the traveling writer often becomes especially aware of its existence. "The attempt to expel this other within," LaCapra notes, " . . . problematizes identity and causes anxiety in the self." Creative travelers find new ways to engage with this inescapable otherness, yet travel can also lead to a dangerous cultural scapegoating when people lapse into a simplistic "binary opposition between self and other (or 'us' and 'them')."[41] Travel writing that constructs such absolute dichotomies is neither interesting nor valuable, but LaCapra's emphasis on the anxieties that grow from the troubling recognition of a fragmented self suggests how a traveler's encounters with other people or cultures contribute to new identities, creativity, disorientation, and fear.

Although the following chapters discuss nineteenth-century travelers rather than modern cultural theories, the travelers' lives and texts often connect with analytical frameworks that recent theorists have used to explore the linguistic, gendered, racial, and psychological aspects of travel experiences and travel literature. These traveling writers could thus be used as cultural exemplars for engaging in broader theoretical debates, but I want to stress instead that they were specific *persons* whose stories and multifaceted lives also complicate all the cultural theories and historical presuppositions that might categorize, condemn, or ignore them.

Nineteenth-Century Travelers on the Long Journey toward Selfhood

This book examines eight diverse travelers from France and the United States. They can be described by gender identities as four women and four men (divided equally between French and American national origins) and by racial identities as two African Americans and six who were white Americans or white Europeans. They all traveled extensively in foreign countries and wrote journals, articles, books, and letters that were published in various formats during their lifetimes or after their deaths. Each part of the book focuses on the travels of one man and one woman from the same home nation. Their experiences and writings can thus be compared through contextual references to these shared national origins, and their ideas can be analyzed through a careful reading of their published texts.

The first chapters compare the French travelers Victor Jacquemont (1801–32) and Flora Tristan (1803–44), who grew up in different social milieus as part of the "French Generation of 1820" and who differed from the other travelers in that they made long trips outside the North Atlantic world. Like other Europeans, Jacquemont and Tristan both visited the Americas, but Jacquemont's most influential travel experiences (after a trip to the United States) took place in India, and Tristan traveled in Peru. Both writers, however, found new opportunities to affirm their French identities and ambitions from places far outside France.

The next section describes the journeys of the European American writers Margaret Fuller (1810–50) and Randal McGavock (1826–63), whose texts show how the different sectional origins of people from northern and southern American states influenced the contrasting political and cultural perspectives of mid-nineteenth-century travelers. Fuller and McGavock also differed in that she became far more famous in later American cultural history, but they traveled through many of the same European cities, and they both wrote about their home nation's global significance in newspaper articles that were republished as travel books.

The third section of the book analyzes the transnational experiences of the free Black American writer Nancy Prince (1799–1856?) and the enslaved (but later free) Black American writer David Dorr (1827?–72?), who both challenged the barriers of nineteenth-century racism by asserting their freedom and social status during long journeys outside the United States. Prince and Dorr wrote about entirely different places in Russia and Jamaica (Prince) and in western Europe and the Middle East (Dorr), yet they used similar cultural strategies to move outside the gender and racial hierarchies that blocked their aspirations to establish independent, respected social identities within American society.

The final section of the book discusses the North American cultural explorations of the French Jesuit priest Nicolas Point (1799–1868) and the French feminist-journalist Olympe Audouard (1832–90), who both crossed the Atlantic because they faced personal and professional obstacles at home and because they were looking for new places in which they could pursue their religious or literary ambitions. Their political and personal ideas (except for a shared belief in Catholicism) diverged as widely as their professional goals, but they explained their American experiences in self-defining texts that declared their independence from French constraints and affirmed the autonomy of their lives in the United States.

The eight writers thus came from different social origins and pursued different personal goals as they traveled through foreign cultures, so you may wonder why or how these specific individuals might serve as exemplary interpreters of nineteenth-century journeys. They lived through identity-shaping social and political events that influenced most people in the United States and France during the century after the American and French Revolutions, but I chose to focus on these particular men and women because they all used travel experiences and travel writings to describe their national cultural identities and to redefine their individual selfhood (most people constructed a sense of selfhood without leaving their home countries). They are thus significant because they exemplify wider patterns in the modern search for selfhood and because each set off on long journeys with goals or ambitions that have also inspired countless other modern travelers.

Like all once-living figures whom historians analyze, these writers were complex individuals with distinctive life experiences who also expressed the ideas and customs of wider cultural systems and social structures. Their travel stories show how people from diverse national cultures, social classes, and racial groups could use long journeys to pursue personal aspirations or to escape from home-country distress. They were constantly entangled with all the broader identity-shaping components of their historical era (nationalism, race, gender, wealth, education, religion, language, science, political conflicts, professional status), yet they were always struggling to define or defend a unique sense of selfhood as they traveled to unfamiliar cultures and responded to the postrevolutionary transitions of the wider social world. Many other exemplary nineteenth-century travelers could be included in this book, but every historical narrative requires a limiting framework. I have therefore chosen to discuss eight specific individuals whose travel writing points to broader cultural patterns in Europe or America and to the personal complexities of cross-cultural experiences.

I "met" each of these writers somewhat haphazardly through historical studies, collegial conversations, and classroom teaching, as you might meet someone in a passing encounter while traveling to visit others at a different destination. You continue with your own preplanned trip after such encounters, of course, but you may also think, "It would be interesting to know that person better or to extend the conversation." I thus eventually found research pathways back to these diverse, intriguing travelers, whom I would like for you to meet or know better by joining this historical dialogue and by thinking about the convergences or differences in their lives and journeys. The writings of nineteenth-century travelers tell us about the ideas and conflicts of people who lived in a different historical era, but they also raise enduring questions about the construction of our own identities or selfhood and about the meaning of our own journeys toward unknown places.

I first learned about Jacquemont through his family's connections with Lafayette and early French liberalism, and I first encountered Tristan when I read about Saint-Simonians and early feminists in July Monarchy Paris. Conversations with a departmental colleague, Charles Capper, led me into the fascinating trajectory of Margaret Fuller's transnational life, but it was my long-ago study of southern American history that somehow gave me a memorable introduction to Randal McGavock's travel writings and his early life in Tennessee. I came upon Nancy Prince and David Dorr when I started teaching university seminars on modern travel writers and discovered that neither of these exceptional authors had entered the canon of American travel literature. Finally, I read some comments about Nicolas Point and Olympe Audouard while I was researching the history of nineteenth-century French nationalism and looking for critics who had opposed the evolving secularism of France's national culture or the exclusion of women from France's public institutions.

Each writer "stuck in my mind" and became more engaging as I began to note unexpected connections between their historical contexts, their ideas about national cultures, and their desire to travel. They all used their journeys to affirm or criticize earlier national identities, to compare home cultures with the customs or ideas in other cultures, and to seek new social recognition by demonstrating an experiential knowledge of foreign societies. They all hoped their accounts of other cultures would ultimately enhance their public status, but their travels in unfamiliar foreign lands also carried them into previously unknown places within themselves. Their stories, in short, showed how travelers explore and reconstruct their own identities and selfhood while they are describing, praising, or criticizing the people they meet in other countries.

All of these traveling writers pursued self-conscious searches for new knowledge and new kinds of social or cultural recognition. They never knew one another or read each other's texts, but their social trajectories overlapped in some notable convergences. Only one of the men (McGavock) would ever marry and none had children, whereas all the women married and all but one (Prince) also had children. Many of the travelers left home after the painful breakup or failure of romantic relationships, and the French women used long trips to escape abusive husbands because divorce was illegal in France between 1816 and 1884. The physical challenges of difficult journeys, unsettled social relations, and divisive public conflicts affected the health and well-being of all these adventurous people. Although they were energetic transnational explorers, they died at ages (listed here in parentheses) that seem remarkably young by the averages for twenty-first-century life expectancy: Jacquemont (31), McGavock (36), Fuller (40), Tristan (41) Dorr (around 45), Prince (around 57), Audouard (57), and Point (69). Drawing on a familiar cliché that portrays life itself as a journey rather than a destination, we might say that these travelers made relatively short lifetime trips.

They nevertheless visited or lived in more places than most other people would ever see because voluntary, transoceanic travel was possible only for those who had the time and money to take long voyages. During the decades before steamships began crossing the Atlantic in the 1840s, a "packet boat" sailed for about three weeks to reach Europe from eastern American ports, and the westward trip could take as long as five or six weeks (depending on the winds).[42] Steamships reduced the travel time between New York and Liverpool to about twelve or fourteen days, but European and American journeys to Asia were much longer, and Jacquemont needed nine months for a trip from France to India in 1828–29. International travelers were out of contact with friends and families for weeks or months at a time, so the news from home was always out of date (telegraph cables did not provide reliable, rapid transatlantic communications until the late 1860s). Travel in this era was thus neither spontaneous nor casual, and it usually required personal wealth, family money, or institutional support. A round-trip fare between the United States and Europe in the 1850s cost roughly $350, which is equivalent to more than $12,000 in today's money. International travel grew steadily throughout most of the nineteenth century, yet the expenses kept the lower classes at home—unless a traveler worked on ships or made a one-way emigrant passage in the miserable lower-deck steerage.

The people with whom we are "traveling" in this book obviously found the financial means to make long journeys, but they rarely said much about the costs in their published writings. They liked to portray themselves as competent or respectable travelers, even when they traveled in search of financial support. Although commercial motives were less important for ambitious writers than for traveling merchants or shipowners, the traveling writers shared many of the other common motivations for prolonged nineteenth-century trips: the desire for scientific knowledge or religious proselytizing, the desire to explore famous cities or to visit famous historical sites, the desire for literary or political experiences that could be described in written texts, the desire to gain home-country recognition for expertise on foreign history or distant societies, and (above all, perhaps) the desire to find liberating opportunities for more personal, social, and intellectual freedom. This search for new freedoms was particularly important for women and for enslaved men, but the most privileged male travelers also sought new avenues for self-advancement and new personal escapes from homeland constraints.

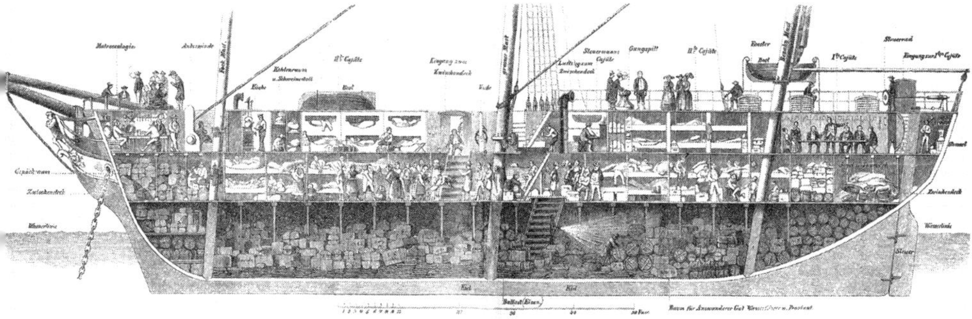

Inside a Packet Ship. Illustration by an unknown artist in *Die Gartenlaube Leipzig Fruft Neil,* 1854. Most travelers crossed the Atlantic before the 1850s on ships that used sails rather than steam power. This German depiction of a packet ship shows how shipping companies separated wealthy passengers in the upper-level cabins from poor people in the crowded steerage level and from the packets and cargo in the hold of the ship. The Mariners' Museum and Park, Newport News, VA.

The travel experiences discussed in this book, to reiterate earlier points, therefore differed from the journeys of enslaved workers or migrant laborers, and each writer carried distinctive personal ambitions as well as the cultural influences of Romantic literature. Travelers in this era, however, also left home with anxieties, ideas, and identities that reflected the wider conflicts, ideologies, and social systems of the Atlantic world. The history of travel, in other words, was always linked to larger historical transitions that deeply affected the meaning of freedom, social status, and individual selfhood.

Postrevolutionary Selfhood, National Identities, and Nineteenth-Century History

French and American writers who traveled between the 1820s and 1860s had grown up in societies where the legacies of the European Enlightenment and the late eighteenth-century Atlantic revolutions continued to shape the national cultures and politics. This postrevolutionary context influenced every sphere of nineteenth-century cultural life, including the Romantic quest for exotic experiences, the changing perceptions of science and religion, and the growing market for books and newspaper articles about other nations. Travel writing therefore contributed to transnational cultural exchanges, but travel writers were rarely original thinkers who proposed new political or philosophical theories to explain the evolution of politics or culture.[43] Their narratives were nevertheless historically significant because they showed how eighteenth-century ideas and conflicts continued to affect every thoughtful writer who traveled from France and the United States into foreign countries.

Travel in this era became part of a transition in the meaning of selfhood that followed the breakdown of prerevolutionary social and political systems. These earlier systems had defined people through their connections with social estates or corporate groups rather than through claims for an individualistic selfhood. As the historian Jan Goldstein has argued in a perceptive analysis of the changing "post-revolutionary self," the demise of long-existing legal hierarchies produced a disturbing "specter" of life outside the traditional "corporate matrix" and provoked the influential French philosopher Victor Cousin (1792–1867) to assert that the formation of a new "unitary self" might overcome the spreading dangers of self-fragmentation. Although contemporary thinkers now mostly accept the reality of a multivalent, multilayered self, Goldstein offers good evidence to show that "the rupture represented by the Revolution" brought a new "self-talk into prominence" and led to an educational system that followed Cousin's ideas in attempting to create a unified French (male) selfhood. Travelers could not construct a unified self by simply writing about their journeys, but they often affirmed what Goldstein describes as the belief in a new self that "effectively supplanted the structuring principle of Old Regime Society: the corporate order that the Revolution had abolished."[44]

Goldstein focuses on the "Cousinian *moi*" in France, but her description of the quest for an individualized bourgeois self (mostly denied to women and impossible for all enslaved people) might also explain the less philosophical aspiration for a coherent, autonomous selfhood in the early American republic. The revolutionary legacy reshaped or expanded the meaning of a "traveling self" in both France and the United States, and it connected travel to a wider "self-talk" that appeared in both personal lives and public debates. The legacy of the Atlantic revolutions also affected French and American travelers, however, through the diffusion of nationalist political cultures, the belief in human progress, the struggles to abolish slavery, and the campaigns to expand the rights of women and low-wage workers.[45]

Nationalism developed rapidly during the early nineteenth century as new schools, newspapers, political leaders, public rituals, and historical books taught people how to understand themselves as "French" or "American" or any other nationality that might coalesce in a sovereign nation-state. National identities came to be viewed as collective and personal expressions of shared cultural traits that emerged from distinctive national languages, political ideas, economies, social customs, literary texts, religious traditions, and landscapes. Nationalism thus influenced almost every traveler's narrative because writers wanted to describe national differences for readers in their home nations and because travelers became more aware of the national cultures that had shaped their own education and political ideas.

This nationalism contributed to popular ideas about modern progress, which European and American travelers regularly evoked whenever they discussed the civilizing achievements of their own national cultures. Nations were defined as "modern" if they promoted scientific knowledge, expanded their commerce into global markets, developed new technologies or factories, opened new schools or universities, and established constitutional systems to guide their government policies. Travelers used these criteria to place various nations at different historical ranks in a hierarchy of progressive modernization and then used the rankings to justify European imperialism in Asia or the displacement of Native American tribes from their homelands in North America. Travelers from the United States usually claimed that their nation was making more political and economic progress than any other country in the world, though they might concede that their national cultural achievements still lagged behind the impressive history of European high culture. Travelers from France usually claimed that their nation had made the most progressive advances in scientific knowledge, literary creativity, and (universal) political theories, though they might concede that the United States was making exceptional progress in commerce and industry. The views of French and American travelers, however, tended to converge in critiques of the regressive, antimodern social system that denied all basic human rights to millions of enslaved people.

The continuing defense of the racist slave system in the United States and in a few South American nations provoked commentaries or criticisms from almost everyone who traveled in the Atlantic world during the decades before 1865. Travel literature therefore provides transnational perspectives on the struggle to abolish slavery because it shows how cross-cultural comparisons forced travelers to analyze the ways in which slavery contradicted America's claim to represent the progress of modern democracy. Europeans constantly asked Americans about this contradiction, thereby pushing writers such as Margaret Fuller to understand more clearly that slavery was destroying America's global reputation for political progress. The traveling Tennessean Randal McGavock also had to respond to European critics of the slave system, which he defended by claiming that American enslavers were more enlightened and progressive than English factory owners or slave traders in the Ottoman Empire. African American writers, by contrast, mocked all such arguments for a more humane slave system in the United States; but nobody could read nineteenth-century travel literature without encountering impassioned discussions of slavery. Most travel writers viewed the buying and selling of human beings as a key example of deep national flaws, so the ubiquitous engagement with slavery became connected with other debates about politics, progress, or the meaning of human rights.

American travelers, for example, wrote about ongoing struggles to expand the political rights of European workers or to improve the social conditions in European industrial cities; and women writers on both sides of the Atlantic often criticized the degrading blockage of women's rights. The nineteenth-century struggle to expand the rights of women thus generated another recurring theme in travel narratives that ranked the historical progress of different nations by comparing the social status of women. These reports sometimes argued that women had more freedom outside their home countries, yet the praise for other cultures as well as the transnational critiques confirmed the importance of cross-cultural comparisons in all of the era's struggles to implement the spreading belief in equal human rights.

Political and cultural arguments for the rights of women could thus converge in travel narratives with the critiques of slavery, the belief in modern progress, or the nationalist desire to defend abstract political ideals in stronger national institutions. Even more generally, however, the traveling writers' cross-cultural interests in the ways that different nations denied or promoted human rights, social progress, and postrevolutionary political aspirations show why their accounts of nineteenth-century journeys can still speak to our twenty-first century lives.

The Personal Meaning and Cultural Significance of Traveling to Unknown Places

I began this introduction with general observations about how modern people travel and how travel affects personal and cultural identities. I now want to add a more specific personal explanation for my own interest in travel writers and note why travelers provide important subjects for continuing historical study. Like all other travelers, I came from a particular homeland and moved on to other places. I was born in a small Tennessee town and received my youthful education in central Arkansas, southern Indiana, and eastern Tennessee. Young people in these mid-twentieth-century communities and their segregated white schools were taught that America's political, economic, and religious institutions made the United States the greatest, most prosperous nation in all of world history. Other countries seemed far away, and nobody said that we had *a lot* to learn from foreign nations and cultures.

I eventually made a brief trip to Mexico, visited a world's fair in Montreal, and traveled on two college "study trips" to the Middle East and England. These journeys helped me see more clearly that I had come from a very small sphere of human history, and I started to imagine a trip that might take me completely around the globe. Several years later—after finishing college and some graduate work in history—I was able to launch such a journey when my wife and I found teaching positions at a postsecondary school in Hong Kong.[46] This two-year experience became a cross-cultural immersion in new foods, friendships, languages, ideas, classrooms, and crowded city streets that led me far away from my earlier all-American life. We also traveled extensively during holiday breaks in the Philippines, Thailand, Malaysia, Laos, and Vietnam (shortly before the final American military departure in 1975). Living and traveling in Asia took me to previously unknown places and pushed me to rethink the meaning of my American cultural origins and social privileges.

After working in Hong Kong for two years, we decided to travel overland to Paris, so that we could live in France and learn about European cultures we had never visited. We therefore set off on a long, low-budget journey across a continent whose people introduced us to more unfamiliar languages, political cultures, religions, and local customs. Asians and young European travelers had created an informal, low-cost "travel culture" that facilitated our trip and also forced us to recognize our inescapable American identities. We met people who were deeply suspicious of Americans and met others who welcomed us warmly into their towns and social lives. Among the many unexpected experiences of these cross-cultural travels, I especially remember three moments when I was forced to confront my national identity as starkly as earlier travelers had confronted their identities during long journeys in the nineteenth century. The memory of these moments connects my life with the historical themes of this book.

Wandering through the streets of Luang Prabang, Laos, in July 1974, I came upon a building that housed members of the communist Pathet Lao political movement (which was then part of a governing coalition in Laos). The Pathet Lao flag was flying above the building, and I naively took pictures like a tourist photographing historical monuments—whereupon I saw a young Pathet Lao soldier rushing toward me and angrily waving me away with his carefully pointed AK-47 rifle. He was of course suspicious of an American who was taking pictures, but he did not pull the trigger; and in those few intense seconds I directly faced the hostile, cross-cultural perception of my national political identity (despite my own opposition to the Vietnam War).

In the following year, as we traveled through New Delhi, India, I was resting on a park bench when a young man sat down beside me and said he thought we had known each other in a previous life. We discussed this unexpected encounter in the here and now—whereupon he invited my wife and me to go that evening to a religious service that would honor his special Baba. We agreed to go, so after a long, meandering bus ride we found ourselves in a room of chanting people who invoked the Baba's name as they praised deities that were new to me. They celebrated religious beliefs that had never entered the Protestant churches of my American youth; they placed a colorful, symbolic dot on my forehead; and they generously shared food after the chanting ended. My new/old friend then told us how to return to the city, and I went out into the hot night with a deeper awareness of my family's religious roots than I had ever felt before.

A few weeks later I was waiting for a bus in a small Pakistani town near the Hindu Kush mountains while my wife waited with women passengers in a separate room. I fell into a lively conversation with a vacationing Pakistani lawyer—whereupon two policemen suddenly approached me and said I must go with them to the local jail. They had heard that young Americans were selling drugs, and I was to be charged with this crime because I obviously had the social identity of a foreign drug dealer. Fortunately, however, the friendly lawyer with whom I had been talking at the bus station came to the jail, affirmed my innocence, and helped me continue my journey. I nevertheless felt a lingering anxiety as I boarded a bus and recounted the whole experience to my wife, because my inescapable social identity had marked me again as a cultural outsider.

Although each of these unsettling encounters with my political, religious, or social origins showed how I was "defined by others," I came to understand from such disorienting incidents that I was also reconstructing my own self-definitions as I moved through unfamiliar places. When other people ascribed unexpected traits to my traveling identity, I had to confront the challenges and influences of otherness within myself, yet these challenges were not unusual because travelers often have such disconcerting experiences. These unexpected encounters nevertheless became part of my own jolting entry into the complexity of cross-cultural exchanges and an experiential foundation for later historical projects that had never yet entered my mind.

The "kindness of strangers" remained a key theme amid the deepening recognition of national identities (in ourselves and others) as we crossed the Khyber Pass and made our way through Kabul, Herat, Tehran, Ankara, and Istanbul on the winding road to France. Traveling everywhere via low-cost transport, we headed toward Paris on a smoky Turkish bus that lacked legal permission to cross the last national border, so we first set foot on French soil by walking over a bridge into Strasbourg and finding a train to Paris. Like other modern travelers over the last two centuries, I had discovered components of national selfhood that I neither recognized nor understood when I lived only within my own nation. Future interactions in other cultures would create more disorientations in later years, and the uncanny feeling that came from living amid different languages and social practices would persist, no matter how long I stayed in foreign countries. The United States looked different too, however, and I found that my travel experiences outside America permanently altered the meaning of my earlier all-American life.

I have summarized this self-referential history of my own cultural starting place and transnational journeys to provide partial contextual explanations for my interest in nineteenth-century travelers and their changing perceptions of identity and selfhood. Following in the distant footsteps of other travelers who were still unknown to me, I began my journeys and my writing in specific historical contexts that shaped my personal and cultural identities; and I came away from my travels and expatriation with new perceptions of myself. My own experiences differed from those of earlier travelers, but all journeys have structural similarities as well as profound differences, and they can be studied historically with careful attention to how they share important continuities and how they also change over time.

Travel continues to influence the lives and ideas of people who visit foreign cities and cultures around the world. Tourism is a major global industry, but it is only one of the modern travel experiences that generate disorienting encounters and redefinitions of selfhood.[47] There are also constant migrations of laborers and displaced workers, political and religious refugees, writers and artists, traders and entrepreneurs, and diplomats and government agents. These travelers all jostle with tourists and struggle to make sense of their lives in new places. Although the worldwide COVID pandemic greatly reduced transnational travel for a time, long journeys still symbolize freedoms, opportunities, and transitions that push millions of people to leave home for faraway places and unsettling experiences. These transformative aspects of human travel have led me to write about ambitious French and American writers whose nineteenth-century journeys can help us rethink our own experiences and recognize still-unknown layers of our own selfhood.

PART I

Travel and the French Generation of 1820

Victor Jacquemont and Flora Tristan

INTRODUCTION TO PART I

Leaving France and Redefining Selfhood

THE YOUNG MEN AND WOMEN who came to maturity in France during the 1820s faced a difficult challenge in defining their collective and personal identities after the revolutionary upheavals that had transformed the lives of their parents' generation. Historians have frequently noted the distinctive struggles of the people who grew up immediately after the French Revolution and the Napoleonic empire, rebelled against the constraints of a conservative Restoration monarchy, and anticipated a better French society that always lay somewhere in the future. Many of the ambitious, educated persons in this early nineteenth-century generation (which Stendhal described brilliantly in *The Red and the Black*) became alienated from a French national culture that had abandoned heroic political action and returned to the public pieties of official Catholicism.[1]

Although they complained about the mediocrity and national decline of post-Napoleonic France, many of these young rebels would eventually settle into careers and communities that provided conventional social integration and economic rewards. Some members of this "Generation of 1820," however, never settled comfortably into French society, or they died before they could receive public recognitions and rewards. They also looked for better lives in this postrevolutionary culture, but their quest for new identities and social recognitions pushed them toward transnational travel. The following chapters focus on two such unsettled persons who died young: Victor Jacquemont and Flora Tristan.

They never knew each other, and they grew to maturity in very different social positions, but Jacquemont and Tristan shared numerous experiences that linked them to their specific generational cohort and connected them to a wider history of European encounters with the non-European world. Their lives also showed how travel to distant places could transform personal identities, ambitions, and conceptions of selfhood. Jacquemont and Tristan followed a generational pattern in their early contacts with repressive government policies, their support for liberal or radical political reforms, and their search for personal or professional opportunities within French society. Yet, in contrast to most persons of their generation, they responded to these typical French problems by leaving France and traveling alone in the Americas and Asia. They both wrote about their cross-cultural encounters in travel narratives that also became stories of self-exploration and stories about aspirations or anxieties they shared with others during the years before and after the French Revolution of 1830. They traveled in the different societies of the United States, India, and Peru, but they began their long journeys toward selfhood in early nineteenth-century France and then redefined their identities by describing people and cultures they encountered far outside Europe.

Transnational travel experiences pushed both Jacquemont and Tristan to develop stronger French cultural identities as they analyzed their disorienting encounters with non-European cultures. Despite their obvious interest in other cultures and their strong desire to interpret cross-cultural interactions, Jacquemont and Tristan drew upon their travel experiences to describe a deepening sense of their inescapable "Frenchness." Wandering in alien environments like cultural outsiders in a Stendhal novel, they increasingly aspired to social-cultural recognition within the French society from which they had departed because of their unsettled personal and generational histories. They both hoped their travel writings might give them a future status in France as experts on the wider world, but their early deaths meant they would reach this goal only through posthumous fame. Jacquemont eventually gained his reputation as a French scientist who knew India, and Tristan eventually gained her reputation as a French feminist who understood the conditions of women in South America and Europe.

Jacquemont and Tristan thus affirmed both enduring and evolving layers of selfhood as they described their cross-cultural experiences in non-European cultures. They wrote about these experiences in texts that resembled other nineteenth-century Romantic narratives of lonely voyages toward unknown places in the wider world or within the self—though neither Jacquemont nor Tristan expressed much interest in the more sentimental forms of Romantic literature. Like many Romantics of their generation, however, they sought to understand how other cultures posed "exotic" challenges to European ideas or social values, and they often referred to the kinds of unexpected encounters that have reappeared in cross-cultural stories and comparisons throughout the modern era. They also reflected on the ways in which material conditions and social relationships influenced non-European ideas about class, race, gender, marriage, religion, politics, and the meaning of human knowledge. Analyzing the differences of other ideas and social systems offered textual opportunities to express new cultural identifications with the historical significance of France's scientific knowledge and modern national culture. Their accounts of the Americas and South Asia therefore followed well-established traditions of travel literature whenever they described unfamiliar cultures through comparisons with well-known European cultural traditions, but they also repeated a key theme of such traditions when they expanded their accounts of cultural differences into wider claims about European cultural superiority. They seemed to become more self-consciously French or European because they perceived Europe as different from other cultures *and* as more advanced, more civilized, and more enlightened.

Jacquemont and Tristan both criticized and fled from specific problems within French society, yet their encounters with cultural differences led them toward two connected French themes and ambitions in their otherwise diverging voyages: the assumption that European values, ideas, or customs were mostly superior to the customs of other cultures (an assertion of cultural identity), and the recognition that cultural differences opened a pathway toward the future exercise of intellectual authority in France (an aspiration of personal identity). In other words, these French travelers in non-European societies discovered that the cultural and personal layers of identity and selfhood could never be simply or finally separated.

CHAPTER ONE

Victor Jacquemont's French Identity in America and South Asia

VICTOR JACQUEMONT was the third son of Rose Laisné Jacquemont and the French philosopher Venceslas Jacquemont (their daughter died as a young child, and Rose Laisné herself died, age forty-eight, when Victor was only seventeen).[1] A strong supporter of the French Revolution, Jacquemont *père* (1757–1834) had served in several government posts, entered the Class of Moral and Political Sciences at the National Institute, and associated with the circle of Idéologues that included liberal critics of Napoleon such as Antoine Destutt de Tracy. The youthful Victor thus grew up in a critical-minded intellectual community that linked materialist philosophy with liberal political theories and thereby provoked Napoleon's authoritarian hostility—as the seven-year-old Victor surely began to learn after his father was arrested and imprisoned in 1808 on charges of political conspiracy.

The Jacquemont family therefore gave their children firsthand knowledge about the political legacies of the Revolution and the French imperial government's repression of dissent. Educated at the École Polytechnique and the Collège de France, Victor went on to study medicine and science in the best Parisian schools, travel in the Alps, write scientific papers, and circulate in the salons of prominent French liberals. His close friends included writers such as Stendhal and Prosper Mérimée and liberal political figures such as Lafayette and Victor Destutt de Tracy. Jacquemont, in short, was well-prepared by the mid-1820s to launch the promising career of a Parisian doctor and scientist, but the failure of a love affair with the Italian opera singer Adélaïde Schiassetti plunged him into such a severe depression that his family urged him to seek diversions on a long trip to the United States and Haiti (1826–27). Jacquemont wrote numerous letters to his family and friends as he reflected on his American experiences with a liberal aristocratic perspective that some historians have compared to the later writings of Alexis de Tocqueville.[2] The trip to North America, however, became the partial preparation for a much longer trip to India when the French Museum of Natural History (part of the Jardin des Plantes) asked him to undertake a scientific study of the Indian subcontinent.

The directors of the museum wanted to collect information about the plants, animals, climate, and geology of India. Jacquemont, for his part, was attracted to an opportunity for expanding his travels and career in directions that would free him from the settled life of a French doctor (he never completed his medical studies). He thus accepted the museum's proposal and returned to France in the late summer of 1827 to make the necessary arrangements. Setting off for India on a French ship in August 1828, he stopped briefly in Brazil (October–November 1828) and eventually reached Calcutta (now Kolkata) in May 1829 after a voyage of nine months. Jacquemont prepared for his Indian land expedition during six months among British colonial officials in Kolkata and then traveled across central India to Benares (Varanasi) and Delhi, wandered far north into the Himalayas of Tibet and Kashmir, journeyed west into Punjab and Lahore, and then headed south to Bombay (Mumbai) in search of every plant, animal, and rock he could identify. He assembled vast collections of specimens for shipment to France; wrote long, descriptive letters to his family and friends; and kept detailed journals of information for future publication.

Traveling through the kinds of places that the literary historian Mary Louise Pratt has called the "contact zones" for interactions between colonizing Europeans and non-European communities, Jacquemont became part of a European scientific project that (drawing again on Pratt's terminology) could be described as an "anti-conquest" narrative. Where the British had pursued a colonial conquest of India, Jacquemont was traveling as a scientist to expand the modern European knowledge of natural history, much as the celebrated naturalist Alexander von Humboldt had traveled earlier in South America (Jacquemont noted their similar scientific interests in a letter he wrote to Humboldt shortly before departing for India). Pratt rightly notes that such knowledge could also contribute to projects of imperial control, but Jacquemont himself did not envision his travels as a political expedition.[3] Although he carefully collected scientific information for future study in France, Jacquemont never returned home from India or wrote the book he had planned to publish. After traveling for more than four years without a serious illness, he fell gravely ill with a liver infection and fever in Mumbai and died there in December 1832, age thirty-one. The journey that became the great transformative event of Jacquemont's life thus ended painfully and abruptly before he could fully explain its meaning to himself or others. His letters and journals, which were later published by his family and friends between the 1830s and 1880s, nevertheless provide a fascinating account of a young French traveler's encounter with Indian cultural differences; and they show how Jacquemont's journey

Victor Jacquemont. Engraving by Ch. Bouvier, after Mme Mérimée, ca. 1840. This idealized portrait by the artist Anna Mérimée (mother of Jacquemont's close friend Prosper Mérimée) suggests the youth and generational identity of the traveler whose posthumously published writings would eventually establish his French reputation as a knowledgeable analyst of North America and India. Old Books Images/Alamy Stock Photo.

led him to redefine his identity as a French European scientist and an ambitious French writer.[4]

A sense of isolation often emerges from Jacquemont's writings—an isolation amid crowds, communities, and customs that seem to intensify the solitary musings that appear throughout his accounts of other people. As Jacquemont left Kolkata for the interior of India, for example, he told a friend that he would see no Europeans in the countryside and that he would feel alone. "I am going to imbibe Asia in this long pilgrimage," he wrote. "I have already broken from Europe." His first trek would take him through heavily populated districts in central Asia, "but how important are people when they are so different from us?"[5] Evoking the religious language of a "pilgrimage" may seem unusual for a scientist, yet Jacquemont seemed to recognize that he had embarked on a transformative journey. He traveled with large crews of porters, cooks, and research assistants, but his letters frequently referred to his solitude and his strange memories of Europe in the heart of Asia. "There are periods from the past," he wrote to his father on 25 December 1829,

> that appear to me like dreams. I sometimes cannot believe that I am the person who did something [in France] or who has been there. . . . I have doubts at some moments about my identity, and I am ready to suspect, in this country of the transmigration of souls, that someone else's soul has expelled my own. The source of [my] enthusiasm is exhausted, and when the cold keeps me awake under my blankets, I contemplate the world not as an actor but as a critical, disinterested spectator of various scenes. I no longer *feel* the things of the past; I simply remember them and therefore judge what used to be inside of me like something that is outside of me.[6]

Jacquemont's description of a personal "transmigration" suggests the disorienting sensations that led him away from his former life, his former activities, and even his former identity. Nothing was quite the same in India, and the Jacquemont who gradually emerged from this migration conceived of himself and his culture with new meanings, new burdens, and new aspirations. His deepening insights into the overlapping levels of collective and individual identities would thus shape his descriptions of South Asia. All travelers begin new voyages under the influence of previous experiences, however, and Jacquemont experienced his first important cross-cultural encounters during his pre-Asian journeys in the United States and Haiti.

Jacquemont in North America: Politics, Culture, and the Contrasts with France

Jacquemont's transatlantic trip became the starting point for a later, more profound departure from the French home, relationships, and social world in which he had once lived and to which he always expected to return. He sailed into New York in early December 1826, carrying letters of introduction from the famous French "hero of two worlds," General Lafayette.[7] The trip's main purpose—in addition to a recovery from emotional despair over his breakup with Adélaïde Schiassetti—was to collect botanical information in rural America, but Jacquemont ultimately wrote to his French friends mainly about American culture and society. He became a sociologist as well as a natural scientist during his months in North America. Although he had planned to travel from New York City into rural western counties, an argument with a former general in Napoleon's army named Charles Lallemand led to an unexpected trip to Haiti. Outraged by the general's positive views of Bonaparte, he planned to stay at the Haitian home of his brother Frédéric Jacquemont and to prepare for a duel with Lallemand somewhere on the island. The duel never took place, apparently because Lallemand decided that a dispute with a young critic of Napoleon was not worth a trip to Haiti or a pointless risk of death. Jacquemont nevertheless remained in Haiti from February to May (1827) and began to develop a new intellectual identity as a French analyst of cultural differences.

Generalizing from his limited contact with Haitians, for example, Jacquemont argued that all human races had the potential to create modern civilizations, even if they might differ in their current achievements and cultural institutions. He thus rejected what is now called "racial essentialism" and assumed that people in every culture shared similar desires for happiness. To be sure, each culture developed distinctive ideas about the specific characteristics of a happy life, as Jacquemont noted by comparing the people in Protestant, commercial northern Europe with the people in Catholic, agrarian southern Europe. Almost everyone wanted to be happy, but they embraced different religions and pursued different activities to reach their goals. Such cultural differences were also evident to any traveler who compared the Haitians with the French, but Jacquemont would not accept racial traits as a causal explanation for the distinctive personal beliefs and social values that evolved historically in different human societies.[8] His earliest forays into cross-cultural analysis, in short, emphasized the potential for universal cultural developments and shared social aspirations rather than inherent racial differences.

This emphasis on the power of culture also shaped much of Jacquemont's discussion of the United States. Although his decision to embark on a scientific study of India shortened his North American travels to little more than a summer visit (June–August 1827), Jacquemont wrote several long letters about the culture he observed during his trips around New Jersey and New York. These letters might have disappointed his friend Lafayette because they were far more critical of the United States than anything Lafayette had written during his lifelong French-American exchanges. Jacquemont's letters on American life were not published until after Lafayette's death, however, so the man who "introduced" him to New Yorkers may have never known that his younger friend used his American trip to begin writing the kind of cross-cultural analysis he would later develop in India.

The historian René Rémond has described Jacquemont as part of an early nineteenth-century generation of French liberal travelers who were theoretically sympathetic to republican governments but unhappy about the social-cultural leveling they encountered whenever they visited America's rapidly developing commercial society. Rémond notes that young French liberals often became more critical of democratic institutions and cultures after they discovered that the citizens in a more egalitarian social system generally rejected aristocratic intellectual values as well as the political and social hierarchies of aristocratic European governments. French liberals, by contrast, identified with various aristocratic cultural traditions they wanted to preserve.[9] These elite intellectual perspectives (which would also become evident in Tocqueville's descriptions of the United States) reappeared often in Jacquemont's most detailed commentary on the new republic's social and cultural life, which he developed in a forty-page letter to Victor de Tracy during September 1827. Writing from the ship that carried him back to Europe, Jacquemont began his extended comments by noting that "American customs generally displease me" and that American manners and appearances were often "cold, flat, and ordinary." If his account therefore showed a certain coldness in its descriptions, he explained to Tracy, it would be "the fault of the subject" rather than the writer.[10]

American government policies reflected the problematic customs and cultural attitudes of the American people because democratic institutions represented the nation's dominant social values. Despite the national Constitution's abstract affirmation of religious tolerance, for example, Jacquemont noted that the evangelical clergy and Christian sects often imposed intolerant religious laws on local populations who were governed by religious-minded state or town officials. "Our Jesuits," Jacquemont explained to Tracy, "are like philosophes in comparison with these Puritans!"[11] American political culture was therefore suffused with an intense Protestant religiosity that undermined the enlightened theoretical principles of the national government. Although there were many Protestant sects, they all agreed on the sanctity of the Bible and demanded that their legislators prohibit every kind of Sunday work or amusements. There was no established national church, but the religious majority was often more oppressive than any European state religion and more intrusive in private lives than the Catholic Church in France.[12] Jacquemont thus concluded that France would not become a more enlightened society by turning toward Protestantism (an idea that French liberals such as Benjamin Constant sometimes suggested). The reputed individualism of American Protestantism obscured the fact that America's religious culture created new forms of intolerance and conformity, which provoked Jacquemont to abandon "all wishes for more Protestantism in our country" and to believe the French "would have nothing to gain from this kind of change. The multiplication of religious sects in the same country only increases the zeal of each sect."[13] This zeal, as Jacquemont described it, led directly to the religious dangers that enlightened thinkers and liberal critics of Roman Catholicism most wanted to avoid.

More generally, this religious-minded political culture exemplified unfortunate changes that had transformed American society since the creation of the new republic. Repeating a common complaint of almost all nineteenth-century French travelers, Jacquemont reported that American politics had declined because the extraordinary men of 1776—who were shaped by English European educations and enlightened knowledge—had disappeared, leaving state power to people who lacked a sophisticated understanding of political theories and complex government policies. Americans now spoke in political platitudes, showed virtually no interest in foreign affairs, argued mainly about who should be appointed to government offices, and learned about public affairs from superficial articles in mediocre newspapers.[14] As Jacquemont explained with comparative references to his own national culture, America's modern political leaders possessed almost none of the knowledge or theoretical insight that could be found in French newspapers, public debates, and political parties; and he had little doubt about the cause of the differences. "There is no intellectual aristocracy in the United States," he wrote in a diagnosis that Victor de Tracy and other French liberals would have understood and appreciated. The wide diffusion of basic education created cultural equalities in America, but this intellectual leveling also produced political and cultural mediocrity because the "enormous" cultural distinctions that characterized different groups of people in France no longer existed in the United States. Although the larger American cities had numerous literary and scientific societies, the members of these organizations spent their time electing officers and praising their leaders in the local newspapers rather than pursuing serious intellectual conversations.[15] Meanwhile, nobody did the hard work of an "intellectual aristocracy" that might rigorously analyze cultural traditions or produce advanced knowledge.

Jacquemont assumed that Americans did not pursue intellectual work because they were obsessed with making money. The main "immaterial pleasure" he could find among most people in the United States was an "ignoble pride in wealth" that blocked their appreciation for the other pleasures of a good life. In fact, he explained in another cultural generalization, much of "the life of feelings and of thought" was simply unknown to Americans, which meant that aesthetic traditions and other valued aspects of French culture were "foreign to their nature" or completely lost in the rush toward wealth. "They have no sense of art or poetry," he complained. "There is no admiration for the beautiful; they do not feel this [sense of beauty], even when it is presented to them in the simplest forms." To be sure, Americans had begun importing sculpture and paintings because they now had the money to acquire fine art from European artists, but they were so uncomfortable with human nudity that they covered the body parts of the statues that arrived from France.[16] Like "savages" in Brazil, they imitated European clothes and material objects, even though they could not understand the culture that created them. These cultural limitations seemed to afflict even the best-educated Americans whom Jacquemont met. "Take some men in all of the liberal professions, bring them together for an evening in a salon, listen to the general conversation that develops in the group or in their separate conversations: [and] I challenge you to find the slightest stimulation for your spirit."[17] Remembering the exchanges at salon conversations he had known in Paris, Jacquemont concluded that the United States still lacked the essential social and cultural foundations for elite intellectual creativity.

In addition to criticizing the obsession with money, Jacquemont lamented the woeful intellectual life among American women and within American families. Men and women were encouraged to marry at early ages in the United States, so the women quickly turned to childrearing as their main activity. "Their virtue," he noted in a simplistic summary of American wives, "is resignation." He observed that men and women rarely spoke with each other about serious issues; and if there were fewer scandalous sexual affairs in American families there was also a certain distance between the sexes that precluded close relationships.[18] In contrast to the French respect for cultural education, Americans worked mainly for the economic advancement of their children and instilled the rigid proprieties of religious morality.

Gender relations thus became another example of how religion pervaded every sphere of American daily life. Religious piety in no way inhibited the quest for wealth, of course, but Jacquemont became convinced that "the Bible seems to be the bane of America." Biblical allusions were repeated constantly in conversations, and the prevailing interpretations of biblical texts shaped the limits of acceptable public opinion and political beliefs. "Every career would be closed to a philosophically honest man," Jacquemont reported, or "to what they call an infidel."[19] Even Benjamin Franklin was no longer much remembered or admired in the United States because of his philosophical proclivities. This endless attention to religion, however, did not make Americans more virtuous than the people in less religious societies. Jacquemont had earlier believed that religion could be a useful moral instrument in modern national cultures, but he came away from America with a new perspective. "I no longer believe [in] this" moral utility of religion, he wrote to Tracy, because religious beliefs ultimately seemed to have "no influence on the private and secret life of individual persons."[20] Americans pursued worldly wealth rather than spiritual recompense in the next life, and reading the Bible never led enslavers to believe that slavery was an immoral foundation for their personal or social lives.

Jacquemont strongly condemned the slave system in America. He saw the system as both immoral and anachronistic, which made its ultimate demise inevitable. The slave states could not compete successfully with the commerce of the free states, and the enslavers' economic-political power would therefore eventually collapse. The injustices of racism and racial discrimination would nevertheless remain embedded in America's political, religious, and commercial systems. Indeed, Jacquemont found pervasive discrimination in the states where slavery had already been abolished. Such inequality might be expected to persist in hierarchical, aristocratic societies, but it obviously contradicted America's democratic ideals. "In a democratic country where the main principle of government is equality," he wrote, "I am disgusted by this horrifying inequality that exists in almost blatant contempt of the law. I have never been able to adjust to this sight with any self-control, and I was as angry about this discrimination on the day of my departure as I had been on the day I arrived." White Americans claimed that nature itself was responsible for the strict racial divisions they had created in their laws, yet this racist argument struck Jacquemont as a "stupid lie" that was disproved every day by the racial mixing he could see in the American cities he had visited.[21] White settlers used similar racist arguments to justify the displacement of Native people from western lands and to prevent the proper education of American Indian children, all of which showed that American racial theories had clear social consequences. The Native peoples of North America could be heading toward "extermination" if the United States did not change its long-standing support for the violent seizure of the tribal lands on which they lived. "The discovery of Columbus," he noted in his unsentimental, analytical style, "has been fatal for a large part of humankind."[22]

Jacquemont wrote about other American social patterns such as the popular consumption of hard cider; and he also discussed the soils, crops, and climate that were the scientific issues he had planned to study on his trip.[23] He was most interested in the debilitating effects of religion and cultural ignorance, however, and he condemned the lack of enlightened intellectual leadership in an American society that hypocritically defended racism and slavery. Despite its theoretical affirmation of human equality, the United States accepted the profound political and social inequalities of a nationwide racial caste system. Many of these themes would reappear when he later described how French society differed from the social system and religious beliefs in India and when he asserted Europe's cultural superiority in his comparative accounts of Asian cultures. By the time he arrived at Kolkata in 1829, Jacquemont had developed a well-honed intellectual proclivity for cross-cultural comparisons and an unshakable confidence in the cultural achievements of modern France.

Jacquemont in India: Material Conditions, Social Classes, and Gender Identities

The European responses to non-European societies have always included commentaries and anxieties about the climate, material conditions, racial or social differences, foods, languages, and gender relations in other parts of the world. These inescapable aspects of daily life made vivid impressions on nineteenth-century travelers and shaped their interpretations of cultural differences. Indeed, the quotidian, material realities of travel are still important for anyone who visits or lives in foreign countries because cross-cultural experiences begin with the body, and everybody talks about the weather. Jacquemont decided that Europeans had exaggerated the physical dangers of India's climate, for example, but he reported that India's weather and geography could never give him the pleasures he found in the climate and landscape at home. He also came to believe that hot weather destroyed most of the creative activity that flourished in more temperate regions of the world. Writing from Kashmir, he reported to his father that the "excessive heat" of summer days had drained his "European energy" and transformed him into "an indolent Asiatic."[24]

India's summer heat, however, was by no means the sole climatic problem for Jacquemont. The high temperatures became more stifling because neither the rain nor the mountains could provide the relief and satisfactions that the weather provided in France. "The land, which exhales such an agreeable smell in Europe when it is refreshed by a storm after a long drought, only emits foul miasmas here," he wrote in one of his descriptions of rural India. These bad smells followed the Indian rainstorms because (as Jacquemont described the problem) the downpours released vapors and "fetid" particles from dry soils that had absorbed vast quantities of animal urine. Fortunately, the "foul miasmas" of vaporized urine did not reach the higher mountains, yet even the most spectacular Asian peaks could not match the beauty he had seen in Europe. "I do not like the Himalayas as I like the Alps," he wrote to a friend in Switzerland. It was easy enough to find plants that resembled the vegetation in the Alps, "but their distribution does not have the same grace; the relief of the mountains also conceals the colossal height of the Himalayas. There are no long valleys, lakes, meadows, or pastures."[25] Jacquemont's senses thus carried him back to memories of rainy days and high mountains in France while his scientific curiosity kept pushing him toward some of the most unknown and beautiful places in Asia.

The differences between European and Asian climates and geography were more than matched by the differences that Jacquemont found in European and Asian peoples. The women of India, as he described them in his journals and letters, appeared to be less attractive than he had expected; the impoverished masses frequently suffered from diseases; and most people rarely washed their clothes or their bodies—especially in the mountains. "Their filth," he complained, "manifests itself far and wide by the most disagreeable odor." Mountain people may have seemed exceptionally dirty to Jacquemont, but he believed their physical movements were typical of all the Indians he met: "The habits of laziness and slowness among these people in the mountains are the same as those of people on the plains," he wrote in one generalizing summary of his demeaning social conclusions.[26] This pace of life often irritated Jacquemont, but he also found the Indians to be more graceful than Europeans and more at ease with the daily motions of their bodies. European obsessions with work and wealth drove them to run like ants through the streets of their big cities. Indians, by contrast, never ran anywhere. "The slow walk and the indolence of an Asian crowd are . . . full of grace and nobility," Jacquemont noted in his journal; "you rarely encounter expressions of grossness, and never those of brutality. . . . The physical constitution of these people is more agile than ours; it is more supple, more elastic; [and] it is this power of continuous movement that gives so much grace to [their] repose."[27] This grace in the movement and repose of Indian people was in fact so striking to Jacquemont that it became one of the few Indian traits that he deemed superior to the traits of European people or cultures.

His own body made Jacquemont feel exceedingly European as he traveled through India. Experiencing a racialized "otherness" he had never known in France, Jacquemont was a tall, thin white man who traveled under the gaze of people whom he wanted to describe and define with his own categorizing observations. His pale skin, however, gave him the conspicuous identity of a racial outsider in every place he visited, and he reported that his passage through small Indian villages was often a local spectacle because none of the inhabitants had ever seen a white man. A simple bath in the mountains attracted crowds of curious onlookers, including women who apparently found the color and appearance of this European male to be altogether strange. "What could be more novel," Jacquemont noted in reference to himself, "what could be more peculiar, what could be more curious for nearly black women, who have always seen only men of their own color, than to see one who is extremely white!"[28] It was, of course, impossible for Jacquemont to know what his observers thought or said about him, but he understood that his strange habits and skin color marked him inescapably as a European; and the critical scrutiny of unfamiliar bodies shaped both sides of his racialized, cross-cultural encounters.

Jacquemont could never have hidden his French origins even if he had wanted to disguise himself, but he expressed little inclination to abandon the outward European identity that he carried so prominently in his travels. He continued to wear European clothing, for example, and he always preferred European food. The Indian diet and eating habits seemed unbearably primitive to this Frenchman who could only dream of typical French meals, a bottle of French wine, and a good French dinner conversation.[29] Eating with other people was for Jacquemont a cultural pleasure that separated human beings from animals and Europeans from the rest of the world. Civilized people, he explained in another generalization, did not like to eat alone. "This universal instinct among the European people is . . . less developed in the other races of the human species," he wrote in his journal; and he attributed at least some of India's social problems and caste divisions to a lack of sociability at the dinner table. "Men eat here like beasts, solitary and silent; and the lower classes, that is to say the immense majority of the population, feed themselves like animals, with the same grain." There was no variety in the diet of lentils and grains, which Jacquemont, Indian villagers, and even their horses consumed with monotonous regularity. Although he sometimes added chicken, rice, butter, and spices to his best dinners, the basic foods at Jacquemont's mostly silent meals never really changed.[30]

The silence at Jacquemont's dinner table may have come partly from his problems with Indian languages. He was surprised to find that few English colonial officials knew how to speak Hindustani or Persian, but he also stressed his own difficulties in learning non-European alphabets, vocabularies, and grammars. "The system of writing in Oriental languages makes them prodigiously difficult to read," he explained as he struggled with language studies in Kolkata.[31] Although his reading skills therefore developed very slowly, he gradually acquired some fluency in speaking and sought to communicate with his Indian assistants in their own language. Recognizing that the inflections of Hindustani words (now usually referred to as Hindi-Urdu or as the related languages of Hindi and Urdu) were "different from those of European languages," he urged his guides to speak often in his presence and thereby help him improve his linguistic understanding and accent. He assumed that Indian languages would provide the best access to people whose culture intrigued him as much as the natural history of their land. "I am trying to penetrate their existence, their sentiments, [and] their ideas," he wrote in a letter to his father. "I am steeping myself in India rather than simply touching it with my fingertip like most of the English who claim to study it."[32]

Indian languages ultimately challenged and frustrated Jacquemont's scientific mind, however, which may explain why he concluded that Indian writings referred mainly to theology, metaphysics, and "other nonsense of the same genre." The study of Indian literatures (including Sanskrit) thus became a "useless science" for Jacquemont because, as he explained it, the "allegorical mysticism of the Orientals" affected every aspect of their languages, including their discussions of science and mathematics.[33] This evolving dislike for Asian languages expressed the typical frustrations of a traveler who struggled to understand alien words and approached unfamiliar linguistic traditions with the cultural presuppositions of a French writer. Yet this difficult encounter with Indian languages, like the encounters with the Indian climate, people, and foods, pushed Jacquemont toward a stronger sense of himself as a European scientist. The deep structures of Indian society and culture, in short, seemed to reveal and intensify Jacquemont's identification with the deep European cultural structures that continued to define his own French identity during all his travel across South Asia.

The differences between India and France also became apparent to Jacquemont as he described the hierarchies of social class and gender relations in Indian society. Drawing on his experiences in both the countryside and larger towns, Jacquemont decided that the social distinctions and caste boundaries in India contrasted sharply with the changing social relations in nineteenth-century France. Jacquemont never fully embraced the class structure in India, but he came to believe that the caste system prevented much of the unrest, anxiety, and unsated ambition that had become more common in France since the revolutionary demise of the Old Regime. At the same time, however, he reported that non-European societies lacked a French-style conception of liberty because they had no middle class of independent workers and businessmen. Although Europeans often used complex political metaphors to explain how the poor supported the wealthier social classes, Jacquemont found that the dichotomous social system in India was far more literal and obvious. "Instead of workers and eaters or governed and governors, which are the subtle distinctions of European politics, there are only the *carried* and the *carriers* in India." Accepting the social power of this distinction, Jacquemont soon identified entirely with the "carried" class. He insisted that his assistants address him with the most respectful language and titles (for example, "your highness" or "your majesty"). "Between the hammer and the anvil, between contempt and servile respect, no neutral position is possible," he explained to his brother in defense of his own drift away from the theoretical human *égalité* of modern French liberalism. In contrast to his deepening identification with French culture, Jacquemont began to doubt the viability of modern French aspirations for legal and political equality. By the end of his long Asian expedition, he found that his social values had become so "completely Indianized" that he felt angry when he saw men of his own caste acting in ways that he viewed as inappropriate for a ruling social elite.[34] The hierarchies of European colonialism thus become more acceptable to Jacquemont as he traveled in India and settled into the privileged, quasi-aristocratic position of an honored European traveler.

Jacquemont nevertheless rejected the claim that India's caste society was somehow rooted in divine origins. On the contrary, he consistently viewed the caste system as an "unjust" human institution that promoted "bizarre prejudices" and destroyed ambitions for social improvement among the lower classes. Yet this destruction of ambition was for Jacquemont the caste system's great advantage in comparison to the increasingly mobile society of modern France, where people sought obsessively to rise beyond their family's past social status. The poorest people in India, by contrast, seemed entirely willing (in Jacquemont's dichotomous narrative) to accept their inherited positions as an inevitable social destiny within an inherited hierarchical system. They were neither embarrassed nor angry about a status that in postrevolutionary France would lead to shame, rebellion, and psychological conflicts.[35] India may not have offered appropriate models for French intellectuals, but Jacquemont suspected that European workers might generally be more content if they could reconcile themselves like poor Indians to the social position and manual labor of their parents. The French traveler who disliked many of the leveling social and cultural patterns in early nineteenth-century America therefore seemed to find a more congenial hierarchy in the enduring repetition of social positions and hierarchies among Indian sons and fathers.

And what about Jacquemont's own restless desire to surpass a scholarly father? Here too, perhaps, one finds a prescription for the case of unrequited ambition that was driving him across India. Leaving Delhi on the last leg of his journey (February 1832), Jacquemont reflected on the possible pleasures of poverty and repose for the Indian lower classes:

> They are absolutely lacking in imagination; but the fumes of tobacco smoke no doubt carry them into vague dreams that are perhaps worth more than the pleasures and pains of the imagination. They don't know the ecstasies of happiness in a more elevated sphere of passions and thoughts; but we who think and feel in this sphere, how much despair, how much sadness we also find there! And they are not aware of these pains.
>
> I would have wanted then to change my existence for theirs, because I suffered acutely from my imagination and my sensibility.[36]

Jacquemont thus perceived the economically impoverished people in India (like the culturally impoverished people in America) as "other" kinds of human beings who were free of the anxieties, despair, and passions that disturbed him and most educated persons in Europe. Cultural difference became for Jacquemont a sign of emotional difference. If the Indians felt few real joys, they were at least saved from great sadness. If they missed out on great love, they were also spared great heartaches. "The exterior form of material existence varies as much, if not more, as it does among us in the different classes of societies," Jacquemont explained to his father; "but the interior life is the same everywhere [in India]. There is almost never any passion to give it some variety."[37]

This alleged absence of passions became an important theme in Jacquemont's explanation for the degraded position of women in Indian culture. Marriages resulted from family agreements rather than from mutual affection, and children were often committed to future marriages by the time they were eight years old. Such customs showed little concern for the sentiments of young people, though Jacquemont conceded that the Indian system prevented the romantic mistakes and despair he had seen (and experienced) in France. More shocking, however, and more typical of attitudes toward women, was the practice of selling young girls to the men of Kashmir. Jacquemont reported that English attempts to suppress the sale of women had not yet succeeded, and young, available women came to his door almost every day. "An Asiatic squire, in my place, would always have about forty of them to sing and dance around him," he explained to his brother; "but I maintain my European integrity in my morals as in my clothing."[38] Adhering to his ascetic commitments to scientific research, Jacquemont steadfastly denied any attraction to dark-skinned, non-European women; but he commented extensively on a pervasive disrespect for women that contributed to both the sale of young girls and the social acceptance of polygamous marriages.

According to Jacquemont, the men in these marriages were mostly indifferent to their own children and contemptuous toward their many wives. "The woman is an impure being whom her husband regards as barely belonging to his own species. The children . . . soon pick up this abominable idea, which separates them from their mother as soon as they can pass from her care." Suffering from the abuse of husbands and children alike, these scorned women were not allowed to read or write or cultivate artistic talents of any kind. This degradation was bad for the women themselves, but Jacquemont also saw a direct link between the low status of women and a general dissipation of morals, a weakness in domestic affections, and a desire for sexual relations between men.[39]

Jacquemont's French judgments thus shaped his strong condemnations of marriages and sexual customs that excluded women from education, freedom, and respect in Asian societies. He could find only a couple of exceptions to the general disdain for Indian women, and both exceptions appeared among women who lived outside the normal structures of South Asian (or French) marriages. He discovered, for example, that the prostitutes in Amritsar were independent, friendly women and that "public opinion does not degrade these prostitutes as in our own country." They were respected members of the community whose social acceptance reversed French social mores in ways that both puzzled and fascinated Jacquemont when he visited the city.[40] This view of prostitutes seemed strange to

Jacquemont because it clearly differed from the usual gender hierarchies in France, but the cultural traditions he encountered in some Tibetan villages diverged even further from the French social meanings of womanhood and manhood. Traveling in the mountains, he came upon an isolated culture in which all the brothers of a family married the same woman. The married men were therefore obliged to compete for the attention of a single woman, which led Jacquemont to wonder how such a society could avoid constant family disputes and marital conflicts (he was assured that nobody felt jealous in these marriages). Although this unexpected reversal of marriage roles struck Jacquemont as "the most ignoble of compensations for the polygamy that prevails in all the rest of the Orient," it also provided a rare alternative to the hierarchical structures that dominated most of India's social life and merged with Britain's colonial political system.[41]

The gender relations and marriage customs in India therefore attracted Jacquemont's critical attention because they differed from the social practices that governed female-male relations in France (where other gender hierarchies were also common). But Jacquemont's commitments to French science and Enlightenment traditions generated even more skepticism and critique when he turned from Indian social hierarchies to the religious beliefs, political institutions, and intellectual traditions that had shaped India's long cultural history.

Jacquemont in India: Religion, Politics, Knowledge, and Literature

The power that was often implicit in Indian social relations became more explicit in religious or political systems and in the cultural organization of knowledge or literature. Jacquemont recognized that Indian social customs and gender hierarchies were connected to religion, politics, and other cultural values, but he also analyzed political and cultural ideas as distinctive shaping forces in Indian society. His cross-cultural comparisons of religion, politics, and knowledge, however, all stressed European superiority, mainly because Jacquemont assumed that modern progress and freedom were unique, positive legacies of the French Enlightenment and Revolution.

The beliefs and rituals of Indian religions offered nothing that Jacquemont could see as valuable for his scientific projects. Traveling around the countryside with a rationalist passion to categorize plants, trees, rocks, and insects, he decided that the spiritual preoccupations of Hinduism were essentially useless for human progress and modern knowledge. "Among all the follies and miseries of humanity," he wrote in his journal, "religion is the one whose history is the most boring and the least profitable." The flaws of religion, which he had also criticized in his

A Hindu Woman. Engraving by R. Woodman, after a drawing by William Daniell, ca. 1836, in Hobart Caunter, *The Oriental Annual, or Scenes in India* (London: Edward Churton, 1836). Jacquemont criticized the marriage customs and family relations he observed in India, yet he was also surprised to find that some Indian women were more respected than French women and that some exceptional women-centered marriages reversed the gender hierarchies of European cultures. This image from an English book shows how European men portrayed the "otherness" of Hindu women during the era in which Jacquemont was traveling in South Asia. Rare Book Collection, Wilson Library, University of North Carolina at Chapel Hill.

descriptions of American Protestantism, seemed especially obvious to Jacquemont in India, where Hindus promoted ideas that offered (in his view) little more than a consolation for early deaths. Indeed, as Jacquemont described it, Hinduism transformed death itself into the most desirable experience of life. "In his entirely negative existence," Jacquemont wrote in an account of the Hindu believer, "rest is the supreme good and the annihilation in death is for him one of the forms of rest. While we conceive of the Brahman theology as something like appalling nonsense, the absorption in Brahma is the most celestial beatitude in the Hindu paradise. But it seems to me that through the absorption in Brahma, one must seek the annihilation of the *me*, the total destruction of the moral being as well as the physical being."[42] Some Europeans might have explored this ostensible Indian serenity in the face of death, but Jacquemont viewed the serenity as an unintelligible, emotional expression of a religion that linked death to the rebirth of life and placed the highest value on the abolition of selfhood.

Few ideas could have seemed more alien or unappealing to an ambitious French scientist who was working to create empirical knowledge and to construct the personal reputation that would lead to a successful future career. Ironically, as a Hindu believer may well have understood, Jacquemont would die before he could achieve his ambitious scholarly or worldly goals. Such ironic (realistic? tragic? Hindu?) perspectives were not part of Jacquemont's journey toward knowledge, however, because he could not understand a religious indifference to science, personal ambitions, and social reform. "In these vast countries," he wrote to Destutt de Tracy, "the human condition does not appear susceptible to any amelioration or any change so long as the religious ideas remain the same, and Hinduism seems to be immutable."[43] Meanwhile, Jacquemont believed that India's only hope for escape from the effects of this "immutable" religious culture lay in the benevolent, civilizing control of the imperial British government.

Jacquemont never assumed that the British ruled India through the general consent of the Indian population. In fact, it was a colonial government whose power rested on conquest, force, and the only principle that a "semi-barbaric" people could accept: despotism. Lord William Bentnick, the wise governor who acted "like a Quaker in Pennsylvania," and his British administration thus used a "paternal despotism" to maintain social order and provide whatever progress one could find in the schools, legal systems, and bureaucracies of Indian society. India's own princes, as Jacquemont portrayed them, were "like children" whose irrationality and poor judgment called for constant supervision. "And it is not just the princes," Jacquemont noted in another critical generalization, "it is the entire population that is deprived of reason and moral sense."[44]

Britain's firm control of Indian political culture was thus for Jacquemont the only defense against violence, brigands, and the petty disputes of local leaders, none of whom seemed to understand the most basic principles of "civilized" justice or rational government policies. Developing themes that French colonizers would later use to justify their own expanding imperial ventures in Africa and Indochina, Jacquemont assumed that British imperialism had become essential for the preservation of peace and order in South Asia. "European civilization is justified in invading the universe," he wrote. "Lacking the *civilization* of the West, people in other parts of the world still receive an immense benefit from this [European] domination alone; and it is probably the only benefit that the [Eastern] religious institutions will allow us to carry into the Orient." Jacquemont therefore believed that European nations played a stabilizing role in Asian politics and made civilizing contributions to human progress throughout the world. He welcomed news of the 1830 July Revolution in France, for example, as new evidence that Britain and France were the two "leaders of modern civilization" and also the most prominent advocates of "social improvements" and "human happiness" for people in all modern societies.[45] The differences that separated these two nations in Europe simply disappeared amid the wider "civilizing" responsibilities that united all Europeans in Asia; and these responsibilities derived ultimately in Jacquemont's view from the superior ideals and achievements of Europe's political institutions. Why, then, could Indian cultures not simply advance on the European political path toward progress and freedom? The answer to that question carried Jacquemont's reflections from society and politics into the realm of intellectual traditions.

In contrast to the many Europeans who traveled across South Asia to establish trading companies or proselytize or build military bases, Jacquemont traveled as a scientist and writer who expressed strong interests in the intellectual life of the societies he described. In this respect, his writings exemplified (as noted earlier) what Mary Louise Pratt has called the "anti-conquest" narratives of natural historians.[46] He did not view India merely or mainly as a geographical space for European economic development. He interpreted his experiences instead through the lens of French literary culture, and he understood that his own intellectual reputation and status could best develop as a representative of Western cultural knowledge in Asia and as an expert on Asian societies and natural history in France. The contrasting intellectual traditions of French and South Asian societies thus opened a space for Jacquemont to pursue his personal ambitions and to claim a new personal identity as a scientific analyst of cultural differences. But Jacquemont (like Flora Tristan in Peru) assumed that French forms of knowledge, education, and literature far surpassed Indian cultural achievements, so that his account of intellectual differences also constructed historical hierarchies that ranked the cultures of the world within a Eurocentric framework.

Jacquemont claimed that Indian culture lacked intellectual vitality because people in India focused constantly on simple physical needs or obscure spiritual myths. The consequence of both preoccupations appeared in a common Indian indifference to the philosophical and scientific questions that animated the transnational cultural life of Europe. Jacquemont acknowledged that such a nonscientific society could be "picturesque," though it struck him personally as a "blank piece of paper on which my spirit finds nothing to read." This strange, "blank" place thus offered no significant resources "for the curiosity of our spirit and the exercise of our intelligence," Jacquemont noted in a journal entry that summarized his low regard for the reputed wisdom of the East as well as his own identity-shaping links to the knowledge and power of French academic institutions.[47] He assured his father's philosophical colleague Destutt de Tracy that even a 120-volume encyclopedia of Tibetan knowledge consisted almost exclusively of reflections on "the attributes of God, the first of which was incomprehensibility." Such doctrines could never produce knowledge as Jacquemont and Tracy defined it, and so the 120 volumes of Tibetan wisdom moved from the attributes of God to a strange "mélange of theology, medicine, astrology, fabulous legends, and metaphysics. This awful nonsense," Jacquemont went on to explain, "does not even have the merit of originality. Like the majority of Tibetan books, it seems to be merely a translation or compilation from Sanskrit that was collected 150 years ago."[48] Given the scientific ignorance that he found in Sanskrit and Tibetan texts (linguistic barriers did not inhibit his evaluations), Jacquemont assumed that Indian society could never make intellectual progress without a massive infusion of European knowledge and education.

Fortunately, as he saw it, this European learning had begun to enter India through the new English schools in which Indian students were taught the European languages and sciences that conveyed true knowledge. The success of this curriculum could be measured by the fact that many students had "naturally converted from Mohammad and from Brahma to reason," thereby proving that European science was more effective than Christianity in bringing India's youth to modern civilization. Although some students complained that their new knowledge isolated them from their own nation, Jacquemont believed that such alienation was an acceptable consequence of Europe's civilizing mission. The English language that separated young people from their families also connected them to a wider cultural world of "European knowledge" that would be essential for the intellectual and social development of modern India.[49] Jacquemont assumed that

The Bernar Pagoda. Engraving by R. Wallis, after a drawing by William Daniell, ca. 1835, in Hobart Caunter, *The Oriental Annual, or Scenes in India* (London: Bull and Churton, 1835). The sacred sites and religious traditions in Indian cultures remained alien and inaccessible to Jacquemont's scientific worldview, but he also wrote about how Indian religious thought deepened his own identification with nineteenth-century French intellectual life. Hindu beliefs and temples symbolized a cultural distance from England or France that European artists tried to portray during the 1830s through pictures such as this engraving of a temple in Benares. Rare Book Collection, Wilson Library, University of North Carolina at Chapel Hill.

the tenets of European knowledge, like the enlightened tenets of liberal politics, came especially from England and France, represented the most advanced stage of civilization, and justified the exercise of European power in non-European societies.

The connections between knowledge and power became obvious to Jacquemont in the course of his travels. He found that his scientific equipment and experiments aroused both curiosity and respect among the common people who watched him work or read his books. "I am an extremely mysterious man for them," he wrote in one of his letters to France; and this mystery, in turn, was connected to another cultural hierarchy that Jacquemont soon came to appreciate.

"Any man here who is a bit less ignorant . . . than the others," he noted, "is a saint."[50] The knowledge that made him mysterious and important to people in the countryside also opened doors to the palaces of British governors and Indian rajahs, all of whom were apparently eager to listen to the conversation of a young French scientist. Jacquemont gradually learned that the independent Indian rulers in Punjab and Kashmir would treat him as a favored guest because he could give them detailed information about European nations—especially facts about populations, tax revenues, civil law, armies, and industrial enterprises. In Punjab, for example, Rajah Goulab-Sing asked his secretaries to write down Jacquemont's lengthy descriptions of European governments and social organizations. "Seated behind us," Jacquemont reported to his father, "[the secretaries] wrote my words in haste. So there I was, taken down in shorthand like the metaphysics of Cousin! But I am more practical."[51] Wandering far from Parisian lecture halls, Jacquemont could deliver his knowledge to the reigning powers in Asian states like an intellectual celebrity in France (as noted earlier, Victor Cousin's influential philosophical ideas helped to reshape French views of postrevolutionary selfhood during the 1820s, when Jacquemont was a student in French schools).

Jacquemont knew what he was doing, and he knew that his "European knowledge" gave him a status in Asia that he might never acquire in France. "I have always thought a European would have to be a fool if he did not know how to hold the complete interest of an ignorant Asiatic in conversation," he explained to another expatriate in India. "Europe is for them, in all its details and in every respect, a world of wonders that they like to hear about with the most lively curiosity... if you know how to choose the subject and the style [of information] that interests them."[52] Jacquemont must have learned how to choose interesting subjects as he explained specific details about Europe, because he reported extensive conversations with local leaders and powerful rajahs in every autonomous region of India he visited; and the proud accounts of his success among the Indian elites conveyed his own recognition that knowledge could provide social privileges as well as intellectual satisfaction.

Despite the pleasures of his status in India, however, Jacquemont always viewed the rigors and loneliness of his Indian journey as a necessary preparation for his main personal goal: intellectual stature in France. Although his knowledge of Europe gave him a gratifying status in the palaces of India, he wanted his extraordinary knowledge of India to grant him the more enviable social and cultural status of a famous scientist and writer in France. He described this ambition most explicitly in letters to Victor de Tracy, who was becoming a prominent figure in the Parisian political and intellectual circles that facilitated advancement in French cultural institutions. Perhaps Jacquemont worried that his Parisian friends were moving forward in their French careers and gaining public reputations while he wandered through India. In any case, he told Tracy that he tried not to worry about the delays and setbacks of Asian travel, partly because he had expected such problems when he left Europe for "these distant countries," and partly because he felt confident about the ultimate rewards of his scientific work. "I hope," he wrote in an early letter from Kolkata, "with some courage and some perseverance to acquire here something that will give me an honorable place in the world when I return." That desire for future recognition enabled him to face hardships with a certain equanimity and optimism. "I feel myself making progress," he wrote to Tracy. "One cannot be unhappy [if one lives] with this feeling."[53]

This sense of intellectual progress may have provided consolation for the lonely days of his trip, but Jacquemont still yearned for the pleasures of Tracy's country home. He looked forward to a time when he could spend winter days there, "rereading my travel journals and preparing some work that would take me out of obscurity!"[54] The escape from obscurity, as Jacquemont began to plan it in India, would come via the publication of a major book that could combine his detailed research on natural science with an extensive analysis of Indian society, culture, and politics. "My ambition," he confided to Tracy, "would be to mix general physics and some advanced analysis of natural history with some descriptions of political history and sketches of Indian customs. But how will I be able to do this without forgetting the simple severity of language in which the sciences must be expressed?"[55]

Jacquemont was never able to answer this question about the literary reconciliation of the natural sciences and social sciences. His family and friends would eventually publish his letters and vast journals without separating his scientific and cultural observations into the different thematic categories that Jacquemont himself wanted to develop in the book he had planned to write. Yet the early death that prevented him from writing his book did not ultimately deny him an "honorable place In the world," though he would reach this place only posthumously and without material rewards. His long, transnational journey ended finally with the French publication of texts that would establish his scientific and literary reputation as a French expert on India's natural history and human cultures. He would thus come "home" to France and a French reputation through an unexpected, circuitous route that became the literary completion of an unexpected, circuitous life story.

In the last year of his Indian trip, Jacquemont wrote to one of his brothers about the unanticipated directions of his wandering life—which was "so completely different, materially and in sensibility, from that [life] for which I had thought I was born and to which I shall return after long voyages."[56] We can now see a poignant meaning in this letter because we know that Jacquemont only "returned" from his voyages through books that appeared after his death. Those books mapped out a kind of homeward journey in the detailed reports of a young French writer who gradually discovered his French cultural identity and a deepening sense of French selfhood as he was also discovering the foreign cultures of India. But Jacquemont ultimately found his place in the French generation of 1820 by leaving France forever.

CHAPTER TWO

Flora Tristan and the Quest for Independent French Womanhood in Peru

FOUR MONTHS AFTER Victor Jacquemont's death in India, Flora Tristan left Bordeaux on an arduous voyage to Peru (April 1833). Her flight from France evolved out of a complicated personal history that reveals many of the differences in social class and gender that separated Tristan's life from the life of Jacquemont.[1] She was the daughter and first child of Anne-Pierre Laisnay and Mariano de Tristan, a Peruvian who had worked for the Spanish king and served as a colonel in the Spanish army. Although her parents met in Spain and were married there by a French émigré priest (her mother had left France during the Revolution), Flora was born in Paris in April 1803. Her father had enough money for the family to live comfortably and enough friends to create a lively household after they moved into Napoleonic France. One of the family's notable friends in Paris was the future revolutionary "liberator" Simón Bolívar, so the Tristans' daughter heard stories about South America from an early age. Mariano de Tristan died, however, when Flora was only four years old, and the Tristan house was soon confiscated and sold by the French government (1808) because it had been the property of a Spanish soldier and because the Tristans' marriage had never received legal recognition in a French civil ceremony.

Following the loss of her father and the family house, Flora Tristan's childhood became a story of migration from Paris into the countryside, deepening poverty, the death of her only brother, and emerging fantasies about a wealthy Peruvian family that lived beyond reach in a faraway, unknown place. In contrast to the well-educated Jacquemont, the impoverished and vulnerable Flora Tristan received little schooling and learned about the wider world mostly through her own self-taught devices. Apprenticed at the age of seventeen to a somewhat older Parisian lithographer named André Chazal, she soon married her boss and fell into a terrible cycle of domestic violence, angry separations, and bitter struggles over the custody of their three young children. She finally managed to leave her husband in 1825 (divorce was illegal in France until 1884) and to work for several years in the service of an English family with whom she traveled in Britain and southern Europe, but this arrangement offered no permanent solutions for her problems with money, child custody, and an angry, estranged husband. Acting finally on some information about her father's influential family in Peru, Tristan wrote to an uncle in search of a possible inheritance from her long-deceased father's estate.[2] This correspondence produced a noncommittal response from her father's wealthy brother, Pío de Tristan (1773–1860), but enough money (2,500 francs) to justify hopes for a significant financial settlement if she could meet her Peruvian relatives.

After months of complex planning, which included the need to find a hiding place for her seven-year-old daughter (one son had died; the other lived with his father) and discreet communications with a sympathetic French ship captain, Tristan left for Peru in search of a family and heritage she had never known. She therefore set off on her extraordinary trip without the official sponsorship, financial support, or scientific agenda that Jacquemont had carried to India. Even more significant, perhaps, she traveled as an unaccompanied woman in an era when only men were expected to make such trips—and she never revealed her marital separation during a voyage in which she was the lone woman aboard a ship with nineteen men.

Tristan's journey thus began as a risky personal quest for family acceptance and financial support, but these goals were never achieved. Responding to her setbacks in Peru, she would return to France with new aspirations to write, enter public debates, and assert her emerging identity as an independent woman. Tristan arrived in South America after a difficult five months at sea and made her way across a desert to Arequipa, Peru (September 1833). She settled into a long stay at her family's home in Arequipa, but her uncle Pío was unwilling to grant her an inheritance or to accept her as a legitimate niece because her parents had never established a legal recognition of their marriage. Despite the intense personal disappointment of this rejection, Tristan remained in Peru until July 1834, observing the customs and politics of Peruvian society, talking with the people of Arequipa and Lima, and keeping a journal in which she described her impressions of Peruvian culture. The personal quest for a lost father's family therefore evolved into a cross-cultural discovery of society, politics, and identity that also transformed Flora Tristan from a wandering, abused wife into a French writer who would forcefully assert that women and workers must attain the universal "Rights of Man." She found in her father's Peruvian homeland that she was really a European, and she found new ways to understand herself as an autonomous French woman through her encounters with women in South America. She therefore reaffirmed her *French* national identity while also creating a new literary identity as an advocate for *universal* human rights.[3]

Returning to France in early 1835, Tristan began to write about women in Europe and Peru and to prepare a book that would report the vicissitudes of her long trip. This book, *Peregrinations of a Pariah* (1838), launched her new career and public identity by describing a non-European culture for French readers and by stressing the shared fates of "pariahs" in other parts of the world. Indeed, her (partial) personal and political identification with marginalized people in South America shaped her deepening political identification with French workers as well as her support for vulnerable women everywhere, and she would devote the few remaining years of her life to writings and organizations that promoted the emancipation of laborers and women alike (she died of typhoid in Bordeaux in 1844, age forty-one). She thus traveled across southern France with the identity and ideas that she had first described in accounts of her trip to South America, advocating for disadvantaged social groups and challenging the privileged power of men and social elites.[4]

Tristan's immersion in Peruvian society provoked the sense of disorientation and isolation that Jacquemont had experienced in India, though her trip was shorter and she was never as far away from European culture; in fact, she lived with her father's Spanish-speaking family or with other Europeans during almost all of her time in Peru. Yet Tristan remembered this trip as an experience of solitude and alienation, and her accounts of Peru conveyed the impressions of a detached spectator and lonely outsider. The "pariah" could not find much comfort in her painful memories of a Parisian past or in the "terrifying emptiness" and "unspeakable sadness" of a Peruvian present in which her uncle Pío rejected her claims for familial legitimacy. "I realized too late," she wrote after describing her uncle's negative response to her requests for an inheritance,

> that, driven by despair, I had yielded too easily and recklessly to my imagination when I came to Peru. . . . Candid to a fault, I felt the need to pour out my sorrows, but when I would have liked to weep upon the bosom of a friend, I was forced to shut myself away and live under constant constraint. I declare that when I left France I had no idea of the tortures the role of *demoiselle* would impose upon me. . . .
>
> The thought of France only recalled my past sufferings. . . . I did not know where to fly or what would become of me: I saw no refuge anywhere on earth. . . . A somber melancholy took possession of me; I grew silent and meditated

> sinister designs. I held life in aversion: it had become an intolerable burden. . . . I spent eight days and nights in the grip of death; I felt its icy hands upon my body.[5]

Tristan eventually came out of this emotional crisis with a new determination to live and to act in the world. Her first plan focused on possible political action in Peru, but she soon recognized that she could not make her way to power in such an alien, masculine world. She therefore turned to writing (another form of power) and decided that she must return to France to pursue new literary ambitions that began to emerge as she abandoned her hopes for a Peruvian inheritance. This quest for the new identity of a French writer thus emerged from Tristan's travels, yet her determined construction of a new selfhood also reflected her deep desire to escape from the social position that had defined her identity during the French prehistory of her long journey to South America.

Tristan in France: Marriage and Women's Rights in a Postrevolutionary Society

Jacquemont's early experiences in Haiti and the United States helped him become more aware of social and cultural hierarchies across the Atlantic world, but Tristan began to develop a critique of social inequalities and cultural problems before she ever left home. Although the French prehistory of her trip to Peru cannot be traced through long letters before 1833, she narrated the story of her earlier self in the foreword and preface to *Peregrinations of a Pariah*. Developing this retrospective account of her pre-trip identity almost five years after her travels, Tristan used historical hindsight to describe a long journey toward personal reconstruction.

These prefatory materials thus introduced autobiographical themes that framed Tristan's interpretations of France and Peru and placed the meaning of her trip in a social context of modern marriage relationships. Like Jacquemont, she began to establish her personal and generational identity within a specific French cultural milieu, which in her case included the much-debated ideas of Henri de Saint-Simon and the Saint-Simonian movement for social reform. As Claire Goldberg Moses and Leslie Wahl Rabine have explained in a well-informed analysis of the Saint-Simonian connections with French feminism during the 1830s, Tristan was influenced by this movement's religious aspects (for example, the expected emergence of a "woman messiah" who would help lead France toward a new social order) and by its Romantic cultural themes (for example, the emphasis on individual rights and freedoms that women could not attain within the gendered legal hierarchies of French marriages).[6] Historians have also noted that Tristan

Flora Tristan. Lithograph by Jules Laure, 1847. Tristan's advocacy for personal independence, women's rights, and the economic advancement of French workers gave her an enduring stature among admirers who continued to honor her work and writings after her early death. Laure's portrait suggests her forceful gaze toward the future. Signal Photos/Alamy Stock Photo.

liked to dramatize her own life story, drawing on melodramatic conventions that portrayed theatrical characters struggling to survive in conflicts between the social forces of good and evil.[7] Such theatrical traditions may have influenced Tristan's retrospective self-portrait of an emerging "pariah," but her self-description of a separated wife and aspiring writer went beyond a theatrical pose by introducing the personal story of a woman's journey toward a more independent selfhood.

The preface of *Peregrinations* began with a general claim that "we all contribute, even if unknowingly, to the progressive development of our species," but Tristan also stressed that some "special agents of Providence" take the lead in charting a path that "humanity will pursue after them."[8] This opening generalization implicitly suggested that the author of this book could well be playing such a path-breaking historical role, in part because the writings that were the "most useful" for social progress were those that showed "the individual in the various positions of social existence."[9] Tristan therefore wanted to publish her travel narrative to show how her own "social existence" provided unique perspectives on the general conditions of modern society.

She insisted that histories of personal experience should not focus simply on powerful people or elite social classes, which male authors often wrote about in traditional memoirs about notable public lives and public actions. An authoritative, *modern* memoir, by contrast, needed to describe life experiences outside high society, and it needed to convey more than mere information. The author who wanted to explain human experiences with complete honesty must "have suffered and suffered greatly, for only misfortune can teach us to know exactly what both we ourselves and others are worth." Such suffering became the best foundation for a wider view of humanity, especially if the author had "seen much" and could "consider humanity from a point of view other than that of our own village bell tower." Those who traveled to distant cultures might therefore help guide others toward the future, yet even personal suffering and travel experiences could not guarantee the honesty that made certain authors "most useful" for all of humanity. "It is, finally, necessary to have the faith of a martyr in one's heart," Tristan argued, because only a "martyr" would defy others, no matter what the social cost, to advance the higher cause of social progress. "If the expression of one's thoughts is stilled by concern for the opinion of others, if the voice of one's conscience is stifled by the fear of making enemies or by personal considerations, one fails at one's mission and repudiates God."[10]

It was this exceptional willingness to accept the role of a martyr that Tristan attributed to herself. She would write honestly about her personal sufferings and arduous travels, and her honesty would expand her narrative from a story of one person's long journey into an account of universal social problems. This book would not just tell the story of Flora Tristan; it would become a story about everyone who suffered and especially a story about all women. By describing her travel toward a new life, Tristan explained, "I am fulfilling the mission that was given to me and obeying my conscience. Hatred may rise up against me; but, *as I am a person of faith* before anything else, no consideration whatsoever can prevent me from telling the truth about people and things. . . . I will have the courage to tell everything I have suffered."[11] Equally important, she promised to tell the truth by naming specific persons, thus rejecting George Sand's literary method of moving oppressive realities into fictional stories. Instead of publishing under a man's name and transforming real people into characters in a novel, Tristan would write unapologetically under her own name and with explicit references to her own life. "I often speak of myself," she wrote in her preface. "I portray myself in my sufferings, thoughts, and feelings, all of which result from the disposition that God has given me, the upbringing I received, and the position that laws and prejudices have made for me."[12]

Skeptical readers of autobiographical narratives know, of course, that the authors of such texts construct themselves and other people with the linguistic strategies that also create the characters in novels, even when (like Tristan) the author describes her own character as a simple "truth-teller" or as a traveler whose life story will speak for the experiences of all unhappily married women. "It is thus not to *myself personally* that I wanted to attract attention, but rather to all the women who are in the same situation and whose numbers are increasing daily. They suffer trials and tribulations of the same nature, are preoccupied by the same sorts of ideas, and feel the same emotions."[13] Tristan's literary mission, in short, was to tell a story about her setbacks on a self-defining journey that might help other suffering women seek and find a freer social identity.

This bold claim for the literary mission of an exceptional writer thus emphasized Tristan's earlier social position as a woman who was oppressed by gender hierarchies and an abusive husband. Her unhappy marriage had given her the personal knowledge with which she began her journey. Where Jacquemont could write as a well-trained scientist and detached observer of alien social mores, Tristan would become a woman writer whose vulnerabilities precluded the abstract scientific reflections or detachment of a male French intellectual. She was fleeing from dangers and seeking a new kind of social freedom, so her self-defined, pre-trip identity differed (in class, gender, and cultural authority) from the identity that Jacquemont had begun to stake out for himself in his early writings from America. Although Jacquemont condemned slavery as a corrupt, hierarchical system in America, Tristan's preface in *Peregrinations* focused on social hierarchies that were much closer to home. She conceded that European countries did not have slave markets in public squares (as in the United States), but she stressed that every nation had "many classes of individuals" who were suffering from "legal oppression." This oppression was especially obvious wherever divorce was illegal (as in France) and wherever marriages could not be dissolved by the free will of unhappy women. This legal injustice sustained a "social order that leaves [women] . . . without professions and keeps them in dependency even as it forges their chains through the indissolubility of marriage."[14]

Tristan illustrated the personal consequences of this oppressive social reality by describing how her mother had pushed her "to marry a man whom I could neither love nor respect. To this union I owe all my misfortune." Although she had left this abusive husband as soon as she was able to escape in her early 20s, her separation could not lead to legal recognition or civil rights or any social means to free herself from the alienated position of "a miserable *Pariah*." The (unrecognized) disintegration of her marriage had therefore placed Tristan on the social margins, where her "life was a torture at every moment" because few people would believe her accounts of the abusive husband and because she faced constant struggles to gain custody of her children.[15] Tristan's "prehistory" to the great Peruvian journey thus became a justification and explanation for the trip itself. Trapped in a legal system that offered women no route to an independent social position, Tristan would use her travels and writings to transform her "pariah" status into a new identity. It was a difficult journey toward selfhood, even as she viewed it in retrospect, but Tristan justified this exceptional flight from her native country and her children by invoking direct comparisons with the slave system in America:

> I resolved to make my journey to Peru only with great regret. . . . To leave my country which I loved in preference to all others, to leave my daughter who had no one but me to lean on, . . . and finally to make all these sacrifices, to confront all these dangers because I was bound to a person who claimed me as if I were his slave! Oh! These reflections made my heart leap with indignation; I cursed this social organization which substitutes the chains of slavery for the bonds of love and divides society into *bondswomen* and *masters*.[16]

The preface to Tristan's travel book therefore set up a personal and social prehistory that would give meaning to much of what she experienced in Peru. It was the "baggage" she carried with her on the longest journey of her life, and it was a personal history that would still affect her when she returned to France. When *Peregrinations of a Pariah* was published in Paris, her enraged, estranged husband, André Chazal, bought a pistol, stalked her in the street, and shot her at point-blank range (10 September 1838). Although she was seriously wounded, Tristan survived the attack and testified against Chazal in a well-publicized trial at which he was sentenced to a long prison term. Her husband's life-threatening violence finally gave her the legal basis for an official separation and the restoration of her premarriage name, so that *Peregrinations* eventually contributed to Tristan's new identity *and* legal autonomy in ways she could not have imagined as she wrote the book.[17]

Tristan's journey to Peru (like Jacquemont's trip to India) was thus shaped by an earlier personal history and by a French social context that would influence her interpretations of the non-European cultures she encountered. She began her subsequently famous voyage after earlier emotional conflicts, travels, and experiences with oppression; and she would face complex, unexpected consequences that evolved from her trip—including Chazal's assault against her in a Parisian street. Her life and travels diverged widely from Jacquemont's social origins and long journeys, yet Tristan shared Jacquemont's aspirations to become more independent, to describe other cultures to French readers, and to attain a more respected social position by claiming the literary authority of a French writer. Tristan's travel experiences shaped all of these evolving personal goals, but (again like Jacquemont) she would never reach a completely coherent identity or gain a prestigious social-cultural position in which she would be recognized and rewarded for her travel writings. She would always describe herself as a pariah within French society. The story of her life in Peru, however, showed how the flight from France led toward little-known parts of her French self and into new processes of personal reconstruction.

Tristan in Peru: Nature, People, Social Classes, and Gender

South American societies were less alien than South Asian societies for a nineteenth-century French traveler, but Tristan responded to her disorienting experiences in Peru by analyzing many of the underlying social and cultural structures that also attracted Jacquemont's attention in India. Her analysis was plotted in a more coherent narrative, however, because she actually published the kind of book that Jacquemont had only planned in his journals and letters. She was therefore able to portray herself as a self-conscious traveler in a quasi-Romantic story about the gradual discovery of a new selfhood. As literary scholars have noted, her narrative resembled traditional accounts of religious pilgrimages in which travelers achieved a higher spiritual consciousness after overcoming the physical and social obstacles of a long journey.[18] In Tristan's story the obstacles included a perilous sea voyage, an all-male crew aboard the ship (and the rejection of a marriage proposal from the captain, Zacherie Chabrié), a dangerous desert and mountain range that had to be traversed on the land trip from the Peruvian coast to Arequipa, and her uncle's devastating rejection of her quest for a familial inheritance. The ordeals of this journey became the difficult but necessary prelude for the emergence of a new self-knowledge that the "pariah" would later use in her French life of social and political action. *Peregrinations of a Pariah* thus narrated the identity-changing experiences of a central character whose personal challenges forced her to travel toward a new inner self while she was also traveling physically between France and Peru—and back to France.

Indeed, it seems unlikely that the story could have conveyed such processes of self-discovery if Tristan had achieved complete familial acceptance, received a large inheritance, and thereby entered a new social position in Peruvian or French society. The story of personal success—the self-affirmation of a new person who became "Tristan" after she was turned away by the patriarch of the Tristan family—required a failure that had provoked the "somber melancholy" in which she had "spent eight days and nights in the grip of death."[19] She eventually emerged from this desperate emotional condition like the self-reflective characters in Romantic novels who explored the deepest internal levels of their emotional and spiritual lives while they wandered through an external world of natural beauty or exotic cultures.

Tristan's contact with the New World began in a geographical context and climate that offered unfamiliar scenes in all directions: sublime sunrises and sunsets in the tropical seas, blinding hot deserts in lowland Peru, wastelands of volcanic rock in the Peruvian hills, and spectacular, snow-covered peaks in the mountains around Arequipa. These extraordinary places offered new encounters with the diversity of nature, but new experiences in the natural world could be dangerous as well as beautiful. Tristan began to learn this material fact of Peruvian life when she became ill during her grueling eighty-five-mile overland trip from the Pacific coast to Arequipa. Setting out on a September morning "as I would if I were going from Paris to Orleans," she soon found that the intense heat and dust of the desert produced terrible headaches, "a raging thirst," tormenting mirages of "liquid fire," and a complete physical collapse. "I was so ill," she explained, "that twice I fainted right away."[20] The cooler night air gradually brought some relief and enough energy for her to reach the treacherous mountain road that ascended to Arequipa—the home city of her father's family and the specific destination of her long pilgrimage.

Throughout this arduous journey Tristan consoled herself with the views of distant mountain ranges and giant volcanoes, all of which evoked a sense of awe to balance her lingering personal anxieties. "At the sight of this magnificent spectacle," she wrote, "I forgot my sufferings and lived only to admire. I let my gaze wander over the bright billowing sand to the point where it met the azure heavens, then upon the lofty mountains which stretched like an endless ladder to the skies, their thousand snow-capped peaks reflecting the sun's rays . . . with all the colours of the rainbow." This natural scene became all the more significant when she could see the "three volcanoes of Arequipa, joined at their base and branching out like a triple candlestick, symbol of a trinity beyond our human understanding."[21] Peru's scenery thus offered the mysteries of a religious experience and spiritual ascent as well as the spectacular beauty of high mountains; yet she also complained about mundane problems that included terrible infestations of fleas in a coastal village, exhausting heat in the desert terrain, and a high-altitude mountain climate in Arequipa.[22] Tristan's accounts of South American geography thus carried mixed messages about beauty and danger that were nevertheless linked through a single unifying theme: she (and her French readers) had never seen a place like Peru.

The people who lived there were different too. They consisted of three distinct races whose social positions contrasted as much as their skin colors. Indeed, the social differentiations were often sharper than the racial contrasts because many of the "whites" had a darker skin color than the categorical term implied: ancestry was the key distinction, and "'white' means anyone with no negro or Indian ascendants." Tristan estimated that by this criterion about a quarter of the population in Arequipa was white, a quarter was Black or "colored" (mixed-race), and the other half was Native American. The demographic statistics lacked precision, but the race consciousness was obvious and fundamental to the entire social order. "In Peru, as in the whole of South America," Tristan reported, "European origin is the supreme *title of nobility*."[23] Enslaved people were of course at the bottom of all social hierarchies, and they were either Black or "colored." Tristan was highly critical of slavery's effects on enslaved people and enslavers alike, but she was especially disturbed by the brutal attitudes and actions of the enslavers. She strongly condemned the slave system because it violated the abstract "Rights of Man" and also because (as she had argued in her book's preface) slavery could be compared to the social organization of marriage, which "divides society into *bondswomen* and *masters*."[24]

Tristan was therefore not really surprised to find that enslavers demeaned and abused their workers, but her racist descriptions of enslaved people suggested that they also remained alien to her in every social encounter—despite her explicit comparisons of oppressed slaves and oppressed wives. Expressing her strong European racial prejudices, she wrote of a "characteristic negro smell" and commented on the "sullen" and "miserable" and "stupid" appearance of the enslaved men and women whom she met. She also suspected, however, that such appearances reflected the brutal conditions of enslavement. "Beneath a black skin," she explained with the generalizing perspectives of a European traveler, "there may well be a proud and noble soul"—which was more than she could say for the souls of aristocratic white people. "All one finds there," she noted, "is the most arrogant presumption joined to the most profound ignorance, expressed in the kind of boastful language which would elicit a pitying smile from the poorest European sailor."[25]

Tristan had less to say about the large Native American population, but she was clearly intrigued by the independent Indian women (called *rabonas*) who accompanied Peruvian armies on military campaigns. "It is worth observing that whereas the Indian [male] would rather kill himself than be a soldier, the Indian women embrace this life *voluntarily*, bearing its fatigues and confronting its dangers with a courage of which the men of their race are incapable."[26] Tristan's praise for Indian women thus carried a parallel criticism for Indian men, who seemed no more attractive to her than Peru's other races and populations. There were nevertheless some specific exceptions to the flaws she ascribed to most Peruvian people.

Two Women Wearing the Saya. Watercolor attributed to Francisco (Pancho) Fierro, ca. 1848. Tristan praised the clothing of Peruvian women who wore a dress (*saya*) and partial veil (*manto*) to protect themselves from the aggressive looks of men whom they met in the streets of Lima. Fierro (1807–79) was an African Peruvian artist whose drawings portrayed the diverse social groups that provoked Tristan's reflections on personal freedom and female autonomy. Heritage Image Partnership Ltd/Alamy Stock Photo.

During a visit to Lima, for example, Tristan found that the clothing of women in the republic's capital city made them more intriguing and impressive than the men in every racial group she described. The unique dress of these urban women (including a *saya*, or outer dress, and *manto*, a veil that covered all but one eye) attracted Tristan's particular attention, and she decided that such clothing gave women a mysterious charm that even style-conscious Parisians could not imagine. "How enchanting they are, with their beautiful black *saya* shining in the sun; how graceful the movements of their shoulders are, as first they draw their *manto* right over their face, then slyly draw it aside!" It was not just the clothes, however, that made the women of Lima exceptional. "What supple figures they have, and how sinuously they walk!"[27] The only possible weakness that Tristan could discern in the appearance of Lima's graceful women emerged in their tendency to be "a little plump" because they liked to eat enormous dinners.

Lima had recently made what Tristan called "remarkable" advances in the preparation of tasty food ("for the past ten years everything has been done in the French style"), but the long dinners lacked the good conversation that French guests would expect. Tristan thus identified mealtime problems that she disliked in Peru for the same reasons that Jacquemont disliked his silent dinners in India. "These banquets are as bad for the mind as they are for the health . . . ," Tristan complained in an account of the dinners she joined in Lima, because "by the end of the meal nearly all the guests are unwell and in such a state of stupor that they are incapable of uttering a word." Similar food issues plagued Tristan at the dinner tables of Arequipa, where people apparently gave even less attention to refined table manners or proper cuisine. Peruvian hosts, for example, liked to place "a choice morsel" on a fork and pass it around to their guests for a sample tasting. Fortunately, "the Europeans were so disgusted by this custom" that it was disappearing; unfortunately, however, no European influence could change the "detestable" cuisine of Arequipa, which consisted of "tasteless" vegetables, "dry" meats, "rancid" cooking oils, "unrefined" sugars, and "heavy" breads.[28] Although Tristan came to Peru from an impoverished social position in France, she responded to Peruvian eating habits like a European aristocrat; and food elicited some of her strongest (French) cultural judgments.

The food in Peru seemed stranger to Tristan than the language, perhaps because she never tried to speak with the Native Americans in Quechua. A sympathetic female cousin in Arequipa patiently helped her learn Spanish, so she was increasingly able to converse with most of the upper-class people she met and to avoid the more intractable linguistic problems that Jacquemont faced in India. Tristan's immersion in Spanish nevertheless led to a new consciousness of her deep connections with the French language and a growing pride in the cultural values it expressed. "The idea of travel makes the French language much in vogue among the ladies," she explained with the nationalist perspectives of her own linguistic identity; "many learn it in the hope that they may need it some day. In the meantime, they derive much pleasure from reading some of our good books, and the development of their intelligence compensates for the monotony of the life the country has to offer. Every well-bred man knows French as well."[29] Her prolonged encounter with other languages thus helped Tristan (like Jacquemont) recognize her inescapable cultural origins and her own intellectual commitments. She reported that French was a language of "good books," which suggests how her Peruvian experiences deepened her linguistic self-consciousness while it also expanded her awareness of different climates, races, and foods. Tristan's trip contributed to her later identification with the poor and powerless in all nations, but it also gave her new insights into her deep allegiances to France. "I was still very narrow-minded," she acknowledged in a retrospective summary of the national attitudes she brought to her transatlantic travel in 1833. "I thought only of my country and hardly considered the rest of the world at all. I judged the opinions and customs of other countries by the standards of my own: the name of France and everything related to it had an almost magical effect on me."[30] This persistent "Frenchness" thus went beyond her cultural response to alien foods and languages to affect almost all of Tristan's commentaries on Peruvian society, including her analysis of the social classes and gender relations she encountered within both her own family and the wider communities in which she lived.

Although Tristan's accounts of women in Peru referred to different social practices that might offer more freedom or autonomy than women could usually find in France, most of Peru's social life seemed as hierarchical as the caste system that Jacquemont described in India or the French marriages that Tristan had seen in Paris. The wealth of Peru belonged almost exclusively to the small social elite, and there was no middle class to provide jobs or circulate money. "So it is not surprising," Tristan wrote in her discussion of a Peruvian civil war, "that the masses who are exploited by the greed of a few should rejoice and give their active support to the military leaders who squeeze the rich, because it is the suffering of the many that has filled the coffers of the few." This pervasive social inequality, from which her father's family also benefited, undermined economic ambitions and prevented the commercial and technological development that was enriching modern societies in Europe. Tristan reported that the "primitive machinery" around Arequipa was therefore "backward in comparison with ours," though she found an enterprising chocolate manufacturer who kept up with the "progress of civilization" by importing his machines from England.[31]

Peru's limited economic development stemmed, in Tristan's view, from the culture's disrespect for physical labor and from the degraded condition of enslaved workers. The slave system in Peru (as described by Tristan) therefore resembled India's caste system (as described by Jacquemont) in diverging from French conceptions of human rights and in undermining both the current initiative and future development of a whole society. Responding to Peruvian enslavers who complained that neither Indigenous nor Black people wanted to work, Tristan set aside her own racial prejudices and denied that race could ever explain economic behavior: "Whether a man is white, black or red, he will not take easily to work when he has not been brought up to it; but slavery corrupts man because it makes him loathe to work, so that it is impossible to prepare him for civilization." Slave societies thus rested on what Tristan called a "monstrous outrage against humanity," which France's revolutionary National Convention had rightly attacked in 1794 when it abolished slavery in all French territories. Napoleon later restored slavery in French-controlled colonies (1802), however, and it remained legal there throughout Tristan's lifetime. But she did not discuss this ongoing contradiction of France's revolutionary principles or analyze her own contradictions as she sought an inheritance from the wealth of her Peruvian slaveholding family. She could therefore describe the French-inspired abolition of slavery as an essential precondition for future freedom and justice in modern social systems; and though she often noted that Europeans suffered from widespread social oppression and economic inequality, she also assumed that even the most destitute European workers did not face the degradation of slave markets or enslaved labor.[32]

The comparative social position of women, however, suggested a different story and offered new perspectives for a critique of gender relations in France. Despite the many constraints on Peruvian women, Tristan decided that they were often freer and more independent than the French women who found themselves blocked in oppressive social institutions. The encounters with Peruvian women may well have been the most important aspect of Tristan's long journey because they helped her gain new insights into the social restrictions on women's lives, the possibilities for freedom in women's behavior, and the emergence of her own identity as an advocate for women's rights. The similar social obstacles and quests for freedom that she found among women in all cultures thus became as important for Tristan as the differences that otherwise separated France from Peru.

In the first place, she found that many Peruvian women felt trapped and abused in marriages that resembled Tristan's own miserable marriage in France. The legal opposition to divorce and the power imbalances that shaped unhappy relations between women and men were obviously more universal than the French legal system. "Married women here are just as unhappy and oppressed as they are in France," she wrote in a description of Peruvian women, "and the intelligence God has given them is doomed to sterility." Her proud cousin Carmen, for example, had to endure the gambling and constant infidelities of a rakish husband from whom she could never escape. "Such is the morality which proceeds from the indissolubility of marriage," Tristan lamented in an ironic passage that clearly referred to women on both sides of the Atlantic.[33] The alternative to marriage, however, was seclusion in a convent, which Tristan deemed to be even worse than living with a bad husband. Her visits to convents in Arequipa convinced her that such communities mostly functioned like women's prisons, except for the fact that the church's "gloomy cloisters" offered no hope for release. One of Tristan's unmarried cousins had in fact managed a spectacular escape from a local convent (by feigning her own death in a fire), but she had to live thereafter in nearly complete isolation for having violated her religious vows and the constricting social mores of her society.[34] Tristan therefore found that neither the households nor the convents of Arequipa offered pathways to freedom for entrapped women—or appealing alternatives to her own debasing marital experiences in France.

Some Peruvian women nevertheless showed Tristan how it was possible to act more freely than most European women could yet imagine. As it happened, she discovered the freest women in Peru amid the elites of Lima and amid the nomadic Indian camps that followed Peruvian armies. Although the two communities could hardly have differed more in their economic status or social customs, Tristan believed that the women in both cases had found ways to escape from the control of men. Their autonomy seemed to come especially from a specific freedom of movement, which the women of Lima acquired through the anonymity of their unique dress (the *saya*) and the traveling Indian women (*rabonas*) acquired through their refusal to marry. Women therefore became free when they were able to move outside the constraining male surveillance and family institutions of Peruvian society.

Tristan's descriptions of Lima repeatedly emphasized the exceptional independence and influence of the city's women. "There is no place on earth," she explained, "where women are so *free* and exercise so much power as in Lima." They seemed to have better health and more intelligence than the men, and their *sayas* enabled them to travel around the city alone and incognito.[35] Equally significant, the women in Lima possessed a "marked inclination for politics and intrigue," so that men apparently relied on their wives to handle negotiations for government appointments and political power. Indeed, this pattern of female dominance extended to the highest levels of government, where the president's wife, Señora Gamarra, exercised more real power than the president himself. At least this was the situation when Tristan arrived in Peru, but a civil war in the spring of 1834 drove the Gamarra party from power, sent Señora Gamarra into exile, and showed the obstacles that a woman of "Napoleonic ambition" still faced in Peru.[36]

Tristan met Señora Gamarra for a couple of conversations after her fall from power (her uncle Pío was on good terms with the Gamarrist faction), and the defeated woman's misery convinced Tristan that the indirect exercise of state power could never offer the enduring satisfactions of personal freedom. The happiness of men or women in government depended too much on the actions of others, whereas the truly happy women of Lima had learned to depend solely on themselves. It was this sense of independence that allowed some Peruvian women to free themselves from social controls that most women were still unwilling or unable to challenge in Europe:

> It is easy to understand that they [the women in Lima] must have a completely different outlook from European women, who from their earliest childhood are the slaves of laws, morals, customs, prejudices, fashions and everything else[,] whereas beneath their *sayas* the women of Lima are *free*, enjoying their independence and confident in that genuine strength which all people feel within them when they are able to act in accordance with needs. In every situation the woman of Lima is always *herself*; never does she submit to any constraint. . . . When she marries she does not take her husband's name but keeps her own; when she is tired of staying in, she puts on her *saya* and goes out, in the same way as a man does when he takes up his hat. Freedom of action characterizes everything she does.[37]

Although Tristan also criticized these free women for their shallowness and obsession with gold, she praised them as an idealized model of female independence and influence that European women should emulate in their own societies. Some Peruvian women, in other words, found ways to escape the daily oppression of a "bondswoman/master" hierarchy that shaped the unhappy marriages Tristan had seen and experienced in France, yet even the free women of Lima remained socially constrained in comparison to the *rabonas*.

The *rabonas* were the previously noted Native American women who camped beside Peruvian armies and provided food, clothing, and sex for soldiers when they were moving around the countryside on military campaigns. According to Tristan, these poor women endured terrible hardships and received no money except for what they could steal for themselves and their children during their migrations. The *rabonas* lacked every comfort of advanced societies, and their work did not lead toward any of the intellectual advancement that Tristan wanted women to pursue; but she decided they had gained a kind of unmarried independence that no advanced society had yet granted its women. Tristan was thus fascinated by stories of their courage, initiative, and freedom. Their precise role in Peruvian society, however, seemed less important to her than the fact that they embodied such an intriguing alternative to the cultures of modern Europe. "They are of the Indian race," Tristan explained, "speak the native language, and do not know a single word of Spanish. The *rabonas* are not married, they belong to nobody and are there for anybody who wants them. They are creatures outside society." Tristan did not exactly recommend this unmarried life of danger and poverty to her French readers, but she used the exemplary strength and independence of the *rabonas* (Peruvian pariahs?) to show how women could survive in difficult social conditions and to propose fundamental reforms in the sphere of education. "I do not believe it possible to adduce a more striking proof of the superiority of woman in primitive societies," she wrote in praise of the *rabonas*' courage; "would not the same be true of peoples at a more advanced stage of civilization if both sexes received a similar education?"[38]

Tristan's reflections on the *rabonas* led toward the most important conclusions she drew from her observations of women in Peru: all women faced prejudices and hardships, but some women in every society could find the means to challenge those obstacles and thereby gain more freedom. The book that Tristan wrote about Peru thus contributed to a liberating process in her own life that replicated the efforts of Peruvian women who were carving out distinctive spheres of female autonomy in a non-European society. *Peregrinations of a Pariah* challenged the social control of women in France by telling the personal story of a free woman's journey toward herself in Peru. Like most self-conscious travel writing, Tristan's book described the place from which she had come as well as the other society in which she traveled. Although some French readers may not have seen how a travel narrative about South America also addressed gender relations in their own society, the message from Peru was clear enough to Tristan's estranged husband. The gunshots he aimed at Tristan expressed his desperate attempt to restore a gendered social hierarchy that the wandering "pariah" had challenged in both her life and her writing; and his violent attack dramatically confirmed Tristan's account of the abusive marital and social constraints she tried to escape by traveling to South America. Tristan's analysis of the social system in Peru, like Jacquemont's account of social hierarchies in India, thus became simultaneously a narrative about the personal aspirations of an ambitious, freedom-seeking writer in France. Despite all their differences, these three societies and two French authors were linked through the constraints and critiques of hierarchical power; and Tristan (like Jacquemont) recognized that the power hierarchies extended from social relationships into religions, political cultures, knowledge, and education.

Tristan and Peruvian Culture: Religion, Politics, Knowledge, and Literature

Tristan's identification with France became most prominent whenever her narrative shifted from social hierarchies and gender relations toward modern Peruvian culture, which she found inferior in almost every respect to the cultural life she described as "French." She came away from Peru with clearly stated beliefs about French superiority in religion and politics that Jacquemont had also affirmed in India, though she did not share his strong aversion for spiritual religions. On the contrary, her complaints about the Peruvian Catholic Church emphasized what she saw as a lack of spirituality in the religious services, festivals, and parades that dominated much of Peruvian popular culture. A typical religious procession in Arequipa, for example, consisted of musicians and dancers who led a "religious farce" through the streets of the city by "writhing and gesticulating in the most shameless and indecent fashion." Large crowds responded to these provocative gesticulations with shouts that were "far removed from any thoughts of prayer" and with behavior that suggested "it will be a long time before their religion has any spiritual meaning."[39] The more formal church services also lacked the spiritual and aesthetic refinement that Tristan believed religion should provide. The monks and their Indian assistants were poorly dressed, the music was always "frightful," and the singing "so ragged" that Tristan could never attend a church service "without feeling irritable" for the rest of the day. "At least in Europe," she explained by way of comparison, "the fine arts lend luster to the sterility of the ritual. But in Peru the church is just a meeting-place and very little else." These unspiritual religious ceremonies, as Tristan described them, impeded the postcolonial nation's social and political progress because they constantly drained money from other institutions (including schools) and enabled the ruling elites to hold power with the help of priests who promoted "superstition and prejudice" among the uneducated Peruvian poor.[40]

The fusion of religious rituals and political power thus exemplified the central political problem that Tristan found in Peru: a complete disregard for both the freedom and the welfare of the common people. It was true that local revolutionaries had expelled Spain's colonial regime in wars that were ostensibly waged for liberty and self-government, but the new political leaders sought only to protect their own power and wealth. If the ruling class "had really wanted to organize a republic," Tristan noted, "they would have sought to encourage the growth of the civic virtues at every level of society by means of education; but as power, not liberty, is the goal of the bunch of adventurers who take it in turns to exercise authority, the work of despotism proceeds."[41] The political elites had thus mobilized the lower classes to escape from Spanish rule, but national independence had fostered neither "the love of political freedom, which they were too backward to desire, nor the wish for economic independence, which most of them were too poor to enjoy." In fact, the new political order had encouraged no significant political ideas or actions except a lingering "hatred" for the "preferential treatment" that Spaniards had received under the colonial system.[42]

The pervasive disdain for liberty meant that the frequent political upheavals in Peru were always power struggles among elites rather than broad-based movements for social and political reform. When a political revolution swept through Arequipa in 1834, for example, Tristan found that "the name of freedom was never mentioned" because people chose their political allegiances solely by calculating their own personal advantages. She saw no political heroism to compare with the heroic Parisian crowds in the French Revolution of 1830, which was the only other revolution that Tristan had previously observed.[43] The contrast between what she saw in French and Peruvian revolutions thus convinced Tristan that Peruvians would never achieve political freedom until they embraced ideas that more closely resembled modern European conceptions of politics and social organization.

Tristan's model for how a non-European society might replicate the more advanced political systems of Europe appeared in a comparative analysis of the political cultures on the two American continents. Warmer climates and hierarchical social customs in South America, she argued, prevented the development of a strong class of independent farmers who could appreciate and defend personal freedom. "In British America, on the other hand, morals and customs evolved under the influence of liberal political and religious ideas. . . . The climate was exacting and the people retained the industrious habits of Europe."[44] Such habits, combined with the wide distribution of land ownership, assured the progress of European freedom on an alien continent and proved that European political ideas could flourish in other parts of the world. Tristan did not mention the spread of slavery in the United States—a strange omission because she strongly condemned the slave system's debilitating effects in Peru and often complained about the social equivalences between slavery and the oppression of women. When she argued for the value of "liberal political and religious ideas," however, she used the United States as a persuasive *American* example of how the Peruvians might have better adapted European principles in their own society.

Tristan seemed always to assume that France had provided the best transnational example of political enlightenment in the Revolution of 1789 and in the subsequently successful export of French principles throughout much of Europe.[45] Her descriptions of nineteenth-century Peru, by contrast, suggested that a comparable infusion of French political ideas would not attract much support in South America. Most people in this society were simply not prepared for European political enlightenment, as Tristan would soon discern in the response within Peru to her own French book. Peruvian critics vehemently denounced *Peregrinations of a Pariah* after it was published in 1838, and Tristan learned that angry crowds burned effigies of the author in the streets of Arequipa and Lima. Reporting these incidents to a French editor, Tristan complained about the "savagery" of Peruvians and wondered how "such people [could] want to be in a republic!"[46] Three centuries of European contact, political development, religious conversion, and linguistic influence had failed to overcome a deep Peruvian resistance to European insights and enlightenment (as exemplified in the reception of Tristan's unwelcome French book). The religion and politics of Peru thus continued to puzzle or threaten Tristan for some of the same reasons that Indian religion and politics puzzled or threatened the scientifically minded Jacquemont. Neither of these French travelers could understand why non-European cultures were unable or unwilling to follow the European pathway toward progress and freedom. But Tristan also sought like Jacquemont to account for the enduring religious and political differences by analyzing intellectual traditions that separated non-European societies from the cultural life in France.

In addition to the deep-seated (though differently gendered) French cultural identity that Tristan shared with Jacquemont, she also wrote the kind of "anti-conquest" narrative that Mary Louise Pratt has found in authors who wrote about the natural world without an explicit interest in European political or economic expansion. I have noted how Pratt's view of anti-conquest writing can be applied to Jacquemont's scientific work (which she does not discuss), but Pratt herself has characterized Tristan's Latin American travel writing as a literary alternative to European male, capitalist narratives that stressed the prospects for the economic development of natural resources.[47] Tristan was not particularly interested in Europe's economic "conquest" of Peru, because she was a "social exploratress" (Pratt's term) rather than a member of the European capitalist vanguard. It nevertheless seems accurate also to describe Tristan as an advocate for nineteenth-century French "cultural conquests" that could advance transatlantic progress through educational exchanges that would introduce more Peruvians to the benefits of European knowledge. Her encounters with Peruvian culture soon convinced her that the non-European society lacked intellectual creativity, useful education, and literary achievements. Although her narrative about Peru would eventually provide literary credentials for her claim to a new social identity within French society, she took her first cultural steps toward the exchange of transnational knowledge as she shared her "insider knowledge" of Europe with the people she met in Peru. Like Jacquemont in India, Tristan could interpret or represent French cultural traditions with intellectual authority only by traveling far outside France.

Tristan's pride in French culture seemed to increase as she criticized Peruvian intellectual life and as she began to formulate her own evolving aspirations to write. However marginal she may have been to influential cultural institutions in France, Tristan found herself admiring, representing, and missing French culture as she traveled with the spirit of a national cultural ambassador. She therefore reported feelings of personal contempt for vacuous conversations in which Peruvians "wore an expression of permanent boredom" and discussed nothing but social gossip, health problems, or the weather. The dullness of these conversations were examples of what Tristan saw as the intellectual emptiness of a culture that seemed unable to generate original ideas in any sphere of thought or the arts. "As the country offers no fruitful topics for discussion," she complained in a specific reference to her experiences in Arequipa, "conversation is always stilted and monotonous." The situation was no better in Lima, where "sensuality reigns supreme" and where nobody seemed capable of truly using their minds. "I have never been more aware of the emptiness and aridity of my surroundings," she wrote in retrospect. It was in fact the "emptiness" of Lima's culture that increased her "impatience to return to Europe, which I loved and appreciated far more since I had left it."[48]

Reflecting on her own dissatisfaction with Peruvian conversations, Tristan came to believe that Peru's intellectual weakness affected everything from social relations to religion to entertainment. The popularity of bullfighting, for example, suggested "the deepest corruption" of an undeveloped culture, but the theater was not much better. Theatrical companies in Arequipa and Lima produced "mutilated versions" of French and Spanish plays, which audiences warmly applauded in all-too-obvious ignorance of flaws that would have appalled anyone who knew European drama. The museum in Lima, by contrast, benefited from the direction of "a learned man who has spent some time in France." Yet he was unable to purchase paintings or sculpture or any of the high-quality art that one would expect to find in a good museum. "A taste for the fine arts does not develop until nations come of age," Tristan explained to her French readers; "it is when people are weary of wars and political upheavals that they turn to the arts and bring new life to their jaded existence."[49] Peru's cultural backwardness reflected more than its political problems, however, because the society also lacked the schools that might have contributed to a more civilized use of the Peruvians' innate intelligence. "Nowhere in Peru is there any institution for the education of either sex," Tristan reported erroneously in her broad critique of Peruvian cultural life. Some interesting and intriguing people lived there, "but the stage of civilization the Peruvians have reached is still far behind ours in Europe."[50] Although her Peruvian uncle could deny Tristan a financial inheritance, she decided that she could fall back on a more important French cultural inheritance that even the wealthiest Peruvians (in her view) could only envy.

This treasure of French culture became Tristan's consolation for the personal, economic, and political problems that dominated much of her long trip. When she was blocked from reaching her goals of full familial acceptance and monetary compensation, she turned to writing and literature as new sources of status and respect. Affirming this new cultural self-recognition, Tristan found that her favorite institution in Lima was a library that offered a rare example of Peruvian intellectual progress because it consisted mainly of French books: "The library has a total of twelve thousand volumes, most of them French: Voltaire, Rousseau, the bulk of our classics, all the histories of the revolution, the works of Madame de Staël, books of travel, memoirs, Madame Roland, and so on. It gave me great satisfaction to see our best authors in this library. Unfortunately the taste for reading is still insufficiently widespread for many people to profit from it. . . . [But] this library is very fine, considering how backward the country is."[51] After living for many months in Peru without finding her social or cultural niche, Tristan seemed finally to discover a new place for herself in a library of French books. She noted the famous French classics, but she also emphasized the collection of travel narratives, autobiographical memoirs, and works by French women—all of which pointed toward her own evolving personal ambitions.

A Peruvian uncle had destroyed Tristan's hopes for wealth, a Peruvian revolution and the fate of Señora Gamarra had exposed the futility of political ambitions, and a "backward" Peruvian culture had given her strong convictions about the superiority of European intellectual traditions. Her life in Peru had therefore pushed Tristan to redefine herself as an emerging French writer, though she would achieve that identity only by returning to France and publishing a book of travel stories that would begin to give her a public reputation. Tristan's Peru thus resembled Jacquemont's India in that it provided a new identification with French culture and a new French selfhood as a knowledgeable writer on non-European lands and people.

EPILOGUE TO PART I

Cultural Identities, Personal Identities, and the French Generation of 1820

THE TRAVEL EXPERIENCES of Jacquemont and Tristan fostered the development of both a broad cultural identity (French European) and a specific personal identity (writer-intellectual) in each of these displaced members of the French generation of the 1820s. Alienated and demoralized by various personal problems and relationships in France, they both set off on long trips to non-European societies where they gradually found emotional and intellectual routes back into French culture and a more self-conscious French personal identity. They also repeated themes that were common among many other nineteenth-century European travelers who concluded from such trips that their own culture was the unique, superior, and inescapable grounding for their own ideas or political commitments. Jacquemont and Tristan were certain that European civilization was more advanced than all other cultures in both its material and intellectual achievements, though Jacquemont could see certain psychological advantages in the Indian caste system's denial of social ambitions, and Tristan could admire the freedom or autonomy of some Peruvian women.

Neither of these French travelers went into non-European cultures with the political or economic objectives of colonizing European explorers. Jacquemont went to North America and then to India to study the natural world and to analyze different social-political systems; Tristan went to Peru to escape an abusive husband, to meet her father's family, and to seek a financial inheritance. Their journeys outside of Europe, however, confirmed or reaffirmed fundamental cultural perspectives that they both noted often in their writings: European civilization was the center of modern progress and creativity, and France occupied an exceptional cultural position in the wider world as well as within Europe itself.

Jacquemont and Tristan both compared non-European cultures to the stages of social and cultural life that Europe had reached in the Middle Ages. Jacquemont, for example, described the rituals and social relations of Indian rajahs as latter-day expressions of medieval feudalism, and Tristan compared Peruvian religious festivals to the superstitious customs in fifteenth-century France. "It was a novel experience for me," she explained, "a child of the nineteenth century newly arrived from Paris, to see a Mystery play performed before such a huge audience . . . whose extreme ignorance and stupid superstition took my imagination back to the Middle Ages."[1] Defining their own cultural identities in opposition to these kinds of alien social systems and rituals, Jacquemont and Tristan wrote narratives about India and Peru that explained what it meant to belong to an "enlightened" culture in France. Jacquemont repeatedly expressed his loyalty to French intellectual traditions and political culture, even though his own family had suffered from Napoleonic political repression and his liberal friends had remained political outsiders throughout the conservative era of the restored Bourbon monarchy. Even more surprising, perhaps, Tristan affirmed her loyalty to a French culture in which the marriage laws and education system had severely impeded her own freedom and opportunities. Yet both authors decided that France offered political and cultural ideals that could best sustain their own ambitions for future careers or future social change. Repressive laws and institutions may have violated France's liberal political theories, but Jacquemont and Tristan believed French ideas still provided an enlightened foundation for the expansion of scientific education or the enactment of fair divorce laws or the abolition of slave systems that both condemned.

This general identification with modern French and European culture therefore became linked in these liberal travelers with evolving personal identities and ambitions. The exploration of cultural differences gave them new experiences and knowledge they could use to advance their personal aspirations for recognition, intellectual status, and new social positions. Traveling far from home and living among unfamiliar people, Jacquemont and Tristan gradually clarified their plans to become writers whose descriptions of other cultures would give them a new prestige within the French culture that always remained (in their view) the real center of modern intellectual life. These ambitions would never be achieved in their own short lifetimes because neither Jacquemont nor Tristan gained personal security or material rewards from their extensive commentaries on non-European societies. Jacquemont died in India before he could write his carefully planned book; and Tristan's published account of Peru brought her new problems when her enraged, estranged husband shot her in a Parisian street and her angry Peruvian uncle severed all remaining connections. In contrast to Jacquemont's never-achieved return from India, Tristan was able to launch a new career as a writer and activist in French worker organizations, but she died (like Jacquemont) before she could reach the ambitious goals that she had begun to define for herself in Peru.

Despite their early deaths, both these traveling writers drew creatively upon their cross-cultural journeys to reshape their personal identities in texts that would ultimately give them posthumous places in French culture. Like the fictional characters in Stendhal's literary portrayals of their post-Napoleonic generation, Jacquemont and Tristan would never quite fulfill their intellectual and social aspirations. Like countless other European travelers in every modern generation, however, both found their deepest cultural identities and clearest sense of selfhood through disorienting encounters with people and places in non-European cultures.[2]

PART II

European Americans in Nineteenth-Century Europe

Margaret Fuller and Randal McGavock

INTRODUCTION TO PART II

Antebellum European American Journeys from the North and South

THE GRAND TOUR of Europe became an important rite of passage for well-educated, nineteenth-century European Americans who wanted to extend their cultural knowledge or social status by visiting famous European cities and historic sites. Most pre-1860 American travelers viewed Europe as the global center of culture, social prestige, and essential intellectual traditions, but they also assumed that their own society was the global center for the most successful, modern political and economic institutions. Americans therefore made the long journey to Europe to see the great achievements of past generations and to compare the social problems of modern urban societies—and most eventually returned home with a confident belief that America was the nation of the future. We have seen how Victor Jacquemont and Flora Tristan compared past and contemporary cultures in the Americas and South Asia with nineteenth-century France, but similar cross-cultural comparisons also appeared often in American travel narratives about the past, present, and future cultures in Europe and the Middle East.

Travel writing was a popular American literary genre throughout the nineteenth century, and many of the era's best-known American writers published notable travel books (for example, James Fenimore Cooper, Mark Twain, and Henry James).[1] Stories about foreign journeys offered opportunities for aspiring authors to connect with stay-at-home readers and to reflect on modern social life or national cultures, but most travel writing flowed from the pens of lesser-known travelers who turned their Old World voyages into articles for local newspapers or now-forgotten books about their quests for European knowledge or their disorienting encounters with other cultures. American travel to Europe became safer and more accessible after steam-powered ships began carrying transatlantic passengers in the late 1830s. More than 7,000 Americans were traveling to Europe each year by the 1840s (most travelers were men, but the annual numbers included about 2,000 women).[2]

Among the countless books that described American travel and cross-cultural experiences, the mid-nineteenth-century writings of Margaret Fuller and Randal McGavock offer both typical and contrasting examples of how white Americans compared the cultural, social, and political meanings of Europe and the United States. Although American travel writing in this era almost always expressed the author's American nationalism, Fuller and McGavock show how nationalist identities and ideas could diverge in different regions of the new nation. Fuller grew up in Massachusetts and lived always in New England or New York before traveling to Europe; McGavock grew up in Tennessee and lived always in the South except for eighteen months when he was a student at Harvard. Fuller's accounts of Europe, which were first published in a New York newspaper, evolved into a critical reassessment of America's failure to support its own political principles at home and abroad. McGavock's travel writings, which were first published in a Nashville newspaper, expressed a deepening belief in the political and social superiority of the United States. Fuller worried after the European Revolutions of 1848 that America was abandoning its historic commitment to social progress and democracy, whereas McGavock never doubted that America embodied the social and political future for all white, European-descended people.

These contrasting responses to European journeys reflected differences in Fuller's and McGavock's regional origins, genders, views of political revolutions, perceptions of slavery, abilities to link personal experiences with wider analytical frameworks, and literary maturity at the time of their travels. When Fuller traveled to Europe in 1846, she had already begun to establish her literary reputation by editing an important journal of Transcendental literary thought (*The Dial*). She had also published a travel book on the American Midwest and an important work on modern women and gender relations, *Woman in the Nineteenth Century* (1845), and she had written numerous articles on contemporary cultural and social life for the *New York Tribune*. Emerging from the intellectual and political milieu of antebellum New England and New York, Fuller would send her commentaries on European culture and politics to the widely read *Tribune*—a liberal newspaper in which readers could expect to see frequent critiques of American society along with a spirited defense of radical European social movements. McGavock, by contrast, set off for Europe in 1851 without a literary reputation or previous publications. He had studied law at Harvard and developed a strong interest in European history and literature, but his own personal history was closely linked to the social and political culture of slaveholding white families in the American South. Emerging from the political and religious culture of the slave-based society in middle Tennessee, McGavock became the first European "reporter" for the

Nashville Union and a staunch believer in the exceptional achievements of the new American nation.

These differences show how previous and diverging personal histories influence the meaning of travel experiences, but Fuller and McGavock also interpreted Europe and America with different perspectives because Fuller became much more immersed in European culture. She lived among Europeans for almost four years and married an Italian; McGavock traveled for about seventeen months and never developed comparable political or emotional connections with European people. For all their differences, however, there were also numerous similarities in the ways that Fuller and McGavock drew upon their travels to redefine their views of America, challenge their personal or familial heritages, and discover new personal freedoms in Europe. Traveling in a time when Americans were asserting their divisive sectional differences, Fuller and McGavock both used their long journeys to reaffirm a shared national history of political ideas and institutions. They also both claimed a new intellectual status as interpreters of non-American cultures (much like Victor Jacquemont and Flora Tristan claimed new intellectual identities by describing other societies to readers in France). Although they came from different spheres of American political culture, they converged in many of their critical responses to European social systems, political hierarchies, and long-established cultural traditions; and like most nineteenth-century American travelers, they defined the distinctive meaning of America and their own lives while they were also describing what they saw in Europe.

Fuller and McGavock also resembled many other Americans in setting off for Europe with laments about disappointing personal relationships, with well-informed interests in European history, and with literary plans to write about their European experiences for hometown newspaper readers. Their journeys to Europe thus grew out of long-developing ambitions for both writers. Their lives never intersected, but they both studied European culture in Cambridge, Massachusetts (though Fuller was not allowed to enter Harvard), and they both believed that travel would provide new self-knowledge and self-improvement. But these overlapping strands of personal history and ambition would *not* lead Fuller and McGavock to similar conclusions about America's place in the world or slavery or male-female relations or the significance of European revolutions and politics. To put the differences most simply, one could say that Fuller became more "European" over the course of her travels, whereas McGavock became more "American." What they shared, however, was a disciplined determination to assert their personal identities as they sought to understand European cultures, become knowledgeable interpreters of European societies, and explain how American democracy and social hierarchies resembled or differed from the European political and social systems they encountered on their transnational journeys. In the end, they also shared the recurring nineteenth-century pattern of early deaths. Fuller would die in a shipwreck at age forty, and McGavock would be killed in a Civil War skirmish at age thirty-six. During the important transitional years before their untimely deaths, however, they both used the experience of European travel to construct and convey their complex quests for a new American selfhood.

CHAPTER THREE

Margaret Fuller's Transnational Declarations of Personal and Political Independence

MARGARET FULLER was born in Cambridgeport, Massachusetts, in 1810. Her parents came from old New England families, and her father, Timothy Fuller, attended Harvard University, but the Fullers did not belong to the elite circles of Boston society. Timothy Fuller was a lawyer whose passions and ambitions led him into politics. He became a Jeffersonian Republican and served four terms in the US House of Representatives (1817–25), staking out his political position as a strong supporter of James Madison and James Monroe. Margaret was the oldest child in a family that would eventually include five surviving boys and two surviving girls, and she remained in Massachusetts with her mother (also named Margarett Fuller but spelled with an extra *t*) and siblings while Timothy Fuller pursued his political career in Washington. From the beginning, however, young Margaret received special attention from her energetic father.

Timothy Fuller decided that his daughter should receive a classical education at home rather than attend school with other children, so Margaret's intellectual training reflected her father's Unitarian religious and intellectual perspectives. Unlike most girls of her generation, she learned to read at a very early age and plunged into the rigorous study of ancient Latin texts as well as modern works of literature, history, and science. Timothy maintained close control over Margaret's education, even when he was in Washington, which may explain why she grew up with an exceptional interest in Roman writers and little exposure to the sentimental novels of the day. She later attended school briefly in Boston, but her education came mostly at home and mostly through the careful study of classical or serious literary texts.[1] Despite this solid intellectual foundation, Margaret was unable to attend all-male Harvard University or pursue any other form of higher education. Her father-directed education nevertheless gave her an exceptional understanding of European intellectual traditions and enabled her to bring deep cultural knowledge to her interactions with the Harvard-educated writers she met in New England during the 1830s and early 1840s.

Margaret's intense connection with her father ended abruptly when he died from cholera in October 1835. Following his retirement from congressional politics, Timothy Fuller had moved his family to rural Groton, Massachusetts, to pursue his Democratic-Republican ideas on an unprofitable farm, and his death left the family with acute financial problems. Fuller *fille* began to support herself and to provide money for her family by teaching at schools in Boston and Providence, but she eventually decided that she preferred to translate European texts and to write literary criticism. She translated works by Goethe, for example, and wrote essays about his concept of "self-culture." She also developed another source of income by creating a series of weekly "Conversations" for women who gathered in Boston to discuss intellectual and social issues; the participants purchased "tickets" for thirteen weekly discussion sessions (two hours per week). These fees, along with other income from her writing and translations, provided Fuller with a steady income for almost five years.[2]

Meanwhile, she also became deeply involved in the creation and editing of a new journal, *The Dial*, which was to serve as the public voice for the Transcendentalist literary and philosophical movement. Working closely with Ralph Waldo Emerson, Fuller found a cultural forum in which she could write literary criticism and develop her analytical skills. Finally, she expanded her writing into the genre of travel narratives when she published her account of a trip to the American Midwest in *Summer on the Lakes in 1843* (1844). This book also discussed the position of women on the American frontier and led toward further commentary on male and female identities in a work that would become her most enduring prose contribution to American feminism, *Woman in the Nineteenth Century* (1845). Fuller argued that women did not have a single innate nature; in fact, she explained, women possessed both the intellectual qualities of analytical thought (the qualities of "Minerva") and the spiritual, poetic qualities of creative visions (the traits of the "Muse"). The challenge for nineteenth-century societies was to ensure that these overlapping feminine qualities could be expressed in both the personal lives of modern women and the institutions of modern social life. A more balanced expression of women's intellectual and spiritual qualities would also produce more balanced, equal relationships between women and men—which would gradually lead to a more enlightened national culture and social system.[3] Transcendental aspirations for a free, independent selfhood, in other words, must shape the lives of women as fully as the lives of men.

Fuller's writing about literature, travel, and American social life attracted the attention of Horace Greeley, the editor of the *New York Tribune*, who was promoting various social reforms in the United States and who invited her to become a literary editor and columnist at his newspaper. Fuller accepted the position, though it required a departure from New England and a transition from the aesthetic theories of high literature to new explorations of the social realities in America's largest nineteenth-century city. After moving to New York in December 1844, Fuller spent the next twenty months writing about the ideas and literary styles of contemporary writers, the position of women in modern urban societies, and the problems of poverty in modern commercial systems. She became the first woman to serve on the editorial staff of a large American newspaper, and her job at the *Tribune* provided new financial stability. Her writing became more journalistic, more accessible to a wide reading public, and more rapid; in fact, she published over 250 newspaper articles during this phase of her career.[4] Despite her growing involvement with New York, however, she retained her earlier intellectual fascination with European culture, and her personal life added new dimensions to her transatlantic interests. In 1845 Fuller developed a close relationship with a German Jewish businessman named James Nathan. Although various conflicts gradually drove them apart, she helped Nathan publish several travel "letters" in the *Tribune* after he returned to Europe. Her desire to continue this relationship may also have contributed to her aspirations for a European trip, but Nathan soon married another woman, and Fuller never saw him again.[5]

The practical arrangements for a transatlantic journey began to develop when two of Fuller's liberal Quaker friends, Marcus and Rebecca Spring, invited her to travel with them and their twelve-year-old son on a tour of Europe in 1846. Marcus Spring was a successful merchant who shared his wife's interests in the social reform movements that were spreading across European nations in the 1840s, so the trip would combine the pleasures of a long holiday with a cross-cultural exploration of new ideas and political activism. The Springs would pay for Fuller's travel expenses, and she would tutor their son while providing friendly companionship for Rebecca. There would also be new opportunities for journalism because Greeley offered to pay Fuller for a series of articles in which she could describe what she observed during her travels and thereby gain new cultural status as the first American female newspaper correspondent in Europe. The advance payment for the first fifteen articles was only $120, but Fuller could expect some modest income if she continued to write her *Tribune* articles, and she arranged to borrow additional funds with the help of friends who were connected to both American and European banks.[6]

A long European trip would pose financial challenges, yet Fuller was determined to follow through on ambitious travel plans that she had set aside when her father died in 1835. The purpose of her trip, as she explained to friends, was

Margaret Fuller in New York. Photograph by John Plumbe Jr., 1846. This portrait shows Fuller as a thoughtful woman and an engaged reader, which was how she viewed herself (and wanted others to view her) when she worked at the *New York Tribune* and when she was later writing articles from European cities. The picture thus conveyed the public identity of an independent woman writer that Fuller had already established before she began her journey to Europe. National Portrait Gallery, Smithsonian Institution, Washington, DC.

to enhance her own intellectual development, but (like Flora Tristan in France) Fuller also saw herself as a woman with a wider public destiny. "There are . . . in every age *a few* in whose lot the meaning of that age is concentrated," she had written to Nathan as their relationship began to break down. "I feel that I am one of those persons in my age and sex. I feel *chosen among women*. I have deep mystic feelings in myself and intimations from elsewhere."[7] This sense of a unique historical calling surely contributed to her desire for transatlantic travel, but she also worried (as she told other friends) that she might have become too old to learn much from her long-deferred journey:

> At every step I have missed the culture I sought in going [to Europe], for with me it [was] no scheme of pleasure but the means of needed development. It was what I wanted after my painful youth, and what I was ready to use and be nourished by. It would have given my genius wings and I should have been, not in idea indeed, but in achievement far superior to what I can be now....
>
> My mind and character are too much formed. I shall not modify them much but only add to my stores of knowledge. Still, ... I wish much to go.... But it must [now] be in the capacity of a journalist, and for that I need this new field of observation.[8]

Fuller thus carried mixed expectations as she set off from Boston with the Springs in August 1846, crossing the Atlantic in ten days on a modern steamer (the *Cambria*). She spent about three months in England and Scotland before moving on to Paris (November 1846) and eventually to Italy (March 1847). She continued to travel with the Springs until July 1847, when they left her in Venice and returned to America.

Fuller was not yet ready to go home. Increasingly attracted to Italian culture and also to a man whom she had met in Rome, she soon found a place for herself in the "Eternal City," immersed herself in the Italian language, and entered into an intimate relationship with Giovanni Ossoli (1821–50). The last months of 1847 became the happiest period of her entire European journey, though she wrote few articles for the *New York Tribune* (partly because of financial misunderstandings with Greeley) and began to complain about numerous illnesses—which intensified after she became pregnant. Although she moved to an Italian village to give birth to a son (5 September 1848), who would be named Angelo, she soon returned to Rome and wrote a remarkable series of political reports for the *Tribune* throughout the winter, spring, and summer of 1849. During these tumultuous months Roman republicans forced Pope Pius IX to flee the city, proclaimed a new republican government, and ultimately surrendered to a French (republican) army that restored the pope's control over Rome. Fuller described these complex events with high democratic hopes and then with intense political despair—before finally fleeing with Ossoli into the countryside and eventually moving to Florence.[9]

Most scholars believe she had secretly married Ossoli in April 1848, partly to ensure that their child could be properly baptized.[10] Meanwhile, Ossoli's support for the defeated Roman republic destroyed his prospects for a secure job, and persistent financial problems forced Fuller toward another journey she had long resisted: she would return to the United States, where she might publish a book on recent Italian political history and where her new Italian family might settle into a safer social life. She had little money for the voyage, however, and the low-fare sailing ship (the *Elizabeth*) on which she crossed the Atlantic ran aground during a storm and sank near Fire Island, New York, in July 1850. Fuller, Ossoli, and young Angelo all drowned within sight of the coastline, so the long journey across Europe (like Jacquemont's travels in Asia) never finally carried her home.[11]

Fuller's extended European trip and her descriptions of other cultures nevertheless helped her redefine her personal, cultural, and political identity. Facing struggles she had never anticipated when she described her sense of a special personal destiny or public duty in a pre-European letter, Fuller came to identify deeply with the Italian people and to declare her vehement support for the republican political movement that she joined in Rome. Her political ideas became more radical, and her connections with both the social mores and the political culture of the United States became increasingly tenuous after 1848. Yet, by the painful political summer of 1849, she was calling on Americans to provide every possible kind of political and financial support to help the suffering Italians as they tried in their own ways to defend political principles that Fuller linked to America's own most valuable national ideals. "I pray you do *something*," she wrote after the collapse of the Roman republic, when sympathetic sentiments alone would no longer suffice. "It ought not to content your consciences. Do you owe no tithe to Heaven for the privileges it has showered on you, for whose achievement so many here suffer and perish daily? Deserve to retain them, by helping your fellow-men to acquire them."[12] This insistence on the need for American political action expressed the multiple passions that gradually emerged in both her travel experiences and her politicized travel writings. Setting aside all pretense of detachment and all interest in conventional travel narratives about historical monuments, she transformed her journey into a new kind of personal, political campaign for American support of radical republicanism in Europe.

The deepening critical analysis of sociopolitical issues in both Europe and America reflected her long-developing view of how travel writers should describe the world by conveying their *inner* thoughts about the places they visited. She had in fact begun to call for a new kind of personally engaged travel writing in her correspondence with James Nathan while she was still working in New York. Nathan had returned to Europe in 1845 to pursue his business interests, but he also wrote about European cities in letters that he wanted to publish in the *New York Tribune*. Fuller arranged for several of these reports to be published, despite her already emerging belief that travel writers should discuss their deeper personal involvement with European cities. "Rome is an all hacknied theme and by the most accomplished pens," she warned, and so a would-be narrator of Roman sights must bring something new to the subject. "Do not describe outward objects.

... But what you see [as] characteristic and your own thoughts will interest [readers]." Nathan's superficial descriptions of famous historical sites did not provide what Fuller requested, however, so she came back to the problem again after receiving a clichéd letter on the Eternal City that she did not publish. "I wish you had sent, instead," she wrote to Nathan, "the letter on Modern Rome, for your observations on what you personally meet are always original and interesting. I hope you will write *yourself* out in letters on Egypt and Palestine."[13] As it happened, Fuller ultimately followed her own advice by writing *herself* into political letters that summarized her personal views of modern European politics as well as her evolving views of America. Rejecting the tourist clichés that she disliked in the bland reports from James Nathan, she showed how a travel writer could find her own distinctive voice as she described both the political upheavals in other nations and the political despair of a radicalized American in Europe.

Fuller's View of European Culture and History

Transatlantic travel had become one of Fuller's strongest personal and professional aspirations because of her deep interest in (and respect for) the rich cultural traditions of European societies. Her early newspaper articles thus focused on intellectual, artistic, and literary achievements that far exceeded the cultural creativity in nineteenth-century America, but the political struggles of European republicanism attracted most of her attention after the Revolutions of 1848 and gradually displaced cultural history in the analytical reports she sent to the *New York Tribune*. Stressing that European cultural life could not be understood without reference to the social and political contexts in which it evolved, she sought to explain how complex sociopolitical conflicts were challenging both the cultural traditions that she admired and the social and political hierarchies that she condemned. Fuller's descriptions of modern Europe thus drifted from her own time of travels (1846–50) into an imagined European future, which could be compared positively or negatively with the history, the present culture, or the imagined future of America. Her travel stories, in short, moved backward and forward across time while they also moved back and forth across political cultures on both sides of the Atlantic Ocean.

Fuller spent many of her days in Britain, France, and Italy visiting museums, theaters, opera houses, art galleries, and famous churches. These cultural sites embodied and symbolized the cultural history of the European societies she had come to see, and she was not disappointed. "The British Museum would, in itself, be an education for a man who should go there once a week," she wrote in one early description of Europe's cultural legacies; but the sheer size of such museums forced even the most energetic visitor to "think and read at his leisure moments about what he saw."[14] Fuller assumed during the early months of her trip that Europeans drew on their museums, art, literature, and history to develop a deeper knowledge of intellectual life than she had found among most people in America. Writing to one of her brothers shortly after she arrived in England, Fuller reported that she had already met "a number of intellectual and cultivated men" whose "habits of conversation [were] so superior to those of Americans." These conversations opened new opportunities for intellectual development because, as she explained to her brother, "I am able to come out a great deal more than I can at home."[15]

This experience with a more wide-ranging cultural freedom suggested to Fuller that people in Britain often differed from Americans in seeing their culture as a path to self-understanding rather than as another commodity to be bought and sold. In Edinburgh, for example, she met the publishers William and Robert Chambers, who insisted that "they could never look on publishing *chiefly* as *business* or a lucrative and respectable employment, but as the means of mental and moral benefit to their countrymen." Such views precisely expressed the noncommercial attitudes that Fuller had rarely found in America, so she emphasized her satisfaction with the literary commitments they affirmed and sustained. "To one so wearied and disgusted as I have been by vulgar and base avowals on such subjects, it was very refreshing to hear this from the lips of a successful publisher."[16] In fact, Fuller seemed to find anti-commercial commitments in numerous spheres of European life, and she clearly appreciated the European interest in critical intellectual perspectives that were so central to her own identity. "I find how true for me was the lure that always drew me towards Europe," she wrote to a friend after arriving in Paris. "It was no false instinct that said I might here find an atmosphere needed to develop me in ways *I* need."[17]

Paris offered Fuller new kinds of personal and cultural liberation, perhaps because she found herself for the first time in a different linguistic context as well as a different intellectual milieu. She wrote about the pleasures of going to French plays and opera "every night" and emphasized that Paris provided a unique cultural education. "Could I remain six months in this great focus of civilized life," she wrote to her mother, "the time would be all too short for my desires and needs."[18] Much of her fascination with Parisian culture emerged at the theater, where she saw the great actress Rachel (stage name of Élisa Félix) in multiple performances and came away with a new understanding of "the true way of viewing French tragedy." Rachel's acting revealed the complexities of human character and transported theater audiences beyond the national limits of French culture itself. "The French language from her lips is a divine dialect," Fuller explained to her *Tribune* readers; "it is stripped of its national genius—the pure music of the heart and soul." Rachel was thus a "true artist" who communicated the kind of universal truths that one might have seen in the great plays of ancient Greece, but the smallest Parisian theaters also offered "excellent acting and a sparkle of wit unknown to the world out of France."[19]

This theatrical vitality contributed to the transnational significance of a Parisian cultural life that regularly surpassed the best cultural work in the United States. "For the first time in my life," she wrote in another article for the *Tribune*, "I saw something represented in a style uniformly good, and should have found sufficient proof, if I had needed any, that all men will prefer what is good to what is bad, if only a fair opportunity for choice be allowed." Indeed, she described Paris as a remarkable "school" for anyone who wanted to explore the deepest questions of human life and to learn from "the experience of others [who] might accelerate our progress."[20]

A similar commitment to enduring cultural work seemed to exist also in Italy, as Fuller noted during her extended travels through Naples, Rome, and Venice. The ancient and premodern history of these cities gave her new reasons to identify with European cultural traditions that she had already praised in Britain and France, so her sense of truly "belonging" in Europe grew stronger as she explored the pleasures and historical complexities of Italian life. "Who can ever be alone for a moment in Italy?" she asked in an article from Milan. "Every stone has a voice, every grain of dust seems instinct with spirit from the Past, every step recalls some line, some legend of long-neglected lore."[21] The cultural depth of this Italian past, however, generally eluded the crowds of English and American tourists who (according to Fuller) traveled through Italian cities with only the shallowest understanding of the past and modern cultures they were encountering.

Fuller thus began to define her own relation to Italy by making sharp distinctions between herself and the tourists who were merely sailing across the surface of Italian life. "I find that it is quite out of the question to know Italy," she wrote soon after her arrival in Rome, " . . . [or] to convey any idea of her spirit, without long residence, and residence in the districts untouched by the scorch and dust of foreign invasion (the invasion of dilettanti I mean) and without an intimacy of feeling, an abandonment to the spirit of the place, impossible to most Americans." To be sure, like other Americans she admired the grandeur of the ancient Coliseum and the artistic genius of Michelangelo and Titian, but she insisted with the typical claims of an "authentic" travel writer that her relation to Roman culture and politics differed from the superficial impressions of an uncomprehending tourist.[22] Addressing imaginary tourists in one of her reports from Rome, Fuller advised "nine-day" visitors on the inevitable limitations of their experience. Although such visitors might vaguely realize that they did not understand much of what they saw, "this consciousness would be most valuable" only if they took the "time to think and study." Careful study provided the means by which all active minds might gradually cure their natural defects, but *only* the long-term resident (such as Fuller) could see what the tourists did not understand.

> You have no time, you are always wearied, body and mind, confused, dissipated, sad. The objects are of commanding beauty or full of suggestion, but you have no quiet to let that beauty breathe its life into your soul—no time to follow up these suggestions and plant for your proper harvest. Many persons run about Rome for nine days and then go away. . . .
>
> No; Rome is not a nine-days' wonder, and those who try to make it such lose the ideal Rome (if they ever had it) without gaining any notion of the real.[23]

Fuller's own quotidian relation to Italian culture gave her a distinctive involvement with Roman social life. She believed that she was learning how to live like a Roman, especially after she settled into her relationship with Giovanni Ossoli during the fall of 1847—though she never mentioned this personal component of her Roman life in the *Tribune* articles.

The foreigner who actually lived within this ancient culture did not have to spend her time visiting tourist sites because the deeper meaning of Roman cultural traditions could enter deeply into her personal consciousness through the experiences of daily life. "I now really live in Rome," she informed her readers in late 1847, "and I begin to see and feel the real Rome. She reveals herself now; she tells me some of her life. Now I never go out to see a sight, but I walk every day, and here I cannot miss of some object of consummate interest." The layers of Roman history and culture gradually folded into Fuller's evolving personal and intellectual life, giving her a new conception of how the old and new overlapped or diverged within Italian society. "As one becomes familiar [with the city], ancient and modern Rome—at first so painfully and discordantly jumbled together, are drawn apart to the mental vision. You see where objects and limits anciently were. . . . When this begins to happen . . . one feels first truly at ease in Rome."[24] This claim for an insider's knowledge of the true Rome (written about seventeen months after her departure from America) expressed Fuller's own growing identification with her new European cultural home. Like the Roman surroundings she described, old and new levels of her identity gradually became "jumbled together" within her evolving self-perceptions.

This transition into European culture required an immersion in European languages, as Fuller herself noted in letters to her friends and family after she separated from her American traveling companions and settled into a different

Margaret Fuller. Oil on canvas by Thomas Hicks, 1848. By the time Hicks painted this portrait in Rome, Fuller had become an experienced reporter on Italian society and public events. The artist placed Fuller in a classical Roman context that confirmed her status as a knowledgeable American participant in Italian culture, but this setting did not convey her deepening engagement with Italian political conflicts. National Portrait Gallery, Smithsonian Institution, Washington, DC, Gift of Constance Fuller Threinen, great-granddaughter of Margaret Fuller's brother, the Rev. Arthur Buckminster Fuller, Union chaplain killed at Fredericksburg in 1862.

linguistic life. She had begun her language studies in Paris with a French tutor, whom she called "an excellent master," but she wanted to reach a level of fluency that would enable her "to learn [and] even *to think* in French." This was an ambitious goal because she could not avoid "thinking in English" whenever she came upon a truly interesting subject to discuss. Her French instructor assured her that she was making progress, yet her three hours of daily study and her regular trips to the theater could not take Fuller across the language barrier that placed her on the margins of French culture. Despite this barrier, she threw herself constantly into French lectures, theatrical performances, and art galleries, all of which deepened her (humbling) self-consciousness about the limits of linguistic competence and identity. "My French teacher says, I speak and act like an Italian," she noted in a letter to Emerson; "and I hope, in Italy, I shall find myself more at home."[25]

It was not easy to change from French to Italian, however, and so Fuller needed more intense language study after she moved on to Italy. Writing to Emerson again on the challenges of learning a foreign language, Fuller reported from Florence (June 1847) that she was able to speak French with educated Italians, but she could not yet communicate with most people in the city. "To know the common people, and to feel truly in Italy, I ought to speak and understand the spoken Italian well, and I am now cultivating this assiduously." This determination to speak a new language reflected Fuller's ambition to escape the limitations of tourism and to enter as fully as possible into a new (and old) European culture. "If I remain [in Italy]," she explained to Emerson, "I shall have, for many reasons, advantages for observation and enjoyment, such as are seldom permitted to a foreigner."[26] Her growing knowledge of the Italian language thus gave Fuller new access to Italian culture, but her expanding language skills, her lengthening residence in the country, and her developing relationship with Ossoli (they met in April 1847) also separated her from most American travelers in Europe and from her family in America. As she later wrote to another American friend who wanted to visit Italy, language offered the only sure pathway into Italian culture, but this cross-cultural journey required a disciplined refusal to speak English. "After leaving the Springs," she remembered in a description of her own linguistic transitions, "I always lived with Italians yet it is only after six months [of] total abstinence from English that I speak fluently and to do so is for many reasons of great importance."[27] Fuller was here referring obliquely to her relationship with Ossoli, yet her recurring comments on language and culture transcended her own life experiences to make a more general claim: nobody could truly understand Italy or other places in Europe without carefully studying the relevant European language. Language—like the streets, the monuments, and the people—could become deeply familiar only through a prolonged encounter with Italian society; and since no tourist could learn Italian on a nine-day trip to Rome, Fuller's knowledge of the language became a key sign of how she differed from the other Americans she saw in the streets and shops of Italian cities.

Her personal relation to languages was complicated, however, because she continued to write English-language articles for the *Tribune* (professional identity) and English-language letters to her family and friends in America (personal identity), even as she settled into her Italian-language relationship with Ossoli (a new emotional selfhood) and with other people in Italy. She always identified herself as an American writer or literary traveler who exchanged ideas with famous European authors. She noted in her early reports from Britain, for example, that she had met William Wordsworth in the Lake District and Thomas Carlyle in London, and she wanted her readers to understand that she was an American writer who could move freely and comfortably in European literary society.[28] She also met well-known writers in Paris, including George Sand, Félicité-Robert de Lamennais, Pierre-Jean de Béranger, and the famous Polish exile Adam Mickiewicz. Fuller seemed to fuse her personal and cultural pride as she described these encounters in her newspaper articles or private correspondence, but her reports on European writers also led to reflections on the meaning of cultural creativity and the qualities of exceptional people. "These are men who need no flourish of trumpets to announce their coming," she noted in an article that discussed her encounters with Lamennais and Béranger. "They are true kings. . . . The hearts of men make music at their approach."[29] Her praise for these "true kings" of Europe expressed Fuller's own conception of the literary calling, which (in her case) may have received its deepest European affirmation from Adam Mickiewicz (1798–1855).

Fuller met Mickiewicz in Paris after sending him some of Emerson's poems, and this literary gift soon led to one of her most emotionally charged friendships with a European writer. She explained to Emerson that Mickiewicz combined "intellect and passions . . . with a soul constantly inspiring," and she regretted that she had not met him earlier because, among the many people she encountered in Paris, "it was only with Mickiewicz, that I felt any deep-founded mental connection."[30] Fuller was already in Naples by the time she wrote to Emerson about her special "connection" with Mickiewicz, but she continued to think about her new Polish friend as she traveled around Italy. She also described her feelings in a letter to Marcus and Rebecca Spring, who had discussed Mickiewicz in conversations with Fuller while they were all together in Rome. "He affected me like music or the richest landscape," she explained to her friends with two of her favorite artistic similes; "my heart beat with joy that he at once felt beauty in me also. When I was with him I was happy; and thus far the attraction is so strong that all the way from Paris I felt as if I had left my life behind, and if I followed my inclination I should return at this moment and leave Italy unseen."[31]

This strong attraction to Mickiewicz thus developed partly from Fuller's perception of him as the poetic embodiment of both the "intellect and passions," but she was also drawn to him because he affirmed her own intellectual talents and insights. After their meeting in Paris, for example, Mickiewicz sent Fuller a summary of her special destiny in Europe. Writing in his distinctive mystical style,

Mickiewicz assured her that she would become a mediator between the "old" and "new" worlds *and* a distinctive, influential female connection between the past, present, and future. "Your spirit is bound to the history of Poland, of France, and begins to bind itself to the history of America. You belong to the second generation of minds. Your mission is to contribute to the deliverance of the Polish, French, and American woman."[32] This flattering description of her exceptional "mission" converged with Fuller's self-perceived cultural identity, so it is not surprising that she immediately admired Mickiewicz or that she would describe him in one of her *Tribune* dispatches after the Revolution of 1848 (when he went to Rome) as "the great Poet of Poland." She reported in another account of Mickiewicz's political interventions in Italy that he was an orator of exceptional "magnetism" who could communicate with almost everyone, including those who did not speak his language. "It is the force of truth, the great vitality of his presence, that loads his words with such electric power," she explained to her American readers.[33] Mickiewicz was therefore a unique poetic genius who knew how to combine the passions of art with the cause of national independence and with religious messages about the universal meanings of Poland's exceptional, suffering, modern history. Equally important for Fuller, he strongly affirmed her own belief that she had a special personal destiny.

The letters that Fuller wrote to Mickiewicz have been lost, but she shared some of his mystical tendencies, and she almost surely praised his prophetic sense of national mission while he was encouraging her to pursue her spiritual ideals as well as her personal and social liberation. Indeed, the literary historian Ursula Phillips has argued persuasively that Mickiewicz's letters challenged Fuller to expand her understanding of womanhood and personal destiny by questioning "the deeply ingrained contemporary conviction that a woman could not play a public role *and* be a mother, *and* be sexually fulfilled."[34] Epistolary advice from a Polish poet cannot exactly explain Fuller's openness to a romantic relationship with Ossoli, of course, but Phillips and others have rightly emphasized that Mickiewicz's letters to Fuller coincided with her rapidly evolving conceptions of selfhood and her subsequent plunge into a risky sexual and political relationship with a younger Catholic man.

Fuller admired Mickiewicz's liberal interpretations of politicized religious ideas, but she was much more critical of the Roman Catholic Church—which was the institution that had long employed men in the Ossoli family, including the father and brothers of the man she loved in Italy. Although her early references to Pope Pius IX portrayed him as open-minded and sympathetic to reform, she quickly changed her opinion when the pope opposed liberal republicanism in Italy and rejected all the revolutionary movements of 1848. Even before those revolutions, however, she was complaining about the Catholic Church and its

Adam Mickiewicz. Photograph by an unknown photographer, ca. 1850. Mickiewicz's ideas and his stature as Poland's most famous exiled national poet influenced Fuller's growing support for democratic, nationalist revolutions after 1848 and may have also contributed to her liberating personal relationship with Giovanni Ossoli. Fuller's self-perception of her public, transatlantic role in the era's political revolutions evolved through the respect and encouragement she received from Mickiewicz's friendship. Pictorial Press Ltd./Alamy Stock Photo.

support for the traditional social hierarchies that Fuller disliked. "How any one can remain a Catholic—I mean who has ever been aroused to think, and is not biased by the partialities of childish years—after seeing Catholicism here in Italy I cannot conceive," she wrote in one angry response to the Italian church. She wanted religion to express a living spirit rather than the power of old "customs," much as she wanted art, literature, theater, nationalism, and political cultures to express a dynamic creative spirit rather than the dead weight of tradition. Viewing Catholicism as a powerful defender of old customs, Fuller became more critical of the Roman Catholic Church than almost any other aspect of European culture (except for repressive kings and superficial English tourists). "Oh awake, indeed, Romans!" she urged in a different kind of religious commentary. "And you will see that the Christ who is to save men is no wooden dingy effigy of by-gone superstitions, but such as art has seen Him in your better mood—a Child, living, full of love, prophetic of a boundless Future."[35] Above all, Fuller wanted the Catholic Church and all religious institutions to move beyond traditional rituals and hierarchies in order to promote a "boundless future" of social equality and spiritual renewal.

Fuller and the Hierarchies of European Social Life

The social and economic distance between rich and poor was the great European problem that Fuller expected religious people to address, but her own inspiration in the campaign for social reform came more directly from the French social theorist Charles Fourier than from specific traditions in Christian theology. Conceding that Fourier was too materialistic and sometimes "uncongenial" to her own religious ideas, Fuller nevertheless insisted that he had correctly shown how religious thought supported social reform: wherever Fourier's ideas for social reform were embraced, "some practical application of the precepts of Christ, in lieu of the mummeries of a worn-out ritual, cannot fail to be felt."[36]

Most wealthy people in Europe and America would resist Fourier's reformist message, yet Fuller believed that anyone who visited cities such as Glasgow, London, Paris, and Lyon would quickly understand both the social urgency and religious dimensions of Fourier's writings. Every European society tolerated or fostered a disturbing gap between rich and poor, which became even worse for women than for men. "I saw here in Glasgow," Fuller reported in an early article for the *Tribune*, "persons, especially women, dressed in dirty, wretched tatters, . . . and with an expression of listless, unexpecting woe upon their faces." Although modern people prided themselves on their progress from earlier stages of barbarism, their social system still consisted of "lords and ladies" who cared nothing about "laborers who . . . starve or are turned into wild beasts." Unfortunately, many people continued to believe that this system simply showed what Providence intended for the poor, but Fuller's religious assumptions led to very different conclusions. The "frightful inequalities" that separated people into modern social classes made it "impossible" for her to "believe that God can smile upon a state of things such as we find existent here."[37] No matter what other American travelers or the apologists for this social system might say, Fuller insisted in her *Tribune* columns that inequality was not the natural state between man and man—or between man and woman.

Fuller's descriptions of European social relations frequently noted the exclusions and hierarchies that defined the social position of women. Indeed, the gender hierarchies were often delineated even more clearly than the social classes, though the hierarchies of gender and wealth merged most notably in the lives of poor women. Fuller's own encounters with social exclusions, however, had less to do with economics than with the traditional institutional constraints on women. In Paris, for example, she was barred from entering the buildings of the Sorbonne when a disdainful guard insisted that women had no right to visit the lecture rooms. The most famous French university thus maintained an "old pedantic and theological character" that defended what Fuller called a "state of barbarism" and that made France's academic institutions even more restrictive than the institutions in Italy. Visiting the University of Bologna after her run-in with the guard at the Sorbonne, Fuller was pleased to discover that Italian women had served as honored professors and active members of the most elite scientific and artistic circles.[38]

The Catholic Church in Italy, by contrast, offered more disturbing examples of gender hierarchies—as Fuller reported in a *Tribune* article about a young woman whose family made her become a nun. "Poor thing!" Fuller lamented in her description of the ceremony that brought the young women into a convent. The family apparently believed that a nun's life was the best solution for a daughter who had never married, but Fuller saw the whole process as "revolting and painful to the last degree." Like Flora Tristan in Peru, she perceived the convent as little more than a prison for women who had no freedom to shape their own lives. The "poor" woman whom Fuller saw in Rome was "taken behind a grating, her hair [was] cut, and her clothes exchanged for the nun's vestments; the black-robed sisters who worked upon her, looking like crows or ravens at their ominous feasts."[39] Fuller in fact decided after watching this unhappy initiation that "no hell could be worse" than the fate of a woman who was forced to enter or remain in a convent. Where some young women were rigidly excluded from universities or barred from schools, others were forcefully compelled to enter religious orders from which they could not escape. In both cases, however, Fuller emphasized (like Tristan) that women lost their freedom of action, which men took for granted and which Fuller herself was asserting through her European travel and writing.

Despite the restrictions on their education and personal freedom, some European women found the means to express themselves in the mostly male world of literature and the arts. In addition to praising the exceptional talents of the actress Rachel, Fuller stressed the literary and cultural achievements of George Sand (1804–76), whom she met in Paris and described in her letters for American friends. Although Fuller may have decided that American readers would not respond favorably to sympathetic descriptions of Sand's character or work (the *Tribune* articles about Paris did not discuss her meetings with Sand), she wrote about Sand in letters that were included in her posthumously published *Memoirs*. Affirming the "*goodness*, nobleness, and power" in Sand's character, Fuller reported that she had overcome her own "bad French" and social anxieties to achieve an immediate rapport with a woman who was usually portrayed as a "vulgar caricature." To be sure, Sand lived independently and defied the reigning social conventions of marriage, but she always had "good intentions" and "bravely acted out her nature."[40]

This assertion of "her nature" offered a European model for Fuller's own ambitions in a male-dominated literary culture. She referred to Sand's distinctive social position as an "intellectual woman and good friend," which she explicitly compared to "my own [position] in the circle of my acquaintance as distinguished from my intimates." Although Fuller criticized the haste and careless use of talent in parts of her writing, she insisted that Sand's larger accomplishment went beyond any narrow criticism that might be applied to her books. Whatever her specific literary achievements, Sand demonstrated how a woman writer could stake out a position for herself in modern cultural life. "She holds her place in the literary and social world of France like a man, and seems full of energy and courage in it. I suppose she has suffered much, but she has also enjoyed and done much, and her expression is one of calmness and happiness." Sand's well-defined (but controversial) personal and cultural identity seemed to fascinate Fuller because it converged with her own aspirations for public recognition of her earlier writing and her recent articles in the *New York Tribune*. Supporting George Sand thus became a way for Fuller to assert the independence and creativity of women's writing in general and also to reaffirm the personal intellectual ambitions that had pushed her to Europe. As she explained in a summary of her conversations with Sand, "I liked the woman in her . . . ; I never liked a woman better."[41] Sand's status as an independent woman pointed toward a future cultural and social world that both American and European reformers wanted to create by establishing more equality between women and men as well as a more equal, democratic social order for the poor and powerless.

Fuller's respect for contemporary authors and activists such as Adam Mickiewicz and George Sand suggests how her European writings increasingly focused on the political and cultural desire to create a different social world. Europe, in other words, was not simply a museum in which travelers could find the classical origins of modern culture. It was also a dynamic, evolving society in which Americans would encounter democratic political movements that were trying to use

America's republican principles in real-world struggles to escape from social hierarchies and governmental oppression. Americans who visited Europe to see the cultural legacies of human history might therefore also see the transatlantic progress toward a more egalitarian human future.

Fuller and the Emergence of a New European Political Culture

Fuller's dispatches in late 1847 began to discuss the growing possibilities for national political upheavals, especially in Italy. She described a widespread anger against the Austrian control of northern Italian cities and against the longstanding Austrian suppression of Italy's sovereign right to freedom. "The Austrian rule is always equally hated," she reported after a long tour of northern Italy, so there were good reasons to assume that important changes were becoming "inevitable."[42] But these changes would have to come from a broad-based popular movement because the Italians could achieve their national independence only by mobilizing the majority of their people. "From the people themselves the help must come," Fuller wrote in the fall of 1847, "and not from princes. . . . From the aspirations of the general heart, from the teachings of conscience in individuals, and not from an old-ivy-covered church, . . . the help must come." This new Italy would thus have to "find the elements of salvation within herself," yet Fuller believed people were already making their way along "an onward, upward road" that could lead the nation to a new era of Italian independence and democracy.[43]

As reports of a new French revolution reached Italy in March 1848, Fuller became even more certain that other political upheavals would soon follow. "Whatever the result," she noted in an article on recent revolutionary events, "France has done gloriously; . . . [and] to stop her march is a vain attempt, though the onward path [will] be dangerous and difficult." The most important consequence of this latest Parisian revolution, however, was taking place in northern Italy, where people were already rising to expel the hated Austrians from their country. Rebellions in Venice and Milan led to political celebrations that Fuller (writing from Rome) viewed as a turning point in modern Italian history. "With indescribable rapture these news [*sic*] were received in Rome. Men were seen dancing, women weeping with joy along the street." Even more important, perhaps, young men were rushing off to join military units that would protect the emerging Italian nation from its powerful political enemies—who included Pope Pius IX after he was forced to flee Rome. The Romans could therefore begin to create a new Roman republic, and Fuller could look forward to a new political era in the ancient city.[44]

This political rebirth of the Italian independence movement coincided with Fuller's personal preparations for her own child's birth, which took place in September 1848. Although she had moved to the countryside during the last months of her pregnancy, she returned to Rome in early December to write about Roman politics and to affirm her solidarity with the Roman people. English and American observers often mocked the Italians for their failure to act, but she wanted her readers to understand that these stereotypical Anglo-American views were wrong. "No one should dare," Fuller argued in December, "after the proofs of the Summer, to reiterate the taunt . . . on foreign lips at the beginning of the contest, that the Italian can boast, shout, and fling garlands, but not *act*."[45]

Fuller was ecstatic about the Roman Revolution because it had apparently released the deepest religious and political instincts of a long-suppressed population. In an article on the new republic (written in February 1849), Fuller reported that this "revolution, like all genuine ones, has been instinctive, its results unexpected and surprising to the greater part of those who achieved them." Referring to political transitions that she could see throughout Rome, Fuller wanted Americans to understand that an almost millennial transformation was taking place as the Italian people realized they were now free from the pope. "The waters that had flowed so secretly beneath the crust of habit . . . have suddenly burst to light in full and beautiful jets; all rush to drink the pure and living draught." There was nevertheless a clear danger that other nations would not allow this beautiful new stream to flow unimpeded toward the promised land of Italian independence. The people of Rome had chosen a new constitutional assembly and set about the business of selecting their leaders, but the French had also mobilized their forces to support the displaced pope; and (ironically enough) a French republican army would in fact soon destroy the new Roman republic.[46]

A French siege in the early summer of 1849 forced the beleaguered Roman defenders to surrender their city, thereby opening the way for Pope Pius IX to regain religious and political control over the capital from which he had fled in the previous November. The earlier republican optimism and institutions now disappeared, but Fuller continued to write about the sacrifices of the Roman people. She described the Italian soldiers who defended Rome during the siege, the bombardments that destroyed Roman buildings, and the wounded men who lay dying in Roman hospitals. Writing from the besieged city in late June, Fuller knew that the Roman republic was probably doomed, yet she continued to praise the steadfast virtues of the city's heroic defenders. "A spirit burns noble as ever animated the most . . . heroic age," she wrote in one of her sympathetic accounts. "I suffer to see these temples of the soul thus broken, to see the fever-weary days and painful operations undergone by these noble men, these true priests of a higher hope."[47]

Fuller's defense of Rome's "noble men" became increasingly passionate because she assumed that few people outside of Italy understood the extraordinary qualities of the republican soldiers or the significance of Italian republicanism. The French occupation of Rome and the pope's return to the city thus became the most crushing, disillusioning political defeat that Fuller had ever witnessed. Abandoned to their fate by the indifferent leaders of other nations, the now-suppressed Romans fell into a despair that was almost overwhelming for anyone (like Fuller) who had lived through the springtime of political optimism. "The men of Rome had begun, filled with new hopes, to develop unknown energy—they walked quick, their eyes sparkled, they delighted in duty, in responsibility; . . . now, dejectedly, unemployed, they lounge along the streets . . . [and] all the ensigns of hope, have been snatched from them."[48] The Roman Revolution passed quickly through the whole cycle of modern political life—from the most optimistic vision of a democratic future to the most intense despair about the repressive authoritarianism and military power of present-day social and political elites—and Fuller herself shared in every emotion of this cyclical political experience.

Throughout each phase of the Roman republican movement, Fuller praised both the anonymous Roman population and the most prominent leaders, especially Giuseppe Garibaldi (1807–82) and Giuseppe Mazzini (1805–72). She had first met Mazzini in London, where he lived as an exile during the 1840s and developed a Romantic, nationalist-religious account of the Italian nation that resembled Mickiewicz's messianic description of Poland. Fuller wanted Americans to know more about Romantic European nationalisms because the idealism of these political-religious movements differed from the mundane, calculating behaviors of typical political leaders in the United States. Despite a lifetime of setbacks, the "noble" and idealistic Mazzini never lost hope that his national dreams (like Fuller's dreams for social justice and an enlightened literary culture in the United States) would eventually be transformed into the real world of modern nations.[49]

This unshakable faith was finally rewarded when the creation of a Roman republic gave Mazzini the opportunity to put his ideas into action. Arriving in Rome for the first time in his life (March 1849), he became a Roman citizen and immediately assumed a prominent public role as the leading advocate and symbol of Italian republicanism. Fuller saw him often during the spring of 1849 and praised his virtues in *Tribune* articles that stressed both his high ideals and unbending political determination. "Mazzini is a man of genius, an elevated thinker," she explained to her American readers, "but the most powerful and first impression from his presence must always be of the religion of his soul, of his *virtue*, both in the modern and antique sense of that word." Although the French army advanced relentlessly against the outgunned Roman defenders and the republican cause became desperate, Mazzini remained Fuller's unbroken symbol of enduring republican aspirations. European aristocrats and their apologists in the European press would never recognize the virtues of such a religiously inspired national leader, but Fuller urged Americans to see how Mazzini embodied the universal principles they had advocated in their own revolutionary campaigns for freedom and republican institutions.[50]

Fuller's descriptions of Mazzini thus expressed both her deep support for his national political objectives and her loyalty to an important friend. Her friendship with Mazzini resembled her close relationship with Mickiewicz in giving Fuller a strong appreciation for the overlapping poetic, political, and personal virtues in the persons who led European nationalist movements. Indeed, she seemed to redefine her earlier American personal and political identities through her relationships with these idealistic (and idealized) European political activists. "Mazzini is a great man," she wrote in a letter to an American friend. She called him a "poetic statesman," and she explained to her friend that his "radiant look" made a "melancholy music" in her soul.[51] The emotional energy in such comments shows how Fuller drew more than new intellectual or political insights from her European life. New meanings of personal freedom and selfhood emerged through relationships that expanded her American identity into a new kind of self that was also "European." Her friendships with Mickiewicz and Mazzini, her Italian husband, her new language, her child, and her immersion in Rome's republican revolution all carried Fuller far beyond her New England cultural origins and created a deep personal identification with Italy.

Fuller's Italian Freedom

Fuller's identification with European political movements appeared in her private letters as well as her published articles on Roman republicanism. Although these letters suggest that Fuller's "European" identity grew stronger after she parted from the Spring family in 1847, she had already begun to describe feelings of personal liberation and opportunity during the earliest months of her European travels. The letters she wrote to Emerson from Paris, for example, noted that she had discovered new ways to express herself in Europe. "I find myself much in my element in European society," she explained. "It does not indeed come up to my ideal; but so many of the encumbrances are cleared away that used to weary me in America, that I can enjoy a freer play of faculty, and feel, if not like a bird in the air, at least as easy as a fish in water."[52] This freedom from past "encumbrances" became a recurring theme in Fuller's evolving interpretation of her European experiences, but her reports on Italy also began to convey a new sense of social and cultural connections. While she was feeling the new personal freedom of "a fish in water," she was also learning how to swim in new social streams of friendship, sustenance, and support.

Fuller summarized her new social connections in the fall of 1847, when she told her mother why she had decided to stay in Europe after her American friends went back to the United States. Explaining that she had found a comfortable home for herself in Italy (without mentioning Ossoli), she stressed that the people there appreciated her personal qualities as well as her political support for their national aspirations. "The Italians sympathize with my character . . . as no other people ever did; they admire the ready eloquence of my nature, and highly prize my intelligent sympathy (such as they do not find often in foreigners) with their sufferings in the past and hopes for the future." So Rome was the place in which she could experience a "flood of joy" that went beyond her feelings for any other city. "To live here, alone and independent, to really draw in the spirit of Rome, Oh! What joy!"[53] This joy and independence stemmed partly from her deepening relationship with Giovanni Ossoli, but it seemed also to come from an evolving sense of her own literary and journalistic vocation. When she informed Emerson in 1848 that she could not yet return to America, she emphasized that she still had "much to do and learn in Europe" and that she wanted to see how the current revolutionary conflicts were going to evolve. She would become either a political participant or an interpreter of these "public events" because, as she continued in her letter to Emerson, "I have *my part* therein, either as actor or historian."[54]

Her reports on transatlantic political events might therefore help Americans understand the public upheavals in contemporary Europe, but she could also find personal satisfactions in the daily activities of Italian life. Even in the small town of Rieti, Fuller noted in still another letter to Emerson, she felt more respect and sympathy than any outsider could expect to receive. Although she did not tell Emerson that she was living in Rieti to prepare for the birth of her child, she assured him that "the Italians love me; they say, I am so *simpatica*. I never see any English or American, and now think wholly in Italian. . . . I am to them a divine visitant. . . . They are people whom I could love and live with."[55] This Italian "love" for Fuller's distinctive personal qualities may have been a discreet allusion to her relationship with Ossoli, but it also explained why her new sense of belonging was stronger than any desire for a return trip to America. "If I came home at this moment," she told her mother in November 1848, "I should feel as if forced to leave my own house, my own people, and the hour which I had always longed for."[56] After years of European travel, Fuller's personal, literary, and political life had merged to make Italy her "home" and America an almost alien land of distant memories.

Indeed, when Americans asked about her plans for coming back to the United States, she repeatedly emphasized that Rome had become her "country" and the center of her deepest affections. "What come back for?" she asked in response to one query about her possible return to America. "Here is a great past and a *living* present. Here men live for something else beside money and systems, the voice of noble sentiment is understood. . . . 'Tis a sphere much more natural to me than what the old puritans or the modern bankers have made."[57] Her European travel and Italian life had made her more aware of her American cultural origins, yet she doubted that she could ever return comfortably to her former place within the puritanical, commercial society from which she had left on her long emotional and political journey. In short, she explained to friends in the United States, "Rome as an abode has taken the strongest hold on my affections," even when she could not find enough money and even when political crises threatened the stability of the city.[58]

This affectionate attachment to Roman life intensified as she developed her deep relationship with Giovanni Ossoli. They had met in a chance encounter at St. Peter's Basilica during her first visit to Rome in the spring of 1847, and Fuller soon learned that he came from a noble Roman family, that his father and brothers worked in the papal offices at the Vatican, and that his liberal political ideas had led him away from a career in the church. Ossoli quickly proposed a permanent relationship, but Fuller resisted until the late fall of 1847 (when she returned to Rome after a tour of northern Italy). Despite the differences in their ages, education, languages, and cultural backgrounds, Fuller always described their relationship as extremely harmonious. "We get along very well," she eventually wrote to her sister in one of the long-deferred accounts of her connection with Ossoli. "The friction that I have seen mar . . . the domestic life of others does not occur with us."[59] In addition to their strong affection for each other and their son, Angelo, they shared a deep commitment to liberal, republican political ideas. Ossoli's political views, however, made it difficult for him to find a job after the Roman republic collapsed in the summer of 1849. Leaving Rome soon after the French army occupied the city, the now-married couple lived for a short time in Rieti before moving on to Florence. In these months after her departure from Rome, Fuller finally began to tell her American family and friends about the man she had married and about the satisfactions that she found in both her husband and child. All of her reports emphasized that Giovanni and Angelo provided a stable emotional base for her new "American-Italian" selfhood and helped her cope with the painful death of the Roman republic.[60]

Giovanni Ossoli. Photograph by an unknown photographer, ca. 1848. Fuller met Ossoli in Rome and secretly married him before the birth of their son, Angelo, in 1848. She described him as a "tender" husband with "unswerving" love, though she also noted that he knew almost nothing about the knowledge "contained in books." MS AM 1086 (Box 2: 102), Houghton Library, Harvard University.

She nevertheless knew that this younger, uneducated Italian man would seem to be an unlikely husband for an ambitious American writer, so her descriptions of Ossoli always stressed his remarkable personal qualities rather than his intellectual training or professional accomplishments. "He is not in any respect such a person as people in general would expect to find with me," she wrote to her mother, because he was "absolutely ignorant" of intellectual life and "of all that is contained in books." Despite this limitation, or maybe because of it, he had a "sweet temper" and much "native refinement"—though his greatest attribute was perhaps his steadfast appreciation for Fuller herself. "His love for me has been unswerving and most tender," Fuller assured her mother. "In him I have found a home, and one that interferes with no tie." She and Ossoli had also discovered the joys of parenthood, and it was this small, happy family that gave Fuller a new understanding of "all that is innocent and sweet" as well as deep personal connections with Italian culture.[61]

Fuller's new domestic life and the unexpected pleasures of childrearing counterbalanced the despair that she felt amid the worsening political conditions of 1849. "In him," she wrote about her son, Angelo, "I find satisfaction, for the first time, to the deep wants of my heart."[62] Although neither her child nor her husband diminished her enduring intellectual ambitions, the "simplicity" and "domesticity" of her daily activities brought an important break from much of Fuller's earlier journalistic work. Contrasting her personal life with the tensions in other people's marriages and the conflicts of public events, Fuller reported that her relationship with Ossoli brought the "pleasure of always being at hand to help one another." The marriage seemed to expand the sense of freedom and acceptance that she had already found during her European travels, but Ossoli also provided an emotional affirmation that her American friends might never understand. "Others have loved me with a mixture of fancy and enthusiasm excited by my talent at embellishing subjects," Fuller told her friend William H. Channing. "He loves me from simple affinity; he loves to be with me, and serve and soothe me. Our relation covers only a part of my life, but I do not perceive that it interferes with anything I ought to have or be; I do not feel any way constrained or limited or that I have made any sacrifice."[63] This emotional attachment and respect more than compensated for the intellectual differences in their relationship, but Fuller worried that American mores and institutions could bring new dangers to her husband and new social threats to her marriage.

She feared that her Italian husband would not be accepted in the United States ("he is very unlike most Italians, but very unlike most Americans too"), yet the inescapable pressure to find a stable income finally pushed Fuller and Ossoli to leave for America. It was extremely difficult for Fuller to make this move, in part because of her anxiety about the voyage itself and in part because of her concerns about a disorienting departure from the social and cultural communities that had helped her create a new selfhood for herself in Italy. "I leave Italy with profound regret and with only a vague hope of returning," she wrote in a final letter to the American chargé d'affaires in Rome. "I could have lived here always, full of bright visions, and expanding my faculties, had destiny permitted."[64] Indeed, if there was any consolation for her exit from the country that had become her European home, it could be found in the fact that she was leaving a reactionary, repressive political culture.

Fuller's final political reports from Europe, however, tried to balance her deep despair about the contemporary political reaction with defiant predictions about the ultimate triumph of democratic and republican political principles. Although the French suppression of republican Rome had been the most distressing political event of the entire revolutionary era, she was certain that anti-republican political

Garibaldi in Italy during the Siege of Rome in 1849. Engraving by William Luson Thomas, after a sketch by George Housman Thomas, ca. 1854. Fuller's reports from Italy praised the republican and democratic ideals of leaders such as Giuseppe Mazzini and Giuseppe Garibaldi because she wanted her readers to understand how the Italians were fighting for ideals they shared with Americans. Like Fuller's *Tribune* articles, this image portrays the human costs of the Italian national struggle as well as Garibaldi's guiding, inspirational leadership. Classic Image/Alamy Stock Photo.

forces could not permanently block the rising political movements of modernity. "That struggle may last fifty years," Fuller wrote in her search for long-term historical consolation, "and the earth may be watered with the blood and tears of more than one generation, but the result is sure. All Europe . . . is to be under Republican Government in the next century."[65] A future generation would overthrow the aging monarchies, destroy the political influence of the Roman Catholic Church, and reopen the historical pathway toward a democratic and socialist European future.

The final article that Fuller sent to the *Tribune* (January 1850) thus laid out her hopes and expectations for the eventual development of democratic socialism. She had assumed even before traveling to Europe that socialist reforms were coming to the modern world, she noted in this last report from Italy, but the popular movements of 1848–49 gave her more reasons to believe that new ideas and political forces would finally overwhelm Europe's ancient institutions and prejudices. World history was moving inexorably toward her vision for progressive political and social reform. "At this moment all the worst men are in power, and the best betrayed and exiled. All the falsities, the abuses of the old political forms, the old social compact seem confirmed. Yet it is not so: the struggle that is now to begin will be fearful, but even from the first hours not doubtful. Bodies rotten and trembling cannot long contend with swelling life. Tongue and hand cannot be permanently employed to keep down hearts."[66] This struggle for political and social reform might well take a long time, and it would require strong support from forward-looking political allies across all of Europe and the Americas. The pressing need for international support would meanwhile give Fuller her new cross-cultural work and identity. She would help Americans understand the rising political storm in Europe and encourage New World assistance for the struggling democratic, republican movements in Old World societies. Seeking to add her voice to this long-term political campaign, she sailed for America with plans to publish a book that would tell her compatriots about the recent Italian revolution. Her travels had given her a new transatlantic intellectual project as well as a new American Italian family, and she was returning to her old national home to describe and promote the new republican political movements she had seen in Europe.

Fuller's Praise and Critique of America

The descriptions of culture and politics in Fuller's analysis of European events always included comparative references to the United States, but after 1848 these comparisons became more political and more critical of America's commercial culture, foreign policy, and indifference to European struggles for republicanism and democracy. Although she continued to praise America's founding political ideas, Fuller worried that the current generation was not really supporting this political tradition within the United States or in Europe. If America's people and government leaders would do more to promote the democratic ideals that flowed from their own eighteenth-century revolution, she suggested, then Europeans might advance more quickly toward the establishment of democratic societies in the Old World. Her European writing therefore evolved from commentaries that focused mainly on cultural issues into specific calls for Americans to support emerging political movements, especially in Italy.

Fuller's early *Tribune* articles expressed the cross-cultural fascination and pride of a traveler who was trying to discover how her own culture was viewed in Europe. She was flattered to learn that British readers responded favorably to her book on women in the nineteenth century, and she was proud to tell her family that one of her essays on American literature was translated into French and published in *La revue indépendante* while she was in Paris.[67] Her work for *The Dial* had also attracted attention in England, and she reported in a *Tribune* article that practical-minded English educators were reading American writers because they recognized that Americans were making valuable contributions to contemporary cultural life. Indeed, after hearing English intellectuals speak at public events, she decided that the "pure eloquence" and "spiritual beauty" of American writers such as William H. Channing and Theodore Parker equaled or even surpassed the eloquence of prominent English speakers.[68]

Anyone traveling to Europe from the United States, as Fuller described the experience, could thus feel a national pride in the ways that American ideas and writers were gaining respect among people in the Old World. Fuller's encounter with European cultures by no means transformed her into an uncritical American nationalist, but she reported that her travels gave her a new understanding of America's rising cultural position in the modern world. "The American in Europe, if a thinking mind, can only become more American," she wrote in one of her reflections on the meaning of a European trip. "Although we have an independent political existence, our position toward Europe, as to Literature and the Arts, is still that of a colony, and one feels the same joy here that is experienced by the colonist returning to the parent home."[69] Yet this complex relationship with the "parent" did not mean that Americans must simply defer to Europeans or that all modern cultural achievements came from the Old World. Those Americans *and* Europeans who made the effort to understand other cultures would therefore recognize that creative people were making distinctive cultural contributions on both sides of the Atlantic, but Fuller's articles in the *Tribune* also argued that Americans especially needed to think more critically about their superficial views of Europe.

Her discussion of unthinking Americans included a sharp-edged critique of tourists who ignored the complexities of European cultures and traveled blissfully across the surface of every foreign country they visited. According to Fuller, there were in fact three general types of American tourists in Europe. The first, which she called "the servile American," visited Europe to shop for fashionable clothes, meet aristocrats, and eat expensive foods. Fuller had no interest in these "shallow, thoughtless, [and] worthless" travelers who simply wanted to imitate European aristocrats or to inflate their own social status among their stay-at-home friends.[70] Since most Americans lacked the money and the leisure to travel abroad, "servile" American tourists could elevate their hometown social or cultural position even when they understood nothing about the places they had visited.

The second group in Fuller's hierarchy of American travelers was somewhat more analytical and reflective, but this group—which she called the "conceited" Americans—viewed their European travels simply as an opportunity to confirm the superiority of everything in the United States. Although the conceited tourist typically mocked the alien traditions of other societies (for example, old paintings, old music, old cultures), this kind of traveler could at least learn to appreciate the complex achievements of old European cultures. Conceited Americans never doubted the superiority of modern American institutions, however, so they rarely reached a higher level of cross-cultural understanding or allowed European ideas to challenge their long-held views of the United States or other national societies. Expressing this kind of conceited perspective on the Roman republic, for example, an American traveler smugly assured Fuller that the republic would fail because Italians were "not like *our* People." Such one-sided beliefs prevented Americans from seeing how different European social or political movements might actually extend America's traditional social and political ideals. "Conceited" Americans, in short, became "more ignorant" in Europe because they overvalued their own "crude impressions and frequent blunders" and then returned home with a "mind befooled rather than instructed."[71]

Neither the "servile" nor the "conceited" American would ever contribute to the cross-cultural project that Fuller wanted Americans to embrace, but she found a third kind of traveler—the "thinking American"—who shared her own approach to Europe. These people analyzed and compared societies on both sides of the Atlantic by "recognizing the immense advantage of being born to a new world and on a virgin soil" and by also recognizing the all-important cultural "seed from the Past." Such Americans knew they could learn from both the past cultures and the modern people they encountered in Europe; and they were willing to draw on European knowledge and insights when they returned to the changing social and political life of the United States. This "thinking" traveler takes back "all that will bear a new climate and new culture," Fuller explained, and seeks to "give them a fair trial in his new world."[72] This task gave "thinking" American travelers a different view of Europe, but it could also place the thinkers at odds with most other American travelers and with much of their own culture at home.

Fuller decided that most American travelers rarely sought to understand European cultures as they pursued what she condemned as an uninhibited quest for commercial gain or mindless pleasures. The mad pursuit of wealth and status thus became the main rationale for travel among those many Americans who left their minds at home while they crisscrossed Europe in search of the fine clothes and expensive objects they could display when they returned to the United States. Fuller criticized these commercial-minded Americans for losing sight of their most important national traditions, and she was soon expressing typical European complaints about American superficiality and money-grubbing. "They have no heart for the idea," she wrote in one critique of her compatriots, "[or] for the destiny of our own great nation: how can they feel the spirit that is struggling now in this [Italian nation] and others of Europe?" This blindness came from a "boundless lust of gain" and from a national vanity "which bristles and blusters at each foolish taunt of the foreign press." America's aggressive desire for "gain" could be seen in many spheres of the nation's life, including the "wicked" war against Mexico and the "horrible cancer of Slavery," but Fuller also insisted that the ongoing struggle to abolish slavery showed that some Americans continued to defend the nation's universal principles. Those abolitionists who had often seemed so "tedious" or "narrow" or "rabid" at home now appealed to Fuller (from her European perspective) as the principled defenders of America's most important political ideals and traditions.[73]

It was this long-developing American commitment to freedom and democracy rather than the misguided support for slavery, territorial conquest, and rampant commercialism that sustained Fuller's complex identification with her own nation. Given their own honorable political ideals, Americans had the most compelling philosophical and strategic reasons to embrace the new political movements for freedom in Europe. Although only a minority of her compatriots could presently see that the "lust for gain" was leading the United States away from "the cause of all mankind," Fuller's transnational experiences convinced her that America's universal principles of freedom and democratic government could help reshape modern European nations. While nineteenth-century Europeans struggled to promote these universal (and American) ideals, however, America's political leaders were aggressively violating these same principles as they conquered large parts of Mexico and extended slavery into new territories across their expanding nation.[74]

Fuller's final dispatches from Europe therefore repeatedly urged Americans to remember and support their own political principles. If they would turn their attention from their territorial conquests in Mexico to the revolutionary struggles in Europe, Fuller argued, Americans could both defend and extend the political principles that had long made their nation an exceptional symbol of freedom for the people of the Old World. Even before the Revolutions of 1848 erupted in Europe, Fuller was encouraging her readers to back the Italian movement for independence and comparing Italy's national struggle against Austria to America's own campaigns for national freedom. "This cause is OURS, above all others," she wrote in the fall of 1847; "we ought to show that we feel it to be so." Despite the official caution of their government, Americans should steadfastly support the aspirations of the Italians and all the other oppressed peoples of Europe. Private individuals or political groups could send a cannon to the Italians, for example, and thus confirm their solidarity with a growing political movement that would eventually rise against the Austrians. "Ah! America," she wrote in one of her calls to action, "with all thy rich boons, thou hast a heavy account to render for the talent given; see in every way that thou be not found wanting."[75] Fuller's remarkable prescience about forthcoming political conflicts developed into even more insistent pleas for tangible American assistance after the Italians began to establish their own republican institutions in 1848–49.

She urged the American government to recognize the new Roman republic in late 1848 and to send a sympathetic ambassador as its representative; she called on Americans to see the Roman struggle as a European version of their own revolutionary struggle for independence; and she advised her readers to ignore the hostile, anti-Roman reports that appeared regularly in the English press or in the commentaries of uninformed Americans.[76] Fuller wanted above all for Americans to see that their own enduring aspirations and ideals had reappeared in the new Roman republic. This recognition of overlapping political principles, as she imagined it, should provoke more active support from an American nation that had become "spoiled by prosperity, stupid with the lust of gain, soiled by crime in its willing perpetuation of Slavery, [and] shamed by an unjust war." Blinded by these distractions, the American people could not see what was now emerging in the new European spirit of freedom and brotherhood—"a spirit which cheers and animates mine," Fuller noted in the spring of 1848. What had happened to this "spirit" in America? Fuller tried to answer this question by calling America's own national spirit back to life rather than by expressing a deep distrust for her native country. America, she wrote, "is not dead, but in my time she sleepeth, and the spirit of our fathers flames no more, but lies hid beneath the ashes."[77]

In the end, Americans did not rise from their ashes to provide direct assistance for the collapsing Roman republic, and Fuller's journalistic campaign to mobilize popular American support for the Italians failed to achieve its transatlantic goals. Fuller's vehement backing of the Italian cause nevertheless gave her new reasons to praise America's universal principles even while she also condemned America for its failure to promote these principles more vigorously in Europe. She was pleased to learn about meetings that celebrated the Italian cause in New York, but she also wanted Americans to take more direct political action. They should, for example, "send money, send cheer—[and] acknowledge as the legitimate leaders and rulers those men who represent the people, who understand its wants, [and] who are ready to die or to live for its good."[78]

The failure to act was a symptom of a political illness that also afflicted every European nation that stood by while the hypocritical French republic crushed the Roman republic and reinstalled a frightened pope. But Fuller believed the greatest contradictions emerged in the United States because American support for Italy should have flowed directly from the stream of the nation's founding ideals. Setting aside her disappointments, however, Fuller still wanted to believe that Americans had never completely abandoned their national principles nor forgotten the European struggle for similar political goals. The struggle for republican political institutions would now continue by other means and in other times, and some Americans would surely support this never-ending campaign for human freedom and democracy. "I love my country for the spirit she has shown," she wrote after hearing about American sympathy for the recently destroyed Italian republic; "it proves that the lust of gold, her peculiar temptation, has not yet cankered her noble heart."[79]

By the end of her long stay in Europe, Fuller had therefore gone a long way toward constructing a new public identity and personal selfhood that merged the American and European components of her private and political life. She had found in Europe a new purpose for her American writing and a new selfhood in her Italian friendships and Italian family.

Her strongest feelings by 1849 were engaged in Italy's republican movement, in relationships with people who defended it (including her husband), and in the literary attempt to explain this political struggle to people in America. Indeed, she set off for America with the hope that her future publications would encourage or provoke new American support for democratic republicanism both at home and abroad.

Although her manuscript for a book on recent Italian history disappeared in the shipwreck that took her life, Fuller's numerous articles in the *Tribune* show how her European experiences stimulated a "thinking" traveler's critique of American commercialism and national indifference to the European struggles that she linked to America's most important political principles. Writing from outside the United States, she established her public role as a woman journalist in a sphere of male writers and as a literary advocate for transatlantic political transformations. Her political prose urged Americans to promote national political ideas that were also becoming transnational ideas in the radical republican movements of modern Europe.

Fuller thus came to believe that Americans might better understand and reaffirm their own republican ideals by giving more attention to the political and social struggles in other nations. These ongoing campaigns for democratic ideals and institutions went far beyond the narrow pursuit of self-interest that had become the modern American obsession, so anyone who viewed the United States from Europe could see that America was by no means the world's only promised land of modern republicanism and political democracy. Fuller's European journey,

European ideas, and European relationships therefore shaped a new historical and journalistic narrative in which she tried to show nineteenth-century Americans what they could learn from social and political conflicts in faraway places. Within a year of Fuller's tragic death, however, the young Tennessean Randal McGavock began writing a new series of traveler's letters that would reaffirm the nationalist belief that Americans had more to teach than to learn in all the other nations of the modern world.

CHAPTER FOUR

Randal McGavock's American Affirmation of Southern White Manhood

About nine months after Margaret Fuller's death off the coast of Fire Island, Randal McGavock (age twenty-four) sailed out of New York City with a group of fellow Tennesseans on his way to Liverpool, England. He had grown up in a prominent Nashville family and completed his legal training at Harvard, but he approached this trip as another crucial step in his education. Like Fuller, he had learned about American politics and religion from ambitious family members, yet (also like Fuller) he became eager to explore a wider world of European culture and history. He also wanted to describe his journey in letters for his hometown newspaper, the *Daily Nashville Union*, which would explain what he observed as a traveling Tennessean in Europe and the Middle East.

McGavock was born in Nashville in 1826. His mother, Ann Grundy, was the daughter of a lawyer-politician named Felix Grundy (1775–1840), whose prominent career as a congressman, US senator, and US attorney general had established a network of family friendships that later helped young Randal meet influential northern and southern Democrats. His father, Jacob McGavock, worked as a clerk in federal courts, but he also owned farmlands in rural Arkansas and used the labor of enslaved people to build the family's wealth and prominence in Nashville's white society. Randal was the first son to survive infancy, though an older sister and four younger siblings would also live into adulthood. McGavock's family had moved to Tennessee from Virginia and Kentucky as the frontier of European American settlements advanced rapidly toward the West, and he grew up in the political culture of Andrew Jackson's Democratic Party. His family belonged to a Presbyterian church, and young Randal received additional religious training at the University of Nashville, where he also studied classical languages and history, participated in a debating society, and prepared himself for advanced training in the law. He graduated from the University of Nashville in 1846.[1]

The intellectual and personal horizons of McGavock's youthful education began to widen after he entered Harvard Law School in the fall of 1847 for an eighteen-month program of legal studies. Although he dutifully went to his law classes, he also studied history and modern literature, attended numerous plays and political events in Boston, and started to keep a journal. He wrote about the books he was reading and the people he met at Harvard as well as the contemporary public debates about slavery and the Mexican War. McGavock's journal entries show that he found the poetry of Lord Byron more engaging than his law books, he read Bible passages almost every day, he deeply disliked Boston's "disgraceful" abolitionists, and he developed new interests in European history, especially after the Revolutions of 1848.[2]

He also launched his career as a tourist, traveling from Cambridge to New York, Philadelphia, and Washington and making other trips to Niagara Falls and Canada. His grandfather Grundy's friendship with James Polk gave McGavock an entry to the White House, and his visits there in January 1848 illustrate the casual access that was available to young men from well-connected families. "I went to the White House and dined there," he wrote in his journal during one of his trips to Washington. "The dinner was splendidly served, and the President and lady performed the honors with becoming style." This dinner invitation for a young law student suggests how presidential access has evolved since 1848, but it is even more remarkable to find that McGavock returned to the White House several times in the next week to collect letters of introduction for a friend and to meet informally with President Polk. "I called on the President and conversed socially about one hour," he noted casually in a journal entry about his busy social life in the capital.[3]

McGavock's interest in Europe evolved into a new career plan during the summer of 1848, when he returned to Washington to visit President Polk and to ask for a diplomatic appointment in a foreign mission. Unfortunately, as McGavock noted in his journal, "there was no vacancy either in the Legations or charges d'affaires." Even the president was therefore unable to provide a job in Europe, though McGavock was certain that he "would have granted my request" if a position had been available.[4] This request for a foreign position may have surprised McGavock's family because his Harvard education was supposed to prepare him for a legal career in Nashville. Within a year after beginning his studies, however, he was already yearning for an extended visit to Europe, and he would try again (unsuccessfully) for overseas diplomatic appointments after his European trip in 1851–52.

Having completed the residency requirement for a Harvard law degree in February 1849, McGavock returned to Nashville, launched a slow-developing law practice, and pursued a new relationship with a woman named Fanny Jane Crutcher. When neither the law practice nor the romantic relationship developed as he had expected, however, McGavock decided that he should travel (or escape) to Europe. His family money facilitated his restless aspirations, so McGavock left Nashville in March 1851; stopped in Washington to see the new president, Millard Fillmore; and went on to New York to board a sailing ship (the *Waterloo*) for Europe. The traveling party included several Tennessee relatives and friends as well as a free African American man named Frank Parrish who worked as a barber in Nashville and who joined the trip to provide "service" for the Nashville lawyer Edwin Ewing.[5]

McGavock described his motives for the trip in both his journal and his first published letters, but he was vague about the personal reasons for his departure from Nashville. Although he noted in an early journal entry that intellectual curiosity inspired him to travel, he also stressed that he lacked a binding hometown relationship. "Having a longing desire to visit the ancient world I have hit upon this period of my life to perform the tour, believing that I can realize more pleasure and improvement than at any subsequent time," he explained to himself in a purposeful, moral justification for his journey; "and at the same time I am better able to leave home, having no entangling alliances or particular object to bind me to Nashville."[6] A European voyage would therefore improve his mind, but it might also be useful for his heart. His published rationale for the trip referred more explicitly to a need to expand his past studies and "to see with my own eyes, and learn for myself, things I have failed to realize in books."[7]

This cross-cultural curiosity, however, did not explain all his motives for a European trip, as he acknowledged in his allusions to incentives that went beyond the cultural lessons of good books. "Through some freak of fortune, or misfortune, as time may determine, I found my inclination to leave home become so strong, I was willing . . . to part with my family and friends, and all who are near and dear to me, and be a rover for eighteen months or more in foreign climes."[8] McGavock clearly felt an emotional push from Nashville that intensified a cultural pull from Europe as he set off on his journey with personal disappointments and with a literary model in the life and writings of Lord Byron, whose influence appears throughout both McGavock's journal and his published articles. While still at sea, for example, he referred to his sad breakup with Fanny Jane Crutcher and the misfortunes that had caused their separation; "I have known no happiness since," he wrote in a melancholy summary of his emotional misery. He doubted that even the long ocean voyage could lift his spirits from a despair that echoed the lovesick sadness of popular romantic poetry. "And today my heart feels sick when I think of the past without any future to cheer me on."[9]

McGavock seemed to imagine that his newspaper articles might help him remain present in the life of the Nashville woman, who, as he wrote in London, "haunts me continually and makes me perfectly unhappy." The precise emotional purpose of McGavock's travel writing is of course impossible to know, yet his early European letters and his memory of a lost relationship were somehow connected. One of his journal entries in Scotland, for example, reported that a letter from his mother assured him "that three of my letters had been published and favorably received" and, equally important, "that my old flame was not so great a belle as formerly."[10] His letters were appearing in the Nashville newspaper, and perhaps his literary presence had provoked "old flame" regrets about McGavock's physical absence? He did not expand on these speculations, but his Romantic sensibility and vaguely rebellious "Byronic" identity would reappear regularly in his European journal.

His personal interest in sustaining relations with hometown people helped McGavock become a hardworking travel correspondent. Although he complained about the time and effort that his writing demanded, he eventually published seventy detailed letters in the *Nashville Union*. Confessing his dislike for the disciplined work of continual letter writing, McGavock struggled to describe his observations and reflections. "I remained during the entire day in my room writing a description of my travels for the *Union*, which I find to be no small job," he noted in the journal entry for a "dark and gloomy" day in London. "It occupies much time and mental labor, and I almost feel conscious that I will never be remunerated." Yet he was determined to push on with the task, even as he continued to complain about the daily challenges of composing travel stories and keeping a journal. "I regret that I ever commenced writing for the papers, as it occupies much valuable time."[11] As McGavock had predicted, he never collected much remuneration for his European letters, but the written remnants of his journey and thoughts gave him an obscure literary selfhood; and the traveling Tennessean left something of himself (like Byron) for people who might read his published letters or encounter his forgotten life in this book.

McGavock's grand tour of Europe and the Middle East took place between April 1851 and September 1852. He traveled through England, Ireland, and Scotland in May and June (1851), moved on for a month in Paris, and then meandered across Belgium, the Netherlands, Germany, Switzerland, and Italy (August to early December). From Naples he went by ship to Egypt and set off on another overland trip through the Middle East, stopping in Palestine, Syria, and Turkey. By the spring of 1852 he was visiting Greece and steadily making his way north into Austria and Germany en route to Russia. The final stages of his long journey included stops in Scandinavia and northern Germany before the return voyage to New York in early October 1852. Traveling to Tennessee by way of Boston and New Hampshire (where he met the Democratic presidential candidate, Franklin

Pierce), he arrived in Nashville on the eve of the 1852 election and soon joined the local celebrations of the Democratic electoral victory.[12]

This extensive travel had no discernible effect on McGavock's political allegiances, but his trip changed him in other ways. He grew a bushy red beard; developed a broader, somewhat skeptical view of some religious or cultural values in middle Tennessee; and gained a new social status at home through the publication of his seventy travel letters in the *Nashville Union*. The author was identified simply as a "Tennessean," but his identity was well known, and he became a local celebrity during his long, well-reported journey. "It was a happy day to me when I arrived at my native city and received the congratulations of my family and friends after having been a rover so long," he wrote in a journal comment about his return to Nashville. "All seemed glad to see me, and many comments were made upon the changes that had taken place in my person and manners since leaving."[13] Although he resumed his interrupted career as a Tennessee lawyer, McGavock's new literary identity and international ambitions by no means disappeared. He found a New York publisher for his European letters and assembled a book titled *A Tennessean Abroad, or Letters from Europe, Africa, and Asia* (1854).

Meanwhile, he also decided that he wanted to return to Europe (the sign of an underlying discomfort in Nashville?), and by February 1853 he was applying to President Pierce for a diplomatic appointment in Europe. He asked well-connected political friends to support his case and even met with the president and several cabinet officials in Washington, but his job-seeking campaign produced only an offer for a diplomatic post in Central America, which he declined. Frustrated by his setbacks in Washington, he went back to Nashville with unhappy feelings about his international ambitions. "Office seaking [*sic*] I regard as utterly disreputable to a gentleman and this experiment has taught me a lesson that I will not soon forget," he wrote after this futile quest to represent the United States abroad. "Hereafter, offices may seek me, I will never again seek them."[14] In fact, he could not abandon his desire to live in Europe until he made a final, failed attempt to gain a European position after James Buchanan was elected president in 1856.

McGavock's personal life had changed by this time because he had married a younger woman named Seraphine Deery (age twenty), established a more active legal career, and become more engaged with local politics. He was elected to one term as mayor of Nashville in 1858, but his political interests also extended beyond his own city. He sought to help Irish immigrants by strongly opposing the anti-immigrant Know-Nothing Party (an example of his international perspectives), and he eventually supported the southern secession movement. As the Civil War began in the spring of 1861, McGavock became a captain in a local company of mostly Irish soldiers that joined the Tenth Tennessee Regiment of the

Randal McGavock in Military Uniform. Oil on canvas by George Dury, ca. 1863. McGavock's letters from Europe in the early 1850s affirmed his confidence in the exceptional political and economic achievements of the United States, and he returned from his travels with a strong belief in the importance of national union. When Tennessee seceded from the Union in 1861, however, he joined the Confederate army (as this portrait emphasizes) and died in a secessionist war against the nation he had continually praised during his long European journey. Maidun Collection/ Alamy Stock Photo.

Confederate army. He was captured by Union forces in Tennessee after the surrender of Fort Henry in early 1862 and sent to a prison in Boston Harbor, thus traveling again to his old "home city" in New England with a southern military identity that had displaced the Byronic literary ambitions of his student days at Harvard. Released from prison in exchange for Union prisoners during the summer of 1862, McGavock returned to his regiment, rose to the position of commanding colonel, and participated in Confederate defensive operations around Vicksburg. He was mortally wounded on 12 May 1863, as he led his troops into a skirmish with Union troops who were advancing toward Jackson, and so the world traveler, writer, and once-patriotic American died fighting against the US Army in Mississippi.[15]

He left only one published book, but his family preserved his journals from Harvard and from the first eight months of his European trip as well as parts of his journal from the later 1850s and the early Civil War. These journals were published in the twentieth century, providing an informative supplement to the public travel narratives in *A Tennessean Abroad*. McGavock's death in the Civil War adds a complex, ironic aftermath to his European writings because he often stressed that travel abroad had shown him America's clear superiority over other nations. "Let those who speak of disunion, who have sectional prejudices, or who are blindly led by party rule, make the tour of the Old World," he wrote in the conclusion of his book, "and if I am not greatly mistaken they will return home with national ideas, national love, and national fidelity."[16] This national allegiance ultimately gave way to a stronger sectional identity and to a life-ending military campaign to break apart the union of American states, but McGavock's travel writings in 1851–52 show how he had first defined his American selfhood by describing the people and cultures of Europe.

McGavock's View of European Culture

If Margaret Fuller had met Randal McGavock or read his commentaries on European life, she might have categorized him as a typical "conceited" American traveler who never doubted his own nation's political and cultural superiority. To be sure, he wanted to understand and explain the distinctive traits of European cultural history, but he also wanted his American readers to know that they lived in the world's best and most advanced modern nation. McGavock generally expressed his greatest respect for high European culture—writers, old monuments, paintings—and the least respect for the current institutions and people in nineteenth-century European societies. Although he did not put his cross-cultural comparisons in precise temporal terms, he seemed to see Europe as the culture or society of the past and America as the culture or society of the future. Each could learn something from the other, yet McGavock assumed that Americans who cared mostly about the present or future would likely come away from Europe with a new confidence in the superiority of American achievements and institutions. He was, in short, one of those travelers who return from international trips with a stronger pride in their home country. At the same time, however, he clearly admired Europe's literary culture and historical significance, which he wanted to explore with all the diligence that a conscientious, traveling letter writer could possibly muster.

McGavock had developed his knowledge of European culture by reading the historical accounts of famous people, the historical novels of Walter Scott, and the Romantic poetry of Lord Byron. The journal in which he described his daily life at Harvard often noted that he was reading Byron's poetry whenever he could take breaks from his legal studies, and he liked to balance his daily religious reading of the Bible with an almost daily unreligious reading of Byron. "I remained in my room and read my Bible and Childe Harold's Pilgrimage," he wrote in a typical journal entry. Calling Byron's work "sublime" and a form of writing "which I admire very much," McGavock also confessed in his journal that he enjoyed "Don Juan" (though it was "a little smutty") and liked to read Byron's "beautiful letters."[17]

His reports from Europe therefore referred often to Byron's greatness and to virtually any historical or natural site that could be linked to the poet's life. He visited Newstead Abbey in England, so that he could see where "the great genius of Byron was first developed" and where the poet's body was placed after his untimely death in Greece. But the physical monuments to Byron's life ultimately meant less to McGavock than the poetic legacy that would continue to "live when all monuments shall have crumbled away." McGavock himself confirmed Byron's immortality through his frequent allusions to Byronic descriptions of specific sights in Switzerland, Italy, and Greece, all of which gained exalted cultural meanings because they were associated with the rebellious English poet. He thus visited Missolonghi to see the place in Greece where Byron had died in 1824, but he also explained how the famous mountains and valleys in Switzerland and Italy inspired a new surge of personal ambition because they evoked his memories of Byron's brilliant poetry. Walking along Lake Leman in Switzerland, McGavock found himself "gazing in wonder and admiration upon the spots that inspired the genius of a Rousseau, a Byron, and other gifted authors. It was an evening for reflection; thoughts of the past, the glories of the present, and the bright hopes of the future, all conspired to create emotions that will not soon be forgotten."[18]

It was in fact the poetry of European sights rather than their natural grandeur that provoked McGavock's deepest touristic engagement. He frequently claimed that Europe's most celebrated scenes of nature were unimpressive for Americans because these natural wonders were almost always smaller than the mountains, rivers, or waterfalls in the United States. No matter what other travelers might write about the often-described waterfalls of Switzerland, for example, the discerning American visitor (such as himself) "who has heard the roar, and seen the mighty rush of waters at Niagara, would pronounce it a swindle, and inferior even to many cataracts in the United States, that have no reputation beyond the sound of their waters."[19]

The monuments of Europe's long *human* history therefore elicited McGavock's most sustained interest, but these symbols of historical greatness also became good examples of why Rome, Florence, Athens, and Jerusalem were cities of the past rather than important places for the present or future. His entry into Rome provoked deep emotional responses, McGavock explained to his readers, because it was the greatest city of antiquity and the famous site for much of the history he had studied at school. Although dramatic recent events had also taken place in the city (including the brutal French suppression of the Roman republic in 1849), the impressive people and events of the distant past represented for McGavock the essential historical and personal meaning of Rome:

> I thought of its antiquity, its renown, its glory, and its present lowly state. Even my own brief history involuntarily passed before my mind's eye....
>
> Here we realized, in one sweep of the eye, all the dreams of our boyish days and the hopes of later years. Like nectar, we drank in... the beauties of a panorama rich in history, in memory, and in truth....
>
> [The Coliseum] is without question the most stupendous ruin in the world. Most things, as seen through the writings of travellers... fall short of one's expectations; but the Coliseum is, in truth, far ahead of any description that I have ever read.[20]

McGavock's praise for the ancient glories of Rome thus expressed a strong identification with European history and with the "stupendous ruin" of a past culture that could still inspire modern Americans. Yet it was also true that perceptive American travelers could see that Rome (like other ancient cities) had fallen from its former greatness and that nobody would visit Italy to learn about the progress of modern world history.

McGavock's respect for Byron's poetry and for ancient ruins therefore carried him to all the usual sites on the "cultural tourist" itinerary, but he also found some impressive modern knowledge on display at the international exhibition in the Crystal Palace.[21] McGavock's tour of London's Great Exhibition of 1851 generated a rare letter of praise for Europe's modern achievements, and (in the presence of this modernity) he compared himself to a rural "*greenhorn*" on his first visit to a large, fancy store. Noting that Americans could gain new practical knowledge about recent progress in English and European machinery, he stressed that the Crystal Palace exhibition was well worth a visit for anyone who wanted to understand the human "powers of advancement." Even in the era of London's Great Exhibition, however, McGavock thought the best education for Americans might still be found among the "relics of antiquity" at the British Museum—where travelers could see the most creative achievements from all of human history.[22] This was the cultural legacy that made Europe so valuable for American travelers and the legacy that McGavock pursued on his visits to every collection of art or sculpture or historical artifacts that his guidebooks recommended.[23]

Although he humbly admitted that his writing could not convey the beauty of the visual arts, he assured himself and his readers that he was gaining new cultural knowledge from his experiential contact with the most famous monuments and literary sites of European culture. "It is impossible to describe the feelings that animated my bosom while gazing on the antiquities of so many ages," he wrote in his journal during his visit to Rome. "I thought of my schoolboy days when I used to . . . recite the writings of Cicero, Caesar, Virgil, and the other writers. All of my early reading came up fresh in my memory and I felt that I was once more a boy." European monuments thus symbolized both past human achievements and his own classical education in America, but they also elicited melancholic feelings about the transience of human life and every kind of human labor. If the famous Colossus of Rhodes showed the grandeur of human creativity, for example, then its disappearance demonstrated the inescapable frailty of all human accomplishments. "But such is the history of the world," he noted in one of his historical reflections; "the greatest works of man must pass away, and vanish for ever, while the immutable creations of God stand the shock of ages."[24]

McGavock's comparison of vanishing human monuments and the "immutable creations of God" drew upon an American Protestant education that also shaped his critical responses to most of the religious practices he observed in both Catholic Europe and the Muslim Middle East. Indeed, his views of Catholicism and Catholic rituals brought him closer to Margaret Fuller on this subject than on almost any other aspect of American or European culture and politics. Like Fuller, he repeatedly condemned Catholic traditions, especially when he wrote about specific rituals such as the popular pilgrimage up the Holy Stairs at the Church of St. John Lateran in Rome. Church authorities claimed that Christ himself had gone down these stairs after Pontius Pilate condemned him to death, but McGavock believed that both the pilgrims and the clergy who encouraged their pilgrimages were completely deluded. "Fifty to one hundred pilgrims, male and female, old and young, may be seen at any time ascending this staircase on their knees. I never, in my life, saw anything else so ridiculous and absurd as this sight—ridiculous in the many incidents connected with it, and absurd in its senseless and unmeaning degradation."[25] Although McGavock occasionally reassured his readers about his own (respectable) religious commitments, he resembled Fuller and the most radical skeptics in denouncing the religious ideas and practices of Roman Catholicism. Unlike Fuller, however, McGavock traveled on to Egypt and Palestine, where his journey provoked more reflections on his own religious culture and where even the revered sites of biblical history could not overcome his aversion for what he saw as simple-minded religious credulity.

McGavock's trip to Palestine retraced the exodus and tribulations of the ancient

Hebrews. Traveling slowly overland from Egypt, he struggled through sandstorms in the desert and faced threats from Bedouin bandits before entering Jerusalem in early 1852. The Holy Land reminded him of childhood religious lessons ("I learned the catechism from my mother's lips") as he visited shrines that had long attracted religious pilgrims from Europe and America, but he confessed his deepening skepticism about the authenticity of sacred places and the religious tourists who flocked to see them. When he visited the alleged site of Christ's burial, for example, he could not actually believe "that this was the tomb in which the body of Christ reposed for three days." He nevertheless assured his readers that his skepticism did not preclude spiritual experiences and that "the sanctity of the place took possession of my soul, and . . . the great Jehovah seemed to rise before my vision like some bright spirit from the dreamy world."[26]

It was therefore possible for a Tennessean to draw inspiration from the sacred sites of Palestine—if he could set aside distracting intrusions from the naive pilgrims and the Christian churches that dominated all of the surrounding religious space. The priests at the Greek Orthodox Church of the Holy Sepulchre provided a good example of the problem by telling "credulous" visitors that fire descended from heaven to light the church's lamps; and the Church of the Ascension added to the religious mythmaking with problematic claims about housing the stone (marked by the impression of a man's foot) from which Christ had ascended into heaven. McGavock doubted all such descriptions of miraculous objects or miraculous events. Although he visited the famous sites that a good pilgrim had to see, he soon decided that the best-known tombs were essentially places where "the curious traveler stops to wonder and to doubt." Religious tourists thus needed to maintain a critical distance from their well-paid guides and to remember that the spirit of sacred shrines was more important than precise locations or the dubious stories that described them. "We are privileged," he wrote during a visit to Bethlehem, ". . . to doubt as much as we please; yet it is pleasant to feel that we are in the vicinity of such places, even if we do not hit exactly on the identical spot."[27]

By the end of his visit to Palestine, however, McGavock had fully satisfied his religious curiosity and decided that he had no desire to convert others to his own religion. Responding to the diverse peoples and faiths in Jerusalem, he concluded that Christian missionaries would never convert Muslims and Jews because the Muslims would never abandon their mosque and the Jews would never turn away from the "Wall" that had survived from the ancient temple.[28] In other words, when it came to religious rituals and proselytizing, McGavock was more pragmatic than devout.

He was nonetheless intrigued by Muslim religious traditions and by the ways in which Arab culture both resembled that of Europe (in its history of *past* greatness) and differed from it (in its adherence to Islam). His racist views of the Arab people reinforced his critical views of modern Egyptian society, but the ancient historical monuments were "far, far more interesting than anything modern. They speak of the past—the mighty past! When Egypt was in the zenith of her glory and Europe in a state of barbarism." By the 1850s, this cultural hierarchy had long since been reversed, perhaps (from McGavock's Christian perspective) because of Arab commitments to the Muslim faith. Yet, McGavock wanted to understand how Muslims used or abused their faith in daily life and to explain how their apparent religious devotion could hide a multitude of sins. The people in Cairo were careful to perform their daily prayers, he explained during his visit to Egypt, but these prayers often failed to produce the kind of ethical behavior that McGavock associated with religious faith: "They evince great devotion and sincerity while on their knees, but as soon as they finish, they are ready to filch your purse, tell you a falsehood, or do any other rascality in their power."[29]

Such complaints expressed typical European American beliefs about the people and dangers in Middle Eastern cities, and they reinforced stereotypical views of the religious culture McGavock sought to understand. As he traveled on a boat up the Nile River, however, he began to see deep religious commitments in the disciplined daily practices of the Muslim crew members, even though he always discussed Muslim practices with the critical presuppositions of American Protestantism: "They first wash their face, feet, and privates, and then kneel and rise on their feet six times, touching their faces to the ground twice every kneeling. According to the Koran, they are required to wash themselves and pray three times a day—first at sunrise, then at 3:00, and at sunset, always turning their backs to the West. Passing along the Nile, hundreds of Arabs can be seen at these hours coming down to the water's edge and going through the forms of their religion."[30]

McGavock's information about the number of daily prayers was not accurate, but he wanted to understand and explain the influence of religious rituals and spiritual commitments in the lives of people he had never previously encountered. His reports on Egypt and Palestine thus included descriptions of meetings with pilgrims who were returning from Mecca and rigorously upholding their religious duties. "It is a solemn and affecting scene," he noted, "to see men out in the still and barren desert offering up to God and the Prophet the earnest devotion of their hearts."[31]

In contrast to the language he used to describe Catholic pilgrims on the church steps in Rome ("ridiculous and absurd"), McGavock rarely mocked or simply condemned Muslim rituals, though he admitted that he sometimes found them incomprehensible. He observed one of these mystifying rituals in Cairo, where he saw a group of pilgrims celebrate their return from Mecca by throwing themselves under the horse of a local religious leader. At the climactic moment of this celebration, "a number of *blind* and foolish fanatics will throw themselves down and be ridden over by a sheik on the sacred horse." Although the custom defied American conceptions of common sense, McGavock took its complexity as the starting point for a more careful analysis of cultural differences. "The Arabs are a strange people," he wrote in his journal, "and the more I see of them the more curious I become to learn their real character."[32] This quest for cross-cultural knowledge pushed McGavock across much of the Middle East and Europe, but his engagement with other cultures, religions, and social relations ultimately confirmed his previous American views of other people and his deep identification with the cultural values he had learned in the United States. Encountering people in other cultures and visiting "inauthentic" holy sites could be unsettling, but these experiences also carried him toward new affirmations of his enduring American selfhood.

McGavock's Critique of European and Middle Eastern Societies

McGavock's reports on European and Middle Eastern cities became more critical whenever he turned from their cultural and historical legacies to describe modern social and political conditions. The superiority of American society, as he perceived it, became more apparent through his daily encounters with contemporary institutions—from hotels and social hierarchies to agriculture and even Middle Eastern markets for the sale of enslaved people. He noted in both his newspaper articles and his personal journal that American travelers needed to be constantly on guard against dishonest hotel clerks, miserable beggars, and repressive police forces. These threats increased as Americans traveled toward the south or the east, but they would also find challenging problems in the most prosperous northern European nations.

Writing from England, for example, McGavock reported that the hotels "are far inferior to our American hotels in every particular. They are nothing more than large coffee-houses with lodging rooms attached." They were also expensive, though in this respect they resembled the hotels in almost every tourist city of the Old World. Overpriced hotels in Switzerland provoked McGavock's warnings about the financial perils that awaited unwary Americans, but the problems became even more annoying in Italian hotels, where McGavock struggled to make his way through a constant stream of "fleas, bad coffee, and dishonesty."[33]

Assuming that such inconveniences were the price that Americans had to pay for visits to the historical sites they had come to see, he advised travelers to expect some physical discomforts as an experiential cost of every transnational journey.

American travelers might also discover, however, that the obstacles on a long European journey created new opportunities for national solidarity, as he noted in an account of some Americans who met in a small-town Italian boardinghouse after a hard, cold day of European tourism. The travelers gathered around a few hot fireplace coals in an otherwise chilly house and fell into a happy American-language conversation about "the inclemency of the weather, our eternal horror of all *vetturini* [guides] . . . [and] the great annoyance occasioned by the nocturnal visits of fleas and other vermin."[34] Such complaints contributed to a shared belief in America's national superiority and suggested that new threats were forever hovering around the famous historical sites that good American travelers wanted to see.

McGavock discovered that these lurking dangers could haunt any place he might visit, including the famous port at Alexandria, Egypt. Coming ashore in a small boat that was supposed to transport him to the city dock, McGavock found himself amid "rascally Arabs" who demanded payment before they would row the boat. The rowers defiantly put down their oars, whereupon McGavock and a fellow American traveler "drew our pistols and told them to carry us ashore or we would shoot them, a threat that soon brought them to their senses." This assertive, American-style arrival in Alexandria was soon followed by an even more dangerous incident on the boat that carried McGavock's American party up the Nile River toward Cairo. The boat's crew fell into a violent brawl with a large group of villagers who wanted to collect pieces of wood that were floating on the water in which the boat was anchored. When the villagers prevented the boat from sailing away, several of the American travelers armed themselves with guns and went ashore with their "servant" Frank Parrish to break up the crowd. An angry brawler hit Parrish with a large stick and wounded him in the neck with his own gun, but McGavock (who was also injured in the fray) fired several shots to push the attackers away. The Americans then returned to their boat, leaving behind several wounded men, one of whom died. McGavock's description of these violent events in his journal and in one of his newspaper letters vividly portrayed the dangers of traveling in alien cultures, but he stressed (heroically) that the conflict had not deterred him from sightseeing in Egypt. Several of the wounded Arabs were brought to a police hearing in Cairo, where (according to McGavock) they "made statements altogether false and ridiculous" and where the local authorities treated the Americans with deferential respect. Indeed, the whole cross-cultural proceeding confirmed the power of reigning social hierarchies because the injured Arabs "were trembling in fear" and an American consul helped the travelers resume their privileged journey across Egypt.[35]

McGavock thus escaped any legal consequences that might have followed from this conflict. He moved on with the personal freedom of a (neocolonial) white visitor, though he also expressed new anxieties about the perils of living in foreign cultures. He was certain that American force had prevented a worse situation from developing, yet he also began to recognize that privileged American travelers could always be vulnerable to local populations. Indeed, he was soon facing other threats from disease (he was quarantined when he arrived in Smyrna, Turkey), from petty thefts, and from pickpockets, one of whom stole his money in Russia and gave him more reasons to worry about the risks in unfamiliar countries. "I tried to philosophize, but it was of no use," he wrote after his money was stolen. "I could not divest myself of the fact that my pocket was empty. Philosophy is a very good horse in the stable, but out on a journey in a foreign land, far away from home, he does not work so well."[36] Although a local American diplomat immediately loaned him the money he needed to continue his trip, McGavock used this crime story to remind his readers that Americans inevitably faced unexpected obstacles as they traveled through unknown, distant places.

Apart from crime, disease, and cheating hotel clerks, the main dangers for conscientious American travelers came in the temptation to drink, dance, and distract oneself in frivolous European entertainments. He found disturbing examples of this frivolity among the beer drinkers of Bavaria, who (as McGavock informed his readers) could often drink ten or twelve quarts of beer per day; and there were other dangers among the celebrated dancers of Vienna. McGavock worried in a self-deprecating letter from Austria that he might have damaged his nation's reputation when his awkward steps at a Viennese dance hall pulled a partner crashing to the floor, "much to the amusement of the by-standers." He eventually escaped from the dance hall without damaging himself or "the reputation acquired by our countrymen of being equal to anything," but the unhappy incident showed McGavock's sensitivity to the different national meanings of social and cultural status.[37]

McGavock's family connections gave him entrée with American diplomats in London, Paris, Rome, Alexandria, Constantinople, Berlin, St. Petersburg, and other cities he visited. These American contacts also provided access to the European upper classes, so it is not surprising to find references to social elites in many of his letters for the *Nashville Union*. Neither the wealth nor the social status of privileged people was especially impressive to McGavock, however, and he tended to belittle the cultural or political significance of the European upper classes. After visiting a law court in England, for example, he noted the elegant clothes and dignity of the judges before concluding that "in this age of progressive democracy in America, all such trappings would be cast aside as utterly useless and anti-utilitarian." The fashionable, wealthy guests in the upscale casinos at Baden-Baden also failed to impress McGavock, and he assured his readers that the finest hotels in Germany were less elegant than comparable American resorts at Newport or Saratoga.[38]

Upper-class hotels and the leisure activities of the idle rich were thus less important to McGavock than the industrial output of English factories or the cloth that was manufactured in the Manchester textile mills. These factories were of course a highly successful component of the English economy, but McGavock reported that Americans had no reason to feel inferior. In fact, he suggested that "our mills can fully compete with them in all respects, and in a few years, I hope to see in operation manufactures on a much grander scale in our own Tennessee."[39] This confidence in the rapidly expanding American economy reappeared often in McGavock's references to European poverty and social inequality, all of which confirmed a nationalist belief in the superiority of American commerce and the future accumulation of American wealth.

The miseries of European poverty became a theme in McGavock's earliest reports from England and Scotland, but the impoverished people in Ireland elicited some of his most detailed accounts of social despair (perhaps because his own ancestors had emigrated from Protestant Northern Ireland). Describing his visit to the city of Cork, McGavock stressed that "the streets . . . are literally blocked up with a variegated mass of squalid humanity that sways and surges around the stranger on every side, pulling his garments . . . and filling his ears with all the discordant sounds of blatant mendicancy." Irish cities were therefore among the most miserable places on earth, but living conditions were no better in the countryside—where Irish peasants struggled to survive in such awful squalor that "no one who has not witnessed it can possibly conceive their manner of living, or realize that they are beings like ourselves, subject to the same diseases and possessing the same wants."[40]

McGavock attributed the Irish poverty to a wide range of possible social causes, including the negligence of absentee landlords, the influence of Catholicism, the failure of the potato crop, and a system of agriculture that had exhausted the land. If the precise sources of the misery were difficult to discern, the consequences were all too obvious in an almost universal social and cultural despair that was driving hopeless people toward America. "Every one that can raise a few pounds," McGavock explained, "immediately sets sail for the new world, which is regarded here as the promised land for the oppressed of all nations."[41] The intractable economic problems of Irish society thus led McGavock into a nationalist theme that helped to shape the broader message of his whole travel narrative: anyone who visited a country like Ireland would understand why so many unhappy people crossed the Atlantic to seek a better life in America.

Ireland offered especially disturbing examples of human misery, but it was only one of the places in which McGavock wrote about pervasive social inequalities. Cities in Italy and the Middle East were filled with equally stark signs of poverty, and there were always beggars who distracted American tourists from the historical sites they expected to enjoy. Stopping briefly in the small Italian town of Fondi, for example, McGavock was quickly surrounded by an assertive crowd that begged for money. "Poor, ignorant, and degraded people!" he wrote in one of his newspaper articles. "They know nothing of the comforts of life, the beauties of religion, or the duties of man."[42] The poverty became ever more conspicuous as McGavock traveled across southern Italy and finally reached Egypt, where he saw desperately poor people in the muddy villages that stretched south from Alexandria along the Nile River.

The degradation in these villages went beyond the misery McGavock had seen previously in Ireland or Italy, and he wondered how families could survive when they slept on the bare ground and suffered constantly from acute hunger or disease. Many villagers had sunk into conditions that (for a privileged American) seemed to approach the degraded existence of hungry animals: "I noticed in several of these miserable hovels as many as twelve or fifteen human beings in a perfect state of nudity, living among yelping dogs and swarms of flies. . . . And their only food seemed to be a few raw onions and garlic. No wonder that famine and the plague make such sad ravages among the benighted people; their mode of life, their filthiness and their indolent habits, all conspire to bring on disease in every shape, and render them miserable and degraded."[43] Although wealthy elites also lived in Egypt, McGavock's letters for the *Nashville Union* gave far more attention to the miseries of Egypt's most impoverished people. The grinding poverty in the cities and villages of Ireland, Italy, and Egypt surpassed anything that McGavock could remember seeing in America, even among factory workers in crowded northern cities or among enslaved people on the poorest southern plantations. This vast gap between rich and poor in Old World societies thus offered McGavock a comparative framework for defending the much-criticized social and economic gap between American enslavers and their enslaved workers. Rejecting abolitionist critiques that condemned the American slave system as one of the most brutal, dehumanizing social systems in all human history, McGavock tried to differentiate the enslavement of African Americans from the social miseries and enslavements he observed in other countries.

A nineteenth-century traveling Tennessean could scarcely avoid questions about slavery, and McGavock soon understood how these questions directly challenged his confident claim that America represented the most advanced development of modern human societies. How could slavery exist in a modern democratic nation, and how could Americans reconcile slaveholding with their often-professed belief in human freedom? McGavock's conversations in Europe forced him to answer these questions and to recognize that international opinion had turned strongly against southern America's "peculiar institution"—and nobody asked more hostile questions than the English critics whom McGavock met almost everywhere: "I feel it my duty to say that all Europe is against us," McGavock wrote from Egypt to his Nashville readers, "and more particularly the English. The subject is introduced on all occasions, and we are asked, even here, in this benighted land if our slaves are not maltreated and abused. Ignorant of our peculiar institution, and I may say of our country, they hold up this subject for contemplation, and say to us that it is a system unworthy of the age."[44]

The challenge for traveling American enslavers was to refute this critique of slavery as a "system unworthy of the age," so McGavock set out to reject the critique with pro-slavery arguments he had surely heard in his Tennessee family. First, he insisted that modern industrial systems produced more human misery than the slave system in the southern United States; second, he argued that American enslavers were far more humane than enslavers in "less civilized" countries around the world; and finally, he used the era's bogus (white) "scientific" arguments about racial differences to justify the enslavement and forced labor of Black workers. These claims were all familiar themes in the southern white defense of slavery, yet the distinctive experience of foreign travel gave McGavock new opportunities and reasons to expand the comparative arguments for his own racist culture's most prominent social institution.

McGavock's cross-cultural comparisons with the English social system emerged, for example, in a letter about English poverty that criticized the hypocrisy of foreign abolitionists, praised the "humane" qualities of the American slave system, and described specific social contrasts that neither the English nor his stay-at-home American compatriots could fully understand:

> Englishmen may write, talk, and preach what they please about the horrors of our peculiar institution; they may send their abolition emissaries across the water, with pockets well filled, to preach a crusade against our liberty and our laws; but they had better consider the deplorable condition of their own [impoverished] population, . . . whose condition both in a physical and moral point of view is far inferior to that of the slave owned by the most cruel of masters. Our colored population are provided with every thing calculated to render them comfortable, and life happy. They are worked moderately, clothed comfortably, fed abundantly, and provided for when they get old and decrepit—while the poor of this great metropolis [London] are devoid of all these blessings.[45]

McGavock's defense of American slavery thus made a straightforward claim for the comparative *economic* well-being of an enslaved population that (in his extremely constricted view) enjoyed more material advantages than the poor people in England. This claim of course blatantly ignored all the personal and social costs of human slavery as well as the denial of wages to enslaved workers, but the comparisons with English poverty enabled McGavock to sustain his broader nationalist belief in the advantageous, modern qualities of the American slave system and to reaffirm his racist belief in the superiority of white American society. The argument for America's "enlightened" modernity carried an awkward contradiction for traveling enslavers, however, because slavery remained legal only in those societies that white Americans and Europeans alike described as "backward," "less civilized," and out of step with the progress of the modern world.

Responding to widespread critiques of this contradiction as he traveled across Egypt and Turkey, McGavock tried to draw sharp distinctions between the slavery in Muslim societies and the slavery in more "enlightened" places such as Tennessee. In the first place, McGavock noted, the Egyptians still cultivated their lands with the kinds of ploughs that had been invented "three thousand years ago" and with agricultural practices that ignored modern knowledge about the management of natural resources. It was therefore simply wrong to believe that "modern" agriculture in the American South could possibly resemble the "primitive" social and economic system in Egypt. "One of our southern planters might come here," McGavock assured his readers, "and with proper attention, and our mode of cultivation, produce the finest staple in the world."[46] The Egyptians themselves, however, failed to achieve this kind of modern production because their "primitive" forms of enslaved labor and social organization could never match the more "civilized" slave system in the American South.

McGavock emphasized the differences that separated these two slave systems after visiting a large slave market in Alexandria. In contrast to what his readers might commonly see in, say, Tennessee, the "less civilized" Egyptian slave traders were selling enslaved people from Nubia and Abyssinia for "a mere song" (about fifty dollars per enslaved person) and treating them with more brutality than southern enslavers would ever use in the United States. "The condition of the Egyptian slave is far worse than you have any conception [of]," he reported in a summary of the Egyptian system. "They are fed on onions, garlic, and stale bread—have hardly a rag to cover themselves, and are worked very hard. Our slaves are perfect lords compared to them; and . . . they are far better off than the slaves in Africa, or the laboring classes of any nation in Europe."[47] Here again McGavock claimed the authoritative, comparative perspective of a well-informed eyewitness whose travel experiences enabled him to defend the modernity of an American slave system that hostile critics linked with a premodern, "uncivilized" slave system in Muslim Egypt.

This modern/primitive dichotomy that McGavock constructed in Egypt nevertheless began to break down as he moved on to Constantinople because the Turks did not collect their enslaved people in the African societies that white Americans called "primitive." The slave markets of Constantinople typically sold people who came from the white populations of Circassia, the Caucasus Mountains, and Greece, thus disrupting what McGavock saw as the proper racial hierarchy in nineteenth-century slave societies. The "modern" slave system—as McGavock understood it in America—adhered to modern definitions of innate racial characteristics and avoided the kind of inappropriate social degradations that appeared in the uncivilized sale of *white* women at Turkish slave markets. The "merciless" Turkish slave trader, in other words, violated "civilized" racial boundaries in ways that made McGavock tremble "with no ordinary degree of emotion." The key flaw in Turkey's "more degrading" enslavement of white women thus stemmed from a lack of racist knowledge about human differences and the dehumanizing racial essentialism that explained and justified slavery in the United States:

> But, horrible as this [slave] traffic is, under any circumstances, to my ideas and feelings, it loses in some degree its horrors when confined to the African race. By physical formation and power of endurance, by their mental inferiority, and their natural disposition to be governed, instead of govern, we are forced to believe that they were intended by a higher power to be hewers of wood and drawers of water until the end of time. But the beautiful Circassian, the lovely georgian, and the unfortunate daughters of poor downtrodden Greece, were created for higher and nobler purposes.[48]

McGavock's distinctions between modern American slavery and a more primitive Turkish slavery therefore assumed the objective reality of racist social and ideological categories that made the enslavement of white people "unthinkable" for a southern American slaveholder. Since only a less enlightened, premodern culture could make such errors (in McGavock's view), America's racist enslavement of Africans showed a scientific "enlightenment" that the Turks had not yet achieved. Although abolitionists would never accept the racial "knowledge" that differentiated American enslavers from the slaveholding Turks, McGavock believed he had found another cross-cultural comparison to support his claims for the modernity of the American slave system.

The Turkish slave markets raised disturbing issues for McGavock because they violated the civilized codes for women's morality as well as the hierarchies of race. The Turks, after all, were selling white women to the highest bidder, so

McGavock's criticism of the slave markets in Constantinople went beyond his critiques in other reports about the conditions of enslaved people in Egypt or the misery of factory workers in England. His discussion of enslaved white women carried a racially charged critical perspective that obviously differed from Margaret Fuller's feminist critiques of gender hierarchies, but McGavock was acutely aware of both gendered and racial hierarchies whenever he wrote about women travelers or the daughters of European aristocrats. He also discussed the lower-class women who worked in European shops and fields, noting, for example, that Swiss women managed the barnyard tasks that men would usually handle in the United States. "Indeed," he noted in Switzerland, "the women of this country do most of the work."[49] Such descriptions of hardworking European women—like his accounts of almost all other people, religions, social hierarchies, governments, and travelers—thus became part of his broader narrative about the social and cultural differences that separated Europe from the United States. Although these differences could appear in every sphere of daily life, McGavock's travel stories continually affirmed that a distinctive American belief in the freedom of white men provided the most important cultural foundation for his national identity and for his own enduring selfhood.

McGavock's Search for Personal and Political Freedom

Like the journeys of many American men in Europe, McGavock's trip offered opportunities for new personal freedom from hometown constraints as well as new encounters with unfamiliar systems of social and political control. He therefore wrote about both the personal freedom of foreign travel and the official restrictions that made him feel less free in Europe. Adhering to the usual reticence of nineteenth-century travel writers, McGavock discussed his opportunities for freer relations with women only in his private journal, whereas the critique of constraints on his freedom of movement became a recurring theme in published articles that also portrayed white American men as the freest people in the modern world.

The failed relationship with Fanny Jane Crutcher added a painful emotional edge to McGavock's departure for Europe, so it is perhaps not surprising that his journey stimulated romantic fantasies and led to at least one brief affair in Italy. His responses to the sexual mores of European women combined a deep fascination with considerable fear, both of which may have gained psychological intensity from his disciplined, youthful training in Presbyterian religious duties. The prostitutes in London, for example, attracted his early voyeuristic attention as "lewd" women who brashly solicited any man who walked by. "They are much bolder here than [in] any city that I have ever seen," he wrote in his journal. "They think nothing of accosting a man on the street and taking him by force of arms to their dens of pollution."[50]

The sexual temptations became even more dangerous in Paris, where McGavock found that French women were happy to amuse any man who would join their parties. He was especially drawn to the open-air "mobile balls" that took place in well-lighted Parisian gardens and offered some of the most uninhibited pleasures he could imagine. At these popular balls, he noted in his journal, there were always plenty of refreshments, games, "and a woman to go home with you if you choose." McGavock clearly enjoyed some Parisian pleasures that helped him break free from the social and religious rules that had shaped his life in Nashville; and he was happy to find that almost everyone in Paris went out to drink, eat, and dance on *Sundays*—the day that was always strictly reserved for religion in his native city. Sundays in France, by contrast, were "a great fete day. The best balls, plays, operas, and amusements of every character is [*sic*] carried on here while the people of our country are worshipping God."[51] McGavock never explicitly rejected or criticized his hometown religious culture, but he wanted to explore the secular Parisian amusements that were so readily available for curious male tourists.

By late July 1851, he was writing in his journal about his frustrated desire to meet women in Paris and commenting on how his American friends had enjoyed themselves at one of the mobile balls—from where they "went with girls to a café and from there to *their apartments, I suppose*." McGavock's description of his friends' activities conveyed the Parisian fantasies of numerous American men, and then he fell into a journalistic silence that may suggest his own adventures with a French dancer. Curiously enough, there were no entries in McGavock's journal for the three days following his reference to the friends' evening "with girls" at cafés and apartments. After this uncharacteristic silence, however, McGavock changed his whole assessment of the mobile balls and began to emphasize their dangers. "These balls are very agreeable for a while, but one of my disposition soon tires. I think I will cease my visits and occupy my evenings more profitably," the young Presbyterian from Nashville wrote in his journal. "Sometimes a man may find a very beautiful and nice woman at such places, but the great majority of them are nothing more than common prostitutes who make their living by entrapping the unwary."[52] What exactly happened to McGavock during or after his visits to the mobile balls? He gave no details in his journal, yet his unusual three-day break from journal writing, his new criticism of the balls, his harsh judgment of himself, and his hostile characterization of the dancing women all suggest that McGavock may have followed his American friends into the real world of Parisian pleasures.

Paris Evenings: Dancers in the Open Air. Lithograph by an unknown artist, after Henri de Montaut, ca. 1850. American male travelers were often drawn to the open-air "mobile balls" that offered nighttime music, dancing, drinks, and food in illuminated Parisian parks and gardens. McGavock visited several of these dances in 1851 but later condemned their distracting immorality. Photo 12/Alamy Stock Photo.

The disillusioning encounter with Parisian amusements, however, did not lead McGavock straight back to religion or destroy his desire for female companionship. In fact, by the time he reached Florence he was happy to discover that the guests at his hotel included "a young lady from England whom I found not only pleasant but particularly agreeable." Although he did not name the woman or describe her personal qualities, McGavock spent several happy days and nights at the Hotel de York in October 1851, pursuing an affair that seemed to liberate him from both the melancholy memory of a failed relationship and the constraints of Presbyterian morality. He noted in one obscure journal entry, for example, that he had "made an arrangement to meet her after going to the opera, an engagement fulfilled to the letter. This night has been the happiest that I have passed in Europe." One of his older American companions apparently condemned the immorality of what McGavock called "an affair in Florence," but this brief Florentine adventure seemed to bring McGavock more happiness than almost any other experience in his long journey. The journal summary of his last day in Florence noted simply that he "saw my *Lord's lady* today and found her exceedingly agreeable. Retired at 2:00." This vague note was followed by a confession that he slept during "the greater part" of the next day's travel toward Rome because he was "feeling much fatigued from the labors of the night."[53]

The new personal freedoms of a European journey may have pushed McGavock away from some of his American social or religious constraints, but his trip never generated any comparable distance from his confident beliefs in the superiority of the American political system or the exceptional nature of American political freedom. On the contrary, his descriptions of European states and political systems invariably emphasized that they were less free and less democratic than the political culture in the United States. He regularly complained about petty harassments from customs officials who searched his baggage and violated his American conceptions of individual freedom. Austrian officials confiscated his pistol as he crossed into Italy, for example, and he was often forced to bribe policemen or local inspectors as he traveled between Italian cities. Although he soon learned that baggage searches could be expedited by bribing the inspectors, he repeatedly complained that the whole system of government regulations reduced his touristic pleasures and forced him into the "necessary evil" of bribery.[54]

The inconveniences of repressive government inspections became even more acute in Russia, which he described as the most repressive political system in all of Europe. Entering St. Petersburg in 1852, he was detained for more than two hours at a Russian police station and subjected to "more searching than we ever underwent before in other countries." His travel experience was transformed into a Russian political inquisition that bombarded him with questions and required his signature on piles of official documents. The strict government controls and interrogations intensified McGavock's patriotic appreciation for the freedoms he took for granted as a white man in the United States. "Oh, what a country to an American accustomed to live, move, and act freely," he wrote in one of his descriptions of the strict Russian travel regulations. "It is utter martyrdom. I would not be compelled to live under such a government for [all] the mineral wealth of Siberia."[55]

The repressive state apparatus in eastern Europe gave McGavock good examples to support his preference for life in America, but his critique of European political systems stemmed from more than a simple hostility toward the constant surveillance of travelers. He also condemned the political and social inequalities in Britain, where Queen Victoria's wealth and conspicuous consumption represented the stark economic divisions and indeed the whole hierarchical ethos of monarchical societies. Writing about his visits to royal castles and the royal stables near Buckingham Palace, McGavock reported that the royal family possessed over 300 horses and far more carriages than anyone could ever use. Although this seemed absurd to an American, it was simply one example of how kings and queens abused the people and resources of their own nations. "But in monarchies," he noted, "the whims and caprices of the sovereign must be indulged—it matters not how foolish and extravagant—and at the expense of *democracy*."[56]

McGavock's critique of European monarchies might have made him more sympathetic to republican states and political movements in France and Italy, but he soon decided that European republics were no more effective than the monarchies in promoting the kind of democratic political institutions that existed in the United States. The political future of the Second French Republic seemed particularly bleak because the republican leaders could not understand the orderly political processes that a stable republican state would require. Reporting on a visit to the French National Assembly, McGavock dismissed the new republican legislature as little more than a chaotic debating society in which the nation's elected representatives made "more noise than any set of men I ever saw assembled to legislate for a nation's weal." The noise produced neither clear ideas nor strong action, and McGavock quickly decided that French republicans were "unfit for self-government."[57]

The realities of French republicanism thus diverged from France's lofty political theories, but McGavock eventually found more eloquent republican speakers in the Greek parliament—where he discovered that memories of Byron circulated in a national political culture that reminded him of ancient times, "when Greece was in the zenith of her glory." There were also passionate republicans in Italy, but McGavock described the recent demise of the Roman republic with none of the political grief that Margaret Fuller had expressed in her sad letters about the French destruction of Italian republicanism. Although McGavock found that the republican spirit had not disappeared from Rome, he reported that the city had simply been "too weak to govern herself" or to resist a foreign army. His conversations with a passionate republican in Rome, however, suggested that resentment toward the occupying French army and a weak pope might soon lead to new political upheavals. "The people want a republic," McGavock reported in a summary of the political situation in Rome, "and they are only waiting for an opportunity to renew hostilities."[58]

McGavock thus assured his readers that America's political system was far more successful than any monarchy or republic in the Old World. Indeed, he reported that Switzerland was the only European country in which people were beginning to create the kind of free government that flourished in America. Yet even in Switzerland an American visitor would soon realize that the citizens did not yet appreciate the political value of modern democratic institutions. Like everyone else in Europe, the Swiss still needed to learn about democracy from America's superior political achievements and governing system. "The more I see of the governments of Europe," he noted in one of his references to the political lessons he was learning from his travels, "the more I admire and appreciate our own; and there is nothing in my opinion so well calculated to make a man patriotic and attached to the union of the States and the perpetuity of our institutions as a tour of observation among the nations of Europe."[59] McGavock's journey may have given him new personal and religious freedoms, but his experiences in both monarchical and republican countries simply confirmed his belief in American exceptionalism and constantly reinforced his nationalist political identity.

McGavock's Pride in America

Other Americans accompanied McGavock on every phase of his long journey, so he had much less interaction with local people than Fuller experienced during her prolonged immersion in Italy. His inability to speak foreign languages also limited his comprehension of other cultures, as he acknowledged after he failed to understand the "chattering of business men in French" and when he noted in his journal that many Americans traveled around Europe "without speaking any language but their own." This language barrier gave McGavock good reasons to spend much of his time with American friends at European restaurants, hotels, and tourist sites. He noted that some 8,000 Americans were reportedly in Paris while he was visiting the city, and there were other American tourists in all the towns of Switzerland. "Here as at almost every place I have visited in Europe," he wrote from Geneva, "I find a crowd of Americans."[60]

Like most tourists, McGavock enjoyed being with his fellow national travelers because he could talk frankly with them about the challenges of foreign journeys, reminisce about the pleasures of life in English-speaking America, and agree on the freedoms or accomplishments of the American people. McGavock thus found frequent opportunities to reaffirm his American cultural identity and personal selfhood, but he was especially happy when he discovered unexpected connections between Europe and the people of Tennessee. He was proud to report from Vienna, for example, that the imperial palace displayed coal and "other valuable minerals from our state" because a professor at the University of Nashville had sent a collection of rare stones for display in the royal household. This surprising glimpse of Tennessee's scientific knowledge became for McGavock a flattering confirmation of his own state's cultural status and another example of how Tennessee's people were as talented as anyone he met in Europe.[61]

McGavock's narrative about Europe and the Middle East therefore included a parallel narrative about Tennesseans who were living abroad. He reported proudly from St. Petersburg that America's ambassador to Russia was a distinguished former governor of Tennessee who was "agreeable in conversation and fully alive to the interests of his country."[62] The commendable qualities of such diplomats showed that Tennesseans could hold high-status positions in European society, and McGavock's later quests for diplomatic appointments would show his own desire to become the kind of honored, high-status American he had seen in St. Petersburg and other capital cities.

Although he was not representing the United States in any official role as he moved across national borders in Europe and the Middle East, McGavock liked to claim social prerogatives as a white American man who traveled with a confident belief in American superiority. He seemed to relish his run-ins with hotel clerks, guides, shopkeepers, and rural villagers because these incidents (and his newspaper reports about them) provided opportunities to assert his national identity. The Moscow railroad station became one of the many places in which McGavock demonstrated his confident American assertiveness. An American friend told him that he should claim a seat by boarding the train before the Russian military officers, who always had priority over other passengers. When a guard attempted to block the train's entrance door, McGavock's friend simply took the guard's collar "and held him out at arm's length, until we walked through. It was an amusing scene, and created great commotion among the passengers." The Russians wondered how someone could act so aggressively with a railroad guard until they learned "that he was an American, which explained the whole affair."[63]

McGavock liked to tell such stories about forceful American interventions, perhaps because he wanted to emphasize a unique American ability to take decisive action in both daily life and global affairs. The people who had to stand aside when Americans wanted to board a train were also (in McGavock's narrative) lagging behind the commercial and technological power of the United States. Americans had gone a long way toward establishing their dominance in modern economic life, and McGavock's praise for this commercial progress became another nationalist theme in his cross-cultural comparisons. American technology, as he described it, seemed superior to almost every kind of technology he saw in Europe. The German boats on the Rhine River were "good" but still inferior to American "boats on the Cumberland and Mississippi Rivers"; the Russian railroads were built with the help of American engineers, yet the most advanced Russian train tracks were no better than what "we would term second class in the United States"; and a visit to one of the most modern English warships in the Mediterranean simply showed that "they did not keep their decks in such order or manage their guns so dexterously as our American sailors."[64]

The transnational comparisons in McGavock's newspaper reports therefore stressed America's modernity and efficiency, but he wanted the United States to become more assertive in promoting national achievements and in preparing for future challenges to its global power. He was disappointed, for example, to find that Americans had not displayed their advanced technology at the Crystal Palace exhibition in London, and his travel around the Mediterranean showed him why Americans needed a more powerful navy to protect their commercial and political influence. Although Americans were mostly unaware of their nation's expanding global engagement, the traveling McGavock could now see that "we have a mighty destiny to work out" and "an increasing commerce to foster." A stronger navy would therefore help the United States advance toward a modern "destiny" that was bound to include global commerce, distant wars, and international conflicts that inward-looking Americans could not yet understand.[65]

Foreign travel, as McGavock described it, thus helped Americans recognize their growing national power as well as their distinctive national traditions and commercial ingenuity. Some foreigners criticized the cultural provincialism of American travelers who explored Europe in self-contained, English-speaking groups, but McGavock saw these tourist communities as another sign of American superiority. Drawn together by their national identity, language, and common interests in European antiquities, "no people in the world are so much attached to each other, or evince in foreign lands so much clannishness, as the citizens of the several States of the American Union."[66] Traveling Americans, in other words, discovered their shared and exceptional national identity by meeting their compatriots in other countries—and also by meeting Europeans who viewed the United States as the world's best destination for a better life.

McGavock often noted this European yearning for migration to the American "promised land" as confirming evidence of America's national superiority. Stories about European emigration reinforced the overarching nationalist argument in McGavock's long travel narrative: *Life was freer and better in America than anywhere else in the world.* This claim obviously ignored the oppressions of the profoundly unfree slave system and the ongoing displacement of Native Americans, but it was a central theme of the American nationalism that ran through McGavock's letters from his arrival in Liverpool to a final stopover in Germany.

His first report from England, for example, described emigrants on a passing westbound ship who began to shout happily from their crowded deck when they saw that McGavock's ship was flying "the stars and stripes of our free and happy country, to whose shores they were going like the Israelites of old to the promised land."[67] This "migration theme" therefore helped to launch the long account of McGavock's deepening national consciousness, which concluded with a final story about a young traveler he met on a train. The young man had emigrated from Germany to St. Louis, and he was traveling to see his family and friends in Baden, but he needed assistance to pay for some travel papers that would allow him to return home. McGavock decided to give him the money—for which he was repaid with the kind of national praise that was worth far more than a full bag of German coins. "There is no country like America," the young German told McGavock; "and if God spares me to return, I will never make another track on this continent!"[68] Hearing this European affirmation of the "American dream" shortly before he recrossed the Atlantic, McGavock shared the emigrant's encouraging cross-cultural perspectives with American readers who could only travel to Europe through books such as *A Tennessean Abroad*. The simple, unsolicited comment of a young European ("There is no country like America") summarized the main nationalist theme of McGavock's whole travel narrative and the essential nationalist truth for both the narrator and his American readers.

The story of an anonymous German traveler became the prelude for McGavock's concluding reflections on the meaning of American history. He knew he was returning to a country in which many Americans were promoting national disunion or what he called "sectional prejudices," but he was coming home with an experience-based confidence that a European journey could show Americans why they should remain committed to a strong national union. "With such a country, and so much to make one happy," he asked in the conclusion of his book, "how can any sensible American ever wish to abandon it?" This question—and the answer it implied—gave a coherent nationalist theme to McGavock's often diffuse travel writing and showed how his journey strengthened his patriotic belief in the exceptional qualities of his home country. McGavock's trip gave him all kinds of evidence to reinforce his view of America as the greatest country in the world, but he worried that non-traveling Americans could not see the truths that his experiences had so clearly confirmed:

> Nature has given us a country of virgin soil, capable of producing every variety of products, and our mountains are filled with untold wealth. The rivers of the United States are more numerous and better fitted for navigation than those of any other country in the world. Our government is the perfection of human wisdom, and our people are not only familiar with its principles, but able and always willing to defend them. Some of our colleges will compare favorably with the oldest and most renowned in Europe, and in point of general intelligence, no country can claim superiority over us. In the sciences and fine arts we, of course, cannot set up our claim for eminence, but in a short period we may even boast of these things.[69]

McGavock thus returned to Tennessee with deep confidence in his national identity and his allegiance to national unity—which he would soon abandon to join the Confederate army.

He could not imagine the coming upheaval in his national loyalties while he was completing his travel-shaped portrait of the United States as the modern "promised land." His journey had taken him deep into his own American selfhood and given him a vision of America's future global influence, so perhaps he would have responded differently to southern secession if he had fulfilled his post-journey ambition to become an American diplomat in a European city. But there would be no more foreign travel. Settling back into his home-state culture of white enslavers, McGavock turned away from his earlier national identity and eventually joined a traitorous war against the national union to which he had pledged a deep allegiance throughout his European trip. He had seen a wider world and written about his own search for freedom, but he could never stop defending the slave system; and his long, national-minded journey reached its final anti-union destination on a Civil War battlefield.

EPILOGUE TO PART II

European American Travelers and the Exploration of Antebellum National Identities

DESPITE OBVIOUS differences in their sectional origins, early education, gender identities, and political ideas, the life histories and international travel of Margaret Fuller and Randal McGavock converged in numerous shared experiences. They both grew up in politically active Protestant families, developed their intellectual interests in Cambridge and Boston, expressed a strong appreciation for European cultural traditions, traveled to Europe after disappointing romantic relationships, published letters about European societies in American newspapers, and described the meaning of American national traditions through comparative, cross-cultural accounts of European institutions and leaders. They also both died young as they pursued their evolving political goals in new public actions they had never imagined before their European travels.

Their social communities pushed them toward opposing political beliefs, however, and their travel experiences only deepened their political differences. Their political perspectives diverged on most key issues (including slavery), but Fuller and McGavock both affirmed their strong affiliations with American political culture and claimed authoritative personal identities as knowledgeable American observers of European history and culture. They both explored the new social and psychological opportunities that could emerge from long transnational trips, thereby freeing themselves from various American constraints (for example, the social conventions of northeastern American womanhood or the religious conventions of southern American Protestantism) and interpreting foreign societies to American readers who would probably never visit a foreign country. They often addressed different public issues, but their writings showed how American travelers became more aware of their own national identity and selfhood as they analyzed the people, cultures, and conflicts in other societies.

Although they could not openly describe new personal experiences in their published travel narratives, Fuller and McGavock both wrote clear public statements about America's exceptional political and international significance in the modern world. Both writers strongly identified with America's republican and democratic political traditions, yet they disagreed almost completely about how these traditions should be interpreted and used in nineteenth-century political conflicts. Fuller expressed growing concern that America was betraying its own best ideals and traditions in the expansionist Mexican War, in the immoral slave system, and in a rampant, apolitical materialism. McGavock, by contrast, repeatedly assured his readers and himself that American social traditions and political institutions were superior to the culture of every other nation he visited, thus bypassing critical questions about the slave system's racist denial of human freedom and political betrayal of national ideals.

Fuller's European writings urged Americans to recover their best liberty-loving aspirations, which she thought they could revive by abolishing slavery or addressing new economic inequalities or improving the position of women or supporting democratic political revolutions in Europe. She therefore wanted Americans in the late 1840s to defend and extend the revolutionary political ideas that earlier Americans had forcefully asserted in the 1770s and 1780s. She also assumed that American support for new European political and social movements might well be forthcoming if Americans knew more about what was actually happening in Rome and other European cities, so she wrote impassioned political commentaries for the *New York Tribune* and sailed for the United States in 1850 with a still-incomplete manuscript about the recent Roman Revolution. Modern Europe could be compared and connected to modern America because people on both sides of the Atlantic yearned for more political democracy, more freedom, and more social equality. The greatest challenges emerged, however, when people in any country tried to put these political ideals into practice—by abolishing slavery, for example, or by creating stable republican governments.

McGavock also wrote about the future while he was describing the European past and present, but he assumed (more optimistically than Fuller) that the United States had already made great progress in creating the society and political culture that other nations should emulate. He believed that Americans were developing the advanced economic and technological skills that were essential for modern social life. At the same time, he was certain that the American system of constitutional government had successfully established the political order and freedom that people in most other nations could only imagine. Confirmation for America's extraordinary achievements appeared, among other places, in the constant flow of emigrants from Europe to the United States. McGavock also used racist arguments to claim that the American slave system reflected the advanced nature of American society because enslaved people lived among enlightened American enslavers rather than under the brutal, unenlightened slaveholders in Egypt and Turkey. McGavock's comparisons of Old and New World societies (as in the discussion of different slave systems) almost never criticized the United States and almost always placed white Americans in a more advanced historical position. Although he recognized Europe's much longer and more influential cultural history, McGavock confidently asserted that Americans had already developed more of the social and political attributes that would be essential for the future evolution of modern societies: economic development, agriculture, technology, and political democracy.

Fuller and McGavock therefore represent two of the most common personal and public responses to prolonged travel experiences. Like many other modern American travelers and expatriates, Fuller drew on her European travels and relationships to call for a critical reassessment of America's role in the world; she wanted to bring the *critical* outsider's perspective back to America. McGavock also resembled many other modern American travelers and expatriates, but he drew on his travel experiences to assure his readers and himself that American society and political culture represented the most advanced achievements of a modern nation-state; he wanted to bring the *admiring* outsider's perspective back to America. These important differences thus provide contrasting historical examples of how travel influences and reshapes the meaning of national identities. Fuller worried more than McGavock about growing threats to America's republican and democratic political culture and about American indifference to republican political movements in Europe. McGavock, for his part, worried about the growing threats to the (exceptional?) institution of American slavery and about the growing threat of national disunion—which he eventually embraced by joining the Confederate army. The European journeys of both writers, however, became experiential provocations for redefining and defending America's distinctive national identity as well as liberating explorations of the personal desire for a new and freer selfhood.

PART III

Affirming the Freedom of Nineteenth-Century African American Selfhood outside the United States

Nancy Prince and David Dorr

INTRODUCTION TO PART III

Antebellum African American Journeys from the North and South

Travel became an appealing, transformative experience for nineteenth-century writers as diverse as Victor Jacquemont and Flora Tristan or Margaret Fuller and Randal McGavock because cross-cultural encounters and explorations opened new opportunities for personal freedom and empowerment. Although French and American travelers came from different social backgrounds and carried different "cultural baggage" on their trips, most men and women set off from Europe and the United States during this era with a post-Enlightenment confidence in an autonomous self. Travel for such persons offered new social and cultural experiences that expanded the expression of individual freedom and the meanings of independent selfhood, even for the women who ran into gendered social obstacles that men did not face.

Foreign travel could thus deepen or reshape the self-perceptions of almost everyone who made long transoceanic journeys, including African Americans whose travel experiences both resembled and differed from the experiences of Europeans and European Americans. The era's pervasive, transnational racism posed special challenges for nineteenth-century Black travelers, but the published accounts of their trips show that they also used the mobility and cultural self-estrangement of long journeys to redefine their distinctive conceptions of selfhood, freedom, and national cultures. Most African Americans could not travel within or beyond the United States before the Civil War, of course, because they were enslaved in the South or struggling with social and economic obstacles in the North. Indeed, the most likely voyage for enslaved people was a trip "down the river" to another enslaver or a distant plantation.

There were nevertheless determined, independent African American travelers who made long trips abroad and described their journeys in books that were published after they returned to the United States. Historians have become increasingly interested in the transnational experiences of Black travelers such as Phillis Wheatley, William Wells Brown, Martin Delany, and Frederick Douglass, who traveled in Europe before 1860.[1] The following chapters, however, discuss two lesser-known African American writers who challenged the long-delineated gender and racial boundaries of international travel: Nancy Prince and David F. Dorr. Prince and Dorr both wrote about their travel to distant cultures that few nineteenth-century African Americans were able to visit; and they affirmed their conceptions of personal freedom and independent selfhood in narratives that also described the freedom and identities of other people they met. They both published their distinctive travel books in the same decade (1850s), they both strongly supported the abolitionist movement, and they both died in complete obscurity. Much like Fuller and McGavock, they grew up in different northern and southern regions of the United States and faced different challenges as they struggled to define an autonomous "American self" during their long trips to foreign countries. The lives and writings of Prince and Dorr therefore offer intriguing themes for comparative analysis of how the era's racial and gender hierarchies influenced identities and conceptions of selfhood. Like the other nineteenth-century (white) French and American travelers who made identity-shaping journeys during the decades before 1865, Prince and Dorr sought to redefine their public identities and to create a freer personal selfhood, but they faced the additional social challenges of racism and the American slave system.

Prince was a free woman from Massachusetts who described her experiences in Russia and Jamaica as a story of personal tribulations, social service, and religious mission. Her travel book, *A Narrative of the Life and Travels of Mrs. Nancy Prince: Written by Herself*, was published in Boston in 1851, revised for another edition two years later, and published again in 1856. Although Prince wrote about numerous adventures and cross-cultural relationships, her overarching theme portrayed a virtuous (religious) journey toward autonomous Black womanhood. Dorr, by contrast, was an enslaved man from Louisiana who narrated his trip across western Europe, Egypt, and Palestine as a story of personal pleasures, cultural enrichment, and rising social status. His travel book, *A Colored Man round the World*, was published in Cleveland in 1858, shortly after he had escaped from slavery. Although Dorr provided detailed accounts of famous sites and interesting people, his broader theme portrayed an unconventional journey toward a "colored man's" freedom and self-assertion. Prince and Dorr wrote from different gender positions, but they both exemplified what the historian Joseph Miller has called a "consistent theme" in the biographical works of "Black Atlantic" historiography: the "determination" of Black and enslaved people "to make the best of a bad situation."[2]

Prince and Dorr never wrote other books before or after the publication of their travel narratives. They both therefore remained almost invisible in American cultural history until late twentieth-century literary historians began to examine the Black Atlantic as a thematic framework for analyzing modern Black history and transnational cultures. Paul Gilroy's influential work on early nineteenth-century Atlantic migrations, for example, argued that Black people in both the Americas and Europe repeatedly expressed a "double consciousness" in which their African heritage and identities were linked to a complex, overlapping history of European cultures and political ideas. These cross-cultural exchanges brought African cultural traditions into contact with Christian religious traditions as well as Enlightenment or revolutionary conceptions of reason and human rights. Gilroy did not refer specifically to either Nancy Prince or David Dorr, but their biographies and books show some of the ways in which a cross-cultural "interweaving" could influence the public aspirations and cultural "hybridity" of African American writers who traveled across the Atlantic world.[3]

It might be a misleading historical generalization to categorize Nancy Prince and David Dorr as simply antebellum American representatives of a wider Black Atlantic culture, but their autobiographical accounts of the search for a freer selfhood offer fascinating examples of how transoceanic travel could contribute to the reconstruction of personal and cultural identities. Their descriptions of exceptional travel experiences provide an intriguing counterpoint to the writings of white northern women such as Margaret Fuller and of white southern men such as Randal McGavock whose European journeys also pushed them to redefine their American identities in the era of deepening national crises before and after 1850. Prince and Dorr wrote books that went beyond the work of most other contemporary authors in showing how travel experiences were entangled with the social and cultural history of race as well as the complexities of gender, nationality, and intellectual traditions. The racial boundaries in antebellum American society shaped the lives and writings of every Black and white American traveler, yet the transnational journeys of Prince and Dorr showed a particular determination to expand their personal ambitions and self-perceptions beyond the racist constrictions of the national culture in which they were born.

The long trips of these pre–Civil War African American travelers therefore offered new opportunities to claim a new personal freedom and gendered selfhood, which they both affirmed by describing their status and respectability within white-dominated social hierarchies. Their personal quests for an independent, respectable womanhood and manhood also led each of these traveling writers to develop a more general analysis of public issues such as slavery, politics, and the different attributes of European or African cultures. Prince and Dorr wrote about these subjects with African American or Black Atlantic perspectives that shaped their distinctive interpretations of personal experiences and foreign social systems.

Going well beyond the traditions of genteel travel stories, they wrote about individual actions and freedoms that neither racism nor slavery nor political exclusions could ultimately control or destroy. The experiences of foreign travel, in short, expanded their understanding of womanhood and manhood, slavery and politics, modern religion and modern knowledge. But they were both concerned above all with the meaning of modern human freedom—a freedom they defined in their own voices by leaving their homes in America and then returning with the critical insights of ambitious, cross-cultural travelers.

CHAPTER FIVE

Nancy Prince's Journey toward Selfhood and Freedom in Russia and Jamaica

NANCY PRINCE was born Nancy Gardner in Newburyport, Massachusetts, in 1799. According to the family history she provided in *A Narrative of the Life and Travels of Mrs. Nancy Prince*, her father was a man of "African descent" named Thomas Gardner. Her mother (unnamed) embodied a more diverse family background that included an enslaved African maternal grandfather named Tobias Wornton and a maternal grandmother (unnamed) who "was an Indian of this country." Nancy's enslaved grandfather was originally brought from Africa and sold to a military officer, but Wornton himself also served in America's early revolutionary army at the Battle of Bunker Hill. All of Nancy Gardner's extended family apparently became free persons before she was born because slavery was legally abolished in Massachusetts by the early 1780s. She thus grew up in a community of free African Americans that comprised about 6,500 people in her home state at the beginning of the nineteenth century.[1]

Her family was thus in a better legal and social position than was the enslaved population of other American states, but economic problems and racial discrimination created constant obstacles throughout Nancy Gardner's early life. Indeed, her youth could scarcely have been more different from the childhood of Margaret Fuller, who also grew up in early nineteenth-century Massachusetts and whose father-directed education carried her into a world of European literature and classical languages. Nancy's own father died when she was only three months old, leaving her mother alone to care for two small children (Nancy had a sister named Silvia, who was five years older). This was the second time that the young widow had lost a husband, which may explain why she quickly married again and gave birth to six more children. The new husband worked as a sailor on merchant ships and provided essential financial support for the growing family—though he was often away on risky sea voyages. Indeed, he died shortly after the British captured his ship during the War of 1812. The premature death of her third husband was a devastating loss for Nancy's mother, who struggled with so much emotional stress that "she never again was the mother that she had been before." Although Nancy later described her stepfather as an abusive man who was "not kind to me or my sister," she also emphasized that his death and the loss of her grandfather Wornton at almost the same time brought a deep sadness to the whole family and then destroyed their "humble home" because her impoverished mother had to send her older children to other caretakers.[2]

Nancy never explained how she learned to read and write. She may have gained these skills with the help of family members or through her connections with a church, but her formal education must have been quite limited. Given the family's dire financial situation, young Nancy began to work as a domestic servant for a white family in Salem, where there was much emphasis on prayers and religious rituals but a complete indifference to the arduous conditions of her job. "Hard labor and unkindness was too much for me," she noted in her later summary of this phase in her life; "in three months, my health and strength were gone. I often looked at my employers, and thought to myself, is this your religion?" Moving on to other domestic jobs, she worried constantly about her older sister, Silvia, whose flight from unhappy domestic labor led her into even more miserable work at a Boston brothel. Silvia's situation became so distressing that Nancy went directly to the brothel, confronted the managing "mother of harlots," and fled with her sister back to their family in Gloucester. Nancy described this rescue as "a great victory," even though it did nothing to improve the family's finances or their mother's mental health. A younger brother soon found work as a merchant sailor and never lived at home again; other siblings lived unhappily in the homes of strangers; and the emotionally unstable mother remained a vulnerable outsider in her own community. Nancy herself felt "oppressed" by her family's misery, until she converted in 1819 to an evangelical Christian faith at the Boston church of a Black pastor named Thomas Paul.[3]

This religious conversion became a key event in Nancy Gardner's life. "Never shall I forget the place or time when God spake to my troubled conscience," she explained later in her travel book. "Justified by faith I found peace with God, [and] the forgiveness of sin through Jesus Christ my Lord." This newfound faith could not overcome family problems, however, especially after her sister Silvia returned to Boston and, as Nancy recalled, "my mother, in one of her spells of insanity," traveled to find her. Meanwhile, another brother left home for a sailor's job on the high seas, presumably looking for his own escape from the family's financial and emotional desperation. The endless family problems may have contributed to the emotional intensity of Nancy's religious conversion, but the ongoing "trials" with her sister and troubled mother finally forced her to reshape her own life through even more decisive actions. Noting that by 1822 she felt a "determination to do something for myself," she wrote in her *Life and Travels* that she set out to learn the "trade" of a seamstress and then after "years of anxiety and toil, I made up my mind to leave my country." Like the male sailors she had known from early childhood, Nancy Gardner found a way to escape from the landlocked world in which she had always lived. She accepted a proposal to marry an older African American named Nero Prince, who had recently come back to Massachusetts after a long stay in Russia. "Mr. Prince" (as his wife always referred to him in her book) had worked on a ship that sailed to Russia in 1812, but he soon left the ship to work for a noble family in St. Petersburg.[4]

Although little is known about Nero Prince's life or travels, there is clear evidence to confirm that he was active in Boston's African lodge of Freemasons before 1810 and that he later served as one of the Black Guards at the Russian tsar's imperial court. Nancy also reported that he had known her family before he went to Russia, which suggests how she might have met him when he returned to Massachusetts in 1823. Despite the lack of details about her decision to marry (a "determination to do something for myself"?), the author of *The Life and Travels of Mrs. Nancy Prince* reported that she wed "Mr. Prince" on 15 February 1824 and that two months later the newly married couple "embarked on board the Romulus . . . bound for Russia."[5] Nancy Gardner thus became Nancy Prince, thereby taking the married name she would use for the rest of her life and eventually place on the title page of her book about journeys and experiences in foreign countries. In contrast to the many travelers who set off on transnational trips with the sadness of a broken love relationship, Prince began her journey with a new partner who offered a much-desired escape from economic problems and family despair.

The Princes stopped briefly in Denmark during their trip to St. Petersburg, where they arrived in late June 1824 and settled into a new life at the Russian imperial court. Moving away from the anxieties she must have felt as she left her mother, sister Silvia, and other members of her family, the future author of *The Life and Travels of Mrs. Nancy Prince* found a freedom and social identity that had always eluded her in Massachusetts. Her descriptions of the Russian court conveyed a new sense of independent selfhood that began to emerge when she saw that she could be a respected woman, wife, and religious benefactor among the people she met in St. Petersburg. She remained in Russia for more than nine years before she decided to leave her husband and return via Denmark to the people she had known during her earlier life in Boston. "Mr. Prince" planned to follow her back to the United States within two years, but he soon died in Russia. Nancy Prince thus faced many of the challenges that had destabilized her mother's life after the deaths of her different husbands. Like her mother, Prince became a widow in search of the financial means to launch a new life, yet (unlike her mother) Prince would never remarry or have children. She moved instead into other activities that included abolitionist politics, Christian missionary work, and travel writing. The return to Boston, in short, did not bring her back to her former life, partly because her mother, older sister, and much-respected pastor had all died while she was living abroad and partly because she could not find a stable social position in a hometown that had inevitably changed since her departure in 1824.[6]

Prince's attempt to construct a post-Russian life ran into new obstacles when she was unable to find steady work, a congenial church community, or a comfortable niche in the antislavery organizations that she now supported. She collaborated with William Lloyd Garrison as she joined the expanding abolitionist movement and became a member of the Boston Female Anti-Slavery Society. Although she strongly endorsed the society's campaign for "the amelioration of the nominally free colored people of these States, and the emancipation of the slaves in other States," she was soon immersed in the conflicts that emerged when opposing activist groups disagreed about how women should participate in abolitionist activities. A devout religious faction did not want women to speak at public events, whereas others (including Garrison) argued that women should be active, public spokespeople for the antislavery movement. Prince sided with the Garrisonians and supported a public role for women, but the conflict challenged her religious identity because many of the most devout Christians and ministers opposed her views.[7] Meanwhile, Prince struggled with other setbacks as she tried to establish an orphanage for poor homeless children. Lacking the funds to create and maintain this kind of sheltering institution, Prince began to believe that her aspirations for both child welfare and antislavery activism would be continually stymied or misunderstood. It was also difficult to make money as a seamstress in a competitive urban market, so (as in 1824) a journey to foreign places could offer an attractive escape from the unsolvable hometown problems that Prince faced during the late 1830s.

The obstacles of daily life in Massachusetts may well have contributed to Prince's growing interest in the conditions of recently emancipated slaves in faraway Jamaica. This interest brought Prince to a church meeting at which a white Congregational minister named David Ingraham spoke about his experiences at a mission station near Kingston, where more religious-minded workers were urgently needed. Ingraham assured Prince that she could make a valuable contribution to the mission's work because "the moral-condition of the people was very bad, and [they] needed labor aside from any thing else." Despite her concern that she "was very limited in education," Prince left for Jamaica in November 1840 (presumably drawing financial support from Ingraham's church funds) to pursue mission work and to see how former slaves were making the transition to freedom.[8] Arriving on the island with optimistic religious and political expectations, she ran into unexpected conflicts that quickly undermined her work with both Black and white Christians. As Prince explained the problem, Jamaican Christians spread misinformed religious ideas and focused mostly on collecting money from impoverished, formerly enslaved workers. She also faced other frustrations when she tried (and failed) to establish a school for destitute girls and when she was almost enslaved during return-trip stopovers in the port cities of Florida and Louisiana (August–September 1842). The story of Jamaican disappointments and dangers thus became a history of endless struggles in which righteous suffering opened a painful pathway to personal redemption and eternal salvation.

Prince's account of Russia had portrayed a liberating journey to a freer, happier life, but her stories of Jamaican mission work and dangerous Caribbean travels described a disillusioning journey in which the only saving grace came from her unshakable trust in God. "The sufferings of this present life are not worthy to be compared with the glory that shall be revealed hereafter," she wrote after summarizing the constant woes of her later travels. "Who shall separate us from the love of Christ? Shall tribulation, or distress, or persecution, or famine, or nakedness, or peril, or sword? Nay, in all these things we are more than conquerors, through him that loved us, and gave himself for us."[9] Where the long voyage to Russia gave Prince a new sense of social empowerment and personal freedom, the trip to Jamaica gave her a new confidence in spiritual empowerment and religious salvation. Both journeys helped to shape a deepening belief in her exceptional religious selfhood, even though the later sections of her travel book described dangerous threats to her emotional and physical well-being as well as her mostly unsuccessful attempts to help needy people.

Prince's prose always moved rapidly from story to story, thereby creating a textual journey that often lacked the narrative coherence of conventional autobiographies as it carried readers through dreamlike juxtapositions of different scenes and people. Prince liked to place her reader directly into unexpected situations at a Russian court dinner or a Jamaican church meeting or a southern dockside conversation—usually emphasizing her sensory experiences rather than historical details or a broader social context. These dreamlike juxtapositions of barely connected scenes or events suggested the author's personal autonomy or willful determination because each story referred to Prince's own observations and independent actions. She constantly dropped herself into the center of stories that ostensibly described Russia or Jamaica or the American South; and then she drew on what she had experienced or felt to convey an expanding conception of personal freedom as well as an astute recognition of the boundaries that always threatened a Black woman's social independence. Here, for example, is Prince's account of what happened on her ship when it docked in New Orleans as she was returning from Jamaica:

> I was seated on a box, but poorly dressed; the mate had taken my clothes to a washer-woman; . . . he was afraid to send the cook or steward on shore, as they were colored people. I kept still, but the other woman [on the ship] seemed to be in perfect despair, running up and down the deck, wringing her hands and crying, at the thought of all her clothes being destroyed; . . . and she seemed as if she were deranged; she took their attention, as she was white. Soon the washer-woman came with my clothes; they spoke to her as if she had been a dog. I looked at them with as much astonishment as I had never heard of such a thing. I asked them if they believed there was a God. "Of course we do," they replied. "Then why not obey him?" "We do." "You do not."[10]

The account of this disturbing scene clearly diverged from the typical stories of genteel travel experiences in distant lands and cultured cities. The shipboard drama would have been an unhappy example of personal despair and moral hypocrisy in any society, but it took place within the United States, referred directly to controlling racial and gender hierarchies, and quoted verbal exchanges that were painfully *ungenteel*. Like other travel writers, Prince used her sometimes strange narrative juxtapositions to describe her disorienting entry into alien cultures, yet these encounters with other people also carried her into new knowledge of previously unknown strengths within her own spiritual selfhood.

Returning to Boston after her dangerous travel in the Caribbean, Prince began to compile the book she would publish and begin selling in the early 1850s "to obtain the means to supply my necessities." She was by then well-removed from the chronological era she described in her writings, so the narrative became a tale of distant times as well as faraway places. This chronological distance from the earlier narrated experiences suggests how *The Life and Travels of Mrs. Nancy Prince* could become a retrospective literary construction of an independent selfhood and (as she noted in the preface) a self-reliant effort to "support myself by my own endeavors." Prince told a life story that began and ended in poverty, but she also emphasized the richness of her multicultural experiences and the distinctive wisdom that emerged directly from her personal suffering and dislocation. Apart from her reported appearance at a women's rights convention in Philadelphia in 1854, nothing is known about Prince's later years or even the year and place of her death.[11] In contrast to Margaret Fuller's widely reported death in 1850, historians have never found references to Prince's death in newspapers or in the later correspondence of people who may have known her. She was a transoceanic traveler whose narrative of exceptional journeys became the only enduring story and affirmation of her life.

Prince's Affirmation of Womanhood and Respect

Prince's descriptions of diverse places, people, and social experiences all contributed to a broader portrait of the author's struggle to become a respectable and respected woman. Indeed, a modern historian might well cite a song that the African American singer Aretha Franklin made famous in the late 1960s to suggest the intensity of Nancy Prince's lifelong quest for "R-E-S-P-E-C-T," but it was never easy for Prince to find or sustain the respect that she sought.[12] The account of her life before her marriage to Nero Prince (a conventional early step toward "respectability") told a story of constant moves from house to house, tedious domestic labor for white families, a sister's social descent into prostitution, the emotional despair of her widowed mother, and the "unkind" behavior of an abusive stepfather.

Although these problems involved numerous people and different social situations, they converged in a gendered and racist perception of young Nancy as a person who would never take important, respectable action in the wider public world of politics, culture, or religion. With the exceptions of her mother and the pastor who facilitated her religious conversion, most of the people Prince encountered in her youth apparently treated her like the abusive white family that condemned her when "the washing was not done well" or like the stagecoach driver whom she met after helping her sister escape from a Boston brothel. The driver came from Prince's hometown, but he refused to transport the two impoverished sisters out of Boston "unless we would ride upon the top" of the coach. "It was very cold," Prince wrote later, and she was "greatly embarrassed" because she lacked the money for a proper seat inside the coach. Fortunately, a sympathetic "colored man" helped the sisters find another way to travel home on a horse-drawn sleigh, thus offering a kindness that Prince always remembered as a rare sign of respect from the older people whom she met in Massachusetts before 1824.[13]

The trip to St. Petersburg therefore opened a new phase in Prince's life. She had become a married woman who immediately and unexpectedly entered the glittering social sphere that surrounded the Russian imperial court. Few experiences could have transformed the life of an African American expatriate as quickly or dramatically as Prince's journey into a European monarchical society. Nero Prince worked in an all-Black male corps of royal servants who waited on the imperial family, opened the palace doors as the tsar passed between rooms, and assisted the guests at special state events. Nancy Prince thus settled into a "splendid" edifice near the main buildings of the palace, where she would soon find herself standing before the famous Tsar Alexander I and Tsarina Elizabeth in a magnificent throne room. The young woman who could not even persuade a hometown coach driver to give her a seat in the Gloucester stagecoach was welcomed to Russia by one of the most powerful rulers in Europe. According to Prince's retrospective description of this memorable event, the tsar acknowledged her arrival at the court with the ritual expressions of extraordinary respect:

> [On entering the palace] the usual salutation by the guards was performed. As we passed through the beautiful hall, a door was opened by two colored men in official dress. The Emperor Alexander, stood on his throne, in his royal apparel. The throne is circular, elevated two steps from the floor, and covered with scarlet velvet, tasseled with gold; as I entered, the Emperor stepped forward with great politeness . . . and welcomed me, and asked several questions; he then accompanied us to the Empress Elizabeth; she stood in her dignity, and received me in the same manner the Emperor had. They presented me with a watch, etc. It was customary in those days, when any one married, belonging to the court, to present them with gifts . . . ; there was no prejudice against color; there were . . . people of all nations, each in their place.[14]

Prince downplayed the hierarchies and prejudices within Russia's imperial court in this flattering memory of the tsar's "great politeness," but she communicated the essential meaning of her experience: personal connections with people at the Russian court made her a *respected* member of an elite social world. Nobody in this elite society knew where she had come from or cared about her family's precarious existence in America. She was simply a new spouse in the community of royal servants who merited a generous, respectable welcome in the dazzling throne room of the Russian monarchy.

This entry into Russia's imperial culture, as Prince described it, was only the beginning of nine remarkable years in St. Petersburg. In fact, she later developed closer connections to the royal family after Alexander I and Tsarina Elizabeth were succeeded in 1825 by Tsar Nicholas I and Tsarina Alexandra. The new tsar ascended to the throne because his older brother Constantine secretly gave up his inherited claim to the position, but this unexpected transition provoked an unsuccessful "Decembrist revolt" among liberal army officers and nobles who wanted Constantine to lead the Russian government. Prince had only recently settled into the royal court, yet she understood the struggle for power and responded to the conflict with unbending support for Nicholas and his wife, Alexandra (who was the daughter of King Frederick William III of Prussia). Although Nicholas had become an extremely conservative tsar by the time Prince published her travel book in the early 1850s, she drew on her firsthand observations to assure her readers that the "present Emperor and Empress are courteous and affable." Elegant court dinners and theatrical entertainments gave the royal couple frequent opportunities to welcome people to their palace and to display their well-polished courtesies. "When the company are seated," Prince explained in an account of the royal dinners she observed, "the Emperor and Empress walk around the tables and shake hands with each individual." Equally important, Tsarina Alexandra's generous character reappeared in her dignified activities on the days *after* the lavish royal dinners. She had come to Russia from another culture (like Prince), but the tsarina had adapted skillfully to her new environment (also like Prince). "She carries power and dignity in her countenance," Prince continued with obvious admiration, "and [she] is well adapted to her station. And after her late amusements at night, she would be out at an early hour in the morning, visiting the abodes of the distressed, dressed in common apparel . . . [and] either walking, or riding in a common sleigh."[15]

Prince's descriptions of the royal family thus emphasized her links with the most respectable persons in Russia, but the Russian tsarina represented personal and ethical values that went beyond her high status in the court-centered social elite. As Prince later explained in her travel book, she shared Alexandra's concern for the "distressed" people of St. Petersburg whom she also began to assist after quickly learning the languages that were needed for conversations in the Russian capital. Speaking with what Prince called a "mixture" of Slavic and Polish languages, she participated in various "domestic affairs" that included the creation of a boardinghouse for homeless children. This assistance for vulnerable children thus offered further confirmation of her public identity as a respectable woman whose public service demonstrated personal connections and similarities with the empress of Russia. The contacts with Tsarina Alexandra also led Prince into the business of making clothes for children, so if Prince's American readers wondered in the 1850s about her talents as a seamstress, they could find assurance in *Life and Travels* that she had once produced fine clothes for the most prominent family in Russia. "The present Empress is a very active one," Prince noted in another description of her contacts with the imperial family, "and [she] inquired of me respecting my business." This query affirmed Prince's status at the Russian court and soon brought economic benefits because the tsarina offered "much encouragement by purchasing of me garments for herself and children, handsomely wrought in French and English styles, and many of the nobility also followed her example." At the same time, Prince began visiting "the matron of the Empress' children" and developing religious contacts with a visiting Protestant clergyman who helped her

Alexandra Feodorovna with Her Two Eldest Children. Oil on canvas by George Dawe, ca. 1821. Alexandra Feodorovna (1798–1860) was born into the Prussian royal family, but she became the empress of Russia after her husband, Nicholas, suppressed the "Decembrist revolt" and consolidated his power as the new tsar in 1825. Nancy Prince admired the new tsarina (they were roughly the same age) as an example of how charitable work enhanced a woman's social status, and she would remain a respected model for Prince's later charitable efforts to educate poor girls in Boston and Jamaica. GL Archive/Alamy Stock Photo.

distribute Bibles at the palace—until the Orthodox Church leaders stopped the spread of such dangerous materials within the court's hallowed interior spaces.[16]

Recurring efforts to support vulnerable children and to serve Protestant Christianity became important aspects of Prince's long international journey toward the mature identity of respected womanhood. Drawing on her Russian experience of "assisting in forming an Asylum" for needy children in St. Petersburg, she later tried to establish a home in Boston for "poor orphans" who "on account of color [were] shut out from all the asylums for poor children." She managed to bring together eight children in this new refuge, but the project soon collapsed because assistance to needy children seemed to flow more readily from the Russian imperial court than from would-be donors in Massachusetts.[17]

Although this hometown setback by no means destroyed Prince's ambition to help children, it may have pushed her to look for other opportunities outside Boston and to respond sympathetically to the Reverend David Ingraham's description of his missionary work in Jamaica. The British government had abolished slavery in its Caribbean colonies in 1834, thereby generating a new interest in Jamaica among antislavery activists on both sides of the Atlantic. Prince thus became one of the many abolitionists who wanted to see how the recently emancipated Black Jamaicans were using their freedom to advance in a society where they were no longer enslaved. "My mind, after the emancipation in the West Indies, was bent upon going to Jamaica," Prince noted in an explanation for why she set off again from Boston in 1840. "A field of usefulness seemed spread out before me." The meeting with Ingraham offered a new religious purpose for another international trip that she already envisioned as an opportunity to combine abolitionism with her enduring desire to promote the welfare of children. "I hoped that I might aid, in some small degree," she wrote in an explanation for her Jamaican journey, "to raise up and encourage the emancipated inhabitants, and teach the young children to read and work, to fear God, and put their trust in the Saviour."[18]

Arriving in St. Ann, Jamaica, in December 1840, Prince quickly proposed to longtime residents that "something must be done for the elevation of the children," but she ran into vehement opposition from local Christians who had already developed their own methods for teaching religious ideas and protecting their churches.[19] Both the white and Black Christian leaders seemed to be more interested in raising money for their churches than in raising religious-minded children. Prince insisted on the need for proper religious lessons, however, which she thought the Jamaicans could provide through a more systematic plan for childhood education. She therefore began to consult with her "colored friends from America" as she imagined a new educational project that would be aimed specifically at improving the conditions of vulnerable young girls (an echo from her own childhood?). "We thought something ought to be done for the poor girls who were destitute," she wrote in her *Life and Travels*. Local people also came to recognize the special needs of recently emancipated girls and eventually agreed to establish a fundraising society that would support a new Jamaican school. Prince, for her part, would contribute to this ambitious plan by returning to the United States to raise money for what she called "my Free Labor School." She therefore traveled to Philadelphia in the summer of 1841, hoping to collect money and books that could help educate impoverished girls and provide appropriate moral guidance. Her appeals attracted favorable attention in Philadelphia from well-known abolitionists such as the Quaker activist Lucretia Mott, "who took great interest in the cause."[20] Later visits to New Jersey and Massachusetts produced additional funds for the new school and for the fundraiser's travel back to Jamaica.

Prince returned to Jamaica in the late spring of 1842, but she immediately found herself mired in social, political, and religious conflicts that made it impossible to establish the school she had carefully described to sympathetic American donors. In fact, she struggled simply to protect the funds she had brought from the United States because Christian groups in Kingston now asked her to place all the recently collected money under their control. Although Prince ultimately managed to hold on to the money, the local resistance to her educational ideas deepened her personal disillusionment with almost everyone in Jamaica's post-emancipation religious organizations. Her own devout goal was to be a virtuous, respectable woman, but her conflicts with local Christian leaders convinced her that the Jamaican slave system had left a social legacy that even the most determined religious worker could not transform. "A more skilful plan than this," she explained in a summary of Jamaican church proposals to control her money, "Satan never designed. . . . It is not surprising that this people are full of deceit and lies, this is the fruits of slavery, it makes master and slaves knaves."[21]

Despite these satanic threats, Prince eventually distributed her money to American missionaries and other charitable projects (collecting "receipts and letters I have in my possession") before she left again for a demoralized return to the United States in August 1842. She gained much information about the local social and religious situation during her months in Jamaica, but her ambitious plans to create a useful and respected school for girls had collapsed in bitter frustrations.[22] Prince's trips to Jamaica always focused on educational and religious missions rather than on the conventional traveler's search for new cultural knowledge or personal pleasures, yet her Caribbean experiences ultimately reshaped a strong-willed woman's inward journey toward the independent Black American selfhood that she reaffirmed in *The Life and Travels of Mrs. Nancy Prince*.

Prince's Knowledge of Customs, People, Places, and Endless Dangers

The stories of Jamaican setbacks conveyed disappointment and even disillusionment, but they never altered Prince's overall portrait of herself as a widely traveled, respectable woman. She understood that travel provided a kind of "cultural capital" (to use a modern term rather than her own words), which women writers could accumulate when their narratives went beyond reports on the education of needy children to include knowledgeable accounts of foreign social life, ideas, and exotic landscapes.[23] All of these subjects therefore appeared in Prince's travel book, along with the stories about important, respectable people who recognized her talents or expertise both in America and in other countries.

Descriptions of her experiences in St. Petersburg, for example, included reports on what she had learned about Russian burial customs, infant baptisms, holiday festivals, religious life, and marriages; and the accounts of such social practices typically referred to direct observations or firsthand knowledge that could come only from a long immersion in Russian culture. Her concise story about Russian marriage customs shows how Prince used an experienced-based approach to cultural knowledge and how she liked to emphasize the influential actions of respected women. Noting that the "first day of May is another great holiday," Prince explained how this spring festival led to Russian marital negotiations that only a longtime resident could understand: "The merchant's daughters are arranged on each side of a long mall, in the beautiful gardens, and arrayed in their best clothes, under the care of an old woman known in their families; the gentlemen walk round and observe them, and if they see one they fancy, they speak to the old woman; she takes him to the parents and introduces him; if the parties agree, they prepare for the betrothal. It is their custom to marry one of their own station."[24] Prince refused to judge the morality or efficacy of this marriage system. The storytelling method in almost all such reports, however, conveyed her authoritative status and her social message by assuring her readers that she had seen this ritual with her own eyes and by stressing that women played a crucial role in mediating key social relationships. Indeed, she explained that she "was accustomed to attend" all of Russia's holiday celebrations and that her linguistic knowledge enabled her to understand what was happening in all the social interactions of daily life. "I learned the languages in six months," she wrote with pride in her accomplishment, "so as to be able to attend to my business, and also made some proficiency in French."[25]

Prince thus asserted a cultural expertise that grew directly out of her nine-year stay in Russia and exceeded what almost any other nineteenth-century American traveler or writer could have learned from much briefer visits. Equally important, she also wanted her readers to understand that her social experiences, cultural knowledge, and long sojourn among Russian Orthodox Christians had never weakened the American Protestant religious identity that formed another pillar of her respectable womanhood. The Reverend Richard Kenell ministered to a devout Protestant community in St. Petersburg, and under his leadership, Prince reported, "we had service twice every Sabbath, and evening prayer meetings, also a female society, so that I was occupied at all times."[26] Some skeptics may have wondered about the moral fortitude of a woman who lived for almost a decade among Russian nobles and their holiday parties, but Prince offered absolute assurances that she never betrayed her respectable, religious values for the seductive glamor of an imperial court or the distractions of a strange foreign city.

Prince's descriptions of Jamaica included similar cultural information about what she observed in the markets, schools, churches, and towns she visited during her travels around the island. The recently emancipated Black workers faced a more desperate economic situation than she ever encountered at the Russian imperial court, yet Prince stressed that these "worn out," impoverished workers found that "their present state is blissful, compared with slavery."[27] In contrast to her accounts of the tsar's elegant dinners or the popular Russian holidays, Prince's Jamaican travel narrative gave more attention to the landscape, agriculture, mountains, rivers, vegetation, weather patterns, and other geographical features that confirmed her knowledge of Caribbean natural history. Here, too, Prince asserted an expertise that came from her direct observations as well as from the books that North American travelers typically used to understand the unfamiliar Jamaican geography and climate: "The mountains that intersect this island," she wrote in a geographical narrative, ". . . are adorned with a great variety of beautiful trees . . . which are nourished by frequent rains, and flourish in perpetual spring. From these mountains flow a vast number of small rivers of pure water. . . . Along the coast, and on the plains, the weather is very hot. . . . The general produce of this island is sugar, rum, molasses, ginger, cotton, indigo, pimento, cocoa, coffees, several kinds of woods, and medicinal drugs."[28] This guidebook-style discussion of natural history offered a quasi-scientific interlude in her Jamaican story of personal dangers, social injustices, and religious deceptions. Yet Prince's digressions into empirical reports on geography and agrarian products seemed to be emotionally detached from the more obvious personal interests and passions that emerged in her meetings with Russian elites, her plans to help needy children, her critiques of slavery, and her religious responses to the painful constraints of the human condition.

Although she carefully summarized her knowledge of foreign customs and unfamiliar places, the most engaging sections of Prince's *Life and Travels* told a story of endless struggles that began with the hardships of her youth in Massachusetts and continued through the memorable adventures in Russia and the disillusionments in Jamaica. The Russian experience stood out as the "best years" of Prince's eventful life, yet even this era of good feelings brought dangers for which religious beliefs offered the emotional support and strength she needed to survive life-threatening accidents or health problems. A terrible flood in St. Petersburg in October 1824 became an early Russian example of the always-present threats to her well-being. Walking toward a neighbor's apartment on a stormy night, she suddenly sank into a deep pit of muddy water in which she felt she was drowning until she miraculously grasped the leg of a dead horse that kept her afloat. "Had not the horse been there, I should never again have seen the light of day, and no one would have known my fate." This miraculous survival contributed to Prince's confidence in the religious meaning of her travels because (as she remembered it) "through the providence of God, I escaped from the flood and the pit." Meanwhile, the cold Russian winters posed an annual danger to her lungs, which her doctors finally advised her to escape by returning to America, though her departure from Russia's winter weather would also mean her departure from a husband whom she would never see again.[29]

There was in fact no entirely safe place for Prince at home or abroad. She faced an endless economic struggle to make a living in Boston and another dispiriting blow in the collapse of her plans to establish a new urban orphanage. Later, while traveling in New Jersey to raise funds for the much-needed Jamaican school, she fell "through an open trap door, down fifteen feet, on hard coal" as she was walking toward the bathroom in an unfamiliar house. This painful accident caused severe bruises, dislocated her left shoulder, interrupted her fundraising trip, and delayed her return to Jamaica.[30] Economic and health problems thus contributed to the obstacles that continually blocked her ambitions in the United States, yet Prince's travel narrative portrayed her Jamaican journey as the culminating challenge in a lifelong passage through hardships and pain. She worked with a Jamaican church leader who rejected her conception of religious training and forced her to leave his church; she gave away Bibles, "not knowing" how she hurt the unhappy Protestant minister who collected money from his sale of Bibles; she visited markets to discuss religious beliefs with people in the food stalls, but "the Jews and Spanish looked at me very black"; she met with Christian groups to plan for her new school, but these people only wanted her money and "started to plunder me"; she turned to the American consul for advice, but he told her that the "unsettled" times would doom a Jamaican girls school; and she ran into frightening personal risks wherever she stopped for rest or protection. "Houses were broken open and robbed every night," she wrote. "I came very near being shot."[31]

Prince's narrative of her experiences in Jamaica resembled psalm-like tales of a long journey through the valley of despair, but she ultimately encountered the greatest dangers during the voyage back to the United States. This almost fatal trip carried her into a terrible storm at sea and then brought her into the explicit threat of enslavement when her ship stopped for trade and repairs in Key West and New Orleans. "A law had just been passed . . . ," she wrote with reference to Key West, "that every free colored person coming there, should be put in custody on their going ashore; there were five colored persons on board; none dared go ashore, however uncomfortable we might be in the vessel."[32] The dangers of falling into enslavement exceeded all the other tribulations that Prince had faced on her trips; and no other danger could reveal so clearly the social limits to a Black woman's continuing struggle to achieve personal respect and autonomous selfhood. Slavery remained the looming social danger that separated Prince's travels from the experiences of every white woman in antebellum America. At the same time, this dangerous threat (like all others) took on a deep moral meaning for Prince by connecting her life to the classic religious pilgrimage that helped spiritual travelers move through hardships toward a better future place. "Many are the trials and temptations to which we are exposed in this vale of tears," Prince noted after describing her struggles, "but in heaven we shall be freed from the bondage of sin. Nothing can enter there to annoy or molest the redeemed ones."[33] In the meantime, however, there was the earthly struggle to defend living Black people who were still suffering from the dehumanizing sin of slavery on American soil. Prince's journey toward the respected life of an independent Black woman could thus never finally escape the oppressive slave system and racism from which she sought to free herself through all her transoceanic travels.

Slavery, Politics, and Culture

Prince was born to free parents in a free state, but the history of the transatlantic slave trade and the oppressive power of the racist slave system affected every phase of her life. Her own family's history—like the history of virtually all African American families—was deeply entangled with the transnational commodification of enslaved people, as she noted on the first page of her autobiographical narrative. Her maternal grandfather "was stolen from Africa, when a lad," and "although a slave, he fought for liberty" in the Revolutionary War at the Battle of Bunker Hill. Prince therefore gained her earliest knowledge of slavery from family stories that continued to influence her mature abolitionist (and religious) perspectives on America's social sins. "He often used to tell us, when little children," she remembered in a description of her grandfather, "the evils of Slavery, and how he was stolen from his native land."[34]

Similar stories came into the family from Prince's stepfather, who was also seized in Africa when he was a young man. Prince had "often heard him tell the tale" that she passed on to her readers as she explained how her stepfather and his enslaved friend survived their leap from a slave ship that was anchored at a northeastern port. The two friends swam ashore and found refuge with a sympathetic man who discovered them "trembling" under a fence. This defiant escape impressed Prince as an important family example of the ways in which resistance to slavery required personal bravery and determination as well as a passion for freedom: "I have often heard my step-father boast how brave they were, and say they stood like men and saw the ship sail with less than half they stole from Africa."[35] This memory of how "they stood like men" conveyed a strong family legacy that Prince reaffirmed wherever she could stand as a free woman to condemn the brutal slave system and to advocate its complete abolition.

Critiques of slavery thus reappeared throughout Prince's discussion of vulnerable people outside the United States. Traveling across Russia, for example, Prince noted the striking contrasts between wealthy city dwellers and the poor rural peasants who lived in the simple log houses of impoverished villages. "This class of people," she reported, "till the land, most of them are slaves and are very degraded." Prince suggested with such comments that Russian peasants lived much like enslaved people in the United States, but she also found reasons to believe that the Russian system ultimately treated peasants more humanely than the laws of her own country treated enslaved African Americans. In contrast to the American enslavers who routinely broke up enslaved families to enhance their own economic interests, the Russian nobles did not "separate families or sell them off the soil."[36] Travelers could immediately see the vast differences that separated the social classes in Russia, but they could also see that even the poorest, most oppressed Russian peasants did not face the devastating losses that occurred constantly in the cruel American dispersal of enslaved families; and a trip in monarchical Russia could provide critical comparisons for challenging slavery in republican America.

Although Prince's contacts with William Lloyd Garrison and other abolitionists in Boston may have helped her expand both the religious idealism and the cross-cultural critiques she had developed in Russia, her experiences in post-emancipation Jamaica forced her to recognize the limits of idealism as well as the real-world struggles of people who had long lived under the daily surveillance and oppression of enslavement. Slavery was officially abolished in Jamaica on

1 August 1834, yet most formerly enslaved workers remained in temporary "apprentice" positions that were supposed to ease their economic transition to freedom. This plan broke down over the following five years, however, which meant that the English government essentially abandoned vulnerable, recently emancipated people who were still seeking the education, jobs, and income they would need to support themselves and their families.[37] There were also conflicts in the early 1840s between Black Jamaicans who had always lived on the island and recently arrived immigrants called "Maroons," whose Jamaican ancestors had been abruptly deported to Sierra Leone after the British suppressed a rebellion of enslaved workers in the late 1790s. This growing population of migrating Maroon descendants claimed a special status as the true Jamaicans, arguing that "the island, of right, belongs to them" and that their painful family histories should be recognized and rewarded with positions or opportunities that would place them above the Black families that never left the island.[38] Conflicts with both the former slaveholders and the returning Maroons thus placed the long-suffering (but now free) Black Jamaicans in an extremely difficult economic situation. Many of the emancipated workers were "old, worn out and degraded," and their conditions grew steadily worse because even the Christian missionaries exploited their vulnerabilities. According to Prince, "every advantage is taken of their ignorance," and the "same spirit of cruelty is opposed to them that held them for centuries in bondage."[39]

Legal freedom alone thus brought no guarantees for social justice or economic well-being, so Prince soon decided that the true emancipation of impoverished, abused people would require further social reforms and government interventions. Although all emancipated persons in Jamaica had received small cash payments when they became free, "what little the poor people had gathered" in the years after 1834 "was destroyed by violence; their fences were broken down, and their horses and hogs taken from them." It would be impossible for her readers to imagine all the abuses that previously enslaved people had endured, Prince explained, but she had already seen more than she could describe: "Were I to tell all my eyes have seen among that people, it would not be credited." Indeed, most of the free Black Americans who had moved to Jamaica to start new lives in this post-emancipation society became deeply disillusioned with the social problems that left people exposed to new hardships everywhere on the island. Prince thus advised against migration from the United States because she believed that the obstacles for free Blacks in America were less dangerous than the new struggles they would face if they were to "stray abroad and starve in foreign lands."[40] Recognizing the complex legacy of slave systems (which would also become apparent when slavery was later abolished in the United States), she explained why emancipation was only the essential first step on a long, painful march toward social justice and a better economic life.

VISIT OF A MISSIONARY AND WIFE TO A PLANTATION VILLAGE.

Visit of a Missionary and Wife to a Plantation Village. Engraved illustration by an unknown artist, ca. 1843, in James Phillippo, *Jamaica: Its Past and Present State* (London: John Snow, 1843). Phillippo was a white English missionary who went to Jamaica in 1823 and lived there for almost twenty years, preaching Baptist beliefs and promoting new schools for Black Jamaicans after the abolition of slavery in 1834. This image of a white clergyman and Black villagers in Phillippo's book, however, depicted the enduring racial and religious hierarchies that Nancy Prince encountered on the island and condemned in her descriptions of Jamaica's post-emancipation economy and religious culture. UNC–Chapel Hill, Library.

Amid these endless hardships, however, Prince explained how *all* Black Jamaicans agreed that their conditions had been worse under slavery. One formerly enslaved man "told me of the wrongs he and his wife had endured while in slavery" and shared stories that were "too horrible to narrate." If Prince could not reveal everything she had learned, she could at least establish her own credibility as a knowledgeable witness who provided accurate accounts of the new Jamaican society that was emerging after emancipation. "My heart sickens when I think of it," she noted in one of her comments about the stories she heard during her travel around the island. Anyone who wondered about whether life had improved for the formerly enslaved Jamaicans would nevertheless find in Prince's book the strongest possible confirmation that slavery had been far worse than any problems that developed after it was abolished. Visiting the busy marketplace in Kingston, for example, she found the food stalls were all "kept by colored men and women" who worked hard and offered daily demonstrations of how Black people prospered after they escaped the bonds of slavery. Jamaica, in short, had lessons for America:

> Here surely we see industry; they are enterprising and quick in their perceptions, determined to possess themselves, and to possess property besides, and quite able to take care of themselves. They wished to know why I was so inquisitive about them. I told them we had heard in America that you are lazy, and that emancipation has been of no benefit to you; I wish to inform myself of the truth respecting you, and give a true account on my return. Am I right? More than two hundred people were around me listening to what I said. They thanked me heartily.[41]

Such reports confirmed Prince's abolitionist themes by showing the new social autonomy of free persons, but her eyewitness stories also conveyed the author's own exceptional knowledge of how people adjusted to life after slavery. There were all kinds of intimidating challenges for emancipated Jamaicans and for the author herself, yet Prince's trip ultimately revealed the universal truth that abolishing slavery was essential for the future well-being of enlightened societies and for a future global transition that most white Americans were still unable to see or were unwilling to accept. Meanwhile, the humanitarian work of British abolitionists such as Thomas Clarkson and William Wilberforce had shown the exceptional power of moral social movements because "it pleased God to break the chains from 800,000 human beings" across all of Britain's Caribbean and African colonies.[42]

The Long Journey toward Homeland Status, Identity, and Selfhood

Travel narratives often portray the "journey home" as a final confirmation of the new ideas or insights that have been gained from a long voyage. Randal McGavock, for example, stressed that his European journey showed him the superiority of America's political institutions, modern commerce, and boundless potential for future cultural achievements. Prince's description of the homeward journey from Jamaica, by contrast, raised the awful specter of America's social injustices and the constant dangers that threatened Black people in the United States. The risk of enslavement prevented her from going ashore in Florida or Louisiana during her port-city stopovers in those states, but Prince could observe plenty of injustice without ever leaving her ship. Her onerous encounter with racist people in the southern United States brought new dangers, but it also added to her transnational comparisons by showing how the emancipated (though still precarious) social position of Black Jamaicans was clearly better than the position of enslaved people whom she observed in New Orleans. Prince emphasized America's systematic denial of freedom rather than what McGavock described as America's

Enslaved Black Workers Loading Cotton on the Levee in New Orleans. Hand-colored woodcut by an unknown artist, ca. 1850. Nancy Prince's second sea voyage from Jamaica to the United States included a dangerous stopover in New Orleans, where she could not leave her ship because she feared seizure by an enslaver and where she saw enslaved people working on the docks of the bustling port. This portrayal of the city's cotton trade shows the centrality of enslaved labor in the commercial system and illustrates the daily realities of the anti-Black racism that evoked Prince's deepest fear and anger about the possible loss of her freedom. North Wind Picture Archives/Alamy Stock Photo.

"perfection of human wisdom."[43] Passing though the waterways that led into New Orleans, Prince "looked with pity on the poor slaves, who were laboring and toiling, on either side [of the river], as far as could be seen with a glass." Whereas the white passengers freely disembarked as soon as Prince's ship reached the city's dock, she explained, "we poor blacks were obliged to remain on that broke, wet vessel. The people were very busy about me," Prince remembered; "one man asked me who I belonged to, and many other rude questions." Despite the encouraging comments of one white man who became friendly after learning the name of her father (whom he claimed to have known), Prince remained cautious about the motives of this would-be friend and rejected his offer to transport her to New York—fearing perhaps that the offer was a ruse to sell her into slavery after she went ashore.[44]

She noted that white people "watched me very closely" as she observed New Orleans from her boat's deck, and she recognized immediately that a free Black woman would face constant threats if she merely walked through the streets of the city. Prince saw enslaved people "fettered together in pairs by the wrists; some had weights, with long chains at their ankles, men and women, young and old." When she asked why they were enchained, she was told simply that they were deemed to be "impudent" persons because they had (allegedly) stolen something or because they were "free negroes from the northern ships." They were thus enslaved in retribution for "being on shore, some of them at night," which was a common diversion for white travelers at almost any port city in the world. Yet, as Prince noted with harsh honesty and dismay, an African American's dockside visit to New Orleans could easily become a "crime" for which the unwary Black visitor could be imprisoned or enslaved. Angered by this absurd injustice, Prince assured her readers that she voiced vehement religious criticisms of the oppression she observed in New Orleans. "I asked them who made them Lord over God's inheritance," only to receive a warning from the local white people that she was "very foolish" to ask such questions and that she should not comment on the enslaved human beings whom she could see suffering near her ship.[45]

Prince thus challenged the religious hypocrisy of enslavers who called themselves Christians, and then she reaffirmed her own freedom by making defiant comments from her restricted shipboard position. "I am sure . . . the Lord will take care of me," she said during her confrontation with the white Christians whose hypocritical comments and behaviors provoked her anger; "you cannot harm me." This firm assertion of divine protection seemed to draw on her experiences in Russia and Jamaica as well as on her enduring religious faith, and it also showed how her recent contacts with emancipated Black people outside the United States gave her an experiential foundation for challenging white racists in Louisiana. "Every ship that comes in," Prince reminded her readers, entered a danger zone for Black passengers because "the colored men are dragged to prison." Responding to this imminent threat to herself and others, Prince "found it necessary to be stern with them; they [the white passengers] were very rude; if I had not been so, I know not what would have been the consequences."[46]

Prince continually insisted on her social status as a free woman, even and especially when she found herself isolated in a slave-state harbor. White visitors to the ship told her she "must not say any thing to these negroes whilst you are here." They demanded to see her "protection," they asked her to confirm rumors that she traveled "under the Russian government," and they wanted her ship to leave New Orleans. Prince responded to all such hostility with quotations from the book of Revelation and claimed that scripture provided exactly the transcendent protection she needed. Her strong-willed religious claims may have knocked her critics off-balance. In any case, her own "impudent" assertiveness was ignored, and she was able to escape from Louisiana on a different ship—though she lost the money she had already paid for the journey from Jamaica to New York. Sailing out of New Orleans on a dismal rainy day in September 1842, Prince saw another "awful sight" that demonstrated the fragile independence of her own life: a "vessel of slaves [was] laying at the side of our ship! The deck was full of young men, girls, and children, bound to Texas for sale!"[47]

The glimpse of enslaved young people must have strengthened Prince's religious gratitude for her own freedom to travel, no matter how difficult or demeaning the trip might become—and the new ship was also dangerous. The captain made unfair demands for money and then refused to release her baggage in New York until she found the additional funds, but Prince eventually returned safely to Boston in 1843. She had barely avoided enslavement in the American South, and she had come back to Massachusetts "poor in health, and poor in purse, having sacrificed both, hoping to benefit my fellow creatures." Yet she found solace in the belief that her difficult Jamaican journey had been "acceptable to God, who in his providence preserved me in perils by land, and perils by sea."[48] This dangerous and frightening trip, in short, provided the most compelling experiential evidence to confirm Prince's belief that a divine power supported her earthly mission, freedom, and survival.

The struggle against slavery and its post-emancipation legacy in Jamaica therefore led Prince into social and religious experiences that diverged from the conventional "self-improvement" experiences that travel narratives often described. Her account of threats to her social or personal well-being, however, also included other kinds of stories because she wanted her readers to see that (like other travelers) she had gained important political and cultural knowledge over the course of her travels. She therefore became a travel writer whose "dual identity" connected her with influential public leaders *and* with the social groups that challenged powerful political elites. Her admiration for the Russian imperial family, for example, seemed to grow partly out of Prince's social desire for a "respectable womanhood" that became linked to political support for conservative factions within Russia's divided court society. She reported that Tsar Nicholas I was "wonderfully preserved" during the revolt that challenged his claims to the throne in December 1825, and she blamed the Decembrist uprising on a "deep plot" that had developed in Freemason lodges abroad. Her account of the failed revolt thus supported the tsar's repressive actions and conveyed her suspicions about the motives of the Decembrist plotters who had mobilized an anti-Nicholas mob in St. Petersburg.[49]

At the same time, Prince distanced herself from the tsar by describing a brutal repression that cast the "bodies of the killed and mangled" plotters into a river and left "the snow and ice . . . stained with the blood of human victims." She also emphasized that the rebellion's surviving leaders and supporters were treated like slaves as they were sent off to Siberia, thrown into prison, or put to death in public places. "The prison-houses were filled," Prince wrote, "and thirty of the leading men were put in solitary confinement." Almost all of these men died in prison, but Prince reported how several were killed in horrifying public executions. Facing a painful death, "each prisoner was secured by iron chains, presenting a most appalling sight to an eye-witness"—a term that suggested Prince's own possible connection to the events she described. In addition to the "brave men" who were executed, many other high-ranking persons were imprisoned, flogged, or banished to Siberia, where they suffered "heart-rending" separations "from all [their] dear relatives and friends, for they are never permitted to take their children."[50] Prince's personal desire for a respectable position at the imperial court, in other words, did not prevent her from seeing that the tsar's repressive political system delivered awful punishments to anyone who opposed it; and she could write about *both* sides of Russian political culture because her travels gave her "eye-witness" views of miserable, chained prisoners as well as elegant dinners in a royal palace.

A similar "dual identity" emerged in Prince's account of social conditions in Jamaica. Whereas her experiences and ambitions in Russia mostly strengthened her identification with the imperial elite (tempered by her sympathy for severely punished political opponents), Prince's contacts with Jamaicans reinforced her identification with recently emancipated Black workers. This linkage between her African American religious identity and vulnerable Jamaicans reappeared often in her comments about the mistreatment of impoverished Black families, her desire to promote the education of young women, her praise for the enterprising spirit of Kingston's Black merchants, and her insistence that even the worst problems of emancipated persons were less severe than the chains of enslavement. Yet Prince's obvious sympathy for the plight of formerly enslaved Jamaicans constantly collided with her anger about the lack of biblical education among the people whom she met in Jamaican churches and her complaints about self-interested church leaders who wanted to "plunder" the funds she had collected in the United States.[51]

Prince's descriptions of these Jamaican problems suggested that she came to see herself as both an African American abolitionist and a religious outsider from New England. Drawing on her earlier experiences with the Protestantism she had embraced in Boston, Prince was confident that her own (New England) religious knowledge went well beyond the misinformation and religious distortions that local white and Black instructors were teaching to would-be church members in Jamaica. She explained, for example, that she ran into conflicts with one such unnamed instructor almost immediately after she realized that this woman misunderstood the essential spiritual path to Christianity. "I spoke to her of the necessity of being born of the spirit of God before we become members of the church of Christ," Prince remembered, "and told her I was sorry to see the people blinded in such a way."[52] Prince's criticisms sparked an angry response from the local teacher, but this clash was only one of the many conflicts that arose from her sharp-edged advice on proper religious training. She later met another woman who (in Prince's view) wrongly assumed that her grandchild's spirit would haunt her forever if the infant died before she had been baptized. Unfortunately, "this poor deluded creature was a class leader in the Baptist Church," and her inferior understanding of Christian doctrines exemplified the failings of a church leadership that was "blinded to every thing but money."[53] Prince's commentaries on Jamaican religious institutions thus expressed the ambivalence of an African American writer who identified with the emancipated African Jamaicans and also separated herself from their culture by identifying with the religious traditions of New England Protestantism. Although her foreign travels helped to deepen the African American female identity that made Prince an outsider in antebellum Massachusetts, her deep commitments to northeastern American Protestantism also helped to make her an outsider in Russia and Jamaica. She wanted to be a respectable, free woman in every place she lived or visited, but her multilayered cultural and religious identities always gave her a marginal position from which she set out to assert or reaffirm her independent selfhood.

The Life and Travels of Mrs. Nancy Prince therefore conveyed the cultural "hybridity" of an African American woman whose quest for respectability and freedom ran into the inescapable historical obstacles of racism, slave systems, and cultural differences. Her life story nevertheless became a tale of personal empowerment, partly because she always portrayed herself as an independent woman and partly because she described her travels as a religious pilgrimage toward personal salvation. Prince was not a theologian or religious scholar, but she used her travel experiences to illustrate the ultimate religious meaning of her whole life. None of the dangers she faced in her domestic and foreign encounters with racism, slavery, cultural incomprehension, or storms on the high seas could block her from the final destination of her difficult journeys. "O Father," she wrote in the conclusion of her travel story, "fearful indeed is this world's pilgrimage"; yet the long pilgrimage led finally to a stable refuge where "a cloud opens" and "a face serene and hopeful looks forth" on the long-wandering traveler.[54]

Like Margaret Fuller after the painful political failures in 1848–49, Prince anticipated a better future world that (unlike Fuller) she expected to find in heaven rather than in earthly republics or democratic governments. It seems most unlikely that Prince ever reached a serene time or place on the ground in America, but her struggle to achieve an independent (religious-inflected) identity offers an intriguing nineteenth-century story about the personal changes and sense of liberation that could flow from long journeys abroad. Her quest for an autonomous African American womanhood carried Prince far from Massachusetts and deep into a religious self-definition that contrasted starkly with most of David Dorr's secular quest for an autonomous African American manhood, except that both travelers looked abroad for the freedom and respect they could never find in their racist, nineteenth-century home country.

CHAPTER SIX

David Dorr's Journey toward Selfhood and Freedom in Europe and the Middle East

If NANCY PRINCE had been able to go ashore during her dangerous stopover in New Orleans as she traveled northward from Jamaica in 1842, she might have encountered the still-youthful David Dorr, whom the Louisiana businessman Cornelius Fellowes "owned" through the laws of the American slave system. This meeting never took place, of course, yet the life stories of Prince and Dorr overlapped in other ways because both used their antebellum, transatlantic journeys to assert their desire for an autonomous identity and selfhood. Although historical knowledge about both of their lives comes mainly from their own autobiographical books, Prince provided more information about her family and early relationships. Dorr's narrative in *A Colored Man round the World*, by contrast, focused almost entirely on his travels in 1851–53 and offered in the dedication and brief preface only a few fragments about his earlier life.

Dedicating his book "TO MY SLAVE MOTHER," Dorr defined his own authorial identity as "a quadroon" from New Orleans. The term "quadroon" was used in Louisiana to describe people who had one Black grandparent, so Dorr's self-identification indicated that he was a light-skinned "colored man" (to use the racial term of his book title). His dedication also vaguely noted the sadness of losing close family connections by simply stating: "MOTHER! Wherever thou art, whether in Heaven or a lesser world." He did not say more about his unnamed mother, however, and he never mentioned his childhood or his father, which became all the more mysterious when his book preface described Cornelius Fellowes as a "gentleman" who "treated me as his own son, and could look on me as free a man as walks the earth." He also noted later that Fellowes was forty-eight years old when he and Dorr (who was about twenty-four) set off on their European travels.[1]

These ambiguous comments on the age and relationship of the "master" and the enslaved traveler raise an obvious question that Dorr never addressed in his narrative: Was Fellowes his biological father—someone who (in a common pattern of abusive, hierarchical sexual power) had fathered a child with Dorr's enslaved, biracial mother? *A Colored Man* left readers with many such unanswered questions about Dorr's parents and the other unknown members of his family. What Dorr's book did provide, however, was an account of his own quest for an empowering male sexual identity that he sought to establish by pursuing the prerogatives of a free American man "round the world." Where Nancy Prince told the story of a long religious journey through earthly sufferings toward the status of an independent, respected woman from Massachusetts, Dorr portrayed his European travels as a long social journey through earthly pleasures toward the status of an independent, respected gentleman from Louisiana. Although Dorr described this journey in a wide-ranging, unique book, he never mentioned how he might have learned about a free "gentleman's" identity from unexplained links with his enslaver and traveling "master," Cornelius Fellowes.

Dorr also never explained how he learned to read and write, but his travel stories conveyed a knowledge of history and culture that very few enslaved persons were allowed to acquire. His book alluded to writers (for example, Shakespeare and Byron) and to French-language phrases that suggested an earlier literary education. He nevertheless claimed in his preface that he used only a school dictionary as he wrote his book, thereby seeking to show that his knowledge came from his firsthand experiences in European cities rather than from his youthful reading. Despite the vagueness of his life history, Dorr provided a glimpse of his personal struggles in an angry complaint that Fellowes failed to follow through on a promise for freedom that was offered while the two were in Europe. "I called on this original man to consummate a two-fold promise he made me, in different parts of the world," Dorr remembered, "because I wanted to make a connection, that I considered myself more than equaled in dignity and means." The long trip had demonstrated Dorr's inherent human equality and his desire to "make a *connection*" (parent/son?), but Fellowes "refused me on old bachelor principles" after the travelers returned to New Orleans. Dorr did not define the meaning of "bachelor principles." Did Fellowes assume that a passing "bachelor" involvement with Dorr's mother could not justify an acknowledged connection with her son, or did he assume that his promises in Europe had no significance in Louisiana? The meaning of this explanation is ambiguous, but the consequences of Fellowes's comments and actions are clear: the broken promise of emancipation soon provoked Dorr to make another journey toward the dignity and equality that Fellowes would never recognize. "I fled from him and his princely promises,"

Dorr explained in a concise summary of his flight to freedom in northern Ohio, "reflecting on the moral liberties of the legal freedom of England, France and our New England states."[2] Dorr thus explicitly linked his journey out of slavery to the personal freedom he had experienced in Europe and then lost again in Louisiana. Modern travel narratives often describe a traveling writer's new sense of freedom, but the rejection of hometown constraints became even more liberating for a young man whose European experiences helped to explain his eventual escape from slavery.

Settling in Cleveland after the mid-1850s, Dorr compiled his travel stories in a book that was probably published at his own expense. Like other travel writers, he described famous cities and historical sites, and then (unlike most travel writers) he constantly juxtaposed tourist-style information with unconventional passages about unexpected encounters with unfamiliar people and unknown places. Although Dorr's distinctive story of "a colored man's" European journey attracted no attention in national publications or antislavery pamphlets, the book was briefly reviewed in three different Cleveland newspapers. A commentary in the *Cleveland Plain Dealer* of 20 September 1858, for example, described Dorr's work as "a neat little volume" that offered a "graphic and racy sketch of the author's travels in foreign lands—what he saw, heard and experienced." The unidentified reviewer noted Dorr's visits to numerous European countries, emphasized his "thrilling account of the scenes and sensations" in Paris during Louis-Napoleon's coup d'état in 1851, and praised the quality of the author's prose. *A Colored Man round the World* was therefore "an exceedingly interesting work," the reviewer explained, because Dorr "indulges in no pompous rhetoric, but jots down in a free-and-easy, everyday style the incidents of his travel." Equally important, the book demonstrated the exceptional personal qualities of a "Quadroon" who was born to a "slave mother" and yet could "readily pass any where as a white man (and an excellent white man, too)."[3] It is impossible to know Dorr's response to this review, but modern readers of his book can imagine his appreciation for the reference to "an excellent white man" because Dorr constantly asserted his male-gendered social identity and because his skin color apparently helped him "pass" across Europe with an appearance that some nineteenth-century Europeans might have "seen" as the visage of a would-be American "gentleman." The anonymous reviewer in the *Cleveland Plain Dealer* (a personal friend of Dorr's?), however, also confirmed Dorr's manliness by alluding to three more specific identities that Dorr tried to convey throughout his travel book: (1) an educated person who knew European culture, (2) a respectable young man who knew how to be attractive to women, and (3) a free traveler who knew how to escape the social and racial hierarchies of slavery.

Dorr arrived in Liverpool in the summer of 1851, but his book provided no information about why he made the trip or how he crossed the Atlantic. The first-person narrative began abruptly by simply dropping Dorr (and the reader) into the Liverpool Customs House on 15 June 1851 and then introducing Dorr's dreamlike experiences as he walked around the streets of the city and met people at his hotel. He soon moved on to London and Paris before setting off on a typical "grand tour" of other cities in southern France, Switzerland, the Rhineland, and the Netherlands. He never explained how his status as an enslaved man shaped or limited his trip as he traveled from northern Europe into crowded Mediterranean cities such as Naples, Constantinople, and Athens. He spent two winter seasons in Paris and eventually (like Randal McGavock) made an adventurous boat trip up the Nile River, an overland journey across the desert from Egypt to Palestine, and a brief visit to the multicultural capital of Syria. Returning to France by the late summer in 1853, Dorr sailed from Le Havre for New York before he finally reentered his hometown slave society in New Orleans. The precise date of his later flight from Louisiana is unknown, but the place and date of his book's publication confirm that he was living in Cleveland by 1858.

Most of the surviving information about Dorr's personal relationships, public actions, and political beliefs appears in his only published book, which means that historians know almost nothing about his life before or after his European trip. The well-informed, modern editor of *A Colored Man round the World*, Malini Johar Schueller, found scattered references to Dorr in post–Civil War military records, but his name never appeared in the directories of Cleveland residents. There is indirect evidence to suggest that he worked before 1860 as a clerk and clear evidence that he advertised plans to give public lectures on his European travels (a strategy that Prince also attempted in Boston). One of his proposed lecture topics focused on the "Ballet Girls of Paris and the Quadroon Ladies of the South"—a subject that presumably linked Dorr's knowledge of France with his "manly" understanding of European and American women. According to Dorr's own report in a Cleveland newspaper, however, this cross-cultural comparison failed to draw more than two dozen people, so it was canceled, and the speaker turned to other activities.[4]

The Civil War radically transformed Dorr's life during the same time that it also changed and then ended the life of Randal McGavock (though the Tennessean fought of course on the other side). Dorr joined the Seventh Ohio Volunteer Infantry Regiment in August 1862, thereby finding new opportunities to assert his strong opposition to slavery and to affirm his independent manhood. The Seventh Ohio was attached to the Army of the Potomac during the battles at Chancellorsville and Gettysburg in 1863, but by November of that year the regiment had moved to Tennessee for the Union military campaign around Chattanooga. Dorr was seriously wounded in the jaw and shoulder at the minor battle of Ringgold Gap (27 November 1863), where Confederate forces were protecting their retreat into Georgia after decisive defeats at Lookout Mountain and Missionary Ridge. Dorr's wounds led to enduring physical disabilities, a discharge from the Union army in August 1864, and a postwar struggle to recover his health.[5] Army pension records indicate that a doctor granted him "permanent disability" status in 1867, for which Dorr received a modest monthly pension of fifteen dollars. He eventually returned to New Orleans to live as a free man in his native city, yet his health continued to deteriorate. His last request for a pension increase (August 1872) reported that his health had collapsed; and his death was later noted in the pension file without further explanations of when, where, or why he died.[6]

Dorr's obscure death thus differed from the widely noted battlefield death of Colonel McGavock near Vicksburg on 12 May 1863, but both of these "manly" world travelers became casualties of the American Civil War. Although they supported opposing political causes, they both fought for ideas of personal and collective freedom that they had clarified for themselves during youthful, transnational journeys. Their European trips intersected when they were at Constantinople and Athens on the same days in 1852 (there is no evidence that they ever met), yet their travel experiences helped them construct different identities that also carried them into different armies during the Civil War. The southern lives and European trips of Dorr and McGavock therefore exemplify the diverging complexities of gender, race, social hierarchies, and selfhood in America's antebellum southern states, much as the northern lives and foreign trips of Nancy Prince and Margaret Fuller exemplify the diverging complexities of gender, race, social hierarchies, and personal identities in antebellum New England. The social positions and journeys of these four Americans varied enormously, but their lives all show the shaping power of vast historical structures as well as the cultural and personal meanings of cross-cultural travel.

Dorr's Search for a Manly Freedom and Respect

A Colored Man round the World created a book-length portrait of Dorr's longed-for social status by emphasizing his firsthand knowledge of foreign cultures and his respected position among both Europeans and other American travelers. At the same time, Dorr asserted an independent, gendered identity through descriptions of his male social privileges and his references to social and sexual fantasies that nineteenth-century women could never mention in a respectable account of foreign travels. Dorr thus constructed part of his claim to the status and identity of a free man in proud accounts of his diverse (and sometimes dreamlike) encounters with women in almost every country he visited. Sexual freedom could become a sign of free manhood for an enslaved young man from Louisiana, which suggests why the liberty and equality of a masculine trip often differed from the transatlantic freedom of respectable women. (Margaret Fuller, for example, never referred to her relationship with Giovanni Ossoli in her reports from Italy.) Dorr's search for respectability could take on a distinctive, even erotic subtext that connected his much-desired escape from slavery to the freedoms and prerogatives of a traveling American gentleman.

This desire to show a foreign recognition of his independent, manly status provided a thematic framework for Dorr's whole travel narrative, which began and ended with stories about his interactions with *respectable* men. Arriving at the Adelphi Hotel in Liverpool on his first day in England, Dorr immediately received the deferential welcome that European or American gentlemen expected and deserved. A "well-dressed gentleman opened the door and descended the steps with an umbrella to escort me in," Dorr explained with evident satisfaction. "'Come right in here, sir,' said he, leading me into a large room," where the "gentleman took my overcoat and hung it up."[7] The usual hierarchies in the enslaved man's life were therefore turned upside down as he walked into his first European hotel and received the polite service that confirmed Dorr's new stature as a well-respected world traveler. He was soon reading European publications in the hotel's "newsroom" and meeting "noblemen from different parts of England" who freely discussed current affairs. When the conversation turned to slavery in America, one of the "noble-looking" gentlemen argued that a slave rebellion could probably destroy the whole system—a suggestion that (as Dorr noted) would be "treasonable" if the men had been talking anywhere in the southern United States. This early summary of a frank "newsroom" conversation introduced a self-flattering style of storytelling that repeatedly conveyed Dorr's new sense of freedom, his new connections with the social elite, and his own critique of slavery. He could put "treasonable" ideas in the voice of a wealthy Englishman, for example, in a story that linked him simultaneously to the upper-class men in a well-respected European hotel and to the abolitionist sentiments of well-educated English travelers. Like all the other respected guests, Dorr apparently received deferential assistance from the entire hotel staff. Indeed, he reported that these helpful people resembled "the servants of all parts of my own country," which was a bold comment from a man whose own home-country status was far closer to the "servant class" than to the position of European gentlemen in a hotel newsroom.[8]

The opening pages of Dorr's book thus began to construct the self-image of a well-respected traveler whose needs received solicitous attention from men and women alike. "It is impossible for me to do anything for myself," he reported in the present-tense voice he used for most of his narrative. "I have offers from nearly all parts of the Hotel, volunteering to do all that is to be done and more too." Dorr may have found effective ways to encourage this service by adhering carefully to the advice in *Murray's Hand-Book for Travellers* that encouraged guests (as Dorr noted) "to give a small bonus to the menials in public or private houses." Small gifts to "menials" showed that Dorr was a respectable gentleman and enhanced the goodwill of everyone who served him, including the owners of hotels. On the day of his departure from the Adelphi Hotel in Liverpool, Dorr explained, the "landlord" himself walked out to the coach "and wished me a happy voyage to London."[9]

These early stories of respectful conversations with servants and gentlemen in Liverpool became the prelude for social patterns that would reappear in every phase of Dorr's long trip. He soon moved on to a first Continental stop in Paris, where the staff at the "Hotel des Princes" provided deferential assistance with plenty of French *politesse* and where the other travelers in the hotel dining room included "three noblemen of England, one Duke of Italy, three barons of the Rhine, and a broken down princess."[10] Nobody who read such lists could doubt the quality of the people whom Dorr met in European hotels. The guests at his high-class hotel in The Hague, for example, included the father of the Dutch queen—an impressive personage who traveled with his own "guard of honor" and who, as Dorr explained with another reference to social inversions, "bows to me" when going out to visit the city. Such respect was the leitmotif of Dorr's journey. There were no stories about servants or nobles who treated him rudely or simply ignored the enslaved traveling companion of Cornelius Fellowes, and he seemed to get as much respectful service as any American he knew. Although Dorr never explained how he acquired his money or paid his bills, he hired local guides at tourist sites from the Waterloo battlefield to the churches in Jerusalem, he visited American consuls, and he met influential diplomats in Damascus.[11]

Dorr's travel stories therefore suggested that he was respected everywhere in Europe, and even his trip home to America confirmed the cultural status he had gained during his journey. Nancy Prince may have barely avoided enslavement in Florida and Louisiana during her homeward journey from Jamaica, but Dorr traveled across the Atlantic Ocean with distinguished Americans who wanted to hear his views on key European issues of the day. Among the passengers on his ship were "Charles W. March, private secretary of Mr. [Daniel] Webster, and Geo. W. Kendall, the travelling editor of the New Orleans Picayune," both of whom Dorr called the "happiest men aboard." After enjoying their dinners and fine wines they "inquired of my opinion of thousands of little things that I thought hardly worth noticing."[12] The enslaved young man who had traveled for more than two years in Europe and the Middle East was now prepared to offer his well-informed "opinion" to the most prominent fellow travelers on his ship. Although he was still (in 1853) the enslaved servant of a Louisiana businessman, Dorr wanted readers to understand that his European trip had given him a cultural knowledge and personal autonomy that made him socially equal to every American he met in shipboard conversations.

He also asserted his freedom and equality in other stories about his encounters with famous and influential European leaders. Unlike Prince, he could not report on personal experiences in an imperial court, yet Dorr often described the royal figures whom he saw in European capitals. In the summer of 1851, he watched Queen Victoria move through the streets near London's famous Crystal Palace exhibition. A huge crowd had gathered to see the queen, but Dorr was able to observe her face and demeanor as she passed close to him in a carriage—a sighting that became a quasi-mystical moment in his life. "I felt a sort of religious thrill pass over me," Dorr wrote, "and I said to myself 'this is civilization.'" In fact, he elevated the entire English nation to a unique global position as "the most civilized and Christian power on this earth," thus transforming his brief glimpse of Britain's ruling monarch into personal connections with a higher level of "civilization" that most Americans could not understand (perhaps because Britain had abolished slavery in every territory of its vast empire). And what did he see when he observed the royal embodiment of modern civilization pass by on a London street? "Her color was too red and masculine for a lady. She was considerable stouter than I thought she was," yet this famous woman possessed the qualities of a "great Queen." Despite his lack of any direct involvement with European court life, Dorr expanded on this eyewitness description of Queen Victoria in other reports on his encounters with the king of Greece, the sultan of the Ottoman Empire, the pope and cardinals of the Roman Catholic Church, the Duke of Tuscany, and the republican leaders of the French National Assembly.[13]

Streetside sightings of Pope Pius IX and the Ottoman sultan provided especially notable opportunities for Dorr to reflect on the grandeur and power of Europe's ruling elites. Summarizing his impressions of the pope, whom Margaret Fuller had criticized so vehemently in her recent letters from Rome, Dorr wrote that the "great man" wore "a gorgeously jeweled crown" and was carried like a ruling monarch through throngs of worshipping Romans. "The people all would fall on their knees," Dorr explained, "and the great man would bless them in the name of God."[14] The pope's personal grandeur and adoring followers thus impressed the traveler from New Orleans, but Dorr may have been even more fascinated by the Turkish deference to the Ottoman sultan Abdülmecid I, whom he saw traveling

The Interior of London's Crystal Palace during the Great Exhibition of 1851. Colored lithograph by J. McNeven, 1851. Like almost every visitor to London in 1851, David Dorr joined the throngs who toured the display of modern industrial inventions and global products at the famous Crystal Palace. Although he described the social and national significance of objects that can be seen in this illustration of the exhibition's vast interior spaces, he seemed to be more fascinated by his sighting of Queen Victoria in a street outside the enormous glass building. Niday Picture Library/Alamy Stock Photo.

across Constantinople with a sparkling caravan of attendants. According to Dorr, this monarchical procession included several pashas on golden-saddled camels, the sultan's seven wives, troupes of musicians, and a vast crowd of admiring bystanders. Here, too, Dorr seemed to be attracted to the spectacle of royal power, though he expressed a typical European and American belief that the young sultan could never be a symbol of civilization. In fact, as Dorr described him, the sultan seemed to be nervous and fearful; and in obvious contrast to the strikingly masculine British queen, Dorr portrayed the Ottoman sultan as effeminate and weak.[15] His respect for "civilized" rulers, in other words, did not extend beyond the elites of western Europe, perhaps because nineteenth-century American gentlemen were expected to believe that civilization itself flourished only in the great cities of Europe and the United States.

Dorr thus claimed his gentleman status by describing his encounters with famous people in famous places, but he also sought to differentiate himself from less knowledgeable Americans who lacked the culture, manliness, or independence of truly civilized travelers such as himself. His accounts of European cities drew these distinctions through mocking critiques of the kind of American he saw in a large outdoor Parisian restaurant, where people danced or engaged in lively conversations and where "not one gentleman had his foot on the table, except an American quietly seated in one corner in a profound soliloquy." This melancholy solitude seemed even worse when Dorr noticed that the boorish American was chewing tobacco, a vile national custom that violated the mores of cultured gentlemen. "I didn't stop to see where he spit," Dorr explained, "for fear he might claim nationality."[16] The presence of less-cultured compatriots, however, gave Dorr another opportunity to affirm his own respectability by contrasting his more refined behavior with the stupid incompetence of travelers such as the two "broken American youths" whom he saw at the famous German resort in Baden-Baden. The young men had lost all their money in the gambling casino, so they were waiting for funds to pay their hotel bills and embarrassing other American gentlemen who visited the resort. These destitute gamblers were "free men," yet Dorr portrayed them as far less respectable than the enslaved traveler from New Orleans. "I didn't pride myself much here on my nationality," Dorr noted in his description of Baden-Baden, "lest I would have some unprofitable fame."[17]

Such references to unattractive Americans reminded readers that the author of *A Colored Man round the World* was a better gentleman than many of the free men who disgraced their nation in Europe. He became especially angry in Florence when he saw a wealthy man from California (Dorr sarcastically called him Mr. "Bullion") "trying to pass himself off for a real American gentleman." Mr. "Bullion" tried to assert his social status by riding through Florence in an elegant carriage, but his actions showed that he "had more money than brains." The Florentine police asked him to open a space in the street for the passage of the Duke of Tuscany, but the American demanded deference to his national citizenship, rudely threw his legs over the front cushions in his open carriage, and stupidly spat tobacco juice. Although the haughty Mr. "Bullion" finally obeyed the police, his rudeness gave Dorr more reasons to elevate himself above wealthy white Americans who ignored the social codes in European cities. "At first my national pride was somewhat lowered," Dorr wrote after watching Mr. "Bullion" confront the police, "but on second thought, I gloried in knowing that Americans are not responsible for every upstart that goes abroad and violates the rules and regulations of other communities because they are not made to suit his taste, for which no body ever cared but himself. The good people of Europe know full well that there is always thistles among roses."[18] Dorr thus separated his honorable identity from unrespectable (white) Americans by suggesting that his own cultural views converged with the views of "good people" in Europe, who included the African American expatriates he met during different parts of his journey. Among all the other American travelers or residents that Dorr discussed, the African Americans in fact stood out as the most impressive, respectable compatriots he ever met. He constantly portrayed himself as an honorable "colored man," of course, but he also praised other Black Americans who had gained a new freedom and respect they could enjoy only in Europe.

In the outdoor Parisian restaurant that attracted dancers, diners, and a tobacco-spitting white American, Dorr also came upon a "very rich" Louisiana "quadroon" whose life in France differed completely from the misery of the lonely, spitting American. His name was Mr. Cordevoille, and he had been a prosperous tailor who left New Orleans "on account of . . . prejudice to color" in that city. He later settled in Paris, married a Frenchwoman, prospered in business, and made his way into French society. "Mr. Cordevoille was looking the very picture of a gentleman," Dorr wrote in his sympathetic (self-referential?) summary of the Louisiana expatriate's life story; "he seemed to be a great object of respect to those that spoke to the lady he was conversing with in the French tongue. He reminded me more of Prince Albert in his manners than any other person around." This "gentleman" from New Orleans greeted the Louisiana travelers with a handshake that deftly conveyed his social equality, and he invited the visitors to spend a night at his country home outside Paris. Cornelius Fellowes and some of his white friends accepted this invitation because it was "the duty of gentlemen" in France to respond honorably to the invitation of a gentleman whom white people would never visit in Louisiana. The stopover *chez* Cordevoille, in short, showed how Europe could provide new social status for the few American men of color who were able to live far outside their racist home country. Dorr recognized, however, that his white traveling companions had crossed a rigid racial boundary when they visited Cordevoille's home; and "lest it be a censure on these gentlemen," he noted ironically, "I refrain from going any further with a subject so delicate."[19]

The story of Cordevoille's Parisian status and freedom launched a theme of African American independence that reappeared in Dorr's longer description of another American "colored man" he met later in Constantinople and Athens. This independent man was the Tennessean Frank Parrish, who had come to Constantinople after a trip through Egypt and Palestine with Edwin Ewing and others, including Randal McGavock, that McGavock had described in some of his articles for the *Daily Nashville Union*.[20] There is no direct evidence that Dorr met McGavock, but their two southern American travel groups briefly crossed paths in both Turkey and Greece during the spring of 1852. The traveling writers from

Louisiana and Tennessee may thus have seen each other in a Turkish street or at a Greek ruin, because Dorr described multiple encounters with Parrish in two different cities and amid the temples at the Athenian Acropolis.

Dorr reported that Parrish was a "free man" who "owned property in Nashville," and though he specifically noted his connections with Edwin Ewing, he never referred to Parrish as a "servant" (the word that McGavock used to identify him). Dorr explained that Parrish "had come to Constantinople, with a Mr. Ewing from Nashville . . . to recover from wounds he had received from Arabs that shot him through the shoulder with his own gun, whilst standing over the body of Mr. Ewing, who the Arabs were trying to kill, and thereby saved the life of Mr. Ewing." This heroic action in Egypt, which McGavock also described in his private journal and in a newspaper article, exemplified the manly courage that was also obvious in Parrish's manly body. "Frank is a man about 45 or 50 years of age, and looks like a man in every sense of the word. He is not a yellow, or black man, but what we call ginger-bread color."[21]

Parrish's strong body suggested to Dorr the personal character of a bold man who viewed himself as inherently equal to every human being he met: man or woman, European or Arab, white American or African American or the sultan of the Ottoman Empire. Dorr saw Parrish for the first time while he was watching an earlier-noted procession of the sultan and his attendants pass by on a street in Constantinople. Standing in a great crowd that awaited a glimpse of the sultan, Dorr saw a "very large man, from Nashville, Tennessee," who towered above every other person on the street. The stature of this imposing figure immediately impressed the younger Dorr, but the man's exceptional actions said even more than his physical size about his independent spirit and firm sense of equality:

> His name was Frank Parish. He had in his hand as large a hickory stick as ever a man carried to be a stick; he wore Turkish costume from head to foot. . . . The Sultan stopped every fifty yards and listened to the music. When he stopped close to Frank, he cast his eyes on his great form, and seemed to be interested; and Frank had brass enough to look at the Sultan as he did at other people. Frank took his pipe from his mouth and walked up to the Sultan's carriage and offered his hand which the Sultan took, to the approbation of all present. The seven Sultanas [the sultan's wives] were looking at Frank all the time through their eyelits as if they liked the looks of him. . . . The Sultan could plainly see that his loyal subjects were but as infants, by the giant-like man that stood over them. Being surrounded by such dwarf-like men, he showed off to great advantage. The Sultan is a weak-looking man, and has the marks of fatigue well written on his forehead and limbs.[22]

Dorr thus described Parrish as the most impressive person he saw in Constantinople or in any other place he ever visited. This independent-minded "colored man" appeared to embody the masculine strength and confidence that Dorr sought for himself throughout his European travels; and even the sultan of a great empire seemed to be "weak-looking" when he shook Parrish's strong African American hand. Parrish and Dorr were traveling in subservient social positions on their grand tours of Europe, but they both used their long journeys to claim the social equality and personal freedoms that were not available to them in antebellum America. Indeed, when Dorr encountered Parrish again on the next major stop of their respective tours, he found that this "giant-like" fellow traveler had brought all his remarkable confidence and personal strength from Constantinople to Athens.

Parrish's striking assertion of social equality reappeared in what Dorr described as "another liberty with royalty," which Dorr observed in Athens as the Greek king Otho I came into a large public area to listen to the music of a national band. Emerging from the crowd that had gathered to greet the king, the free-spirited Frank Parrish suddenly stepped forward with the same boldness Dorr had admired in Constantinople. "As the King and his wife rode up to the band," Dorr wrote, "his horses stopped just at Frank's elbow, and Frank walked to the carriage and offered his red hand to the king, and it was, through courtesy, accepted."[23] Although this sympathetic report on "another liberty with royalty" focused on Parrish, it may well have reflected Dorr's own desire to emulate a social confidence that his age, enslavement, or personal timidity prevented him from expressing—at least in the presence of kings.

Parrish's free spirit extended beyond his penchant for shaking hands with monarchs, however, as Dorr explained in descriptions of other Parrish sightings among the ruins of the Acropolis. The typical tourist tour through the ancient Greek temples led to a large slide-like rock whose magical powers were reputed to provide an antidote to female infertility. This was the kind of magic that attracted Dorr's interest, but he was unprepared for what he saw when he went to look at the people who were sliding on the stone. Frank Parrish was seated near the famous rock, talking with a Scotswoman who had come to Athens as "a lady's maid" and now seemed "to be proud of him as a beaux." The "ginger-bread colored" man who had boldly shaken hands with the imperial sultan was now conversing freely with a white woman from Scotland, and Dorr began to wonder how such a Tennessean could move so effortlessly among European women as well as reigning monarchs. He was therefore "determined to hear Frank talk to this Scotchwoman," and he soon positioned himself close enough to listen to the conversation. "He was telling her of his business, which was still going on in Nashville," Dorr reported. "She believed it all, and Frank was in his glory." When the business talk eventually ended, Parrish moved on skillfully to the more gallant challenge of a sentimental farewell; and he knew, as always, how to take decisive, manly action. Parrish "was well versed for the occasion, in Byron. He took her by the hand and looked her in the face affectionately, and said with emotion, 'Maid of Athens, ere we part, give, oh give me back my heart.'"[24]

The poetry seemed to be perfect for this transitional moment. Indeed, the literary adieu gave Dorr new reasons to respect this African American man who casually greeted European kings and also flattered European women by citing Byronic verse amid the ruins of ancient Greek temples. "As Frank was going to my hotel I thought it well to make his acquaintance," Dorr noted with his usual interest in new opportunities, so the two travelers fell into a conversation. Parrish said that he had noticed Dorr in Constantinople and recognized that he must be an American, but he had assumed that Dorr would have little interest in talking with "a mere barber from Tennessee." He was wrong, of course, as we know from Dorr's commentary on Parrish's forceful handshake with the sultan. Dorr had quickly decided that Parrish was "a man in every sense of the word," to quote again from the earlier assessment in Constantinople, and Parrish seemed to confirm his exceptional masculinity when he informed the younger traveler that "he had been married several times, and was now engaged at home."[25] The multiple marriages and other relations with women (even in Athens) provided final, conclusive evidence of Parrish's enviable, independent manhood, in part because enslaved men could not enter into legally recognized marriages and in part because Dorr's trip across Europe included a self-conscious desire for sensual relations with women.

Dorr's Male Fantasies and the Quest for Independent Manhood

Dorr's arrival in Liverpool led quickly to his first encounters with European women as well as his first contacts with wealthy gentlemen. Barely settled into his hotel room, Dorr struck up a conversation with a young hotel worker named "Mary" who "looked so neat" that he decided to "be polite and become acquainted." The notable theme in Dorr's account of this meeting emerged, however, in his statement that a man was "like a dog in some particulars" and that even the briefest encounter with a potential "sexual mate" could provoke manly curiosity. He therefore told the story of meeting Mary in a first-person narrative that helped to establish his own identity as a man whom European women wanted to serve with respectful attention to all his needs. "I shall be here a week said I, and want you to take care of me." According to Dorr, this comment stimulated Mary's interest, and by the time he saw her again in the hallway "her eyes fell upon me just as mine did on her." The specific information about Mary's "care" remained vague, except for references to Mary's eagerness to collect and wash his clothes. In fact, he assured his readers, "I gave her to understand that nothing would give me more pleasure than to have her return again for them," and this reference to the "pleasure" that Dorr derived from the woman who took his clothes carried the kind of double entendre that he would often use to describe his contacts with women.[26] It is of course impossible to discern exactly what happened when Dorr met European women (as a person of racially ambiguous color, did he try to pass as "white" in such encounters?), yet he sought constantly to portray himself as an attractive young man whom women were eager to please. His much-desired status of autonomous manhood, in other words, depended on a hierarchical view of men and women's relationships and an imagined male freedom that included fantasies about accessible women.

Dorr's description of his early flirtations with Mary set the narrative tone for later stories about his experiences in Paris, where the erotic subtext expressed typical American male ideas about the sexual mores of French women. Although the maids at the Hotel des Princes could barely say an English word, they gave Dorr a warm welcome and "left me pretty certain that I was in Paris." Elegant women also filled the hotel dining room, and Dorr began greeting a mysterious princess whom he passed in the hotel hallways or met in the nearby streets. Indeed, the young (enslaved) man from New Orleans quickly became an independent Parisian *flâneur*, observing well-dressed women on the boulevards and enjoying the social prerogatives of a male gaze. "I stood about, looking! Looking! Looking!" Dorr wrote in a summary of the personal freedom he felt in the city of lights, "seeing what is novel enough to an American in Paris."[27]

Following in the footsteps of countless other American male travelers, Dorr soon found his way to the famous garden dances, where he watched international couples swirling around a "melodious band" and reveling in the "dizziness" of an open-air night party. The women danced in beautiful rhythm with gliding, fashionable male partners, who seemed to come from the whole world to find their pleasures in illuminated French gardens.[28] The nightly dances therefore drew Dorr's manly interests, but he also liked his casual social exchanges in French shops, restaurants, and cafés. Dorr admired the young women he saw in these public places, and he was apparently a happy man whenever he simply ordered coffee in a busy Parisian café. "Then look around, not slyly, but boldly," he advised male readers who might visit a café, "and you see some unassuming French *demoiselle* gazing upon you with such riveted force of interest, that the lashes of her eye moveth not." This was the kind of female attention that flattered Dorr and also suggested freer French sexual mores that became all the more intriguing for a young American man who could not even move freely across his own country. The French were "frank and free," Dorr explained to his American readers. "If one admires a lady, she knows it almost before an opportunity presents itself." Like Randal McGavock (who was also visiting dances in Parisian gardens during the summer of 1851), Dorr emphasized the French passion for leisure, but he embraced this passion without any of the Tennessean's ambivalence or guilt. Remembering the freedom and happiness of his days and nights in France's "legendary capital of the nineteenth century," Dorr praised Parisians for living in the present, ignoring the troubles of daily life, and pursuing the pleasures that flowed from food, wine, and love.[29]

There was thus a distinctive French eroticism that Americans could rarely or never see at home, though Dorr was more than willing to hint at what adventurous travelers like himself might find as they strolled around Paris. There were plenty of famous historical sites, of course, but there were other extraordinary sights for the "curious young men" who preferred the vulgarities of uninhibited spectacles. At one such (illegal) show, for example, Dorr watched "a dozen beautiful women habited like Eve before she devised the fig leaf covering" as they formed a provocative wreath "with each one's head between another's legs." This strange performance continued toward a conclusion that "must be imagined," Dorr explained, because he could not possibly provide other details of the "amusement" he had seen.[30] The story of this unusual nightly "amusement" seemed somehow to extend Dorr's account of Parisian eroticism toward a dreamlike evocation of what later psychologists would call "unconscious desires." Indeed, the narrative in *A Colored Man round the World* sometimes linked people, events, and desires in the odd juxtapositions of a fantasy dream, thereby suggesting that a "colored" American man in France (like Dorr?) could actually live his dreams freely in real life—far removed from the shackles of daily existence at home.

Dorr's descriptions of his activities and fantasies in Paris tended to blur the boundaries between dreams and reality, but these sometimes-tenuous boundaries appeared to break down completely in his narrative of a dream he had one night at a hotel near the Seine. If the word "surrealistic" had been available in the early 1850s, Dorr might well have used this adjective to describe the adventures and desires that his dream conveyed. The surrealistic events took place in a dream, whereas the desires came from a personal life in which the daily constraints were all too real. "Can a man dream with his eyes open?" Dorr asked his readers as he

Café in Paris at Night. Oil on canvas by Giuseppe Canella, 1847. Dorr explored the streets, restaurants, parks, and cafés of Paris with the male gaze of a wandering *flâneur*. Canella's painting of the nighttime social life at a Parisian café suggests why a young enslaved traveler from Louisiana could experience new forms of personal freedom in the crowded streets and restaurants of the French capital. Private collection, DeA Picture Library/Art Resource, NY.

launched the story of his dream, "or can a man see with them shut? Before you say no, bear in mind that man is the shadow of his maker; and life, a dream. . . . Then let me dream of what I saw."[31] The dream and the life of the dreamer could not be separated.

Opening in the midst of an elegant, multicourse dinner at a fancy restaurant or nobleman's Parisian home, Dorr's dream narrative carried him quickly from this extravagant party on to the bustling boulevards and eventually into his seat at a table in a fashionable café. This dramatic transition, however, merely opened the door to new pleasures in a dream that moved through diverse and apparently disconnected (or surrealistic) adventures: "A ballet girl entered and seated herself for *la crème*. I then called for some cream and we eat on the same side of the table. I asked her if it was good? She said she liked it, and asked me if mine was the same. As the color was different I could not say, without tasting hers, and we put our glasses together and satisfied ourselves on the difference, after which we took a *vere du vin* at the expense of one of us."[32] Modern readers of Dorr's dream/story would not need psychoanalytic training to recognize the multiple desires that merge in this vivid scene: desires for the manly power of a wealthy noble, for sexual relations with a young French woman, for crossing or fusing the differences of color, and for providing both *la crème* and the wine that confirms the couple's mutual satisfaction. Above all, Dorr dreamed his desire for the power and freedom of a man who could live outside the racist social constraints that defined his identity in America.

This happy interlude with the ballet dancer then gave way immediately in the dream to another scene in which Dorr again found himself among the wealthy nobles he had already met at the elegant dinner party. The men and women in this congenial group communicated with complete, interpersonal transparency and shared a utopian social harmony. All the usual conflicts of social life and human relationships had vanished in this happy fantasy of male/female symbiosis: "When a gentleman had anything to communicate, he was not obliged to exert himself in reaching, because the ladies would meet him half way. Everything was so harmonious that one could not go through the laborious task of telling his wish, without assistance from the hearer. . . . Every minute or two a couple would rise, and before the gentleman could give his arm the lady would reach for it. Even their tempers seemed to fit, as the ocean does the earth."[33] The harmony that the dreaming Dorr had experienced in his friendly café meeting with a French ballerina now expanded to a whole community of free men and women whose relationships suggested total equality or social reconciliation rather than the real-world hierarchies of power, privilege, and slavery. It was a social dream of an imaginary place where everyone could simply be free, equal, and happy; and it replicated (in a material space) Nancy Prince's religious dream of the serene afterlife that would follow the pains of earthly struggles. The dreamed ascent into a completely harmonious Parisian dinner party differed from the religious stairway to heaven, yet both Prince and Dorr imagined a better place that might exist beyond the racist world in which they lived their real lives before and after their extraordinary foreign journeys.

Despite this satisfying denouement, the utopian dinner conversation was not the last scene in Dorr's long Parisian dream. In fact, after awaking for a brief glimpse of the calm-flowing Seine River, Dorr quickly plunged into another deep sleep and returned to his magical dream world of French pleasures. The new dream scene, "*which pleased me most*" (to quote again from Dorr's narrative), placed him on a Parisian sidewalk amid beautiful women who were all looking for something they could not find. One of the women turned to Dorr and asked in French if he knew the time—though she was not really interested in the hour of the day. When Dorr began to answer her question, she lifted her dress to reveal the "whitest stockings I had seen since I left the Dutch, who don't wear stockings at all." Provoked by this unexpected sight, the dreaming Dorr pursued the woman "to see if there was anything good inside the stockings," only to find that the stockings existed solely in his imagination, "like Santa Claus." This abrupt disappointment jolted him from his sleep, and, as he noted with a whiff of regret, "Thus ends the dream with open eyes."[34]

Social reality flowed back into Dorr's life and travel narrative as he moved on to Italy, Turkey, and other Mediterranean countries. The five-page description of his Parisian dreams thus stood out in his book as a climactic summary of his fantasies and aspirations for independent manhood. He placed the story of these memorable dreams at the exact midpoint of *A Colored Man round the World*, so that the previous travel experiences led gradually to this French dreamland, and later experiences extended the dreamed images of freedom, equality, and male/female relations toward other places and people. Dorr's stories about the free-spirited Frank Parrish's encounters with kings became other examples of how he imagined that his African American dream of social equality could come true in European cities. More generally, however, Dorr's desire for free relations with women, like his reports on equal relationships with respectable men, showed why he believed that travel could lead to a new social empowerment and the liberties of a free, personal life.

Dorr continued to write about women and sexual themes after his Parisian sojourn, but the later stories did not always refer so specifically to the eroticism that fascinated him in Paris.[35] There was nevertheless another remarkable story in the account of his visit to Constantinople, where Dorr's desire to be an independent gentleman shaped new fantasies about a Turkish woman. Arriving in the capital of the Ottoman Empire, Dorr soon encountered the disorienting mystery of veiled women. As he explained the experience, women were the "source of low spirits to a man" because they moved "like spirits or shadows, and cannot be seen." This mystery stimulated his sensual curiosity, however, and provoked his apparent psychological need to find admiring women. He soon projected this need onto a woman whom he saw in a parklike cemetery and whom he imagined to be a potential partner—maybe a successor to his servant-friend Mary at Liverpool's Adelphi Hotel. The Muslim woman was wearing a veil, but Dorr "knew she must have been pretty" after watching her for an hour and sensing that she was also looking at him. Although he heard her voice and saw her "delicate" hands, she was not available for his now-experienced male gaze, and, in contrast to his flânerie in Paris, he could not look at what he wanted to see. The local guide warned Dorr that he could never know this woman, even though her mother had decided that "she was for sale." Only a Muslim would be able to buy the young woman, the guide explained, which meant that Dorr had no chance to make a deal. The fact that this young woman was for sale nevertheless attracted Dorr's perverse interest; and in the strangest possible role reversal, the enslaved travel companion of Cornelius Fellowes wanted to know the cost for purchasing the woman whom he now yearned to meet. His guide suggested a price of roughly twenty-five dollars, thus giving Dorr an idea for how to achieve his goals: he proposed to buy the woman and present her as a gift to his guide. "He said he did not know how it could be done," Dorr explained in a factual summary of his offer, but the impossible purchase led to a new question that conveyed the desire he had carried from Liverpool to Paris to Constantinople. "I asked him if he thought the girl would admire me; he had no doubt about that, and added, I need not have any uneasiness about that, as I could make her love me after she was mine, she was obliged to obey me according to Turkish laws."[36]

The socially ambitious (but legally enslaved) traveler could thus imagine himself to be a desirable, respected man, even when he could not act upon his fantasies or use his money to buy love. Whatever else might be said about the gender hierarchies or cultural misconceptions in this Turkish story, Dorr's proposal to buy another person seems especially paradoxical for a "colored man" whose book began and ended with explicit critiques of slavery. Perhaps the would-be free gentleman wanted to show that he understood how the purchase of women could signify a free man's power and status. In any case, Dorr's desire for manly independence led finally in Constantinople to an imagined inversion of his social position; the enslaved man would own another human being. It should be stressed, however, that this fantasy was by no means the endpoint of Dorr's journey. *A Colored Man* returned eventually to the critique of slavery that emerged in the book's preface, reappeared in Dorr's Parisian dreams, and concluded in the author's claims for the existential selfhood of a free man.

Dorr's Journey from Slavery to Freedom and American National Identity

Dorr's criticisms of slavery never evolved into a systematic, abolitionist critique of the slave system. In contrast to the more militant arguments of other abolitionists, Dorr's antislavery themes emerged somewhat indirectly in his accounts of free Black men such as Frank Parrish or in his passing references to the oppression of African Americans in the United States. His strongest abolitionist statement eventually came in his escape from Louisiana rather than in the words of his book about Europe. He lived again in New Orleans for a short, post-journey time before he fled from Cornelius Fellowes on his defiant escape toward the "legal freedom of England, France, and our New England States."[37] Although this prefatory reference to the greater freedom in European nations was a somewhat oblique challenge to American nationalist assumptions about the homeland of modern freedom, Dorr's later critiques of the slave system show how his European travel became a key experiential step on his long journey toward self-emancipation. His discussion of the American exhibitions at London's Crystal Palace, for example, noted sarcastically that an enslaver from South Carolina had "proposed taking half a dozen haughty and sinewy negroes to the Fair, but was only deterred from that proposition by the want of courage to risk six fat, strong healthy negroes to the chances of escape from slavery to freedom."[38]

Dorr went on to emphasize the broader social opportunities that would follow a transition "from slavery to freedom" when he reported in Athens that the entire population of modern Greece was only one-fourth as large as the number of enslaved African Americans in the United States. The emancipation of America's enslaved people, he pointed out, would thus create a new, free population whose numbers and achievements could far exceed the social and political significance of modern Greece. "Our slaves would make four kingdoms as powerful in population as Greece," Dorr explained, thus suggesting how the American slave system limited the nation's potential power in the wider world. In addition to undermining national strength, however, slavery revealed America's profound national hypocrisy. "Oh, when," Dorr asked, "will we be the 'Freest government in the world'?"[39] Indeed, America's self-congratulatory praise for its exceptional freedom made it impossible for white people within the United States to see how the European rejection of slavery made European governments superior (in this respect) to the oppressive flaws in the social and political system he had seen and experienced at home. Among all "the German kingdoms," he reported in one of his cross-cultural comparisons, "the most despotic is Austria; but she hates slavery more than the 'freest government in the world.'" Dorr's references to American politics set up a self-conscious, critical distance by always placing the phrase "freest government" in quotation marks and by suggesting that even antidemocratic European regimes showed how the systemic oppressions of slavery undermined America's social-political ideals. "Austria tyrannizes over man," he explained, "but she cannot tyrannize, chattelize, and prostrate their rights with impunity, any more than Washington, Jefferson, or Henry could."[40] The hypocrisy of America's liberty-speaking, slaveholding Founding Fathers became all too obvious for an American "colored man" in Europe; and who among his white or Black readers could deny this historical fact?

This emphasis on the contradictions of American slaveholders extended from the history of the nation's founders to the social lives of people Dorr knew in his own daily life, including his enslaving "master," Cornelius Fellowes. Indeed, his description of Fellowes resembled his fantasy purchase of the young Muslim woman in that he placed both the unknown woman and Fellowes in the position of a material object under his own gaze—much like upper-class southern gentlemen described the enslaved persons whom they bought and sold in local slave markets. The meaning of Dorr's challenge to his hometown's slave-system hierarchies becomes more obvious when his text is compared to some reports that the French traveler Elisée Reclus wrote during and after he lived in Louisiana in 1853–55. Reclus would later become a well-known geographer and political anarchist in France, but his opposition to Napoleon III's coup d'état in the early 1850s led him to seek safety and freedom in Louisiana, where he worked as a tutor and traveled around the state on a kind of mirror-image reversal of Dorr's travel in Europe.

The blatant hypocrisies of American republican society both disillusioned and angered Reclus, as he noted in reports such as this account of an auction he observed in New Orleans:

> On a platform stands the auctioneer, a large, red-faced, bloated man with a booming voice. "Come on, Jim! Get up on the table. . . . Look how strong he is! He's got good teeth! Look at the muscles on his arms! . . . "Then it is a Negro woman's turn. "Look at this wench! . . . Look at her strong back and sturdy chest! She's a good wet nurse, and a good negress for work!" And the bidding starts again amid laugher and shouts. Thus all the Negroes of Louisiana pass in turn on this fateful table: children who have just ended their seventh year and whom the law in its solicitude deems old enough to be separated from their mothers; young girls subjected to the stares of two thousand spectators and sold by the pound; [and] mothers who come to see their children stolen from them, and who are obliged to remain cheerful while threatened by the whip. . . . According to the advocates of slavery, all this is willed by the cause of progress itself, the doctrines of our holy religion, and the most sacred laws of family and property.[41]

Reclus lived in Louisiana during the same years in which Dorr returned to the state as an enslaved man, so Dorr understood exactly how his description of Fellowes inverted the racist, dehumanizing hierarchy that Reclus described in his report on the New Orleans slave market. "He is rather more than a medium size man . . . with handsome limbs," Dorr wrote in his narrative portrait of the man who controlled his life. "He cannot be justly termed handsome, without adding *man*. His face was the color of last year's red apple all free from decay; his hair is light for black, and not very thick on top, and he is aged 48 years."[42]

Sale of Estates, Pictures and Slaves in the Rotunda, New Orleans. Engraving by J. M. Starling, 1842. Despite his self-representation as a free traveler in Europe, Dorr was still an enslaved man who remained acutely aware of how the slave system (and Cornelius Fellowes) denied the rights, freedom, and humanity of Black people in his American home city. This disturbing picture shows the brutal, dehumanizing treatment of enslaved human beings whom auctioneers "sold" to bidders as if they were insentient objects in a Louisiana enslaver's collection of material possessions. Pictorial Press Ltd/Alamy Stock Photo.

Dorr thus defined Fellowes as a rather *ordinary* kind of man, though the explicit reference to his age (roughly twenty-four years older than the author who portrayed him) suggests why he could have embodied an *extraordinary* "connection" to Dorr's life: as his never-identified biological father. Although the exact link between the two men remains obscure, Dorr ultimately asserted his own independence by writing about Fellowes with the kind of objectifying language that a "gentleman master" might have used to describe enslaved persons he was ready to sell and send away forever. Equally significant for a psychological reading of this word portrait, Dorr's narrative moved quickly from the body and face to a more detailed discussion of how Fellowes had achieved his success in business and maintained his superior position in the social hierarchy: "He is a very liberal and extravagant man . . . but he is by no means a benevolent man." He could thus be generous with others, but only on his own terms and only in ways that complicated Dorr's own (respectful/rebellious) relationship with this older white man.[43]

It seemed to be difficult for Dorr to speak honestly and completely about his complex, personal relationship with Fellowes, yet his travel stories clearly suggested that a disconcerting hierarchy shaped all the interactions between the older man and the younger man. "He is so proud, or haughty, or perhaps I had better say, naturally aristocratic," Dorr explained, "that he can descend from his sphere to vulgar without knowing it, and joke, laugh, and even offer some of his drink, but if you forget yourself, he will recollect himself." No matter how friendly the two men became, in other words, there were certain lines that Dorr could never cross or challenge without hitting the limits of his lower social identity. "He can treat a free colored man as polite as he can a poor white one," Dorr continued, but this generosity always depended on the mutual recognition that Fellowes stood on higher racial and social ground. When Fellowes felt comfortably in control, he was "happy" and "jovial" and "scarcely ever disappointed with his calculations of things and people."[44] The social boundaries of this joviality nevertheless became obvious whenever the hierarchical order began to break down, as Dorr showed by describing how Fellowes responded to the beggars who approached him throughout his European trip.

Fellowes liked to give coins to people who begged for money, perhaps because his generosity also confirmed his position in social hierarchies; but his typical goodwill disappeared when he encountered an assertive group of young beggars on a beach in Holland. Although the interactions began happily enough because the Dutch boys misidentified Fellowes as a prominent "count" from New York, Dorr's "master" soon lost control of the situation. "About sixty or seventy had circled him" to demand money, Dorr noted, but none of the other American travelers came to help him. In fact, Dorr and his unnamed travel companions simply began "laughing to ourselves because we saw he was vexed and felt himself in a dilemma." The beggars began to dig in Fellowes's pockets, looking for coins he would not give and making demands he could not answer. Faced with this unruly crowd, "Mr. Fellowes showed tokens of fear" and called for the Dutch guides to free him from the swarming supplicants whom he accused of robbing him. The usually "jovial" Mr. Fellowes "tried to put on a pleasing countenance," but his struggle to escape left him so shaken that he wanted to return immediately to his hotel for safety. His self-confidence seemed to dissolve as the young beggars crossed the boundaries of a social hierarchy in which Fellowes always wanted to live his comfortable life. Indeed, Fellowes was still flustered when he reached his hotel, climbed out of his coach, tripped over his Dutch guide's wooden shoe, and struggled to regain his dignity as he headed into the hotel, muttering "in an undertone, d——n the

Dutch."[45] Dorr described these events with the bemused tone of an observer who enjoyed a social inversion that his "master" could not control, but Fellowes himself was not amused. He quickly decided that the Dutch "were not in his opinion, as agreeable as they might be. [And] he left next day, although he intended staying a week."[46]

Dorr's account of Fellowes and the Dutch beggars became a semi-carnivalesque example of the author's interest in overturning traditional hierarchies that always placed the "master" in confident command and the younger, enslaved man in a subservient social position. The older gentleman from Louisiana could not tolerate questions or actions that destabilized the conventional social order, but Dorr's European trip helped him transgress some of the boundaries he would later cross again when he demanded (and then fled to) his freedom in America. Where other American travelers often wrote about the oppressive social hierarchies in European societies, Dorr found that European travel mostly freed him from the oppressive social hierarchies that blocked his life in the United States. These hierarchies, as Dorr showed through descriptions of his disoriented "master," began to break down during a journey that enabled Dorr to act as independently as anyone who lived freely in Europe or America. The European trip, in short, became the foundation for Dorr's future life as a free man.

Dorr's portrayal of Fellowes thus provided another opportunity to assert both his personal equality and his desire for the public identity of an American gentleman. There were in fact some striking countercurrents in the themes and perspectives of *A Colored Man round the World* because Dorr bracketed his critiques of American racism and slavery within an otherwise optimistic narrative about his home country's future social and political evolution. Like Fuller and McGavock, Dorr repeatedly stressed his strong identification with American culture and conveyed a remarkable pride in America's potential for future national achievements—if only the United States would abolish slavery. Summarizing his own political vision for America, Dorr assured his readers that the "author of this book, though a colored man, hopes to die believing that this federated government is destined to be the noblest fabric ever germinated in the brain of men or the tides of Time."[47]

This optimistic view made a clear distinction between the future "federated government" and the nineteenth-century government that most (white) Americans already called the world's "freest government"—a popular nationalist phrase that Dorr always placed within his ironic quotation marks. Despite America's obvious flaws in the 1850s, however, Dorr drew on both his abolitionist perspectives and European travels to explain why people in the United States could expect a better national future. "Though a colored man," Dorr continued, "he believes that he has the right to say that in his opinion, *the American people are to be the Medes and Persians of the 19th century.*" The United States was fast becoming an impressive political and economic power that other nations would have to respect (as the non-European Persians were respected in antiquity), yet this international respect would never really develop until the American government represented the "*will of the whole people.*" Dorr claimed that his optimistic vision for the American future was based on what he had "seen in the four quarters of the globe" and on what his travels had taught him about the political advantages of adhering to a sovereign popular will.[48] European nations faced multiple social or political obstacles that impeded their efforts to implement the sovereign will of the people, but Dorr saw the injustice of the slave system as the great, *specific* obstacle to full popular sovereignty in the United States.

Although the continuing defense of slavery was the greatest impediment to America's quest for international respect, Dorr wanted his American readers to understand that their global reputation also suffered from an inability to convey their innovative economic achievements in European venues. London's Crystal Palace exhibitions offered one example of the problem. He explained in his eyewitness account of this famous international spectacle that he could see no evidence of American economic ingenuity in a national display that simply exhibited "all the most worthless trash to be found in the States": piles of cheap shoes, clothing, clocks, boots, and saddles. Noting his shame as he looked at such worthless objects, Dorr yearned to see an impressive American steamboat or other inventions that might better represent the nation's economic creativity. His report suggested that he was as patriotic as any white American citizen who had ever walked into a world's fair, but he conveyed his patriotism by frankly explaining how Europeans perceived the limitations and flaws of America's commercial products.[49] There were in fact plenty of misperceptions on both sides of the Atlantic, yet Dorr was most eager to correct the racist misperception of himself as a lesser man. He therefore sought constantly to affirm his independent American selfhood by showing how his trip "round the world" had given him the cultural knowledge and elevated status of a patriotic, free American gentleman.

Dorr's Claim for Knowledge of History, Politics, and Culture

Dorr was proud to claim a traveler's special expertise on almost everything he saw in Europe, including historical sites in famous cities and the ruins of ancient civilizations. Europeans may not have known much about America, but Dorr was more concerned about American misperceptions of the freedoms and achievements in other cultures. He therefore wanted to expand his own nation's cross-cultural knowledge by sharing what he learned from traveling to distant places his readers would never see. Many of Dorr's reports, however, simply repeated the traditional clichés of books about a European Grand Tour as he dutifully described the historic monuments that Americans needed to visit on a journey toward the status of a cultured, transatlantic traveler. He also laced his commentaries with the obligatory allusions to Byron, Shakespeare, and Homer to convey a kind of guidebook veracity.[50] These descriptions of famous sites showed the range of his tour, but they lacked the passion that reappeared whenever Dorr discussed people or events that connected with his self-conscious quest for an independent, manly identity: the descriptions of Frank Parrish, for example, or the reports about meeting European women or the summary of his vivid dreams in a Parisian hotel.

Dorr's favorite knowledge came from personal experiences rather than from history books and tourist guides. Other travel writers might summarize the *grande cuisine* or images on the menus at expensive restaurants, but Dorr preferred to provide the inside information that the popular "rabbit" dishes in some Parisian eating places were really roasted cats. How, then, could skeptical Americans trust such statements? "Now reader," Dorr responded in one of his typical, first-person dialogues with an unknown audience, "don't accuse me of trying to become conspicuous by asserting more than others, for you know nothing about it, and I do." His stories, in other words, shared a distinctive, hard-earned knowledge that came directly from personal experiences that most Americans could only imagine in their dreams. "I have dined," he noted with a traveler's pride, "at the *Maison Dorée*, *Trois Freres*, *Café Anglaise*, and *Vachettes*." If this list failed to convince those who doubted that well-sauced "rabbits" were often disguised "cats," Dorr could back up his culinary revelations with assurances that he had eaten at all kinds of French restaurants "down to the lowest grade." This was the experiential base for his European knowledge and for his often-stated personal opinions, all of which rested on the first-person claim that "I ought to know something about it."[51] You had to be there to know about Notre Dame Cathedral, the Vatican Palace, or French restaurants, and nobody who lived only in America would ever see ancient architecture, famous monarchs, or political battles in the streets of Paris.

Although Dorr liked to describe his sightings of European royalty, he also encountered other political actors when he became caught up in the French uprising against Louis-Napoleon's coup d'état while he was visiting Paris in December 1851. France was known for its revolutions, so the opportunity to view political clashes in the French capital added valuable "I was there" credibility for a writer from Louisiana, especially when the most prominent figure in this conflict was a nephew of the famous Napoleon Bonaparte. The ambitious, authoritarian-minded Louis-Napoleon Bonaparte had been elected president of the Second French Republic in 1848, but the constitution restricted him to a single four-year term. When the republic's legislators rejected a constitutional change that would have allowed another presidential term, Louis-Napoleon launched a military coup and then declared himself to be Emperor Napoleon III of a Second French Empire (claiming public support through a national plebiscite).[52]

The coup provoked sharp resistance in the provinces and in Paris, where Dorr saw the French army crush the anti-Bonapartist protests and take control of the city's streets and public spaces. Dorr identified with people who were struggling to be free, so his account of the street battles condemned the brutal military repression in which at least 150 protesters were killed in Paris alone. He saw an older man pleading with soldiers for their political solidarity as they threatened to fire on protesters near the barricades in a crowded street, and he watched in horror as the commander ordered his troops to shoot the man dead. Dorr fled along with other angry, frightened people who had gathered on the Boulevard des Italiens, but he could not easily escape the violence or get around the wounded protesters who were falling everywhere into bloody, lifeless heaps. "I fell," Dorr reported in his description of the battles, "and a dozen or so [other fleeing people] leaped over me. Like a tangled rabbit I rose and went faster than ever." He eventually reached the safety of his hotel, yet the memory of the violence was so haunting that he was determined to see other parts of the city over the next few days. Wherever he went in the usually gay metropolis, Dorr remembered, "Paris looked as if it was mourning for those thousands that were fleetly moving on to eternity."[53]

The human costs of Bonaparte's coup were immediately obvious to anyone who dared to walk through the damaged city streets, but the political costs of the coup became equally visible as Dorr reflected on what he called the "cruel" repression of innocent people. Bonaparte's overthrow of the Second French Republic became another nineteenth-century example of France's enduring deference to "royal blood" and of the recurring French hostility for what Dorr called the "seed of republicanism."[54] These historical generalizations were debatable, but Dorr's reports on a suppressed political rebellion showed again that he had gained exceptional, firsthand knowledge of European cultures and social conflicts.

Dorr also liked to claim superior knowledge whenever he criticized misinformed guides for distorting the history of famous places they described to foreign visitors, and he decided that the guides in Palestine were among the most impressive experts in the high-paid work of historical lying. A local expert at the sacred site of Mount Sinai, for example, told strange legends "without the least shadow of history for support," and other guides in Bethlehem and Jericho recounted "absurd" religious stories that no educated person could possibly believe. Dorr repeatedly ridiculed the alleged expertise of almost everyone he met in the "Holy Land," thus establishing his own cultural stature by diminishing the knowledge of guides who "could not read" and monks who devoted their lives to collecting money. "I was not inclined to believe anything I heard from the people about here," he wrote of his Holy Land pilgrimage, "because I knew as much as they did about it. I came to Jerusalem with a submissive heart, but when I heard all the absurdities of these ignorant people, I was more inclined to ridicule right over these sacred dead bodies, and spots, than [to] pay homage."[55] This was a bold claim for a superior knowledge that meant more to Dorr than religious piety or the sanctity of the sacred places he visited. He wanted to explain how the guides in Palestine told myths rather than history, in the same way that he wanted to show how Europeans and Americans wrote myths when they devalued the history of North Africa.

Dorr argued that Black North Africans had been the most accomplished people in the early Mediterranean world and the source for much of the knowledge that would later shape the greatest ancient civilizations. "Here it was," Dorr explained after his arrival in Egypt, "that Greece and Italy were schooled in all that they excelled; here it was that Moses obtained his fundamental rules of governing nations of people."[56] No traveler who saw the grandeur of the Egyptian pyramids, Dorr noted in his report on the enormous stone constructions, could doubt that this ancient African society had mobilized exceptional power and knowledge to transform natural environments as well as the social organization of human labor. The grandeur of the pyramids confirmed the "talent, intelligence, and power" of ancient Egyptian kings, who organized thousands of workers to move huge stones across the desert. These vast armies of Egyptian workers and soldiers contradicted the historical lies that regularly disparaged Africa's extraordinary cultural achievements, but who were the Egyptian people? "Egypt was a higher sphere of artistical science than any other nation on the earth," Dorr noted in his historical summary of the culture's significance. "This will naturally convey an idea to the world that the black man was the first skillful animal on the earth, because Homer describes the Egyptians as men with wooly hair, thick lips, flat feet, and black [skin], and we have no better authority than Homer."[57]

Dorr never referred to slavery in his allusions to Homer or in his descriptions of ancient Egyptian kings, yet there was a clear subtext for readers who reflected on the implications of his historical narrative. Evoking the kind of argument for racial equality that Nancy Prince also developed in her account of emancipated Black people in Jamaica, Dorr insisted that early North African civilization equaled or exceeded the accomplishments of every other ancient Mediterranean culture. Although racist American enslavers wanted to ignore these irrefutable facts, Egyptian history demonstrated that free Africans had long flourished outside oppressive slave systems and long before Americans had ever established their modern racial and social hierarchies. A trip to Egypt therefore revealed both the historical significance of African civilizations and the historical lies of American slaveholders.

Dorr's Affirmation of His Free Selfhood

The enslaved young man from Louisiana thus used his journey through Europe and the Middle East to show the injustices of slavery and to assert his personal claims for the identity of an autonomous American traveler. By the time he reached the final paragraphs of his book, Dorr was affirming what might be called the "proto-existential" celebration of a free self. Writing the story of his travels, as he described the process, had enabled him to take additional *intellectual* steps toward his long journey's ultimate destination: the self-emancipation of a once-enslaved person and the emergence of independent manhood. "I feel in taking leave of this work," he wrote in a concluding summary of the book's meaning to its author, "as if I was parting with an old and familiar friend that I could stay much longer with, but I am afraid to stay much longer lest I enhance its value as a friend. *A Friend*? Yes, a friend."[58]

Like other authors in different times and places, Dorr realized that he had developed an intense intellectual and emotional relationship with his own book, so that leaving his written work resembled the sadness of ending long conversations with a best friend. Dorr never read Friedrich Nietzsche, of course, but his ambivalence about "parting" from his book anticipated Nietzsche's famous, ambivalent farewell to his own words in *Beyond Good and Evil* (1886). Writing almost thirty years after Dorr said goodbye to *A Colored Man round the World*, Nietzsche also spoke of his own text like a linguistic friend who must inevitably set off for unknown places. "Alas, what are you after all, my written and painted thoughts! It was not long ago that you were still so colorful, young, and malicious . . . you made me sneeze and laugh—and now?" Nietzsche went on to compare his evolving, written thoughts to the bright morning colors that change all too quickly into the shadowy colors of a late afternoon or the late autumnal colors of a withering plant. The metaphors in his literary farewell were thus more poetic than Dorr's allusions to a parting friend, but Dorr would surely have understood the later German philosopher's last words in a text that had also become his friend: "Nobody will guess . . . how you looked in your morning, you sudden sparks and wonders of my solitude, you my old beloved—*wicked* thoughts."[59]

Linking Dorr to Nietzsche makes an unlikely connection between two writers who lived in very different social-cultural contexts and confronted extremely different personal and intellectual issues. Dorr's concluding affirmation of his own, independent selfhood nevertheless carried a surprising "proto-Nietzschean" emphasis on the noble quest for a free, self-defined ethical code and personal identity. Stressing his desire to "tell the thing as I saw it" rather than to repeat the clichéd stories of other writers, Dorr praised his self-defined interests in the "strange places" he visited while he was still a "young man." He viewed his trip as exceptional because he had been an enslaved traveler whose voyage "round the world" showed the willful determination of youth rather than the limitations of his dependent social position. His adventures thus confirmed that "youth must find his own crag on the mountain, rivet his eye of determined prosperity up the cliffy wiles of life, kick asunder impediments and obstacles, and climb on."[60] There was a typical nineteenth-century (Byronic) Romanticism in this assertion of youthful independence, but the themes also anticipated the later Nietzschean or existential insistence that free persons must "climb" beyond the obstacles that emerge in every human life.

Dorr therefore believed that his long journey offered useful lessons for others who yearned to be free, including enslaved persons in the United States. The challenges and opportunities of a long trip, as he explained in his concluding reflections, pointed the way toward a new life for anyone (enslaved and free alike) who decided to take self-creating personal actions. "When you hear *can't*, laugh at it; when they tell you *not in your time*, pity them; and when they tell you *surrounding circumstances alter cases*, in manliness scorn them as sleeping sluggards, unworthy of a social brotherhood."[61] Although Dorr returned here to his personal emphasis on "manliness," his larger theme emphasized the free human being's ability to construct an independent identity—a strong, noble self that evolved on the margins or even outside the constraining "circumstances" of conventional social life.

This argument evoked "proto-Nietzschean" themes because, like Nietzsche, Dorr downplayed the inescapable social components of human action. He insisted that a self-defined (noble) person must "kick asunder" the reigning social "impediments" and ignore all those who answered "can't" to the demand for a free life. When close-minded people denied the equality of human rights with racist claims about the meaning of skin color, for example, the independent, self-defined person must assert the deeper unity of all human races. Indeed, Dorr claimed that the French scientist George-Louis Leclerc, comte de Buffon, had shown already in the eighteenth century that the individuals on each continent were "nothing but the same man differently dyed by climate," thereby providing scientific proof for underlying similarities that were far more significant than superficial differences in the color of human skin. Ignorant people would always look for racial differences or oppose the free actions of bold, independent persons, but Dorr dismissed such people as mere obstacles to bypass on the journey to manly independence. "Then away with your *can't,*" he concluded; "when backed to the wall by the debater, you had better say, as I say while taking leave of you, *au revoir.*"[62] This last sentence reasserted Dorr's claim to be equal with anyone who read his book. He had been an enslaved man who now refused to be a slave and who would no longer allow others to define the limits of his freedom. This already bold assertion became even stronger as Dorr noted that he had *chosen* to leave the book and his readers. Only a free man could *choose* to leave others or decide when it was time to say goodbye, *au revoir.*

The farewell to his own book and his imagined readers thus became Dorr's final assertion of personal freedom on a long journey toward "manly" independence that began during his trip to Europe, expanded during his self-emancipating flight to Ohio, and reached a public destination in the self-referential narrative of *A Colored Man round the World.* Dorr transformed his voyage into a gendered (male) narrative about distant countries and cross-cultural experiences, but his book also showed how long voyages to unknown places could take *any* modern traveler into new conceptions and personal experiences of autonomous selfhood.

EPILOGUE TO PART III

African American Travelers and the Quest for Freedom within and beyond Antebellum America

NANCY PRINCE AND DAVID DORR both had to navigate their lives within and across the sharp racial boundaries in nineteenth-century American culture, but their quests for respect and equality diverged as they responded to the specific social contexts in which they lived and traveled. Their differences developed from the contrasting personal and cultural experiences that shaped their journeys: the gendered constraints and opportunities that separated a woman (married and then widowed) from a single man; the legal distinctions that separated a free person from an enslaved person; the sectional and regional traditions that posed different problems for African American families in Massachusetts and Louisiana; and the social-cultural-political histories that made a journey into Russia or Jamaica different from a journey across western Europe or the Middle East. Setting out from different social positions, their travels and ambitions also led them toward different identities as they responded to the racism and racial hierarchies that influenced every aspiration and social reality they sought to affirm or escape. Wherever they went, however, both traveling writers looked for new opportunities to assert their personal and cultural freedom.

Prince's travel narrative, for example, linked her experiences to the traditional religious story of a pilgrimage in which personal afflictions and painful, public setbacks would lead ultimately to a final reconciliation with God. Although she vividly described the endless hardships that threatened her during every phase of her eventful life (a broken family, the death of a husband, poverty, hostile religious leaders, slave traders in port cities, and so on), every painful struggle gained spiritual meaning as a prelude to the "glory that shall be revealed hereafter."[1] The earthly days before that eventual "glory" meanwhile carried moral imperatives for decisive public actions, as she explained in her accounts of recurring attempts to provide orphanages for needy children, schools for emancipated girls, and religious instruction for poorly educated Christians. The often-painful journey toward eternal spiritual salvation and the struggle for religiously inspired social reforms ultimately merged in Prince's self-defined identity as a virtuous, respectable woman.

The manly self-identity that Dorr sought to construct through his accounts of an almost-free traveler in Europe, by contrast, emerged from a narrative that gave relatively little attention to the hardships of his own enslavement. Dorr focused instead on the pleasures of a would-be gentleman (flirtations with European women, visits to dance gardens and cafés, conversations with wealthy people, knowledgeable tours of historic sites, good service in nice hotels), but these pleasures gradually took on wider social meanings as examples of his evolving escape from the chains of enslavement. Each of his interactions with the free persons he met on his travels provided more evidence of the free life of a young gentleman who chose to "laugh" whenever he was told that he could not act independently in his American hometown or in the European cities he visited during his long trip. Prince referred to her benevolent, womanly attempts to help other people, whereas Dorr wrote about his personal attempts to live the free, uninhibited life of a (somewhat unconventional) American gentleman.

These contrasts in Prince's and Dorr's self-constructed identities suggest the important differences in their gendered social lives and travel experiences, but the similarities in their long journeys and complex lives may have been more significant than their differences. Both these writers wanted to leave the racist hierarchies that shaped their early lives; and they both embraced travel (and travel writing) as a social experience that could help them develop a new social status as respected, independent people. Travel to foreign lands gave them a cultural experience from which they claimed an expertise that white American writers also claimed for themselves whenever they wrote about other societies. The cultural expertise in an African American writer's travel narrative took on additional social-political meanings, however, because the accounts of new knowledge about distant places opened new opportunities to assert the autonomy and equality of a free Black personhood that was not accepted within antebellum American society.

Independent, well-informed "colored" travelers (to use Dorr's self-definition) therefore used both their personal lives and their stories of foreign societies to demonstrate the injustice and absurdity of racism and the oppressive slave system. Prince and Dorr shared a deep desire for freer social conditions that would enable them to break away from the confinement of families or poverty or slavery or dependence on other people. Although they held diverging views of religion and leisure-time pleasures, they were united by abolitionist views of slavery that grew even stronger over the course of their travels. In this respect, Prince and Dorr clearly resembled Margaret Fuller rather than Randal McGavock, but they also resembled most other thoughtful American travelers (no matter how they otherwise differed) in developing a deeper awareness of their distinctive *American* identities as they made their way across unfamiliar foreign societies and cultures.

The changing identities and social status of a respected traveling writer became especially valuable for African Americans who could not gain comparable recognition of their independent selfhood within the United States. Prince and Dorr both used a somewhat disjointed, even dreamlike prose style that plunged readers into disorienting scenes and then quickly moved on to other stories about unfamiliar places, people, or social customs. The writing itself often conveyed the meandering freedom of an open-ended journey. Their narratives also emphasized the independence and cultural achievements of free Africans in Europe, Jamaica, and Egypt, giving readers a social and racial perspective that rarely appeared in the travel books of white American writers. In contrast to the prevailing European American assumptions about modern world history, these African American writers showed how people in other nations could be freer or more enlightened than most people within the United States. Black Americans, as their travel books confirmed, found more freedom abroad than they could ever find amid the slave system or racial prejudices at home. Prince and Dorr always faced the enduring obstacles of social and racial hierarchies, but their unconventional travel books showed how "Black Atlantic" travelers could also defy the constraints of racism and slavery by living in cultures and societies far outside the United States.

An evolving sense of personal freedom helped Prince and Dorr challenge the social hierarchies and the reigning ideas about race, gender, religion, and national citizenship that threatened both travelers before and after their journeys. The cross-cultural experiences of self-conscious travelers could thus offer both liberation and empowerment, even though there were always social constraints and cultural codes that shaped travel as fully as they shaped every other human activity. No traveler could really escape from the hierarchical social structures that existed everywhere in the world. Travel nevertheless fostered a deepening belief in the "free self" and helped to create empowering new identities for women as well as men, for religious persons as well as scientists, and for ambitious Europeans as well as white and Black writers from the northern and southern United States.

PART IV

Redefining French Selfhood in Nineteenth-Century America

Nicolas Point and Olympe Audouard

INTRODUCTION TO PART IV

French Journeys into American Cities and the Far West

French travelers began visiting North America in the early seventeenth century, and they continued to travel across all parts of the continent long after France had given up its colonial territories in Quebec and Louisiana. Some later travelers retained a strong interest in the French-speaking regions of Canada, but after the American Revolution most transatlantic visitors from France wanted to understand how the United States was developing its new national government, commerce, and culture. In addition to ambitious entrepreneurs and exiles fleeing revolutionary violence, America in the late eighteenth and early nineteenth centuries attracted French writers such as François-René de Chateaubriand, scientists such as Victor Jacquemont, political leaders such as Lafayette, political theorists such as Alexis de Tocqueville, and a steady stream of merchants, missionaries, and alienated radicals—most of whom assumed they would discover new social or political freedoms as well as new perspectives on the European culture from which they had come. Although a few of these journeys became famous, most French visitors who wrote about their American experiences have largely disappeared from historical memory.[1]

A comprehensive account of these mostly forgotten French travelers could lead readers into almost every sphere of modern American or French culture, but this concluding comparison of nineteenth-century writers focuses on how the journeys of Nicolas Point and Olympe Audouard helped both travelers affirm French cultural identities and claim a new cultural status as eyewitness experts on lesser-known people or places in North America.

Point was a Jesuit priest who moved to the United States in 1835, became a missionary during the 1840s among North American Indians in areas that would later become the states of Montana and Idaho, wrote long letters and journal entries about his missionary work, drew pictures of Native Americans whom he met on open prairies and in high mountains, and ultimately died in Quebec without ever returning to France. Point thus traveled with the goal of converting others to his religion. Audouard, by contrast, was an energetic travel writer and novelist who visited New York in 1868, set off on a long trip to the far west, developed a particular interest in western American Indians and in the Mormon communities of Utah, and wrote two travel books about the United States after she returned to France in 1869. Although she spent only about a year in America, Audouard drew on her travels to demonstrate (like Tocqueville) an experience-based expertise on the country she had come to know in railroad cars, hotel dining rooms, and conversations with local leaders.[2]

Point and Audouard differed in their views of politics, gender relations, and Native Americans, but they were both French Catholics who used their American travel experiences to develop critiques of their home-country society and to connect their views of religion (Point) or gender relationships (Audouard) with cultural differences they discovered in America. Despite the many divergences in their personal lives and American travels, they both sought to construct a more respected public identity and a more secure religious or cultural selfhood. They both also felt stymied or harassed by political and social forces in France, so their long trips opened alternative opportunities for the blocked aspirations of a Jesuit missionary and an independent woman writer. They never knew each other, of course, and they would surely have disagreed if they had ever discussed the divisive religious and political issues in nineteenth-century France. At the same time, however, they might well have agreed that their American travels gave them much-needed alternatives to the constraints they had faced in their home country: the repression of the Jesuits and the secularization of French society (for Point) and the inequality of women in French politics, education, marriage laws, and economic life (for Audouard). Personal disappointments and cultural obstacles thus pushed both Point and Audouard to explore new public identities and new meanings of selfhood that could emerge through the experiences of transatlantic travel. Their journeys into remote regions of North America led them also into some of the remote places within their inescapable French selfhood. In most general terms, however, their evolving cultural identities and self-definitions can be seen in the different ways they drew on their American travels to discuss the transnational meaning of modern civilization (and their places within it).

French travel writers in the eighteenth and nineteenth centuries often debated whether America revealed the traits of past phases of human civilization (the "prehistoric" era of "noble" or "savage" people) or the likely pathway toward future phases of modern civilization. An important transition in French views took place during the first half of the nineteenth century, when America came to be viewed mainly as an example of modern economic and political systems.[3] Alexis de Tocqueville's descriptions of the United States are the best-known example of this new French perspective, but many French travelers continued to look for a distinctive American past while they were also speculating about America's future international influence.

These parallel interests emerge in the contrasting narratives of Nicolas Point and Olympe Audouard, both of whom wrote about vulnerable, "premodern" Native American cultures as well as the dynamic "modern" society that was shaping a new national culture while it expelled American Indians beyond the social-political boundaries of an expanding national state. Point and Audouard defined their own identities by writing in different ways about the contrasting aspects of the "premodern" and "modern" American people and cultures they encountered. Point linked his aspirations and identity to the Native American cultures he found in the northern Rocky Mountains; Audouard, by contrast, linked her aspirations and identity to the social and political cultures of European American communities she visited in both the eastern and western American states. These two traveling writers therefore described different patterns of "premodern" and "modern" social life in the United States, but they both assumed that Europeans could learn useful lessons from the diverse historical layers and social systems they encountered during their transnational journeys.

CHAPTER SEVEN

Nicolas Point's American Journey for Religious Truth, Cultural Knowledge, and Social Recognition

Nicolas Point was born in 1799 and grew up in the small French town of Rocroi, which is on the Belgian border northeast of Reims. Point's father died in 1804, leaving his wife, Nicole Point, to raise three young children with little money—but with the support and encouragement of the local Catholic church. The Point family thus developed close connections with the church, and all the children would pursue Catholic vocations; Nicolas had an older sister and younger brother who would also join religious orders and eventually immigrate to North America. An energetic priest began to organize new schools at Rocroi after Napoleon signed the Concordat of 1801 with the pope, but the local religious community became even more active after a new Catholic *collège* was established near Point's home at the beginning of the Bourbon Restoration era.

Young Nicolas Point therefore received most of his education from devout Catholics who encouraged him, in 1819, to enter a Jesuit seminary called Saint-Acheul. Studying at this seminary near Amiens, Point developed an admiration for his Jesuit teachers and the desire to become a priest. He soon entered a Jesuit novitiate at Monterouge in suburban Paris (1822), but the rigorous Jesuit training provoked an emotional and physical crisis that forced him to withdraw in despair and return to less demanding work at Saint-Acheul. He later returned to Monterouge (1826), however, and took his vows to join the Jesuits in March 1828 amid an intensifying French hostility for the society. Assigned to further theological and scientific study at Saint-Acheul, Point was still living at the seminary when an anti-Jesuit mob destroyed most of the school in July 1830.[1]

French animosity for the Jesuits continued to grow after the Revolution of 1830. The Saint-Acheul seminary was permanently closed, and the wider political and intellectual currents of the early 1830s gradually pushed Point to believe he was becoming an outsider in French society. Although he was a chronological member of the "Generation of 1820," his staunch Jesuit allegiances separated him from the liberals who wanted to reshape French political culture and develop a more secular educational system. After further theological study in Switzerland, Point was formally ordained to the priesthood in the spring of 1831 and sent to teach at a Jesuit *collège* in Fribourg, thus beginning his religious career as a teacher in Jesuit schools outside July Monarchy France. He later worked briefly in Avignon before moving to another Jesuit school near San Sebastian, Spain, but more political upheavals provoked a liberal Spanish government to suppress all Jesuit *collèges* by the mid-1830s. Point moved back to France in July 1834. Facing more obstacles to his search for a stable teaching position and recognizing the strong anti-Jesuit sentiment in France, Point finally received an assignment to work at a small Jesuit school in Kentucky, with the expectation that he might later contribute to missionary outreach among the western American Indians. Point crossed the Atlantic from Le Havre to the United States in October 1835 and turned his back on a secularizing French culture that had become increasingly hostile to his religious and professional commitments. America represented a wide range of personal and political aspirations for Europeans of his generation, but for Point it became the country in which he could best pursue his vocation as a Jesuit teacher and his spiritual ambition to become a missionary for the Catholic Church.[2]

He did not know, of course, that he would never return to France, yet he felt conflicting religious and nationalist emotions during his transatlantic voyage. "I am a priest," Point wrote in a journal he kept while he was aboard the ship. "All of my life I have felt my heart throb at the very sound of the word, 'America.' So, I do not understand what secret seduction now draws my heart back toward the east. When I am not consciously thinking of that other country, all my affections converge on France."[3] After arriving in New York, Point quickly traveled to St. Mary's College in Kentucky (near Louisville), where he taught for a year before moving on to Grand Coteau, Louisiana, to establish a new Jesuit school called St. Charles College. Point wanted the curriculum at St. Charles to include classical Latin and Greek, but his Jesuit superiors decided that such subjects provided an impractical education for students who would be living and working in the United States. They also decided that Point lacked the personal skills needed for effective administrative leadership, and in July 1840 he was removed from his position at the college after three challenging years.[4]

Point was thus compelled again to leave a school in which he had tried to implement his ideas about religious education (the government's closure of his Jesuit school in Spain had forced his return to France in 1834), and he long harbored anxieties that stemmed from his difficult experiences at St. Charles. Each of his "expulsions" resulted partly from his determined opposition to the political and economic transitions of his era, including the secular revolutions in modern Europe and the commercial transitions in modern America. Both his religious-minded contemporaries and modern historians, however, have agreed that Point often lacked the emotional ability to work well with other people. One of his biographers notes that he was "frightfully insensitive to the subtleties of human relations" and also "destitute of any critical judgment for opinions at variance from his own."[5] He worried that he might continue to fail in his assigned tasks, and he feared that he might be expelled from his religious vocation (replicating his painful experience in the Jesuit novitiate at Monterouge in 1822).

Following his departure from Louisiana, Point was assigned to a new Jesuit mission among people whom Europeans called the "Flathead Indians" and who now identify themselves as the "Confederated Salish and Kootenai Tribes of the Flathead Reservation."[6] (Current tribal names are used throughout the following discussion of Native American people and cultures, except for some quoted passages from nineteenth-century texts.) This missionary role offered an attractive alternative to Point's previous problems at schools in Europe and the United States because he had long expressed a desire to work among Indigenous people in North America. He admired the Romantic writings of Chateaubriand and the idealized images of Native Americans that appeared in such books, but he also saw American Indian tribes as cultural groups in which he might promote the religious instruction and conversions that had become so difficult in modern, secular societies. Point thus set off from Missouri in May 1841 on a missionary expedition that would become the most important travel and work experience in his life (the well-traveled Belgian Jesuit priest Peter de Smet led five other Jesuits on this mission). Living among tribal communities for almost six years (1841–47) on Salish, Kootenai, and Blackfeet lands in areas that would later become part of Montana and Idaho, Point baptized hundreds of new Christians and gradually acquired a religious and cultural status he had never found in other places. Yet his relations with Jesuit colleagues were often difficult (one reported that Point had "something wanting in his head"), and his Jesuit superior, Father Joset, was authorized to expel Point from the society if he deemed such action necessary.[7]

Point seemed to understand that his Jesuit colleagues were always evaluating him, but he developed his own artwork and other methods of communication as he pursued his missionary work among the people whom he called the "Flatheads" (Salish), the Blackfeet, and the Coeur d'Alenes (who are also known as the Schitsu'umsh).[8] He traveled with these tribes on long hunts and worked constantly to persuade people of all ages that Catholicism offered the essential pathway to religious truth and personal salvation. Finally, in response to a request from Point himself, his Jesuit superiors reassigned him to Canada, where he spent the last twenty years of his life at various missions and at a Jesuit novitiate near Montreal. Here, in the years after 1859, Point drew upon his earlier journals and letters to compile six manuscript volumes he titled *Recollections of the Rocky Mountains* (*Souvenirs des montagnes rocheuses*). These memoirs carefully explained how the western American Indians lived before they learned about Christianity and how the Jesuits had introduced Christian beliefs in various tribal cultures because (as his brother Pierre reported) Point wanted to show "the glory of God and to save the history of the [western] mission for future generations."[9] He also illustrated the social life of American Indian villages as well as his own missionary work by including numerous artistic images he had drawn or painted during his western travels. Neither the *Recollections* nor his letters about Indigenous Americans were published in his lifetime, but twentieth-century American historians eventually translated and published much of Point's work, thus bringing the narratives of his cross-cultural travels into a public literary sphere that he was unable to enter himself.[10] He died on 4 July 1868 in Quebec.

Point's Views of "Modern" and "Premodern" America

Point was most interested in the Native American tribal cultures that he described as "premodern," but he understood of course that a different kind of "modern" society was spreading rapidly across the North American continent. He traveled through bustling commercial cities such as New York, Philadelphia, and Pittsburgh, and his work at Jesuit colleges in Kentucky and Louisiana required constant contact with the surrounding European American populations. He would ultimately write far more about Native Americans than he wrote about European Americans, yet his commentaries on the white communities in Kentucky suggest that he was intrigued or at least bemused by the social and cultural habits he saw there. "Kentuckians smoke pipes, spit into the fire, and cross their legs, usually taking the most comfortable position they can," he wrote later in a memoir about his work in Kentucky.

> Even at the table of the most well-bred there is no napkin, no soup, no dessert; there is a two-pronged fork and knife with a huge blade that substitutes for a spoon. The same plate is used for every course; the most diverse foods are put on the same plate! While their mouths are busy eating—that is to say during the whole meal—their tongues stay silent and their eyes rove. One has to . . . have an American stomach or resign himself later on with a bout of indigestion. We Europeans thought we could eat at our host's table as we do

> at home, presenting platters of food to those sitting next to us, and carrying on polite talk during the course of the meal. But if we did that here . . . [the] wagons would have departed, leaving us to carry on politely at table.[11]

Modern American society, as Point described it, thus consisted mostly of busy people who gulped down their food, worked constantly to make more money, and ignored most of the polite conventions he had known in Europe. It was also a society in which the Protestant population's anti-Catholic religious prejudices made it difficult to develop Catholic schools or to bring Catholicism into rural European American communities.

French missionaries therefore achieved greater religious success among Native Americans who had long been more willing to accept Catholic religious truths—especially when they learned about Catholicism from French priests. Discussing the earlier history of French encounters with Indigenous people in North America, Point emphasized that French travelers always encouraged Native Americans to embrace Christianity and that "it is, after God, to the French that we [missionaries] are indebted." This debt was not owed to the modern (anticlerical) people in France but to earlier generations of French Catholics and "to Indians converted by French missionaries. These *voyageurs*, whom Providence scattered throughout these regions, did not . . . always conduct themselves in conformity with their faith, but none of them took it upon himself to speak disrespectfully either of his religion, of the priests, or of his country."[12] French behavior on the American frontier thus contrasted with the hostility for Catholicism that Point had seen in the attack against Jesuits at Saint-Acheul, and his account of the respect for priests in America suggests why he could find his travel in the western wilderness more appealing than the political and cultural life in the cities of France.

Converting American Indians to Christianity still offered plenty of challenges, however, and Point's reports on his religious work often referred to the hardships of eating unfamiliar food, suffering from extreme cold, and wandering on horseback through dangerous mountain passes. These were the "daily trials" of missionary life. "Add to them the ignorance of the language," he explained, "[and] being far away from one's own country, civilization, [and] friends, and perhaps it will seem that altogether the conveniences and inconveniences bear no faint resemblance to what we call the cross of the Apostles."[13] This allusion to the early Christians suggests how Point viewed his work among Indigenous peoples as the continuation of a long history of religious predecessors. Like the first apostles, he was preaching on the frontiers of his own civilization to people who had never known Christianity and whose religious beliefs seemed as wrong to the Jesuits as the ideas of "pagans" whom Christians had converted in ancient Rome. It was precisely these Native American societies, however, that offered Point an exceptional nineteenth-century opportunity to pursue his religious aspirations. "Left to himself," Point noted with some of his own culture's most common stereotypes, "the savage has not been able to make any marked progress toward civilization. Still, however degraded he may be, when it is a question of passing from the most abject kind of natural life to the most noble supernatural life, the savage always offers less resistance than the man perverted by civilization."[14]

Point never accepted mythical ideas about an imagined "noble savage," but he believed that American Indians possessed a deep human dignity and "moral aptitude." Europeans often overlooked these qualities, so they could not see how Indigenous people both resembled and differed from the people in more "modern" civilizations. Where, then, did the American Indian's moral sensibility come from? "It was a vestige of natural law," Point wrote, "whose author, end, and sanction they, of course, did not know, but which nevertheless sufficed to give their actions a kind of natural rectitude, which always prevailed except when . . . the passions asserted themselves."[15] Although missionaries from France had established promising early contacts with these "natural" peoples, Point believed the increasingly secular French nation had abandoned its God-given mission to enhance the "natural rectitude" of Indigenous communities. Given this national failing, nineteenth-century Jesuits might reaffirm France's religious traditions if (as Point envisioned) they could bring Catholicism to the "premodern" people of America.

He reflected on this religious duty in one of his numerous comments about the failures of his own nation. "Oh France," Point lamented, "what have you done with the domain Providence entrusted to your keeping! What have you done with your divine mission which fell to you to catholicize all this new world and to save millions of Indians[?] Your infidelity has all but annihilated them."[16] French secularism was bad enough in Europe, but it was even worse when the Native people in America also became victims of a French "infidelity" that stemmed from the Enlightenment, the French Revolution, and the democratic critiques of Catholic Christianity.

The most comprehensive modern analyst of Point's ideas, Cornelius Buckley, has astutely summarized how this perceived cultural tragedy weighed on Point and drove him toward his religious mission in the western wilderness: "For him, France was more than a country with a particular flag [and] language. . . . He believed that Providence had given France a destiny: France was the transmitter of western civilization, and western civilization was Catholic Christianity grafted onto the culture of the Graeco-Latin World. . . . History showed that during the eighteenth century France repudiated her vocation; her subsequent humiliation was willed by Providence in order to bring her back to her destiny."[17] Buckley argues persuasively that Point drew his religious interpretations of French history from influential, anti-revolutionary writers such as Chateaubriand, Joseph de Maistre, and Louis de Bonald. All of these early nineteenth-century conservatives believed that modern France had fallen into political and cultural chaos because it turned away from its earlier religious traditions, and Point carried these ideas on his transatlantic journey to America.

Point could of course find many of the same disconcerting political and social trends in the "modern" United States, including a social obsession with materialism, a secular rejection of established churches, and an evolving system of democratic government. At the same time, however, the vast territories of the United States contained a large "premodern" population that might still be saved from the secularizing culture of modernity, if only the Jesuits could reach them first. Point's journey to the American West thus took him into tribal cultures where he could act upon his self-defined national, religious, and personal mission: he would convert and save people who had not yet been lost to the secularizing, anti-Catholic forces of modern civilization.

Point's Description of America: Geography, People, Social Institutions

Although Point was mainly concerned with the religious conversion of Native Americans, he also wrote about the distinctive social and cultural beliefs of the Indigenous people who lived amid the spectacular western mountains. Recognizing that Native Americans had long sustained a rich cultural and material existence through complex institutions and traditions, Point became a kind of early anthropologist as he described the political power of local chiefs, the rituals of religion and family life, the methods for hunting animals, and the relationships that grew out of storytelling or smoking in a social circle. His careful analysis of Native American cultures always had a religious purpose, however, because he wanted to integrate his own Christian message into Indigenous cultural traditions that people already used and understood in their daily lives. Conversion to Christianity would inevitably lead Indigenous people away from their traditional religious beliefs, but Point also understood that successful missionaries solidified the most enduring conversions when they were able to fuse the new faith in Catholicism with familiar social customs or long-established cultural practices.

Point therefore attempted to learn American Indian languages (though he usually relied on translators for religious communications), and he used his artwork to illustrate abstract religious principles for people who could not read or write or understand his spoken words. His paintings portrayed biblical themes and the rituals of Christian worship, but he also drew pictures of tribal social activities, buffalo hunts, dwellings, and people, which he sometimes presented as gifts to his Native American friends and sometimes kept as illustrations for the prose accounts of his mission work. Both his written descriptions of different tribes and his colorful illustrations became some of the earliest surviving documents for historians who have studied the cultural evolution of northwestern American Indians. But Point (the anthropological observer) understood that he was always being observed by the people whom he was also watching, and he knew that his presence as an outsider could be disconcerting for everyone in the tribal communities he visited. He noted, for example, how he had studied the appearance and behavior of the families in a Kaw village after he left Missouri on his westward journey, and then "I became aware that I, myself, was becoming the object of attention, almost the occasion for hilarity on the part of the Indian children. For some days I had given no attention to the matter of shaving." A bearded man apparently struck the Kaw children as strange because "in their estimation, the acme of beauty was the complete absence of hair from the chin, the eyelashes, the eyebrows, and the head."[18] Such encounters helped Point to view himself from the perspective of Native Americans and to deepen his awareness of his own European origins as he wandered ever farther from both France and the European American communities in the eastern United States.

Point departed on his missionary journey from Westport, Missouri, in early May 1841. He had lived in Westport for the previous six months, maintaining a small Catholic mission for French Canadians and developing contacts with some tribal groups in the area. The nearby Osage Indians attracted Point's attention because in 1827 a French fur trader had taken six people from this tribe to France and put them on display for curious Europeans. Abandoned by their "handler," they eventually received funds to return home, but Point found in 1840 that only three of the six travelers were still alive. They lived in what he called "an evil tribe, as are all those who are not Catholics, and live on the fringe of civilization." Although this critical description suggests that Point's first contacts with Native Americans did not lead to conversions, he set off on his mission to the western American Indians with optimistic expectations about what lay ahead. After twenty years of studying and teaching in Jesuit colleges, he was finally heading toward what he called "a beautiful perspective for a missionary"—an open land and thousands of souls to bring into the Catholic Church. "At the sight of the azure distances, so pleasing to the eye," Point wrote later, "I thought I could perceive what is most attractive about the beautiful ideal of the apostolic life."[19]

Point traveled in a wagon train caravan with seventy people who were heading for settlements in the far west. The leader of the six Jesuits, Father de Smet, encouraged Point to keep a journal, so he wrote detailed descriptions of what he saw on a trip that lasted from May to early September, when the priests (after breaking away from the main caravan) reached the site for their mission encampment in Montana. He described vast open prairie lands, unfamiliar plants and flowers, impressive streams such as the Platte and Green Rivers, and wildlife that ranged in size from mosquitoes and hummingbirds to prairie dogs and large buffalo. Although almost every aspect of nature seemed to interest him, he was most impressed by the expanse and altitude of the Rocky Mountains: "But who could describe the majesty of the wilderness as we then saw it?" he wrote in his first account of the Rockies. These towering peaks evoked such strong religious feelings that he "carved into the bark of a cedar which overlooked all this majesty the ever-adorable Name at which every knee in Heaven, on earth, and in Hell bends."[20]

This desire to honor God on the land as well as among the human beings who lived on it became a recurring motif in Point's account of all his western travels. The following year, for example, as he accompanied some Salish hunters on a search for highland animals, Point ascended a mountain from which he could see for great distances in all directions. Standing on the summit, he "made and planted a cross, to take possession, in the name of the Lord, of a land which undoubtedly contained many souls to be saved. . . . How ardently did I wish that I might, from this lofty position, make them hear the victorious cry of the Great Archangel, *Quis ut Deus*." Like the first European explorers arriving in North America, Point believed he was claiming both open land and Native peoples for an extraordinary civilizing mission. The western geography itself beckoned the European traveler on to a snow-covered "plain so vast that except for the color, it looked like a sea," but this sea-like space was actually "a mass of rocks shaded in red, yellow, blue, and everything that autumn has to offer of the richest in color and form."[21] This vast space was more than a landscape painting, however, because people were always migrating through the valleys or setting up small camps or hunting for animals. Indeed, as Point followed his guides into the wilderness, he began to worry that tribal hunting practices were gradually destroying the very animals that were needed for survival. "Poor buffalo!" Point wrote in one of his descriptions of a large winter hunt. "What a slaughter! And poor Indians! If you continue in this way, within a few years you will search in vain for your daily bread, your shelter, your clothing—for everything that the buffalo lavishes on you today."[22] In other words, the anthropologist could also write about nature like an early environmentalist.

Point's interest in the intersection of human life and the natural world developed over the course of his extensive contact (1841–47) with the Salish, the Coeur d'Alenes, and the Blackfeet, all of whom brought together several related tribal groups for warfare or hunting expeditions. Although Point noted that these tribes had significant cultural differences, he reported that they all shared physical similarities ("[skin is] the color of copper; cheekbones are prominent, eyes are brown or black, hair is long and straight") and numerous character traits. As he explained later in his *Recollections of the Rocky Mountains*, these traits created resistance to the Jesuits' work, but they also showed why the whole missionary project was so important. "Common to all three [groups], with some exceptions among the Flatheads [Salish]," Point noted in a general characterization, "is an unrelenting spirit of independence, laziness, a passion for gambling, cruelty to the vanquished, very little regard for women, forgetfulness of the past and improvidence for the future. While all of these traits were true of them before their conversion, since their baptism an admirable transformation has taken place in their entire manner of life."[23] These character "traits," as Point identified them, made it easy for even the most conscientious converts to fall away from the Christian beliefs and social values that Point was encouraging them to embrace. Many men in American Indian tribes practiced polygamy, for example, and their verbal "dissimulation" in response to certain questions might strike most Europeans as simply a clever way to lie.[24]

As he enumerated the character flaws among the Native Americans he met, however, Point also emphasized that neither individuals nor social groups could ever be reduced to a list of essentially good or bad traits. In a typical summary of human complexities, he described one of the groups that was allied with the Blackfeet tribe as people who possessed "a goodness of soul which constitutes the core of their personalities," and, despite an unfortunate tendency to beg for favors, they clearly demonstrated the virtues of "rectitude, tractability, and courage."[25] The personal behavior and social mores of other tribes, by contrast, struck Point as highly unpleasant or altogether "savage." His assessments of tribal character typically suggested that virtuous Indians were most receptive to Christianity, whereas the more "savage" groups were most resistant to his Christian messages.

The Salish received Point's highest praise because they were eager to learn about Catholicism; indeed, they had invited the Jesuit "Black Robes" to establish their missions for religious instruction. The Salish engagement with Christianity thus differed in almost every way from the attitudes of the recalcitrant Coeur d'Alenes, whom Point came to know during a special mission trip in 1842. After describing their dirty faces and disheveled hair, Point summarized the other shortcomings of the people he met in a Coeur d'Alene village:

> While eating, foul sounds came from the nose, the throat, from the mouth; in fact, from any part of the body capable of producing them. This gives

> some idea of the visible squalor, but it is a feeble image of the pitiful state of their souls. For even at this time there still prevailed an idolatry which went so far as to render homage to the vilest of animals. There was a shamelessness of habit which knew no check other than caprice or passion. . . . They emerged from their sloth only when the pangs of hunger made themselves felt. Finally, there was a constant inclination to dissimulation, to gluttony, to everything base.[26]

This tribe almost surely gained its negative reputation by resisting Point's religious instruction, and their leader, a chief named Stellam, was unusually hostile to the Jesuit mission. Yet the influence of such leaders within the "virtuous" and "savage" tribes alike forced Point to examine the Native American institutions that could either promote or impede the Christian message he was preaching.

The key institutions and traditions of most Indigenous people in the Northern Rockies supported or celebrated the annual summer and winter hunts. Point learned about the cultural significance of both the hunters and their prey by accompanying the Salish on a long winter hunt (December 1841–April 1842) soon after the Jesuits had established their first mission village, and he joined other long hunts while he was working among the Coeur d'Alene and Blackfeet tribes. He therefore saw firsthand how these hunts served overlapping material and cultural needs for food, for animal hides (which were used for clothing and tents), and for horns, tails, or feathers (which were used for ornaments and dances). Tribal social life was organized to ensure successful hunting expeditions and to facilitate the all-important search for buffalo. According to Point, there was "no fatigue he [the Native American hunter] will not endure, no enemy he will not defy, no form of death he will not face to get the great beasts." Although the actual hunters were usually young men, the social organization of the hunt depended mainly on women and on the leadership of competent chiefs. During the long winter trek with the Salish, for example, Point found that women managed all the baggage, took charge of the pack animals, repaired broken equipment or poles, and cared for all the children. When the tribe finally reached a good campsite, "the women are obliged to erect the lodges, cut the wood, and prepare the food."[27] The women thus created an essential infrastructure for the whole tribal community as they moved across the open spaces of the Northern Rockies and set up temporary shelters in the valleys where buffalo herds might appear.

A successful hunt, however, also required the wise leadership of a good chief, in part because he and his scouts would direct the tribe toward the animals and in part because his military and negotiating skills were needed whenever the tribe approached the hunting lands of another tribal group. Hunting demanded

Details of a Buffalo Hunt. Ink on paper by Nicolas Point, ca. 1842. Point lived among Native American tribal groups that depended on long annual hunts for their food and for the vitality of their social and cultural communities. In the winter of 1842, Point joined members of the Salish tribe on a typical buffalo hunting expedition, which he portrayed in this drawing of hunters and their families near a mobile encampment that sustained the social relationships that Point sought to understand as he pursued his Christian mission. Courtesy of the Jesuit Archives and Research Center, St. Louis.

talented political leaders as well as energetic young hunters, so a well-respected chief wielded enormous influence over the collective life of the tribe. Point quickly understood the importance of winning the chief's goodwill and, if possible, his high-profile conversion to Christianity. He knew that the conversion of the most powerful person in the community would almost certainly bring other conversions in its wake; and at the very least, a cooperative chief was essential for any missionary who hoped to reach the most cautious members of a tribe. If a chief welcomed Point's mission, most of his tribe immediately became interested in learning about Christianity. One of Point's notable converts, for example, was a Nez Perce chief who brought his tribe into the Salish camp for part of the winter hunt in January 1842. This chief, Point reported, "was to be named Charlemagne, a name that suited him in every respect, for he was great in stature, in courage, and in authority"; equally important, his conversion prompted many others in the Nez Perce tribe to request immediate baptism for themselves.[28]

Chiefs played a decisive, authoritative role in the religious and political practices of every tribe, but the annual hunt provided some of the most important occasions for the specific exercise of the chief's power. "After the women," Point explained, "the grand chief has the most responsibility on his shoulders. He must lead the group, choose the campsites, [and] show to everyone an example of courage and vigilance."[29] This courage became even more important when several tribes were hunting in an area where the buffalo roamed because the search for animals could easily lead to the kind of military conflict that Point heard about when he joined the Salish for a hunt in 1846. A group of Crow Indians challenged the Salish as they moved onto land that the Crow had claimed as their tribal hunting ground, and a battle soon ensued. The Christianized Salish hunters were fortunate to have a decisive leader named Titiche Loutso, "or Moses, as he was named at baptism," who rallied his troops like Roland or Charlemagne in their early medieval Christian battles against the Saracens. "If God wishes us to be victors, that we shall be," Moses told his warriors. "If He does not, may His will be done." Inspired by their courageous, devout leader, the Salish fighters routed their enemies, ensured the safety of their tribe, and then celebrated their good fortune in festive dances. Although some Salish women had also bravely joined the battle, Point believed that divine support and the chief's inspired leadership ultimately brought the military victory.[30]

Chiefs thus helped to shape collective tribal identities because their imaginative, inspired leadership in hunting and warfare influenced the whole community. In this respect, the political concerns of American Indian tribes did not differ much from the political stories people told in other human societies. "Here there is just as much a question of politics as in civilized countries when it comes to discussing victories, defeats, battles, engagements, etc.," Point wrote in a description of his visit to a Blackfeet camp in 1846. "And since news of such happenings affects them greatly, they spend three-fourths of their lives doing the war dance, mourning their dead, or plotting revenge."[31] They also told stories about hunting exploits, but the battles received most of their attention and gave the chief a political status that enabled him to claim or buy numerous wives.

This pattern of polygamous marriages was a disturbing issue for Point because it was the kind of traditional social custom that made potential converts resistant to Christianity. The "great men" in a tribe who were accustomed to buying young women from their own parents, sometimes for a mere trinket, did not want to give up the social and economic advantages of their polygamous relationships for the more ethereal, eternal rewards that might eventually follow from a Christian baptism. Point stressed that polygamy led to a "shocking abuse of morals" as the men in Blackfeet and Coeur d'Alene villages collected or abandoned their wives. Christian marriages thus became for Point the moral and social means for improving

Camping for the Night. Ink on paper by Nicolas Point, ca. 1841–47. This drawing of an unidentified Native American campsite shows the important social and economic contributions of women in all the Indigenous communities that Point described. His written reports noted how women set up camps, organized food supplies, managed animals, and participated in the preparation for battles, but Point criticized the polygamous marriages that made women vulnerable to the power of men who could abandon their wives or barter for new spouses. Courtesy of the Jesuit Archives and Research Center, St. Louis.

the position of American Indian women and transforming the personal behavior of their husbands.[32] Polygamy had evolved for specific social reasons within Indigenous cultures, but Point could never reconcile this tradition with his understanding of Christian ethics. There were other tribal traditions, however, that he was more willing to accept and even praise because he believed they resembled or supported his own religious ideas.

Point was impressed, for example, by the chiefs' custom of smoking a pipe with strangers or would-be enemies whenever they wanted to establish new friendships or negotiate peaceful solutions to impending conflicts. Chiefs did not just lead warriors into battle. They often smoked a "calumet" (medicine pipe with tobacco) to greet emissaries from other tribes, to welcome visitors into their communities, or to reaffirm their respect for old friends. This ritual produced a mutual respect that reduced hostilities between rival leaders and created new social bonds for everyone who joined the circle of pipe smokers. Point quickly recognized the importance of this ritual and understood its social utility whenever he entered a new tribal village or met a new chief. His cross-cultural interests thus merged with his religious concerns in a description of how Blackfeet Indians smoked together at a typical calumet ceremony:

> To be properly lighted, the instrument of peace has to pass from left to right until it comes to a person of lesser distinction. . . . After this man lit the pipe it went back, passing from mouth to mouth, the way it came until it arrived at the extreme left. . . . Then it was handed back in the opposite direction, this time passing only to the great medicine men . . . [who] smoke double rations and they are waited on but do no serving themselves. The solemnity of this ceremony, which usually lasts a long time, had destroyed the usual chattering.[33]

The silence and solemnity of a calumet ceremony therefore resembled a religious ritual, which may explain why Point soon understood its useful role in fostering peaceful, intertribal relations. Equally important, a chief who demonstrated his respect for solemnity, for other human beings, and for the repetition of a symbolic ritual might well come to appreciate the religious rituals and messages of an itinerant French priest.

It was more difficult for Point to place social rituals such as eating or dancing in a religious framework. Wandering with Indigenous people in the wilderness, he did not find much religious meaning in a diet of simple bitterroots (which "a civilized mouth can scarcely bear") and the roots of the camas plant. This root tasted somewhat like a prune, "but its digestion is accompanied by very disagreeable [and] . . . strong odors" and by "the sound that accompanies them." The more pleasant eating came after successful hunting expeditions returned to camp with fresh meat. Point described one such feast, which occurred soon after the funeral of the first baptized member of the Blackfeet tribe. Despite their grief, the Blackfeet joyfully celebrated a successful hunt by roasting buffalo and feasting late into the night. "Such is the Indian!" Point explained. "Yesterday he was in the depths of sorrow; today his joy is boundless! We should overlook this abrupt change of moods, remembering that before his conversion the Indian was a child and even now that he has become a Christian he retains a certain childishness."[34]

Behaviors that Point described from his French cultural perspective as "childish" carryovers from the past could also reappear in the dances that Point identified as another source of tribal social solidarity. After the great victory that Salish warriors (led by the converted "Moses") and their allies won against the Crow, for example, Point watched the victors—men and women alike—join in a long, celebratory dance. Moving in step to a steady drumbeat and wearing eagle feathers

Blackfeet Chiefs Smoking . . . in the Jesuits' Tent and Promising They Will Henceforth Pray the Prayer of the Flatheads. Ink on paper by Nicolas Point, ca. 1841–47. Native American leaders participated in the smoking rituals of calumet ceremonies to affirm social bonds, converging beliefs, or military alliances. Point admired the solemnity of these ceremonies and sought to bring different tribal groups to his own religious views in smoking circles that might share (as in this image) a common prayer and thereby avert future conflicts. Courtesy of the Jesuit Archives and Research Center, St. Louis.

on their heads, the dancers formed an undulating circle that became smaller and larger as they pushed forward and backward for hours on end. There was nothing lewd or explicitly pagan in these dances, Point reported, yet he knew that some Catholics would wonder why he was so willing to condone such irreligious behavior among his recent converts. "To those who would blame a Catholic missionary for going along with the Indians in these circumstances," he wrote, "we would answer: with the Indians particularly, it is better to graft than to fell."[35] The idea of grafting the new faith on to older traditions suggests the strategy that Point used in much of his missionary work. His goal, after all, was to bring American Indians to Christianity, and he was pragmatic enough to follow any strategy (drawing pictures, condoning dances, smoking a calumet pipe) that might encourage this grafting to take place. No matter how much he might tolerate cultural grafting, however, Point never doubted that Christianity was the only path to truth, salvation, and the higher forms of human civilization.

Point worried that American Indian culture could disappear if tribal hunting practices continued to deplete the number of animals, but there were few alternatives to the trade and food that came from hunting. "Since their soil does not naturally produce the food which could, as in other cultivated lands, take the place of buffalo meat," Point noted, "they would have no alternative [to hunting] other than exile or death." Yet Point interpreted this dire situation as more evidence to support his belief that missionary work contributed to a broader civilizing mission. The decline of hunting would inevitably push people to live in more settled communities, where missionaries could more readily introduce "civilized ideas" through their religious teaching. "Religion will bring civilization in its train," Point noted, "and civilization will do for their lands what religion has done for their souls."[36]

Point's view of the relation between civilization and religion carried an ironic tension, however, because his own French civilization had increasingly rejected much of his religion. If religious beliefs (as Point understood them) offered all-important guidance for civilizing "savages," it was also true that modern civilization was pushing people toward a new hostility for Catholicism's traditional cultural and religious authority. Modernity seemed to be undermining its own civilizing foundation. Point's mission, in short, brought an endangered religious civilization to an endangered people. This cross-cultural project gave him a daunting religious task, but Point pursued the work with great diligence because he believed deeply in the historical significance of the Jesuit missionary enterprise. American Indians could not escape from their dangerous situation by trading more buffalo hides or receiving money from the government or even hearing the evangelical "error" of Protestant preachers. "There is only one means of preventing . . . the annihilation of these poor peoples already so reduced numerically from what they were at the beginning of this century . . . ," he wrote in one explanation of his work. "This is to make of them good and true Christians. That is what we are trying to achieve with the help of God."[37]

Point's definitions of both Native American vulnerability and religious solutions for the danger show how his travel in the western lands of North America enabled him to reaffirm his deep religious selfhood, defend his conception of a religious civilization, and gain an authoritative public identity he had never found in Europe. Despite the hardships of buffalo hunts on cold winter days and isolated encampments in remote mountain ranges, Point had reached a place where his personal and cultural aspirations could finally come together in a Jesuit mission.

Point's Mission: Religion, Knowledge, and Authority

Nicolas Point understood that religious conversion would require cultural fusions, or the grafting of new beliefs onto traditional beliefs and social practices. Religious grafting differed from the forceful imposition of religious ideas, and it was most likely to succeed if the Jesuits could show how Catholicism offered more benefits than either the respected medicine men in Indigenous tribes or the itinerant Protestant preachers who were also proselytizing in western lands. Point's quest to convert American Indians thus became a cultural quest to establish the religious authority of Catholic priests over religious rivals among people who were unaware of the Jesuits' history or traditions. Religious conversions were complex cultural translations, so the "Black Robes" had to begin these translations by understanding tribal beliefs that had existed long before the European Christians arrived.

Point reported in his *Recollections of the Rocky Mountains* that he found the religious beliefs in Indigenous communities to be a "veritable chaos" of hazy notions about the spiritual sphere and the meanings of divinity. The "infirm intellects" of the American Indians, he explained in one of his racist generalizations, "having lost the idea of the true God, thought to see the divinity where its shadow scarcely even extended. . . . They called 'manitou'—that is 'spirit'—such apparently animated objects as the sun, thunder, and so forth, and the cult they practiced they called 'medicine.'"[38] Native Americans were thus more interested in how spiritual forces shaped the material world than in the spiritual ascent to a higher metaphysical realm, and their conceptions of the afterlife resembled their descriptions of a good life on earth. The Blackfeet, for example, believed in the divinity of the sun and often expressed their devotion to this sacred power. But if "someone"—Point?—"spoke of heaven to them, they would ask very seriously whether in our heaven there were buffalo, unable to believe that without them there could be anything good there." When they were told that heaven lacked this kind of material reality, they decided that heaven must be a "visible atmosphere," which they described simply as "the blue."[39] So the missionary had to give repeated lessons on the spiritual essence of Christianity while emphasizing that belief in a transcendent divinity would also provide material benefits for people who wanted to live a good life on earth.

Successful Jesuits therefore knew how to link abstract descriptions of good and evil with vivid, specific examples from daily life. "How difficult it is," Point noted, "to make souls still dominated by the senses see what is meant by purely spiritual happiness." A few spiritually minded visionaries might accept the belief that "the Great Spirit must understand things we do not" and recognize that Christian ideas were true "because it is God who has revealed them."[40] Yet the message would come across more clearly for most people when they saw images of what the scriptures had revealed (hence, the value of Point's artwork) and observed how Christianity improved the real-world lives of its adherents. Point assured potential converts that both the benevolent and all-powerful attributes of God could be evoked through Catholic sacraments and sacred objects that would replace traditional tribal medicine and demonstrate greater efficacy in healing the sick, hunting for animals, and protecting vulnerable children. "What admirable fruits were produced in their souls, not only by the sacraments of baptism, penance and Holy Eucharist, but also by the simple sign of the cross, the use of holy water, [and] the mere sight of a medal."[41]

According to Point, Indigenous people were drawn to Christian rituals and medallions when they saw that Christian converts often enjoyed better fortunes than those who clung to non-Christian beliefs. Indeed, the worldly value of otherworldly Christian powers, as Point described them, became more obvious after every conversion:

> All that was vicious or tended toward vice has been punished. Such a standard of punishments and rewards is in perfect harmony with the concepts of these people who are still so childlike. Moreover, sickness or health, abundance or famine, victories or defeats—in fact, almost every type of worldly blessing or evil is judged in the light of two great historic facts. After the coming of Catholic missions to the Rockies there was, on the one hand, the increase of the Flathead [Salish] population, and on the other, the tragic decimation of the Blackfeet [who were slower to accept Christianity].[42]

This evidence of punishments and rewards contributed to conversions among the Blackfeet because even the anti-Jesuit skeptics began to notice that "good fortune followed good conduct and misfortune trod on the heels of evil actions." Impressed by the (Christian) Salish victories in military conflicts, some Blackfeet leaders decided they should convert to Catholicism and ally themselves with their former Salish enemies. Christian conversions could thus foster the reconciliation of long-hostile tribes, but Point reported that conversions to Christianity also helped to ensure military success for those who went into battle beneath a cross.[43]

He described a notable example of such religious-military success in his account of the conflict in which the converted Christian leader "Moses" inspired the Salish to gain control over disputed hunting lands in a battle against the Crow Indians. The attacking Salish fighters did not lose a single man, but nine of the non-Christian Crow were killed and fourteen others were wounded. The Salish "attributed their good fortune to the fact that they had made the sign of the cross before engaging in combat," and this assumption was confirmed when they heard about the death of a Nez Perce ally who had gone into the battle without crossing himself. The Salish expressed their religious appreciation for their military success and then "offered seventy-six of their children to be baptized."[44]

Conversion to Christianity also gave the Salish some exceptional rewards on their hunting expeditions, as Point noted in his description of how they had killed 153 buffalo immediately after devoting an entire Sunday to the worship of God. This remarkable hunt, however, was only one example of the good fortune that regularly followed upon Christian conversions. Point reported in other letters that the baptized babies in Blackfeet families had lower mortality rates than the non-baptized infants, that a stampeding buffalo turned away "within an inch" of the son of two devout Christian parents, and that other Christians won military victories in ways that seemed "miraculous in the eyes of those to whom they were granted." More generally, Point noted that conversions to Catholic Christianity began to foster numerous social advances, including a steady growth of the Salish population. This tribe flourished as converted Christians developed new "respect and gentleness toward women; better care for children; more freedom in the choice of spouses; [and] better care and more solicitude for the sick." They also waged "fewer wars, but when wars are unavoidable, [their victories demonstrated] the undeniable fact that heaven protects the Christians." The good fortune of the Salish could be seen even more clearly in Point's contrasting stories of non-Christians who suddenly fell dead from diseases or died in battles or found their villages destroyed in earthquakes. Point and his Catholic converts interpreted all such events as signs of divine judgment and as proof that Christian baptism produced real-world rewards or averted looming dangers.[45]

Some potential converts nevertheless rejected Point's Catholicism and turned to religious alternatives that Point sought to discredit as he traveled among the most skeptical Indigenous tribes. His quest for conversions thus required a two-pronged religious campaign. First, he had to show that Protestant missionaries offered an erroneous Protestant path to Christian truth, and then he had to show that highly respected tribal medicine men were not telling the truth about the healing and religious powers of their medicines and spiritual objects. Although both these religious traditions challenged his personal claims for Catholic spiritual authority, Point found that Protestant missionaries were easier to discredit. Early Presbyterian "evangelists" (as Point described them) alienated influential tribal leaders who had known about the Jesuits in Canada and who therefore traveled to St. Louis with an invitation for the Jesuit Black Robes to come to the Northern Rockies. The Protestants had brought misguided religious beliefs to Indigenous communities, so Point found that some American Indians who "had been half civilized by Protestantism" later became "more difficult to lead to the true faith than the idolaters themselves." Fortunately for the Jesuits, most people who encountered the Protestant missionaries were "disgusted with everything having to do with Protestantism," which meant that Point could still teach disillusioned people to pray in what he called "the Catholic manner." Protestant falsehoods had to be corrected through new instruction, but Point could convert misinformed Christians as they came to understand why Catholic prayers were "the most influential and most esteemed in every respect."[46]

The more difficult religious challenge for Catholic missionaries came from Native American spiritual leaders, whose healing medicines gave them great prestige. Not surprisingly, these medicine men saw how the Black Robes were undermining their own tribal position, and they warned that bad fortune would soon come upon anyone who turned away from traditional spiritual beliefs and objects. Point recognized that American Indians conceived of medicine as a spiritual force rather than as a system of scientific knowledge. "To be 'strong in medicine,'" Point explained in one account of his rivals, "is to be at one and the same time a prophet, a miracle-worker, a kind of pontiff . . . [and a] recipient of revelations."[47] It was of course difficult to achieve this kind of medical/religious reputation, but a few men in each tribe attained this status after they had miraculously cured a wounded or sick person, often by emulating the actions of a wild animal.

The treatment itself depended on the medical healer's ability to evoke the right animal spirit, which he brought into his patients by dancing, by imitating the animal's call, and by breathing aggressively on the afflicted part of a sick person's body. If the person recovered after this medical/religious treatment, the medicine man gained respect for his healing powers and an elevated spiritual status in the community. Responding to the medical and personal problems of people in the tribe, he would recommend the use of a powerful "manitou" and magical objects such as a sacred stone or an eagle's feather or a special herb. The appeal to animal spirits and the use of mysterious relics suggested to Point (despite the long tradition of sacred relics and crosses in French Catholicism) that a "satanic power is firmly established" in the behavior of these medicine men, who were often able to "enslave the gullible and take advantage of their credulity." In any case, most people in every tribal community were reluctant to abandon or alienate their traditional spiritual and medical authorities by embracing the new faith of the Black Robes. "It is, therefore, not surprising," Point noted, "that the more the missionary endeavors to save the people from their gullibility, the more resistance he meets." Point was nevertheless able to discredit several medicine men who claimed they could turn charcoal into a bullet or move a boulder by merely using their breath. When a public demonstration of these magical powers failed to produce the predicted transformations, Point believed his own message began to convert people who wanted to find new solutions to their material, medical, and spiritual problems.[48]

There was always a risk, however, that pragmatic, practical-minded conversions would not last because the recent converts might face new material problems. After the Coeur d'Alenes began to convert to Catholicism, for example, their hunters were unable to find enough animals to feed the tribe. The medical healer said the hunt was failing because people had stopped honoring the long-revered animal spirits. Point quickly saw how this claim threatened his religious mission, so he inverted the medicine man's explanation for the tribe's problems. The real threat, Point explained, came from members of the tribe who were hiding their "manitou" or still expecting protection from stones and feathers that were not truly sacred. Instead of appealing to the alleged power of these objects, he urged every member of the tribe to get rid of false, non-Christian religious relics. "From then on," Point reported with satisfaction, " . . . medicine sacks, an animal's tail, a feather, or some similar object—which . . . had received the veneration due only to the Sovereign Master—were brought to the missionary's lodge to be thrown into the fire." As the old relics disappeared, hunting and fishing rapidly improved, the medicine man lost much of his prestige, and new converts requested baptism.[49]

Point understood the powerful role of material objects in human spiritual life, so he assumed that conversions were not really completed until the sacred stone or feather gave way to a sacred cross. But Point's greatest triumphs came whenever a medical healer renounced his own religious practices and threw away his traditional healing objects. One such conversion occurred when a medicine man in the Coeur d'Alene tribe accompanied Point on a visit to an injured man in his own family. The man quickly recovered from his injuries after Point's visit, whereupon the medicine man immediately announced his own desire to be baptized as a Christian. This remarkable conversion was as valuable to Point's work as the conversion of a tribal chief, and it "made such a strong impression on the stragglers, that they decided to visit the Blackrobe, announcing that they, too, desired baptism."[50] Where the conversion of a chief gave Point authoritative recognition from the tribe's political leader, the conversion of a medicine man could transfer his healing powers and spiritual authority to the Catholic priest.

Healing the sick thus became another belief-enhancing component of Point's missionary work because his medical interventions suggested that he was a new kind of medicine man who possessed mysterious knowledge or magical powers. When he met with a group of Gros Ventre Indians, for example, he was asked to help people whose eyes had become infected from the red paints they placed on their eyelids. He washed the infected areas, relieved the irritations, and enhanced his growing reputation as a miracle worker. "How easy it is to acquire a reputation for scientific knowledge among the ignorant!" he wrote in one of his rare, self-congratulatory letters. He was soon besieged by people seeking cures for all kinds of ailments, and even his repeated declaration that "cures for them were beyond my power" could not stop the stream of visitors that flowed to the fort where he was staying. Point's reputation for medical knowledge rose even higher in another Blackfeet village, where he visited an apparently dying child, bathed his feet in warm water, and revived his breathing. By the next day the child was running around the village and Point had become known as the master healer. "'What power the Black Robe has,' everyone declared."[51] Although Point did not explain what this popular declaration meant to him, the priest who escaped anti-Jesuit crowds in France and unsympathetic Jesuit superiors in Louisiana would surely have felt some personal vindication and some sense of higher social status as he became known for his healing power within the Blackfeet tribe.

Whatever Point may have thought about his modest ability to heal the bodies of Indigenous people, he clearly wanted his growing religious authority to heal their souls and reduce their social conflicts. He was asked to pray for solutions to urgent problems (one family requested prayers for a lost warrior, who was miraculously found within an hour) or to give advice when rival tribes were on the brink of war. The healing priest also became a peacemaker, especially when he was able to forge an alliance that united the Christian Salish with their longtime Blackfeet enemies. Seated between emissaries from the two tribes, Point heard the warlike Blackfeet announce their attention to abide by a common faith: "'From this day forward the prayer of the Flatheads [Salish] will be the prayer of the Blackfeet.'"[52] The alienated priest who had lived on the margins of modern French society and then fled from his own nation had become an esteemed peacemaker between American Indian nations in the far western mountains of North America. Gaining the respect he had never felt at home and mediating between people who apparently trusted his judgment, the traveling priest finally found an essential religious task that neither his French compatriots nor his Jesuit superiors could easily dismiss, duplicate, or surpass.

Point believed his authority among Native Americans derived from his ability to interpret European Catholicism to non-European people who had no prior knowledge of Christian ideas or rituals. Moving among diverse Indigenous communities as an honored teacher, he taught Catholicism to converted "students" who (in his view) responded more positively than European American students in Kentucky or Louisiana had ever responded to his lessons on Latin and Greek cultures. "I taught the children the prayers," he noted in one account of his work among the Blackfeet; then there were "instructions for the men," and finally he explained to the women what it meant to be Christian "wives and mothers." Intergenerational learners listened to the Black Robe's words and prayers, but they also learned from his drawings. When he reached the limits of what could be conveyed in words, he continued to communicate with "pictures of the Passion which my interpreters explained as best they could."[53] This combination of words and images gave Point the means to translate apostolic traditions from a French Catholic culture that was losing its influence in Europe into Native American cultures that were losing their lands, resources, and freedom in North America. Point and the people in Indigenous tribes grew up in vastly different cultural contexts, but they may have connected through the shared experiential knowledge of social and cultural loss.

While Point was reshaping his spiritual tasks and self-definition in the western mountains, he was also constructing a new cultural identity as an eyewitness expert on Native American societies that were mostly unknown to his Catholic colleagues in Europe and the United States. Collecting his memoirs and paintings into carefully organized manuscripts after he left the Rocky Mountains, Point urged the Catholic Church to send new missionaries to Indigenous communities throughout the remote territories in which he had traveled. He offered specific advice on American Indian languages and customs to help would-be missionaries understand Native American societies; and he wanted his pictures of the social life in these cultures to serve as an inspiration for future religious work. If the paintings "should prompt you to do for our poor savages even the hundredth part of the good I wish for you," he wrote in an introduction to his illustrated memoirs, "then, certainly, you would receive a hundredfold [blessing] in this world and in the next."[54]

Although his memoirs were not published in his lifetime, the two-sided task of explaining Christianity to American Indians and Native American cultures to Europeans gave Point a sense of public authority, religious purpose, and cultural status that he could never find in other contexts. The precise psychological meaning of this work cannot be known, of course, yet Point's writings suggest that his travels among the western American Indians became a journey toward his own deepest self. "Only a mother knows what she feels at the return of a long-absent son," Point wrote in one attempt to convey the importance of his life-changing experiences. "Does she know what a missionary experiences when he sees himself, for the first time, surrounded by a numerous family, whose members he has never seen before, but who are, nevertheless, completely devoted to him?"[55]

Point's long trip among the Indigenous people of the Northern Rockies thus resembled an emotional homecoming in which a mother is reunited with her son, or a long-lost relative finds his place in a previously unknown family. This new "family" gave Point a temporary emotional "home" in Native American villages and affirmed his religious identity amid soaring American mountains that nobody could ever see or comprehend from the highest church towers in France.

CHAPTER EIGHT

Olympe Audouard's American Journey toward Independent Womanhood and Literary Status in France

OLYMPE AUDOUARD was born in Marseille on 11 March 1832, but she described herself as a child of Provence and of the mistral—the famous late-winter wind that sweeps across southern France. Audouard's memoirs and travel books are the main source of information about her life, but she was often vague about specific events and dates (including the year of her birth). Although she became a prolific author, published more than twenty-five books, edited four different journals, and argued forcefully for expanding women's rights in France, her eventful life and literary career largely vanished from historical memory until the late twentieth century. Her liberal Catholicism and forward-looking feminist ideas were laced with nineteenth-century French racism and anti-Semitism, so she may have lost visibility because she cannot be easily placed in the political, cultural, or feminist categories of modern historical analysis.[1]

Her birth name was Olympe de Jouval, and she grew up in the countryside near the town of Apt in the Vaucluse. She had two older brothers who died before she was born. Her mother, Marie-Thérèse Fortunée Audouard, died when she was very young, and an older sister was sent off to live in a convent. Young Olympe therefore grew up essentially as the only child of a liberal father, Jean-Baptiste Camille de Jouval, who liked to travel and who encouraged his daughter to travel too. Olympe's affectionate descriptions of her father did not explain exactly how he supported himself, but she noted that Jouval lived in a small chateau, liked to discuss political ideas, admired American republicanism, hosted a Polish exile in the 1830s, and always remained a "philosophe" who abhorred provincial prejudices. Having lost his two sons, he taught Olympe to hunt and encouraged her to wear male clothes, which caused a scandal in the family. Yet Jouval—fearing for his daughter's health and perhaps for her mind—did not want Olympe to read books.

She was therefore unable to read until the in-house Polish exile taught her how to decipher some of the journals that arrived regularly at the family chateau. Her father soon accepted his daughter's new skills and then encouraged her to develop intellectual, literary, and political interests that would enhance her later passion for travel. "My father inspired all of these instincts in me," Audouard wrote in her memoirs, " . . . and this is why I have been able to face energetically . . . the prejudice that says a woman should never be an author or public speaker, never launch out on perilous voyages, and never discuss politics."[2]

Audouard's father thus pushed her beyond the cultural world of most nineteenth-century French girls, yet he retained entirely traditional assumptions about the social roles of men and women. When she was twelve years old he sent her to study in a Catholic convent, but he removed her from the convent after he learned that she was beginning to think she should be a nun. Olympe had developed a strong, enduring Catholic identity, which Jouval now wanted her to transfer from the cloisters of the convent to the traditional domestic life of a French wife. "In the American mores that he liked so much," Audouard explained, "my father criticized only one thing: the liberty that allowed young women to choose their husband."[3] He therefore arranged for the youthful Olympe to marry a first cousin from her mother's family, Alexis Audouard, who was a notary in Marseille. The marriage disintegrated after about five years, however, partly because Alexis found that the "career of Don Juan appealed to him far more than the duties of a father and husband."[4] Seeking a legal separation, Olympe Audouard went through prolonged court proceedings that finally gave her the right to leave her husband.

Like Flora Tristan, Audouard was constrained by the post-Napoleonic marriage laws that made divorce illegal in France until 1884, so her marital separation finally became a legally recognized divorce in 1885. Although she gained custody of her two young sons, Louis-Marie and Camille, after the legal separation from her husband, Audouard faced permanent restrictions on what she could do to earn a living or support her children (who both died young when she was later living in Paris). She could not enter a business or any kind of commercial activity, for example, without authorization from the magistrates or from her estranged husband.[5] These constraints and the growing recognition that women were permanently relegated to the position of "a minor" in French society pushed Audouard to seek a new life and new work in Paris at the beginning of the 1860s.

Moving to the French capital stimulated her intellectual ambitions. She brashly developed a plan to create a literary journal, despite the financial risks and despite the fact that she had to go through another legal proceeding because her distant, unhappy husband objected to the use of his name in a publishing venture. A panel of magistrates eventually decided, however, that editing a literary publication could be a legitimate activity for a "separated" woman, so she established a new journal called *Papillon* (Butterfly) and began to recruit prominent writers. Théophile Gautier, Alexandre Dumas *père*, Jules Janin, and other well-known authors agreed to become collaborators, thereby helping Audouard attract several hundred subscribers and launch the journal in January 1861.[6] She also met the Parisian publisher Édouard Dentu, who encouraged her to write a travel book about a trip she had taken to Constantinople with her father in the late 1850s. This book, *Les mystères du sérail et des harems turcs* (1863) (Mysteries of the Serail and Turkish harems) marked the beginning of Audouard's career as a travel writer, and she soon wrote other books about her travels in Egypt and the Middle East.[7] Travel writing gave Audouard a genre in which she could tell stories, describe different people and customs, gain some income, and claim a distinctive intellectual and literary authority on the basis of her own experiences.

Her trip to the United States in the late 1860s therefore extended her earlier work as a travel writer whose cross-cultural observations shaped a comparative analysis of French society—often with particular attention to different gender roles and marriage customs. As she explained in one of her books about America, she crossed the Atlantic in the late winter of 1868 and remained in the area around New York until she left for a long trip to the West in the late summer of that year (like all her writings, Audouard's accounts of the United States provided few chronological details).[8] Her journey across America was thus far briefer than Nicolas Point's extended travel in the 1840s, but the trip contributed valuable "cultural capital" to her evolving career as a writer and social critic. Audouard emphasized in her memoir (1884) that her father had often talked about America when she was a child, and she had learned from him that Americans cared more about practical freedoms than about traditions.[9] This historical generalization, which reappears often in her commentaries on American society, suggests her own cultural and political motives for a trip to the United States as well as the lasting influence of her father's ideas.

The journey to the United States thus evolved partly from memories of childhood conversations, but it also affirmed the more autonomous personal and professional identity that Audouard was constructing for herself throughout the 1860s. Following her trip to America, she expanded her literary identity in other books about later travel across central Europe and Russia, but she also became a prominent activist in campaigns to change the divorce laws and overturn restrictions on women's rights in France. She criticized these restrictions in works such as *La femme dans le mariage, la séparation et le divorce* (1870) (Woman in marriage, separation and divorce) and *Gynécologie: La femme depuis six mille ans* (1873) (Gynecology: Woman for the last 6,000 years), and she spoke about the status of women at well-attended public lectures—some of which were suppressed by the French police.[10] Audouard's trip to America and her two books about the United States therefore came at a crucial time in her developing critique of the gender hierarchies in French social and political life. Her cross-cultural comparisons discussed women's education, professional opportunities, and family relationships, all of which had become key home-country concerns during the years when she struggled to establish herself as an independent writer after separating from her abusive husband. She wanted her readers to see that the changing public roles of women in the United States offered examples that could help the French create a more enlightened, egalitarian society for women who suffered from the social and legal inequalities in nineteenth-century France. Much as Point viewed the conversion of American Indians as a gratifying alternative to the anti-Jesuit culture in France, Audouard found that gender relations in the United States (and her narrative about them) offered valuable, real-world alternatives to the male-dominated social, political, and intellectual life she had encountered in Marseille and Paris. Travel provided both an escape from that oppressive French milieu and an opportunity for her to establish her own status as an authoritative writer and international social critic.

Audouard's first book about America actually described the later months of her travels in the United States, perhaps because writing about the "Far West" was more exotic than writing about urban life in New York. She told stories about her long trip from New York to Salt Lake City, comparing life on the American frontier to social life in France and describing what she had learned about American railroads, western cities, open landscapes, towering mountain peaks, "uncivilized" American Indians, and the religiously sanctioned polygamy in Mormon families. Narrating this long journey gave Audouard a literary structure in which she could reflect on a wide range of differences that separated America from Europe, but this book, like a second book that focused mainly on New York, culminated in a cross-cultural analysis of the issue that evoked Audouard's strongest personal and political passions: the position of women in America and the relative backwardness of women's rights in France.

In later years, however, she turned more of her literary attention to spiritualism (through which she believed she could communicate with her two deceased sons) and to writing her memoirs. Her final book was the first volume of the never-completed autobiographical narrative that concluded with a clear statement about how travel had changed her life's trajectory: "My life has had two very distinct parts: one part, which took place in France, was dull and painful; the other part, which I spent traveling, was sunny and gay. I have now finished with the first [part], and I am now, happily, going to recall the second."[11] But this second volume

Olympe Audouard. Photograph by an unknown photographer, ca. 1860s, in *Portraits d'écrivains . . . du XIXe siècle*, vol. 1 (Paris, n.d.). Audouard's independent life as a traveling writer could begin only after she separated from an abusive husband and started to write books about her journeys and her feminist ideas during the 1860s. This picture from that era seems to express her desire for direct engagement with her readers and for long journeys beyond the gendered social conventions that had shaped her earlier life in France. The Picture Art Collection/Alamy Stock Photo.

never appeared. Audouard died of influenza in Nice on 13 January 1890, leaving a remarkable record of her travels and the unfinished story of other life events. Although she wrote extensively about her long trips in the Middle East and Russia, this chapter focuses on her two books about America because these works offer intriguing comparisons with Point's writings and excellent examples of her specific, critical commentaries on France. More generally, these books show how Audouard drew (like Point) on her American journey to analyze the meaning of "modern" or "premodern" civilizations, to claim a higher-status identity in France, and to describe her own evolving sense of independent selfhood.

Audouard's Description of the United States as the Future of Human History

Audouard saw America as the land of a "younger" people, but she saw this "youth" moving into the twentieth-century future rather than living in the prehistoric past. In her book on American social and cultural life, she claimed that civilizations and races pass through four stages: birth, height of powers, decline, and finally decadence. Although she worried about where Europe might now stand in this cycle, she was certain that America was at the vigorous beginning of its national ascent. Immigrants from all races and nations were creating an innovative American society that could now give cultural lessons to other societies that were too deeply rooted in the past. "It has produced a young, vigorous people," she wrote in one of her descriptions of America's dynamic national culture, "who have resolutely freed themselves from the routine of old ideas and hardily thrown down this victorious cry: forward!" This progressive development posed a problem for Europeans who were still unwilling to admit that "if we want to advance, if we want to march with our century, we must copy America!" No nation could readily concede its cultural shortcomings, but transnational copying would be especially difficult for the patriotic French, whose long-admired scientific and cultural achievements were increasingly "left behind by this cosmopolitan people."[12]

This American cosmopolitanism was for Audouard a key source of national creativity because she assumed that a multicultural mix of people made Americans less beholden to the kinds of oppressive national traditions that had stymied her in France. Stressing an openness to change in the United States, Audouard told her stories about America to challenge and criticize social constraints in nineteenth-century France, much as Voltaire had written his *Letters on England* (1734) to challenge and criticize French intolerance in the early eighteenth century. As Audouard explained through her cultural comparisons, the progressive aspects of American society appeared most notably in American views of women and men. "These men of the twentieth century," she wrote in a typical chronological reference to the social advances in America, "have understood that the human soul has the same essence, whether it is under a feminine or masculine envelope. They have understood and admitted that knowledge, science, erudition [and] intelligence have no gender and are an attribute of both sexes."[13] This broad claim surely exaggerated the typical American male's view of gender equality in the 1860s (as Voltaire had overemphasized English tolerance), yet it became a key theme in Audouard's argument for the influence of "twentieth-century" ideas in American institutions, families, and schools.

Audouard also wanted to show how these people of the "next century" educated their children to think more freely than the children in any of the older, lagging nations in Europe. Intellectual and academic life in France, for example, was so centralized in Paris that French students elsewhere simply withered on the provincial intellectual vine. The decentralized American system, by contrast, allowed for more independent thinking among both the teachers and students who lived far from the major eastern cities. Each American state developed its own schools and sought to create its own innovative methods of instruction, which meant that Americans "educate their youth through neither obedience nor commands. They teach them simply to know how to be free." This fundamental lesson was of course not taught everywhere (only about 78 percent of America's school-age children attended public schools in 1870), and Audouard did not describe the widespread racial and economic exclusions that contradicted her optimistic account of post–Civil War education. Setting aside these structural inequalities, however, she could optimistically argue that schools in the United States nurtured the "democratic sentiments" and egalitarian spirit that made America "a beautiful example" for French people who were still trying to understand how they could create a better government and how they could educate their students for "twentieth-century" social institutions.[14]

Audouard's travel commentaries thus criticized France more than the United States, but her mostly sympathetic summaries of American life also referred to specific aspects of this advancing social system that were not so attractive. One recurring problem appeared in the American preoccupation with money, which suggested to Audouard that "this is what we will be in the twentieth century: a fanatical worshiper of gold." The United States was filled with people who preferred to amass a fortune rather than spend time with their families, thereby pursuing one of the "modern" behaviors that Audouard would not endorse. Meanwhile, "cosmopolitan" Americans were also becoming indifferent to what people in other parts of the world might think of American affairs. This self-satisfied ignorance of European perceptions was confirmed in the typical "Yankee's" assumption that Americans were "the greatest people in the world; and he will repeat this to you at every turn."[15]

Yet these materialist and cultural shortcomings did not undermine Audouard's broader assessment of the future-oriented, "twentieth-century" Americans who were open to social change, new opportunities for women, and a democratic-minded system of public education. In contrast to Point's travel through a partially imagined "premodern" America in which he could defend his religious values and reaffirm France's essential Catholic identity, Audouard traveled (in 1868) through a partially imagined "twentieth-century" American society in which ambitious women like herself could pursue public activities that were still closed to women in nineteenth-century France.

Audouard's Description of America: Geography, Social Institutions, and Republican Political Culture

Like most Europeans who traveled across North America, Audouard believed that America's vast geographical spaces contributed to many of the social differences that separated the United States from Europe. She also stressed, however, that the scenic, sparsely inhabited western lands (where visitors could see how the natural world must have looked before the development of modern civilizations) were completely different from the crowded, urban spaces of cities such as New York and Chicago (where visitors could glimpse the next century). Audouard found something to admire in both the rural and the urban geography, but she emphasized the differences by dividing her long narrative into a first book that described the "Far West" and a second book that mainly discussed New York. The accounts of these different geographical regions nevertheless converged in similar arguments about distinctive, "untraditional" cultural patterns that existed throughout American society. Audouard shared some of Point's interest in "premodern" Native Americans, yet (unlike Point) she condemned Indigenous cultures and wrote mainly about the "modern" social life of American immigrants, merchants, educators, and families. Her travel writing combined forward-looking claims for women's rights with semicolonial, racist views of non-European people and societies, which suggests why she found the most important and advanced social groups in American cities.

Audouard portrayed the streets of New York as a carnivalesque "fairground" in which the walls were covered with colorful advertisements, and everyone had something to sell. New York's busy people showed how Americans acted on their belief that "time is money," but their mad pursuit of riches also produced a striking social gap between the rich and the poor. Although some wide streets were filled with great mansions, a visitor who wandered a few blocks from the rich neighborhoods would soon enter the altogether different social world of crowded, smelly tenement houses. New York thus introduced foreigners to extraordinary social distinctions that most well-traveled Europeans did not expect to find in a society that had rejected both aristocratic titles and monarchical governments. "I have never seen such a distressing sight," Audouard wrote after describing a jammed, smelly New York tenement house. "I have never had a glimpse of the human species fallen to such a level of degradation." Noting that more than 300 people sometimes lived in packed houses that were originally built to lodge about 10, Audouard wondered how such an advanced society could tolerate this human misery in its largest cities.[16] She could not provide specific answers to this social question, but she assumed that one explanation might be found in the vast landscapes of the American frontier, where city dwellers could flee from crowded tenements toward a new freedom in the underpopulated wilderness.

Although Audouard was both drawn to and disturbed by the bustling social life in New York, she expressed a tourist-style fascination with the very different frontier wilderness of the far west. America's western lands were vast open spaces that could scarcely be imagined in Europe, Audouard explained, but no one could understand America without seeing the huge scale of its remote landscapes. "In order to get a correct idea of the immensity of this new world," she reported, "you have to cross its entire breadth; you see a land without end." American nature was "grandiose," which meant that the sheer size of America's natural wonders spread far beyond any open spaces that travelers might see in western Europe. Indeed, America almost needed a race of giants to populate "this world that was so different from the one in which we [Europeans] now live." Niagara Falls was an immense waterfall, the western plains were immense open lands, the antelope and buffalo wandered the prairies in immense herds, and the Rocky Mountains were an immense range of rugged, snow-capped peaks.[17]

Almost every aspect of the American wilderness "spoke to my imagination," Audouard told her readers, but the Rocky Mountains apparently impressed her more than anything else she saw; and, like Point, she described the mystical awe she felt when she first viewed the towering ranges in northern Colorado.

> To describe the appearance of these mountains is extremely difficult; they have something strange and fantastic, which amazes and moves you. I have seen many famous mountains and traveled through many picturesque places . . . [yet] I can say that neither Mount Olympus, . . . nor Mount Blanc, nor Mount Athos, nor even Lebanon can be compared to the Rocky Mountains.
>
> Imagine a series of mountain chains extending back-to-back without end. The highest have a crown of eternal snow; this white mast is surrounded by azure skies which are reflected on the snow and colored from the beginning of the day by the sun and by a thousand rays of fire. . . . All the colors, all the nuances [of light] come together and combine, so that you would believe they are forming an immense rainbow. These chains fold and bend and twist themselves into narrow gorges, forming inaccessible peaks and plateaus . . . [and] the most bizarre, fantastic shapes.[18]

The Rocky Mountains, in short, offered both spiritual and aesthetic mysteries, as she learned by descending from mountaintop views and entering caves that resembled the most beautiful "art" and "poetry" or the sumptuous furnishings of an elegant palace.[19]

In contrast to the congested streets and smelly tenements of New York City, the peaks and caves of the western mountains provided unparalleled beauty for adventurous travelers and untapped mineral wealth for ubiquitous American fortune hunters. The territories of Colorado and Utah were already swarming with miners, fur traders, railroad workers, Mormon farmers, and energetic entrepreneurs who were trying to extract profits from these vast spaces and displacing Native Americans, who struggled to protect their ancestral lands. Reporting on all these people and their diverse social customs, Audouard defined a place for herself that was both inside and outside the "modern" and "premodern" cultures she described.

Audouard's account of the American people often compared their cultural values and social hierarchies with the culture and institutions of France. She seemed to assume that the United States would become more comprehensible if she could show her readers how Americans resembled or differed from Europeans, but she never forgot that she was writing for a French audience. The key cultural differences between America and France, as Audouard described them, emerged in the contrasting views of inherited social or political conventions and long-honored cultural traditions. Arguing that America achieved both economic and political success because it was not oppressed by the traditions that weighed so heavily on France (she did not examine America's oppressive history of racism and slavery), Audouard emphasized that the United States could fully develop its human and material resources because it "had no past. This cosmopolitan American [nation] has not had to struggle against history or against traditions. It has not had to fight against old routines; it could throw itself boldly into the new; [and] it was easily able to make innovations."[20] This freedom from traditions led to extraordinary economic achievements that older nations were now seeking to copy, but it also led to the political creation and defense of a successful republic.

The contrasting political histories of France and America appeared most clearly in the different historical fates of their republics. Reflecting on the vulnerabilities of French republicanism as France struggled to establish its Third Republic in 1871, Audouard compared her own nation's republican failures to the political achievements of the United States and doubted whether the French would ever establish a stable republic. "I am a democrat and republican," she explained, but the French nation had repeatedly embraced authoritarian political actions that rejected her own aspirations for a stable republic as well as the political traditions of American republicanism. The typical French citizen or government official was a "budding Caesar," and every French bureaucrat liked to flaunt his power as a local despot, so republican constitutions had never overcome France's cultural resistance to the checks and balances of a successful republican government. After multiple republican failures, the French needed to learn American lessons about dividing power among different branches of government, avoiding excessive or corrupt government expenditures, and preventing government surveillance of individual citizens.[21]

Audouard conceded that republics also had their flaws and that America had by no means created the perfect political system. There were corrupt government officials, for example, and both political parties rewarded their own political hacks with unmerited appointments to government offices. More generally, American political life often degenerated into bitter factional battles between Democrats and Republicans or into the conflicts between rural and urban economic interests that had culminated in the recent Civil War. Despite these continuing problems, Audouard assured her French readers that her "long stay in the United States" had finally enabled her to understand the meaning of "a true republic." Americans recognized the perennial human desire for power, so they had carefully created constitutional institutions to control both the individuals and the social groups that sought excessive power for themselves.[22] These institutional constraints had survived the Civil War, and they continued to protect Americans who used their practical, innovative skills to pursue their social and economic aspirations. Nobody expected the government to solve all their problems, which she confirmed by reporting that even decorated Union veterans of the Civil War armies did not believe they should receive permanent government pensions (as military veterans in France would undoubtedly demand).[23]

The stability and success of America's republican political institutions allowed people to work freely toward their personal ambitions, which for most Americans meant a daily quest for more wealth or personal freedom. Here too, Audouard argued, American achievements contrasted positively with social and economic behaviors she had observed in France. Americans had a natural talent for building new machines, creating new cities in the wilderness, introducing innovative new commerce, and mastering the complex process of laying a transcontinental railroad, all of which demonstrated the freedom and anti-traditional ethos of American life. This unconventional freedom seemed to extend beyond almost every social or natural boundary when she reported that she had joined with fellow passengers to shoot antelope from a moving train on the western plains. This gunplay on an American train was remarkable in itself, but Audouard was even more surprised when the conductor stopped the train and allowed her to retrieve an antelope she had shot from her train window. The cultural differences for a European traveler were both stark and strange: French train conductors would never allow passengers to fire hunting rifles or stop their trains for the collection of dead animals, but Americans carried guns on train trips, shot animals on the prairies, and collected carcasses along the tracks. The far west of America, in other words, was far, far away from the people, parks, and police of Paris.[24]

Audouard's Description of America: Wealth, Immigration, and Racial Hierarchies

The comparative openness of American society also became a key theme in Audouard's discussion of how social classes interacted in the United States. She described the social mobility of people who quickly made or lost their fortunes and the social dignity of poor people who assumed they would soon be rich. A general in the Union army could return to the humble station of a cobbler, for example, and the lowest-ranking servants or cab drivers demanded respect from the people they served—a social expectation that visitors from the more hierarchical class system in France often failed to understand. Audouard observed the social consequences of this cultural difference during her stay in New York, where she saw a Frenchman expelled from a hotel after speaking rudely to waiters in the hotel's restaurant. The American democratic sensibility, as she explained in her firsthand account of this incident, instinctively recognized and resisted the disrespectful attitudes of European travelers who could not comprehend how a deeply felt democratic spirit shaped the social exchanges of daily life.[25]

A similar demand for respect appeared among American women, who (according to Audouard) enjoyed a personal security and independence that women in France could scarcely imagine. It was much safer for women to travel in America than anywhere in France, so Audouard was able to travel with railroad workers on western trains and to stay alone in rowdy western hotels. Men treated her with a *politesse* that made her feel safe and respected and free to go wherever she wanted to be. Women traveled alone "across all of America," she explained to her French readers, "and went out alone at night without the least apprehension." Finding that Americans did not view a traveling woman as dangerous or immoral, Audouard decided that she could make her way into the most remote territories of the western frontier. "I understood that a woman could really travel alone in America," she wrote, "because in every social class she only encounters the greatest respect and deference."[26]

Audouard's descriptions of politics, economics, and social relations in the United States thus suggested that the French had much to learn from Americans, but Audouard complained that most people in France were profoundly ignorant of American culture and society. Although this French ignorance gave Audouard a strong justification for her travel books about a distant, unknown society, it also helped to explain a wider problem in modern French history: unlike the other nations of Europe, France sent few emigrants to America, and poor French people rarely took advantage of transatlantic opportunities to improve their economic condition.

Audouard therefore urged the French to consider moving to America, where the skills of artisans, bakers, and creative people would be well rewarded. Tens of thousands of Irish and German immigrants had settled in New York City and entered every kind of economic activity. Meanwhile, the French community in New York consisted of barely 5,000 or 6,000 people who mostly kept to themselves, learned little English, and complained about American vulgarity. Both the resistance to emigration and the French isolation in America would break down, however, if French workers could learn about American conditions and if French immigrants would enter more energetically into American life. One of Audouard's literary goals was thus to make the French more receptive to the American ideas and social practices she discussed in her cross-cultural comparisons and critiques. "The French character is so different from the American character," Audouard reported, "that our compatriots cannot assimilate with the people of the New World; they become bored in America, and they feel ill-at-ease. Their favorite distraction is to bitterly or happily criticize the mores and habits, the people, and things [in America]." Condemning this "chauvinism," Audouard urged the French to embrace the cosmopolitan ideas of modern times and move like the Germans and Irish into the heartland of America. There would be fewer unhappy people in France if low-paid workers and poor farmers began migrating to the United States, though Audouard realized that her proposals would make sense only to people who learned the truth about American society (for example, by reading her books).[27]

If French emigrants moved to the United States, however, they would likely find that the pursuit of economic opportunities required some tolerance of America's less attractive social customs. A realistic account of migration should therefore include honest warnings about the problems of American life as well as descriptions of its liberating attractions. Audouard's discussion of the poverty in New York tenement houses, for example, emphasized the problematic economic gap between America's rich and poor, but this conspicuous economic inequality was only one of the social problems that French immigrants would encounter. They would also meet a nation of tobacco-chewing men who were forever spitting in public and private places; they would have to get used to whiskey-drinking passengers on trains, noisy people in hotel bars, and "Yankees" who loved to put their feet up on tables or chairs; they would have to go to social events with people who did not know how to dance properly or drink a good wine; and they would have to eat food that caused the most acute indigestion.[28]

American meals posed a particular challenge for Audouard because she soon realized that the food and service in American restaurants threatened her sympathy for "democratic" ideals. Although the people she met in restaurants were usually friendly and helpful, they passed the food around in large serving dishes, they never changed the plates between courses at dinner, they wiped their fingers on the tablecloth, and they piled fish bones in a heap on the table. Restaurants typically served poorly cooked meats and soups that consisted of "hot water in which someone has thrown a little Cayenne pepper." The chickens always arrived in the same "white or black sauce," which you washed down with pitchers of milk or lemonade. Wine was available only as an "extra" and served like a liqueur, but there were plenty of "heavy, unhealthy" pastries for dessert. Audouard reported that she had never seen "human beings eat in such a fashion" at even the humblest or most rushed peasant dinner in France. Perhaps the Americans ate quickly because the food was so bad, or maybe they simply rushed through their meals to get those heavy sweets for dessert. In any case, Audouard decided that "it is easy enough . . . to understand why the Americans all complain about dyspepsia. What stomach could withstand such a diet?"[29]

Fine food and long dinner conversations would in fact have kept Americans from their deepest personal passion, which was the endless quest for money. French travelers and immigrants needed to understand that Americans were willing to sacrifice home life, family stability, artistic creativity, and personal morality as they pursued their dreams of getting rich. It was therefore impossible for the French to match the Americans when it came to commerce, but she also suggested that maybe the Americans should learn something from the French about the noncommercial satisfactions that came from maintaining an old home or preserving ancestral furniture or protecting certain continuities in family life. They might also learn that the freedom of endless movement carried some unacknowledged social costs. "The Americans have some of the instincts of the nomadic races," Audouard explained, "[and] the love for family is killed by the desire to earn money."[30] Children regularly abandoned their parents and hometowns in search of more money (hence the crowded boardinghouses), and few people worried about the moral character of anyone who got rich. Audouard's support for a more open, democratic society thus sometimes collided with her own desire for a more settled European respectability or her class-conscious disdain for rootless people.

To illustrate the pervasive and even immoral American respect for wealth,

Audouard told the story of a New Yorker named John Allen who became rich by operating a house of prostitution. Business began to decline, however, whereupon he announced his conversion to Christianity, set off on speaking tours to explain how he had been saved by his new religious faith, and collected money from people who were moved by his story of sin and salvation. Returning to New York with $150,000, he built a luxurious new house in which he installed forty women from Paris and reopened his old business. This created a scandal, of course, but Audouard reported that many New Yorkers admired Allen's ingenuity.[31] Americans were often religious people, but their deep faith in money could make almost all rich entrepreneurs respectable, even if they became wealthy by telling lies.

This tolerance for wealthy people reflected the widely held belief that every hardworking or lucky American could soon become a very rich person. The prevailing cultural assumption suggested that there were only two social groups in the United States: the rich and those who were on their way to becoming rich. Such ideas prevented the development of the class resentments that existed in France, but they also diminished or even destroyed American respect for creative cultural and artistic work. Audouard met people in Chicago, for example, who assumed that Paris was an insignificant place because it had fewer large businesses than other cities; and when she defended the French capital's global importance by referring to its history, cultural achievements, and famous monuments, she was told that art was worthless for anyone who faced practical problems or needed to eat. Americans who defined a city's historical significance in terms of its wealth and commerce could happily claim that Chicago had already surpassed Paris as a center of transnational influence. Audouard rejected these materialist rankings for urban or national achievements, however, and (in this case) affirmed her French identification with proud references to her home city's art, literature, and culture.[32] Defining her own "Frenchness" against American commercialism, Audouard repeated typical French views of American vulgarity and stressed the cultural meanings of modern nationhood, but her later travel through the western frontier brought her much closer to America's enduring racial definitions of social and national identities.

Although would-be French immigrants needed to prepare themselves for American food and materialism, it was perhaps even more important for them to understand that they would encounter a more multicultural mix of people and races than they had ever seen in nineteenth-century Europe. Audouard's own views of America resembled the racist and colonizing assumptions of most Europeans in her era, but she had supported the Union cause during the American Civil War because she strongly opposed slavery. Noting the huge number of casualties in the war's major battles, she wrote in the preface to *Le Far-West* that the Union army had made "the greatest sacrifices to abolish slavery and achieve a victory for one of the most beautiful principles of humanity: individual liberty." The northern section of the nation had been willing "to rally all of its forces [*lever en masse*] to smash this final vestige of barbarism."[33] Despite her sympathy for the Union war against the southern slave system, Audouard's belief in racial differences blinded her to the contradictions between her fervent support for women's rights and her mostly indifferent or hostile attitudes toward disenfranchised African Americans and Indigenous people.

In contrast to her descriptions of European Americans, Audouard's discussion of other racial groups never suggested that they might provide useful cultural lessons for her French readers. Comparing the social position of the formerly enslaved African Americans to the servant class in wealthy Parisian neighborhoods, she argued that many "freedmen" still identified more with their former masters than with the other workers or abolitionists who had opposed their enslavers. Her conversations with a Black male hotel worker in Cheyenne, Wyoming, for example, somehow gave Audouard the impression that some recently emancipated persons lamented the insecurities of their new social freedom. There were obvious injustices in the slave system, yet the enslaved male worker had always known (according to the man she met in Wyoming) that he would have food, shelter, and medicine, whereas his new status as a free man forced him to work and struggle like a "slave" to support his family.[34] Audouard noted that she was surprised when the hotel worker described the problems of a free life, but she also reported that other Black people expressed a similar nostalgia for their former lives on southern plantations. Although it is impossible to know why a Black man might have expressed such views to a European traveler (was he being careful with an unknown white hotel guest or perhaps simply ironic?), this conversation gave Audouard some firsthand evidence to support a white racist assumption about social differences: African Americans differed from European Americans because they did not share the white population's passion for work and money. Such ideas show how the era's racist ideology helped Audouard forget her concerns about American materialism and define civilization, progress, and modernity as distinctive achievements of European and European American cultures.

Her conception of this racial and cultural hierarchy became most apparent in Audouard's racist account of Native Americans, whom she located in an ambiguous biological or cultural sphere somewhere below other human beings. Unlike Nicolas Point, who sought to understand and protect American Indians before and after they converted to Christianity, Audouard portrayed Native Americans as "wild animals" (*bêtes fauves*) that an advancing white civilization would inevitably displace from open western lands. The Indian tribes in nineteenth-century

America, she explained to her readers with uninformed racist generalizations, lived exactly as their ancestors were living when Europeans first arrived on the North American continent. Civilized peoples changed as their cultures evolved across time, but American Indians "remained what they [always] were, despite two centuries of contact with the Europeans."[35] Claiming that she had gathered firsthand information from her travels through the lands of Indigenous people and from her conversations with Jesuit missionaries and American soldiers, she reported falsely that almost all tribal cultures had similar traditions, legends, and customs. She also expanded on her racist themes by portraying Native Americans as dirty, prone to violence, and stubbornly attached to a wandering, nomadic life of hunting and gathering food. In fact, as Audouard described them in her dehumanizing summaries, they preferred to live in misery rather than to settle on farms or attend schools, which did not make sense unless one understood their unchanging racial traits. "They are beastly and ferocious, [and] they commit evil acts because of their natural needs," she wrote in another disturbing racist critique. "People ask if they have a soul, and nothing proves that they do."[36]

The Jesuits nevertheless believed in the humanity of the American Indians, and they had made valiant, sometimes successful efforts to convert the western American Indians to Christianity. Unfortunately, in Audouard's view, these conversions were usually insincere because Native Americans often embraced Catholicism as an opportunity to receive blankets, rifles, or other gifts. If the gifts disappeared or stopped arriving, most converts abandoned Christianity and returned to their former religion. Despite these recurring setbacks, the missionaries steadfastly pursued their civilizing work, sometimes at the cost of their own lives. Meanwhile, the Indigenous population steadily declined, in part because of a passion for the only product of modern civilization they truly accepted: whiskey. Although the American government wanted to bring these "vagabonds" into a modern, civilized life, it appeared to Audouard that the expanding "Yankee" society would soon destroy the Native American race, "because, in my view, it is impossible to civilize them." Audouard acknowledged that white American agents sometimes deceived the Indigenous communities and violated their own earlier treaties, yet she placed more blame on an inherent tribal tendency to lie or ignore previous agreements, which made it virtually impossible for advancing European American settlers to establish stable relations with the migrating tribes.[37]

Audouard thus expressed almost no sympathy for the displaced "premodern" cultures in which Point pursued his work and identity as a priest. She was looking for the future in America, so Indigenous people entered her narrative mainly as a vanishing remnant from the past. Indeed, her racist, demeaning descriptions of Native Americans suggested that their only resemblance to other cultures appeared in their love for whiskey and their condescending view of women. She noted that women carried the heavy baggage and performed most of the hard work whenever a tribe set off to travel or hunt. "The woman is treated like an inferior being," she wrote, "[with] a logic worthy of the civilized countries!" This "logic" of inferiority prevented women from practicing the magic rituals and healing arts that medicine men performed for their tribes, but these exclusions merely confirmed that gender "prejudices are the same everywhere."[38] The escape from such prejudices would therefore have to move women beyond the Native American past and the European present into a future society that was emerging in the modern United States. She recognized some of this society's most notable social flaws, yet this "modern" or "future" American civilization offered Audouard a cultural position from which she could affirm her identity as an independent woman writer and imagine a gender equality that had never existed in France or among American Indians on the western American frontier.

Audouard's View of Women, Men, and Marriage in the United States

Audouard's discussion of marriage customs and the status of women in America merged with her critique of gender relations in France and provoked her reflections on the social and intellectual obstacles she had faced in her own life. Although her descriptions of nineteenth-century American women often exaggerated their independence and professional opportunities, Audouard drew on what she learned about American education, divorce laws, and even polygamy among the Mormons in Utah to criticize the gender ideologies and hierarchies of modern French society. In addition to her feminist analysis of transnational differences in women's rights, however, she strongly defended her own evolving status as a knowledgeable writer and social critic in French literary culture.

The social advantages for American women began in Audouard's view with a widespread male appreciation for women's abilities and minds. The American man, as Audouard explained in one of her optimistic reports to French readers, had "a great respect for woman in general" because he assumed that females had "more refinement" and "more compassion" than males. Americans thus tended to believe that woman was "superior to man." This view of the two sexes was bound to surprise people in France, where women were treated as "weak" beings and permanent minors who could never exercise the "privileges and rights" that were routinely granted to adult men. The famous gallantry and *politesse* of French men was therefore simply an elegant mask for the hierarchical French view of women's inferior talents and personal fragility. American men, by contrast, had moved beyond such attitudes and accepted a more equal social role for women. "In America," Audouard wrote, "they do not call the woman a weak creature [who] is inferior to men; no, she is treated by men as an equal"; and though she still needed some special laws to protect her interests, one could say that "the woman is queen in America."[39] This generalization would have surprised most women who actually lived in America (including activists in the campaign for women's suffrage), but Audouard's view of the American woman's queenlike status depended on comparisons with France rather than on an absolute claim for female emancipation in the United States.

American girls began with an advantage over the girls in France because American schools introduced students to the social world in which they would actually have to live. Where the French isolated young girls in their families and single-sex schools, the Americans sent their daughters to schools with boys. This kind of education helped girls learn about male traits they would confront in later life, and it showed that Americans knew how to "combat the demoralization of women through work and instruction." By studying and working with boys from an early age, American girls learned useful skills and prepared themselves to deal intelligently with both well-educated and dishonest men when they became adults. The isolated French girls learned fewer practical skills at school and remained more vulnerable to the unscrupulous men who might seduce or deceive them as adults. Young American woman also emerged from their schools with the freedom and ability to choose a husband whose "affections" and "esteem" would make him a suitable partner for life. This freedom to choose a husband gave the American woman an extraordinary independence and contrasted starkly with the unhappy circumstances of Audouard's own unhappy marriage. "The parents leave her entirely free to choose her spouse," she noted in a description of the young American woman's autonomy, "and do not seek to impose an old millionaire on her."[40]

The familiar American obsession with money thus gave way in the sphere of male-female relations to a sensible recognition that happy marriages did not depend simply on wealth or financial speculations. Audouard's difficult marriage and separation obviously shaped this idealized image of marriage customs in America, but she also stressed that the freedom to choose a husband would not in itself improve a woman's social position. Women needed a good education, social experiences with men, and personal autonomy before they could make sensible decisions about potential marriage partners. The French should therefore learn from the Americans what Audouard's own father had not understood when he chose her awful husband: "the authority of parents" need not extend to the point of controlling the "happiness or unhappiness of their children's entire life."[41]

French families and teachers might also learn some relevant educational lessons from the American colleges and universities that had opened their doors to women. Professors at these institutions confirmed that women were intellectually equal to men, no matter what subject or academic field they chose to pursue. Women at Vassar College, for example, mastered the most advanced scientific knowledge and showed every day why Americans wisely ignored all the old arguments about the limits of female intelligence. American men did not oppose or ridicule women who sought higher education, and they rejected the absurd French argument that educated women would abandon their children and families.[42] They understood that well-educated women could be good mothers, just as well-educated men could be good fathers.

American men had thus learned from experience that educated women became more interesting, competent marriage partners, and they were quite willing to accept women into most professions. Audouard met women doctors, for example, and she found that American women often preferred to receive their medical advice or treatments from female physicians. The education of women thus encouraged better health care, more social equality, and more happiness among both women and men in the United States. "The Americans have understood something that the French have unfortunately not wanted to understand," Audouard explained in another pro-American summary of cultural differences; "intellectual idleness is very unhealthy for the woman. Her lively imagination needs a serious purpose because otherwise she throws herself into sentimental stories."[43] This weakness for romantic dreaming led French women into unhappy marriages or adultery rather than practical work or happy families, but well-educated American women knew there was more to life than sentimental love. They found more realistic outlets for their dreams or ambitions, and they could use their minds.

Americans therefore expressed pride in the intellectual achievements of women, especially when they matched or went beyond what most men accomplished in education or the professions. "Thanks to the legal emancipation they have granted to their women," Audouard reported with transatlantic admiration, "the feminine intellectual level is now higher in America than the masculine intellectual level."[44] The intellectual, professional, and political opportunities for American women still lagged far behind the opportunities for men, of course, but this was not the comparison that Audouard wanted to emphasize. She preferred to compare her idealized view of American women with the debilitating position of women in France, and she was certain that America's commitment to female education and freely chosen marriage partners gave women greater freedom, better marriages, and more control over their own lives.

Education and the freer choice of marriage partners also reduced adultery, which, Audouard assured her readers, was strongly condemned by all respectable

Americans. When an American discovered that an adulterous spouse had betrayed the marriage vows, he or she had the right to divorce and the right to marry another person, so American marriages reflected mutual affections rather than the constraints of a rigid legal system. These freedoms did not destabilize American marriages. Audouard learned that American divorces were less common than marital separations in France because successful marriages (in her view) grew out of the mutual consent of the partners, the greater equality of legal rights, and the better education of women. This education benefited American women both before and during their marriages, but it was especially helpful when a woman's husband died. Unlike most women in France, American women knew how to manage household finances and pursue an independent life. "In the New World," she explained in another (idealized) description of American gender relations, "the woman is truly the companion and the associate of the man."[45] Whatever the precise truth of these generalizations, they clearly expressed Audouard's anger about French marriages, adultery, and gendered social hierarchies. More surprisingly, perhaps, Audouard extended her claims for the social advantages of American women into her detailed reports on the (happy) polygamous marriages of the Mormons in Utah.

Audouard's interest in polygamy reappeared throughout her travel books, beginning with her descriptions of social life in Turkey and continuing in her book about the "Far West" in America. Although most European travelers viewed polygamy as a prominent example of women's degradation in non-European societies, Audouard developed a distinctive feminist account of how women could use polygamous marriages to serve their own interests and to avoid the dangers of marriage in France. She argued that women who shared the same husband could protect some spheres of personal autonomy and ensure both legal and financial protection for their children. Describing her visit to a "harem" in Constantinople, for example, Audouard reported that the women were smiling, singing, and enjoying the companionship of the other wives; and they most definitely did not look like "poor captives" in a prison. This apparent happiness became less mysterious, however, as Audouard learned about the rights that Turkish women retained in polygamous marriages. Parents arranged their children's marriages, but the daughter had the right to reject the man whom her parents selected (Audouard did not say how often such rejections occurred). When the woman gave her consent for the marriage negotiations to go forward, her family made sure that she would receive adequate financial compensation if the marriage eventually failed. In contrast to the legal vulnerability of women in monogamous French marriages, a Turkish woman could be granted a divorce if she were mistreated or if her husband abandoned her for other women. Judicial councils would then ensure that the divorced woman received adequate financial support and physical protection from her former husband, all of which suggested to Audouard that there was no other country "where the woman is protected more effectively than by the laws in Turkey."[46]

These earlier descriptions of Muslim social practices therefore included the kind of critical comparisons that would later emerge in Audouard's writings on America. In both cases, she attacked French marriages and gender hierarchies by praising the protections or opportunities for women in other cultures, though she also recognized various flaws in the other cultures' social life. The Turkish women who could divorce their husbands, for example, received no education, learned almost nothing about literature or art, and rarely developed any creative talents. The husbands in these polygamous marriages used their wives mainly to gratify their sexual lust or their pragmatic desire for heirs, so neither the men nor the women in Turkey understood the higher pleasures of a love relationship between equals.[47] Yet Audouard never wanted her readers to assume complacently that French marriages and gender relations were superior to the customs of other societies. No matter how much they might ridicule Muslim harems or Mormon polygamy, the French must also recognize the barbarity or absurdity of their own approach to marriage and divorce.

Audouard knew that American Mormons had gained notoriety in Paris, and she may have assumed that this notoriety would enhance her readers' interest in what she had observed during her visit to Utah. It was easy enough to ridicule the Mormons in Paris, she explained, but when you actually went to Salt Lake City you could see that both the Mormon religious ideas and polygamous marriages were more complicated than most French critics imagined. She doubted that Joseph Smith had in fact received divine revelations on golden tablets, but she was even more skeptical about a later revelation that sanctioned polygamy. This providential advice on marriage nevertheless offered a useful social strategy for a new religion that was seeking to gain more adherents. Mormon men could rapidly add children to their new church by marrying several women, and the women themselves were persuaded that polygamy had become a religious duty rather than a male scheme to harm their own interests. Other Americans vehemently rejected the whole idea of polygamous marriages, however, thereby forcing the persecuted Mormons to migrate to the undeveloped lands of northern Utah and to develop an innovative hub for their religious and economic life in Salt Lake City. Neither the dress nor appearance of the Mormons would look out of place in Paris because they were a thoroughly "modern" people in their approach to farming, business, and urban planning.[48]

Although she therefore respected the Mormons' economic activity, Audouard was more interested in their view of marriage and their strong commitment to

Women on the Board of Directors at Deseret Hospital. Photograph by Charles R. Savage, ca. 1882. Audouard argued that Mormon women in Utah were more independent and better protected in polygamous marriages than the vulnerable women who were regularly betrayed in the "monogamous" marriages she had observed in France. The women in this picture supported the creation of a new hospital in Salt Lake City shortly after Audouard's trip to the far west, and their confident presence conveys some of the independence and financial well-being she had found among Mormon women who liked their polygamous marriages. Courtesy of the Utah State Historical Society, Salt Lake City.

women and widows who might otherwise lack financial support. Rejecting the French and American criticisms of Mormon polygamy, she found that the women in such marriages enjoyed considerable autonomy and lifetime financial security. They could choose their own husbands, seek a divorce if the marriage failed, and devote most of their time and attention to the well-being of their children. They did not face the burdens of endless labor on their family farms, and they were not forced to work in commercial enterprises outside the home. Mormon men typically had about three wives, but she reported that the most important Mormon leader, Brigham Young, was married to seventeen women who accepted their marital position without jealousy or resentments toward the other wives.[49]

Audouard noted that Young's wives, like the other women she met, seemed to be happily married. "I was never able to find the least sign of jealousy," she reported in the account of her conversations in Utah. Mormon women expressed a common Protestant disdain for sexuality, and "if you speak to them about jealousy, they become upset and ready to shout: *shocking*." Jealousy would imply moral impurities and suggest that they were "too attached to carnal love, which would be cause for severe reprimand." Women also influenced their husband's later marital decisions because the man had to gain the consent of his wife (or wives) each time he added another spouse to the family. As the man brought new wives into his household, he was never allowed to abandon older or less attractive wives for younger women, which meant that "Mormon polygamy is completely opposite to Muslim polygamy." Where the Turk's sensual preoccupations caused him to lose interest in his early wives after their youthful beauty began to disappear, Mormon men continued to honor their first wives long after the women reached middle age and long after the men married other women. This enduring respect ensured that Mormon wives were never forgotten or ignored, and it gave women a permanent security in their polygamous marriages.[50]

Long-term security for Mormon women was matched by an equally important long-term security and stability for all their children. In contrast to the men in European cities, where the streets were filled with abandoned children and with mothers who prostituted themselves to feed their hungry infants, the men of Salt Lake City provided a secure home for every child and woman. Although Audouard acknowledged that European men pledged their marital allegiance to only *one* woman, she stressed that they often betrayed their oaths, pursued other women, and pushed their one legal wife into the disillusioned misery of poverty and insecurity. This European social reality amounted to a European "Mormonism" that allowed men to enter relationships with multiple women while they left their wives and children alone in an unsupportive economic system and an unresponsive legal labyrinth.

"European Mormonism" thus placed French women in a degraded, desperate position for which neither the self-interested men nor their government would take responsibility. Why then, Audouard asked, should French critics feel superior to a Mormon social and religious system that carefully protected women and children from the misery that was so common in Europe?

> In Salt-Lake, there are no degraded women; there are only women who are respected by everyone, carrying the name of the man with whom they live; their position as one-fourth spouse is in no way humiliating because it is a legal status; the man who has married these women can never abandon them; he is obliged to work in order to feed them, and the women are never forced into misery; all the children they bring into the world have a legitimate position and the name of a father who is required to feed them and to raise them.[51]

Audouard's account of polygamy, like many of her generalizations about American life, surely glossed over the complexities and problems in Mormon families, but, as always, she was most interested in identifying new (unexpected) allies to support her critique of gender relations in France. Indeed, the final paragraph of *Le Far-West* came back to a comparative view of polygamy and French marriages that she had repeated since her earliest travel writing in Turkey. Polygamy was often a "horrible thing," she wrote, because it precluded pure love relationships between two people, and it could permit men to pursue brutish behaviors. Given the persistent male quest for polygamous relationships, however, it would be good for Europeans to think about what they could learn from the Mormons. "I prefer the legal polygamy of the Mormons over the illegal, tolerated and protected [polygamy] of the Mormons of Paris," she concluded, "because . . . this latter [polygamy] has far more unfortunate consequences."[52] The French would continue to condemn the immorality of polygamous marriages, but they should at least recognize that Mormon men respected their wives, took care of their children, and honestly defended their unconventional families with deeply felt religious commitments.

Audouard's Claims for Cultural Knowledge and Literary Status

Audouard's sympathetic account of Mormon polygamy became a notable example of her unconventional feminist perspectives and her critical analysis of women's position in different cultures. At the same time, her claims for firsthand knowledge of Mormon marriages enabled her to enhance her literary status as an expert on subjects that the most celebrated Parisian writers did not understand. This claim for intellectual expertise fused with Audouard's social critique of gender relations because she always described the meaning of social or cultural institutions from the position of a traveling *female observer*. She saw what male travelers often overlooked, and she ignored the literary conventions of (male) academic writing. She liked to write in an anecdotal, free-flowing prose style that she defended as a distinctive form of women's writing. This kind of prose included reflections on the specific challenges of writing a travel book and referred explicitly to hostile male critics, but it also developed a more informal, friendly dialogue with her imagined readers.

She admitted, for example, that she found it difficult to speak and understand the English language, which she described as a practical language for business and daily life. English therefore lacked the spiritual nuances that she drew from French conversations, and she discovered that her American travels produced a linguistic fatigue, even when she felt the deepest attractions to America's landscape or social life. A chance encounter with several French Canadians at Niagara Falls reminded Audouard of how her own language gave her both a deep pleasure and a deep sense of cultural difference from English-speaking Americans. When your own language "no longer rings in your ears," she explained, "you become aware of your isolation and you feel sad."[53] Travel writers inevitably struggled to overcome the language barriers that hindered their understanding of an unexpected conversation or their desire for a casual exchange of ideas, and nobody could become an authoritative interpreter of other cultures without recognizing the power of linguistic differences or the influence of language on cultural life.

Yet the challenges of speaking another language were ultimately less problematic for Audouard than the challenge of writing books that French critics would take seriously as a valid source of information about American society. Her main problem, as she noted in *Le Far West*, was that she never conformed to the authoritative literary style of male academic writing. Critics complained that her travel books were filled with digressions and anecdotes and stories about herself; or they said she merely provided a superficial "photograph" of other cultures instead of an imaginative interpretation of what she had observed. These criticisms disappointed Audouard (as she freely admitted), but she emphasized that her readers' needs were more important to her than the complaints of her critics. She liked to read the reviews of these critics, some of whom clearly had "a real talent." In the end, though, she had "the greatest respect for the reader; to deceive his confidence, even unintentionally, is an unforgivable sin." Her friendly readers depended on her for a literary companionship that went far beyond the concerns of a typical newspaper critic, "because the person who buys my book gives me the honor of believing that I can be interesting, that I can teach him something about a country that he does not know, or at least that I can help him pass a pleasant hour of his time." This implicit agreement with her reader gave Audouard a deep sense of her responsibility to write accurately and to provide that "photograph" of cultural differences that some critics disparaged. "If you visit an unknown country that an author has described for you in a truthful manner, . . . you say to yourself: that's it, that's truly it. . . . And this author becomes your friend and your advisor."[54] A travel writer who was accused of being a photographer instead of a poet might therefore be giving her readers precisely what they most wanted or needed or yearned to experience with a friend.

As she developed her cross-cultural "photographs," however, Audouard regularly placed herself squarely within the picture, thus attracting the ire of critics who disliked her frequent use of the pronoun "I" and her informal, story-telling prose. Conceding that her books did not use the formal, impersonal voice of academic writing, she insisted that she wrote solely for the benefit of her readers and for herself: "I do not have the pretense of having a very academic style; I admit that

Olympe Audouard. Photograph by Mayer Frères and Pierson, ca. 1870. Although Audouard frequently criticized the gendered social hierarchies in France and claimed that she did not want to write like a male academician, she also sought the social prestige of a knowledgeable cross-cultural analyst. This photograph asserts that honorable position in French culture by showing Audouard with a book in her hands and by offering her direct visual engagement with an imagined audience of readers. PWB Images/Alamy Stock Photo.

this criticism is entirely correct, but I have the habit of saying what I think, and I write in the same way without worrying about my phrase or the effects that it will produce." Unlike the aspiring male writer who labored to imitate traditional scientific or academic prose, Audouard claimed that she wanted to write "without pretension," to "speak with the reader" rather than with academic critics and to "give a body to my thought."[55]

Her literary style thus expressed her aspirations as a "woman writer" and affirmed the public identity that she both defined and defended in opposition to the literary status of authoritative male authors. Gender hierarchies forced women and men to follow different paths to a literary career, and their careers received very different (gendered) forms of reward and recognition:

> If a man attains a certain fame as a result of his studies and careful work, he immediately seeks to fulfill his ambitions; if his work is good, he will be praised and exalted by this free-masonry of authors which only admits those whom it recognizes itself; he will delude himself... with the hope of attaining one of the seats at the [French] Academy, where he will be able to settle into a self-satisfied sleep; the doors of the Institut [of France] will open before him, and, if he has haughty dreams, he will see a piece of ribbon shining on his buttonhole, a large cordon around his neck, or a beautiful plaque on his chest. All work therefore has its rewards for a man.... But nothing is guaranteed for a woman.... First, in place of encouragements, she only encounters mocking minds that are always ready to deny her ability and to diminish whatever merit that she might have.... The right to give a body and a soul to her thought is challenged; she is forced to hide it, at her risk and peril of course.... The confrères assume they do not need to take her seriously, and even if she is—like George Sand—one of the leading writers of France, she would have no ambitions that can be achieved, no hope for rewards that are worthily gained or justly acquired!! No, she is a woman.... This condition is all that is needed for the men to invalidate the writer.... For her there is no Academy and no Institut![56]

These differences in the reception of men and women writers gave Audouard a social and cultural justification for her own literary style. Why should a woman use the impersonal, academic prose of a male writer when her readers sought a more personal narrative, when the official academic world would never open its doors to her, and when she was finding her own voice in the "photographic" images and personal pronouns she used in her books? Why, in other words, should a woman write like a man?

Audouard's defense of her travel writing thus carried the emotional and intellectual energy of a woman who was determined to affirm the unconventional authority of her literary work as well as the independence of her evolving female selfhood. Her books would give her a place in that "twentieth-century" world she liked to describe in her accounts of modern American society—a place from which she could freely express the autonomous voice of a woman writer and also enter into an imaginative dialogue with her critics and readers. This dialogue emerged from Audouard's self-conscious opposition to the male-dominated literary system in France, and the dialogue's authoritative cross-cultural perspectives depended (from her side) on her travels in America and other foreign countries. The "confrères" at the Académie française in Paris would ignore her and her books, but she was writing for other readers and women and armchair travelers who recognized the value of her project and the authority that came from personal experiences. Travel and travel narratives would give Audouard the means to claim a literary position that the guardians of official culture would never acknowledge. Like Nicolas Point (and many others), she had to make her way into another culture and even into a future "twentieth century" to affirm a self that was denied or hidden in nineteenth-century France.

EPILOGUE TO PART IV

French Travelers and the Affirmation of Independent Selfhood outside France

Traveling in unfamiliar countries does not inevitably transform cultural identities or self-perceptions, but the American journeys of Nicolas Point and Olympe Audouard show how nineteenth-century French writers could use long, transnational trips to pursue their personal aspirations and redefine their connections with the cultures in which they were born. America offered alternatives to the prevailing political and cultural systems that for different reasons had relegated both Point and Audouard to marginal or constrained social positions within French society. America has always attracted travelers and immigrants who wanted to escape religious, political, and professional barriers in their own nations, so the journeys of these two traveling French writers resembled numerous other transatlantic migrations and reinventions of selfhood.

Although the experiences of Point and Audouard should be placed in this broad history of transatlantic travel and immigration, their narratives about America also provide specific examples of how travelers bring previous experiences, beliefs, and identities into their encounters with new cultures and unfamiliar people. Both Point and Audouard, for instance, brought their nineteenth-century racist assumptions about non-European people and cultures into their American travels and cross-cultural comparisons. They were often critical of French society, but they continued to share French beliefs about their nation's distinctive history and "civilizing mission." They also drew on their American experiences to affirm their evolving public identities. Point's long-developing quest for productive, satisfying religious work and Audouard's literary aspiration to write unconventional travel books found new public expression through their explorations of the unfamiliar cultures in American society.

They pursued their personal and cultural ambitions in the very different social worlds they found in "premodern" Indian tribes and bustling "modern" cities, but they both discovered that these previously unknown American contexts opened new opportunities to achieve their often-stymied desires for social respect and cultural authority. They developed new critiques of the secularism or gender hierarchies in French society while they also criticized flaws in the European American culture of the United States, which included a rampant materialism, a pervasive indifference to the loss of Native American lives or cultures, and a widespread ignorance of the artistic or literary traditions in western Europe.

The more general, identity-affirming significance of their cross-cultural experiences, however, appeared in the *positive* cultural opportunities that Point and Audouard pursued in North America. This fast-changing continent was a place where (for Point) non-Christian people could still be converted to Catholicism and where (for Audouard) independent women were rapidly advancing toward the less hierarchical gender relations of the next century. These aspects of American society pushed Point and Audouard to defend social practices that other French travelers often condemned as primitive, vulgar, or dangerous. Drawing their own contrasts between Europe and America, they found more to criticize in modern France than in the Indian villages of the Northern Rockies or in the women's schools of New York. Their willingness to defend the lesser-known aspects of American culture thus came partly from their critiques of the religious and social problems in modern France, but Point and Audouard also drew new public identities and a new sense of independent selfhood from their influential exchanges with the different people they met during their American travels. Point could become the respected priest and a much-admired emissary of the Jesuit Black Robes; Audouard could become the authoritative woman writer and an expert guide for her friendly readers in France.

Marginalized in different ways within their own culture, Point and Audouard both redefined or expanded their intellectual and personal ambitions through the unexpected experiences and transitions of long American trips. Although now virtually forgotten, their nineteenth-century journeys still show how French travelers have explored and asserted diverse meanings of selfhood in both the open spaces and crowded cities of modern America.

CONCLUSION

Travel, History, and Selfhood

EVERY TRAVELER'S stories connect personal experiences with broader cultural narratives about the meaning of travel, but even travelers who visit the same places in the same years have different stories and memories. The chapters in this book have therefore discussed the journeys and travel narratives of individuals who always emphasized the uniqueness of their journeys and claimed new insights that emerged from their interactions with previously unknown people and from their observations of unfamiliar places. My discussion of eight diverse writers has thus analyzed each person's distinctive interpretations of specific cross-cultural encounters, and I have also compared each personal journey with the experiences and texts of a differently gendered traveler from the same national culture. I want to conclude my own narrative journey, however, by noting some general themes that connect all the French and American writers with whom we have "traveled" to different countries across the nineteenth-century world.

The various parts of this book have shown how long journeys in foreign cultures generate new knowledge of cultural differences and new insights into the traveler's cultural identity and individual selfhood. Drawing on categorical descriptions from the historical work of Jerrold Seigel, I noted in the introduction that cultural identities form the exterior, public components of a person's self-representation, but a deeper sense of self emerges through interior reflections in which (to use Seigel's words) we all "turn a kind of mirror . . . on our consciousness" and distance ourselves "from our own being so as to examine, judge, and sometimes regulate or revise it."[1] Although other people constantly ascribe exterior traits to each person's cultural identity, everyone seeks to construct their own external self-presentations while they are also reflecting on an inner self that both replicates their public cultural identity and diverges into other spheres of their self-conscious and unconscious mind. The public cultural identity and the interior selfhood are thus connected and somewhat different, yet they both evolve through dialogical interactions with other people. This book has therefore argued that long journeys in foreign countries become important historical experiences because cross-cultural encounters expand personal awareness of the interior layers of selfhood as well as the wider, entangled layers of cultural and linguistic identities.

The processes of cultural and personal discovery become more public and more self-reflective when travelers describe their trips in published texts that gradually *relativize* their home cultures and earlier personal identities through cross-cultural comparisons. Travel has produced unsettling experiences and comparative narratives in many different cultures and historical eras, but I have placed these recurring themes within the context of the Atlantic world during the transitional, postrevolutionary decades between the 1820s and 1860s. I have focused on a few French and American writers whose journeys and texts in this specific era were connected to the wider patterns of modern travel and travel writing. All of these traveling authors understood that social and literary traditions gave travelers a notable cultural status, they all traveled from national cultures that affirmed the political theories of late eighteenth-century revolutions but still struggled to expand human rights, and they all used their travel experiences to pursue new (more honored) public identities and new knowledge of individual selfhood.

The overlapping aspects of their historical contexts and cultural ambitions thus connected personal stories to the broader history of nineteenth-century travel narratives, public debates, and individualist conceptions of human autonomy. Some of their ideas about race, religion, gender, slavery, or non-European cultures are disturbing and unacceptable for twenty-first century readers. The overt racism in the cultures of nineteenth-century France and America, for example, often influenced and distorted the travel narratives of white writers, even when their views of human rights otherwise affirmed postrevolutionary ideas about the value of individual freedom or political democracy. Past authors, however, rarely thought or wrote in exactly the ways we would like for them to view other people or to understand their specific cultural prejudices. Historians, in short, must inevitably engage in dialogues with people whose beliefs differ from their own ideas and cultural values.

The Social and Literary Traditions of Travel

Travelers always began their trips with preexisting ideas about the social status of transnational travelers and with information from previous writers who had described the places that curious people should visit. Earlier travelers had explained how long journeys offered an escape from the tedium of daily life, provided vivid sensory and intellectual encounters with unknown people or cultures, and created opportunities for new social and cultural recognition. Travel was thus a much-anticipated personal experience that free people (with some money) inevitably planned by using their knowledge about long-established social and intellectual traditions.

Every trip was launched from a social and cultural context that influenced the intersecting levels of the traveler's cultural and personal identities, but the journey itself led to new social and personal interactions that challenged or altered earlier components of home-country selfhood. Like other historical structures, the "self" evolved in response to unexpected events that made travelers more aware of the cultural histories that had shaped their public identities, personal memories, or social relations with other people. Long trips brought disorienting social separations from the families, friendships, and institutions that had helped travelers develop a sense of selfhood; and every traveling writer described a growing social distance from homeland cultures and customs. Yet travelers were at least partially prepared for this experience because the literary traditions of travel writing constructed their pre-trip expectations.

Influential literary predecessors therefore contributed to both the travel plans and the travel narratives of French and American travelers who saw their journeys as a cultural process of self-education. The nineteenth-century bildungsroman, for example, gave well-educated travelers a fictional model for describing how a long trip through unexpected social obstacles could become a catalyst for discovering higher knowledge of social or personal identities. Romantic poetry (especially the work of Lord Byron) also encouraged writers to describe their journeys as creative escapes from homeland constraints, and scientific texts taught travelers how to narrate empirical information about urban spaces or remote landscapes. Travel writing thus drew on both the fictional and the nonfictional genres of nineteenth-century literature, but it also resembled historical narratives in translating distant cultures and people into cultural languages that home-country readers could understand.

All of these literary traditions and practices of cultural translation provided textual models for the traveling authors whose journeys have been examined in this book. Stories of self-education appeared in almost every narrative, but women gave particular attention to the social obstacles that could impede the journey toward a freer selfhood. Flora Tristan, Margaret Fuller, Nancy Prince, and Olympe Audouard shared a common struggle to establish a more respected cultural status in male-controlled social and intellectual systems. Men also interpreted their voyages as social experiences that enhanced their previous education or cultural authority. Romantic, Byronic images of the wandering, free man gave a masculine meaning to the new "self-knowledge" that emerged in the travel narratives of both Randal

McGavock and David Dorr, but there were also claims for a kind of independent, masculine knowledge in the more scientific or religious narratives of Victor Jacquemont and Nicolas Point. Although Jacquemont represented the research methods of the Jardin des Plantes and Point represented the religious mission of the Jesuits, they shared common interests in compiling authoritative, empirical information that would enable others to understand what they had observed in the landscapes and cultures of non-European societies.

All transnational travelers, in short, organized their journeys within the social and institutional structures that facilitated modern travel, and they narrated their personal experiences by drawing consciously or unconsciously on literary traditions that had created the formal conventions of modern travel writing. In addition to this inescapable connection with social systems and literary predecessors, however, all traveling writers were also engaged in an ongoing dialogue with the intellectual and political history of the Enlightenment and the late eighteenth-century revolutions that continued to influence new struggles for human rights throughout the Atlantic world.

Nationalist Ideologies, Public Conflicts, and the Ideas of Nineteenth-Century Travelers

The cultural and political legacies of the French and American Revolutions affected the ideas and identities of every nineteenth-century traveler who left France or the United States for long, transnational journeys. Nationalist political cultures made travelers highly aware of their own nation's distinctive language, government institutions, and historical events, but nationalism also shaped the ways in which traveling writers understood foreign people and cultures. Travel writing therefore contributed to an evolving public sphere in which cross-cultural comparisons affirmed nationalist ideologies and defined the meaning of national progress. Interpreting different societies with cultural presuppositions about the universal significance of French and American political theories, travelers could portray other countries as less advanced than their homelands, condemn the blatant injustices of slavery, or criticize the structural blockage of equal rights for women. French and American travelers who went abroad in the four decades after 1825 thus wrote about eighteenth-century conceptions of knowledge, progress, and human rights while they were also writing about the cultures and politics of other societies in their own era.

French authors steadfastly believed in the superiority of France's cultural history, no matter how they criticized the flaws and failures in French politics, laws, religion, or gender hierarchies. Jacquemont and Point, for example, were both deeply engaged with the legacies of the French Enlightenment, though they traveled on scientific and religious missions that grew out of very different views of eighteenth-century philosophes. Jacquemont praised the progressive value of French scientific knowledge during all his travels in the United States and India, whereas Point constantly reaffirmed the anti-Enlightenment spiritual beliefs of French Catholicism during all his work among European Americans and Native Americans in North America. Tristan and Audouard also drew on eighteenth-century ideas when they argued that women had more freedom in the Americas or when they developed cross-cultural criticisms of irrational French laws that blocked women from the right to divorce bad husbands, pursue professional careers, and participate equally in public life.

The French writers all believed that France's cultural or political ideas could contribute to social progress in other nations, but they also used their cross-cultural comparisons to identify problems in their own nation's public institutions or to condemn the enduring French hostility to women's rights. Although they were eager to understand other cultures, they interpreted foreign religious beliefs or political systems by reaffirming French theories about historical progress and national identity that continued to influence French political culture long after the era of the French Revolution and Napoleonic imperialism.

American travelers were also much engaged with the legacies of late eighteenth-century cultural and political revolutions. All the American writers discussed in this book—women and men, Black and white—defended the national political traditions of republicanism and the theoretical arguments for democratic government. Like the French travelers, however, they understood their national traditions through different cultural frameworks. McGavock wanted to limit legal equality and democratic participation to white men, but Fuller, Prince, and Dorr all insisted in their travel writings that the United States must abolish slavery and bring long-excluded people into its democratic institutions. Fuller and Prince also strongly asserted women's right to participate in political and cultural debates by publishing their commentaries on transnational issues and public conflicts. Dorr similarly expressed a wide range of social and cultural opinions to claim that formerly enslaved persons should join in American public life as freely as the white men who had always controlled the nation's political and economic systems.

American writers thus believed (like the French) that their nation could contribute essential ideas to modern historical progress, but except for McGavock they also argued that the United States could never advance or serve as a model for global progress until the government abolished slavery and expanded its protection of inalienable human rights. As these travelers repeatedly noted with references to international critiques, the abolition of slavery would enhance the national commerce and strengthen all the national ideals that Americans liked to celebrate. American writers (like the French) always traveled with racial and gender identities that influenced their national cultural identities as well as their public status and self-defined quests for personal freedom. The meaning of autonomous selfhood was thus always entangled with the social meanings of womanhood, manhood, nationhood, and race—and slavery was an inescapable social and political issue for every American traveler before the Civil War. Transnational abolitionism therefore became the most prominent example of how the previous century's expanding conceptions of human rights and social progress continued to affect nineteenth-century travelers. Yet the interconnected cultural and political conflicts that flowed from these public issues always overlapped with individual ambitions, quests, and fears that gave each journey its distinctive, personal meaning.

The Personal and Experiential Meanings of Nineteenth-Century Travel

Travelers have often left home for long trips because home-country obstacles and disappointments were impeding their personal aspirations or causing emotional anxieties. The search for new places and experiences can thus develop whenever energetic, ambitious persons (such as those discussed in this book) come to believe that their work, their education, their personal relationships, their political ideas, or their opportunities for social advancement have stagnated or reached a demoralizing dead end. Travel becomes attractive in such times as a possible pathway toward new creative opportunities or social status, and traveling writers try to enhance their public identities by describing and interpreting other cultures.

We have seen that some nineteenth-century writers never returned home (Jacquemont, Fuller, Point) because they died on their journeys or settled permanently in another country. Others went back to unstable social positions (Prince, Dorr, Tristan) that they sought to change by publishing books about what they had seen in distant lands; and David Dorr may have achieved the greatest post-trip transformation after he escaped from slavery in Louisiana to gain his freedom in Ohio. Two of the travelers (McGavock, Audouard) returned to more established homeland lives but looked for other opportunities to leave again on long foreign trips. They remained restless within the national cultures to which they returned, and the once-patriotic Randal McGavock would die in a secessionist war against the government of the country he had praised so warmly in his travel letters from Europe.

Traveling and living abroad thus altered everyone's personal life through experiences that pushed deracinated outsiders to rethink their home-country origins, languages, and social systems. An expanding recognition of cultural differences often stimulated new identifications with the national cultures that had shaped the traveler's earlier life in France or the United States, but this immersion also created a new critical distance from homeland customs and ideologies. Travel revealed cultural identities that seemed out of place in foreign countries, and home-country problems could become more obvious from abroad. Margaret Fuller strongly criticized her nation's war against Mexico and the American indifference to evolving democratic movements in Europe; Nancy Prince and David Dorr repeatedly condemned the brutal slave system and racist social hierarchies in the United States; Flora Tristan and Olympe Audouard vehemently denounced the social and legal disadvantages that harmed women in French families and blocked their participation in French public life; Nicolas Point rejected the post-Enlightenment secularism in French culture; and even the more socially privileged writers Victor Jacquemont and Randal McGavock believed that the transnational work of scientists or diplomats offered more opportunities and autonomy than they could find within their own countries. Travel usually began with the desire for a temporary escape from hometown constraints, and then the long journey added a psychological distance that made it difficult or impossible for an evolving traveler to go back to the earlier selfhood of a pre-journey home.

Traveling writers used the freedom and unsettling experiences of their trips to construct new public identities as experts on little-known cultures or as wise commentators on famous nations or as imaginative critics who deserved more cultural status in their own national societies. This desire for public recognition became an influential personal ambition for every traveler who wanted to write new narratives about other cultures and thereby claim an exceptional knowledge of foreign places. Writing about distant people and nations became a cultural strategy for affirming a more autonomous selfhood because travel stories fused a claim for new knowledge with other claims for new social or personal freedoms. The assertion of a new, freer identity became especially important for Prince and Dorr because the racist social hierarchy within the United States constantly restricted their personal rights and their aspirations for public stature. But Fuller also found a new personal freedom in Italy; Tristan asserted a new social and intellectual freedom during her complex journey to Peru; Audouard celebrated her growing independence as a woman writer in the American "Far West"; Nicolas Point found new spheres of freedom and expertise among the Native Americans in the Northern Rocky Mountains; Randal McGavock discovered his Byronic personal freedom in European cities and mountain trails; and Victor Jacquemont finally reached an independent intellectual stature on his long trip through the impoverished villages and luxurious royal palaces in South Asia.

Each writer thus interpreted his or her journey as a new experience of personal freedom, as a new source of knowledge, and as a new opportunity to gain more cultural status. These shared perceptions established an experiential thread that linked their otherwise diverse journeys and diverging literary reflections. Despite the many differences in their personal beliefs and aspirations, all of these nineteenth-century travelers ultimately described a freer selfhood that emerged from encounters with previously unknown people in unfamiliar places. Situated within a wider history of transnational travel, these claims for a new cultural knowledge and a more autonomous self repeatedly expressed a widespread belief in the liberating power of long journeys; and this belief has remained influential in most modern cultures down to our own time.

The Memory and Future of Travel

Travel stories help shape everyone's personal memories, as you must know from your own tales about past trips and fellow travelers. These overlapping narratives of travel and memory contribute to the complex connections between travel, identity, and selfhood that become apparent whenever people talk about what they learned or experienced during long trips to faraway places. Nineteenth-century travelers (like those who travel today) wanted to meet new people whose cities, languages, ideas, and social customs would lead to experiences and knowledge they could not find at home. The reports of traveling writers therefore provoked the curiosity and aspirations of other would-be travelers, many of whom also set off to seek their own unique experiences in places they had only read about in books.

Travel may now seem less important or even obsolete amid the changing social and technological conditions of the present century. Modern technologies make it possible to explore distant countries on the World Wide Web, encounter unfamiliar people or cultures on television screens, and order exotic foreign foods with a telephone call or a click on the computer. Long, uncomfortable journeys might well be losing their allure in this digital era, in the way that the once-popular World's Fairs gradually disappeared when people could more easily fly to foreign lands they used to "visit" only on home-country fairgrounds. Other cultural and social changes have also altered the meaning or appeal of transnational travel. Global pandemics have spread across all national boundaries, creating new risks, obstacles, and costs for even the most carefully organized foreign trip. Meanwhile, cultural critics have made privileged travelers increasingly aware of how modern tourism can transform unfamiliar people into the dehumanized objects of a "tourist gaze," harm delicate environments, contribute to global warming, and disrupt local economies. The negative effects of transnational travel are thus fostering an anti-travel skepticism that encourages people to stay at home and to meet distant persons solely on their computers or smartphones.[2]

The enduring desire for travel, however, will surely remain important in future lives and national cultures for most of the reasons that long trips were so attractive to French and American writers in the nineteenth century. Traveling into foreign cultures gives people a social experience that facilitates the perennial human search for new freedom, new knowledge, new relationships, new identities, and new layers of one's own selfhood. This quest to explore what is still unknown will eventually carry human beings far beyond the earth itself; and boat trips across the Atlantic will seem as remote (and slow) to future travelers as the desert migrations of ancient people seem to us. Yet the diverse landscapes and cultures of our own planet will continue to draw travelers toward the continents, islands, and human societies that have attracted curious visitors throughout modern times.

Indeed, as you read these concluding paragraphs, ambitious future travelers are sitting somewhere in noisy cafés or working in windowless offices or daydreaming in dull classrooms or mourning broken relationships in lonely apartments. They may be looking at maps that suggest the next bold steps toward a different life. Many of these people will eventually find a way to leave for famous or unknown places, and some may never come home again. To quote the parting words of David Dorr in 1858, they will "take leave" of their homelands with a decisive "*au revoir*."[3] But their long journeys to distant places will also carry these restless travelers toward places within themselves that they had never known or understood at home.

NOTES

Introduction

1. Botton, *Art of Travel*, 54, 56, 242.

2. Hulme and Youngs, *Cambridge Companion*, 2.

3. Numerous historians have noted how the term "tourist" began to emerge in the 1780s and how "tourism" appeared by the 1810s, when leisure travel became more common. See, for example, Carl Thompson's discussion of these new words in "Nineteenth-Century Travel Writing," 109. For a good analysis of the contrasting goals of cultural and recreational travelers and their favorite guidebooks, see Levenstein, *Seductive Journey*, xi, 33, 70–81; and there is a helpful description of "reform tourism" in Kilbride, *Being American in Europe*, 96–97.

4. This search for a new postrevolutionary selfhood has attracted the analytical attention of insightful intellectual historians. See Goldstein, *Post-Revolutionary Self*, 1–17; and Izenberg, *Impossible Individuality*, 15. Izenberg summarizes the key transition on this introductory page in his book: "It was the impact of the French Revolution on the Romantics' preexisting struggles for self-definition, freedom from heteronomous authority, and original creative achievement that produced a new idea of selfhood."

5. Don Reid, my colleague in French labor history, helped me understand this significant linguistic overlap. Early connections between the word "travel" and the medieval French word for labor, "travail," also alluded to the human passage into life, which required a pregnant woman's "travail/labor" in childbirth. See the etymological links in the definitions for "travel" and "travail" in the *Oxford English Dictionary* (accessed 13 January 2024), https://www.oed.com/dictionary/travel_v?tab=etymology.

6. Leed, *Mind of the Traveler*, 7–8, 13; the difficult journey of Odysseus is discussed on 8.

7. Clifford, *Routes*, 66.

8. Leed, *Mind of the Traveler*, 5. An excellent historical overview of how the meaning of "experience" has evolved through different eras of Western culture is available in Jay, *Songs of Experience*. Historians have increasingly stressed, however, that "experience" should be understood as "culturally constructed" and not as an unmediated, foundational reality. See, for example, the critical analysis in Joan Scott's essay "Evidence of Experience," 797, where she examines the "discursive nature" of experience and concludes that "experience is at once already an interpretation *and* something that needs to be interpreted. What counts as experience is neither self-evident nor straightforward." This perspective offers a framework for approaching "travel experiences" as interpretations that call for interpretive analysis.

9. Urry, *Tourist Gaze*, 152, 154. Traditional ideas about travel as a "male" activity have been examined in much of the scholarly literature. See, for example, the discussion of "gendered geography" in Buzard, *Beaten Track*, 130–54.

10. Seigel, *Idea of the Self*, 5.

11. Seigel, *Idea of the Self*, 7–8, 12, 17, quotation on 17. Izenberg offers a somewhat similar description of the multidimensional connections between identity and selfhood in his important

book *Identity*, 21: "Our identities necessarily include, though they are not exhausted by, our self-definition in relationship to our sexual bodies; our relationship to the world of subsistence and work; membership in one or more groups who speak the same language and share a common sense of place and time . . . and finally, perhaps, at least in some times and places, the sense of something that makes one a unique self."

12. Taylor, *Sources of the Self*, 36. Historians such as Seigel and Izenberg criticize Taylor's account of the relational self as one-dimensional, one-sided in its psychological claims, and historically inaccurate, but Taylor's emphasis on "webs of interlocution" still offers a helpful image of how relationships affect selfhood. See, for example, Seigel's critique in *Idea of the Self*, 41–43; and Izenberg's critique in *Identity*, 432–35.

13. Coulmas, *Identity*, 95.

14. Leed, *Mind of the Traveler*, 263.

15. Green, "Comparative Gaze," 433.

16. Jerrold Seigel has discussed the experience of moving between two cultures in another valuable book, *Between Cultures*. Examining the development of what he describes as "intercultural identities," he stresses the disorientation that flows from "inhabiting two different and sometimes hostile worlds at the same time." He also notes that "it may well be impossible to carry out [intercultural identities] in a satisfying way." Seigel, *Between Cultures*, 3. The ambiguities of this unstable, in-between cultural position may explain why travelers tend either to embrace the other culture or to identify more intensely with their home culture.

17. Mathy, *Extrême-Occident*, 7.

18. There is an enormous historical literature on the emergence of nationalism during this era, which I have discussed in Kramer, "Historical Narratives" and *Nationalism in Europe and America*, 9–27. That book focuses on the collective construction of nationalist ideas, identities, and public institutions, whereas this book focuses on the personal construction of nationalist ideas and identities among specific nineteenth-century travelers.

19. This summary of the evolving passport system in the United States is drawn from the well-researched account in Robertson, *Passport in America*, 129, 131–33, 141–42, 150, 216–17. The numbers for transatlantic American passengers in the 1840s appear in Kilbride, *Being American in Europe*, 2. On the broader evolution of government identification systems, see Caplan and Torpey, *Documenting Individual Identity*, especially the editors' introduction and the chapters by Caplan, "'This or That Particular Person,'"; and Torpey, "Great War." See also the analysis in Torpey, *Invention of the Passport*.

20. Herodotus described his travels across the Mediterranean world as he narrated the history of the Greek wars with Persia. For a helpful overview, see Carolyn Dewald's introduction in Herodotus, *The Histories*, ix–xli. For the story of the most famous voyage of the Middle Ages, see Marco Polo, *The Travels*. Well-known texts by and about traveling pilgrims during the Middle Ages include the literary work of Geoffrey Chaucer (1340s?–1400) and the memoir by Margery Kempe (1373?–?) about her journey to Palestine. See Chaucer, *Canterbury Tales*; and Kempe, *Book of Margery Kempe*.

21. Among the numerous early modern European accounts of distant people and places, the reports that Amerigo Vespucci (1451–1512) wrote about South America became some of the most influential. His first name became attached to the continent he described in texts that have been collected in *Letters from a New World*.

22. Longino, *French Travel Writing in the Ottoman Empire*, 4, 10.

23. For comprehensive lists of travel books published in nineteenth-century France and America, see Monaghan, *French Travellers*; and H. Smith, *American Travelers Abroad*. Smith summarizes the professional identities of American travel writers on page viii, but even this

exhaustive list is not complete. For example, Nancy Prince (the subject of chapter 5 in this book) does not appear in Smith's bibliography.

24. Blanton, *Travel Writing*, 2, 5. For a helpful exploration of the bildungsroman in various national cultures, see the collection of essays in Graham, *History of the Bildungsroman*; but the possible links with travel literature are not explored in this interesting volume.

25. For a concise, abridged edition of the famous scientist's travel narrative, see Darwin, *Voyage of the* Beagle. Discussions of Darwin's travel appear in Blanton, *Travel Writing*, 20; and in Leed, *Mind of the Traveler*, 210. Leed also examines the links between travel and scientific fields such as botany and geology in the same book, 193–201. For an insightful, broader analysis of the connections between science, travel, and European imperialism, see the discussion of scientific explorations and Alexander von Humboldt in Pratt, *Imperial Eyes*, 15–36, 109–40.

26. MacCannell, *Tourist*, 102.

27. Buzard discusses the desire to separate "travel" from "tourism," the influence of Wordsworth and Byron, and the broader significance of Romanticism for nineteenth-century travelers in *Beaten Track*, 29–30, 81–94, and 114–30.

28. Buzard, *Beaten Track*, 121–22, 130.

29. Youngs, *Cambridge Introduction to Travel Writing*, 87–90, 101, quotations on 87, 101. Like many other scholars, Youngs argues that "the importance of Romanticism to the representation of modern travel cannot be overstated," 54. The quoted words of Jim Morrison come from a song recorded by the Doors in 1967. For the lyrics to "Break On Through (to the Other Side)," see the website AZLyrics (accessed July 30, 2023), https://www.azlyrics.com /lyrics/doors/breakonthroughtotheotherside.html.

30. Green, *Limits of Transnationalism*, 40. The interest in transnationalism has generated methodological debates as well as innovative research. See, for example, the exchange in "AHR Conversation: On Transnational History." Patricia Sneed noted in this conversation (p. 1443) that transnational history's "most important contribution" emerges in the historian's "ability to follow *people* (wherever they moved)"—a theme that runs through the whole historiography of travel. For influential examples of transnational historical analysis, see Chakrabarty, *Provincializing Europe*; and Subrahmanyam, *Three Ways to Be Alien*.

31. For an introduction to this genre of historical work, see Moyn and Sartori, "Approaches to Global Intellectual History."

32. I draw this phrase from an influential book by Lowenthal, *Past Is a Foreign Country*, which analyzes how people yearn for, dispute, understand, and remake the past in present-day remembrances. Lowenthal explains (p. 3) that he drew both his title and the phrase "they do things differently there" from the novel by L. P. Hartley, *The Go-Between* (1953), which is set in England during the late Victorian era of Hartley's childhood (c. 1900).

33. Said's *Orientalism* and his later book *Culture and Imperialism* reshaped the cultural study of colonialism and postcolonial societies, but Said himself was clearly influenced (like many historians) by the work of other theorists noted in this paragraph, including key themes in Foucault, *Order of Things* and *Power/Knowledge*; Derrida, *Of Grammatology* and "White Mythology"; Lévi-Strauss, *Structural Anthropology* and *Tristes Tropiques*; and Saussure, *Writings in General Linguistics*.

34. MacCannell, *Tourist*, 110, 128, 137, quotations on 110, 137.

35. Culler, "Semiotics of Tourism," 160.

36. Few women traveled between the United States and Europe in the early 1800s, but they made more trips during and after the 1840s, when steamships became widely used for transatlantic travel. Women may have accounted for 30 percent of the passengers who crossed the Atlantic each year in this later era of faster travel. See Kilbride, *Being American in Europe*, 2.

37. Kaplan, *Questions of Travel*, 2, 50.

38. Pratt, *Imperial Eyes*, 156.

39. Segalen, *Essay on Exoticism*, 20, 67.

40. Porter, *Haunted Journeys*, 13. Porter evokes a Freudian conception of the unconscious to analyze the layers of selfhood that travelers encounter in places where "we discover much that is strangely familiar" and where this discovery "may destabilize inherited categories as well as confirm them" (188–89).

41. LaCapra, *Understanding Others*, 2.

42. This paragraph's summary of nineteenth-century travel times and costs for transatlantic travel draws on helpful information in Kilbride, *Being American in Europe*, 3–4. Expenses for transnational travel were clearly significant, but they may seem less extravagant when compared with common purchases today (for example, the cost of a new car).

43. For informative accounts of the cultural traditions and literary conventions in which these writers all worked, see Thompson, "Nineteenth-Century Travel Writing"; Forsdick, "Travel Writing in French"; Guentner, "Nineteenth-Century Travel Writing"; Bendixen, "American Travel Books"; Obenzinger, "Americans in the Holy Land"; V. Smith, "African American Travel Literature"; and Roberson, "American Women and Travel Writing." See also the insightful analysis of other notable American travel writers such as Mark Twain and Henry James in Ziff, *Return Passages*.

44. Goldstein, *Post-Revolutionary Self*, 9–11.

45. There is wide-ranging historical scholarship on each of these themes in nineteenth-century Atlantic history, but for introductions to the key contextual influences that affected the era's traveling writers, see Kramer, *Nationalism in Europe and America*, especially chapters 1–6; Nisbet, *History of the Idea of Progress*, especially chapters 5–7; Oldfield, *Transatlantic Abolitionism*; Drescher, *Abolition*, especially parts 2 and 3; and Sklar and Stewart, *Women's Rights and Transatlantic Antislavery*.

46. Replicating the pattern of most people who travel or live outside their home countries, I shared my experiences with a fellow traveler: my wife, Sally Barbour. We traveled together on numerous transnational journeys between 1973 and 1981, so I want to acknowledge her influence and insights—though we later divorced and moved thereafter in different directions. She would go on to serve as a longtime professor of French literature at Wake Forest University. Our travels were not unique. Young, middle-class Europeans and Americans were constantly crisscrossing Asia and Africa on low-cost buses and trains during that era. For a French example, see the insightful reflections in Bouvier, *De Dakar à Tokyo*.

47. Global tourism is a huge industry. According to the World Tourism Organization (an agency affiliated with the United Nations), there were 1.5 billion international tourist arrivals across the globe in 2019—the last year before the COVID disruptions. This included 743 million international arrivals in Europe, 364 million in Asia, 220 million in the Americas, and 71 million in Africa. For detailed information, see the UN World Tourism Organization's *World Tourism Barometer*, 5. According to other data from the World Bank, France annually receives the most international arrivals (212 million in 2019), and the United States is the second most-visited nation (166 million in 2019). The full list for 2019 can be found at the website of the World Bank (accessed 1 August 2023), https://data.worldbank.org/indicator/ST.INT.ARVL.

Introduction to Part I

1. Stendhal's great novel *The Red and the Black* focuses on the stymied ambitions of the fictional character Julien Sorel and the sense of loss in post-Napoleonic France. For insightful

historical accounts of this transitional era, see Spitzer, *French Generation of 1820*; and Fritzsche, *Stranded in the Present.*

Chapter One

1. There are several studies of Jacquemont's life and work, but his career has attracted less attention than the best-known French writers of his generation. See the detailed biographical work by Maes, *Un ami de Stendhal*; and the scholarly essays in a collection published by the French National Museum of Natural History and simply titled *Jacquemont.* Among the well-researched essays in this volume, see especially Chinard, "Les expériences américaines"; and A. Brown, "Jacquemont et l'Inde anglaise." Other useful information appears in the introductions to Jacquemont, *Lettres à Stendhal* and *Letters to Achille Chaper.* More recent, well-informed perspectives on Jacquemont's American experiences are available in Craiutu, "Precursor of Tocqueville." My biographical summary draws from all these summaries, but particularly from Maes and the essays in the National Museum's *Jacquemont.*

2. See, for example, Craiutu, "Precursor of Tocqueville," 137–41; and the discussion in Rémond, *Les États-Unis devant l'opinion française*, 2:677–83. For the details of Jacquemont's failed love affair, see Bronner, *La Schiassetti*, 115–326.

3. Pratt, *Imperial Eyes*, 8, 24–38. Jacquemont often criticized the British colonial authorities for their preoccupation with money and their apparent indifference to the Indian people. See the discussion of these themes in A. Brown, "Jacquemont et l'Inde anglaise," 366, 379. For analysis of how the British gathered and distributed information for colonial purposes during the era of Jacquemont's travels, see Bayly, *Empire and Information*, especially chapter 6. For Jacquemont's communication with his famous scientific predecessor, see Jacquemont to Alexander de Humboldt, 31 July 1828, in Jacquemont, *Correspondance inédite*, 1:239–44.

4. These published letters and journals appeared in several editions, including the two volumes of *Correspondance inédite* cited in the previous note. Other works include the letters in Jacquemont, *Correspondance de Victor Jacquemont avec sa famille et plusieurs de ses amis pendant son voyage dans l'Inde* (hereafter *Correspondance pendant son voyage*) and his detailed reports in a journal, which was sent back to Paris after his death and published in six volumes as Jacquemont, *Voyage dans l'Inde.*

5. Jacquemont to M. de Meslay, 17 November 1829, in Jacquemont, *Correspondance inédite*, 1:328–29.

6. Jacquemont to Venceslas Jacquemont, 25 December 1829, in Jacquemont, *Correspondance pendant son voyage*, 1:173. Jacquemont's description of his separation from a previously existing identity seems to anticipate the views of the modern philosopher Derek Parfit, who argued that personal identities (like national identities) lack the coherence and continuities that people typically imagine identities to embody. When "psychological connectedness" is reduced and "when there has been any marked change of character or style of life, or any marked loss of memory, our imagined beings would say, 'It was not I who did that, but an earlier self.' They could then describe in what ways . . . they are related to this earlier self." As Parfit notes in a statement that might be useful also for analyzing Jacquemont, "If we thought of ourselves in the way that I proposed, we might be less likely to take our own identity for more than what it was." Parfit, "Personal Identity," 25, 27.

7. A letter from Jacquemont to his father, dated 12 December 1826, in Jacquemont, *Correspondance inédite*, 1:77–78, reports the arrival and notes the use of letters from Lafayette, who had recently completed a triumphal tour of the United States in 1824–25. See Chinard's detailed discussions of Jacquemont's North American travel in "Les expériences américaines,"

139–73, 179–98; and the summary of Jacquemont's view of America in Craiutu, "Precursor of Tocqueville,"122–41.

8. Jacquemont to Prosper Fouchard, 3 June 1827, in *Correspondance inédite*, 1:117–24.

9. Rémond, *Les États-Unis devant l'opinion française*, 2:679–83. Although Tocqueville's social milieu differed from Jacquemont's, his moderate liberalism was also linked to aristocratic cultural traditions. See, for example, Jaume, *Tocqueville.* Jaume's study of Tocqueville (like Rémond's earlier work) also provides helpful insights into several other French writers who made the American trip. The most notable other traveling authors in this generation of French visitors were Michel Chevalier, Guillaume Tell Poussin, Jean-Jacques Ampère, and Ernest Duvergier de Hauranne, all of whom are discussed in a perceptive essay by Jennings, "French Visions of America."

10. The full letter to Victor de Tracy (dated "at sea, September 1827") can be found in Jacquemont, *Correspondance inédite*, 1:152–95; the passage quoted here is on 153. The detailed commentary in this long letter suggests that Jacquemont may have intended to use it for a future publication, but it was eventually published only in this later collection of his correspondence. Victor Destutt de Tracy (1781–1864) was the son of Antoine Destutt de Tracy (1754–1836)—a prominent philosopher in the Idéologues group that included Jacquemont's father. The younger Jacquemont met Lafayette through these connections. He once stayed at Lafayette's country chateau, LaGrange, while recovering from a laboratory accident, and Victor de Tracy's sister, Emilie, married Lafayette's son. Jacquemont wrote letters to both older and younger members of the family, so the father is identified throughout this chapter as Destutt de Tracy, and the son is identified simply as Victor de Tracy.

11. Jacquemont to Victor de Tracy, September 1827, in Jacquemont, *Correspondance Inédite*, 1:156.

12. Jacquemont to Victor de Tracy, September 1827, in Jacquemont, *Correspondance Inédite*, 1:157.

13. Jacquemont to Victor de Tracy, September 1827, in Jacquemont, *Correspondance inédite*, 1:160. This critique of Protestantism separated Jacquemont from Benjamin Constant and other French liberals who argued that the Protestant emphasis on individualism and *personal* religious beliefs offered a better foundation than Catholicism for liberal democratic societies. For more on these themes, see the insightful analysis in Rosenblatt, *Liberal Values*, 192–233.

14. Jacquemont to Victor de Tracy, September 1827, in Jacquemont, *Correspondance inédite*, 1:166, 168–71.

15. Jacquemont to Victor de Tracy, September 1827, in Jacquemont, *Correspondance inédite*, 1:166–69, quotation on 168–69.

16. Jacquemont to Victor de Tracy, September 1827, in Jacquemont, *Correspondance inédite*, 1:173–74, quotations on 173.

17. Jacquemont to Victor de Tracy, September 1827, in Jacquemont, *Correspondance inédite*, 1:165.

18. Jacquemont to Victor de Tracy, September 1827, in Jacquemont, *Correspondance inédite*, 1:160–61.

19. Jacquemont to Victor de Tracy, September 1827, in Jacquemont, *Correspondance inédite*, 1:158.

20. Jacquemont to Victor de Tracy, September 1827, in Jacquemont, *Correspondance inédite*, 1:159.

21. Jacquemont to Victor de Tracy, September 1827, in Jacquemont, *Correspondance inédite*, 1:179–181, quotation on 180–81.

22. Jacquemont to Victor de Tracy, September 1827, in Jacquemont, *Correspondance inédite*, 1:192–94, quotation on 193.

23. Jacquemont to Victor de Tracy, September 1827, in Jacquemont, *Correspondance inédite*, 1:184–88, 190. Jacquemont's critiques became common themes in later French accounts of American society. See, for example, the comprehensive analysis of such criticisms in Roger, *American Enemy*. Roger's wide-ranging book never mentions Jacquemont, but Mathy refers to him as one of the early French liberals who "became disenchanted with the American dream." See Mathy, *Extrême-Occident*, 29, 32.

24. Jacquemont to Venceslas Jacquemont, 31 October 1830 and 8 August 1831, in Jacquemont, *Correspondance pendant son voyage*, 1:334, 2:147.

25. Jacquemont, *Voyage dans l'Inde*, 1:455; Jacquemont to Jean de Charpentier, 16 February 1831, in Jacquemont, *Correspondance pendant son voyage*, 1:389; see also Jacquemont to Achille Chaper, 25 June 1830, in Jacquemont, *Letters to Achille Chaper*, 250.

26. Jacquemont, *Voyage dans l'Inde*, 1:238, 2:111; Jacquemont to Venceslas Jacquemont, 19 July 1831, in Jacquemont, *Correspondance pendant son voyage*, 2:129.

27. Jacquemont, *Voyage dans l'Inde*, 1:492–93.

28. Jacquemont, *Voyage dans l'Inde*, 2:338, 356, 3:181. Jacquemont's friend Prosper Mérimée described him as tall and thin with curly, chestnut-colored hair. See Mérimée's introduction in Jacquemont, *Correspondance inédite*, 1:ii–iii. Although Jacquemont traveled as a scientist, his reports often conveyed the kind of gazing male perspectives that have been analyzed in recent studies of European tourism. See, for example, Urry, *Tourist Gaze*, 145. As Urry notes, "Gazes organize the encounters of visitors with the 'other,' providing some sense of competence, pleasure and structure to experiences. . . . It is the gaze that orders and regulates . . . what is visually out-of-ordinary, what are the relevant differences and what is 'other.'"

29. Jacquemont to Porphyre Jacquemont, 10 May 1832, in Jacquemont, *Correspondance pendant son voyage*, 2:338.

30. Jacquemont to Venceslas Jacquemont, 24 December 1829, in Jacquemont, *Correspondance pendant son voyage*, 1:167–68; Jacquemont, *Voyage dans l'Inde*, 2:62–63.

31. Jacquemont to M. de Meslay, 6 September 1829, in Jacquemont, *Correspondance inédite*, 1:283; see also Jacquemont, *Voyage dans l'Inde*, 1:220.

32. Jacquemont to Venceslas Jacquemont, 25 December 1829, in Jacquemont, *Correspondance pendant son voyage*, 1:171.

33. Jacquemont to Venceslas Jacquemont, 22 June 1830, in Jacquemont, *Correspondance pendant son voyage*, 1:250.

34. Jacquemont to Venceslas Jacquemont, 17 March 1830, and to Porphyre Jacquemont, 20 May 1830, in Jacquemont, *Correspondance pendant son voyage*, 1:204, 227–28; Jacquemont to M. de Meslay, 11 August 1832, in Jacquemont, *Correspondance inédite*, 2:247.

35. Jacquemont, *Voyage dans l'Inde*, 3:526–27. Some French liberals later became interested in how the hierarchies of India's caste system might help the French understand the flaws of both excessive individualism and radical egalitarianism, but Jacquemont never viewed Indian society as a possible model for addressing social problems in France. For examples of this later French interest in India's social hierarchies, see Bouglé, *Essays on the Caste System*; and Dumont, *Homo Hierarchicus*. On the importance of India for twentieth-century French theorists, see Collins, "French Liberalism's 'Indian Detour.'"

36. Jacquemont, *Voyage dans l'Inde*, 3:326.

37. Jacquemont to Venceslas Jacquemont, 8 August 1831, in Jacquemont, *Correspondance*

pendant son voyage, 2:150. Jacquemont had also decided in the United States that the relationships between American men and women lacked the intimacy that developed between men and women in France, mainly because Americans were more concerned with money than with deep communication; see Jacquemont to Victor de Tracy, September 1827, in *Correspondance inédite*, 1:161–62.

38. Jacquemont to Porphyre Jacquemont, 14 May 1831, in Jacquemont, *Correspondance pendant son voyage*, 2:70; Jacquemont, *Voyage dans l'Inde*, 1:329.

39. Jacquemont to M. Narjot, 22 December 1831, and to Mme Victor de Tracy, 26 May 1831, in Jacquemont, *Correspondance pendant son voyage*, 2:91–92, 244–45; Jacquemont to Destutt de Tracy, 27 May 1831, in Jacquemont, *Corresondance inédite*, 2:86–87. The British tried to ban polygamy in India after 1860, and the Hindu Marriage Act of 1955 outlawed polygamy in postcolonial India.

40. Jacquemont, *Voyage dans l'Inde*, 3:61–62.

41. Jacquemont to Victor de Tracy, 7 October 1830, in Jacquemont, *Correspondance pendant son voyage*, 1:323.

42. Jacquemont, *Voyage dans l'Inde*, 2:63, 91; and see the earlier critique in his journal, 1:360.

43. Jacquemont to Destutt de Tracy, 27 May 1831, in Jacquemont, *Correspondance inédite*, 2:86.

44. Jacquemont to Victor de Tracy, 1 September 1829 and 28 May 1831, in Jacquemont, *Correspondance pendant son voyage*, 1:97, 2:103. See also Jacquemont, *Voyage dans l'Inde*, 3:568.

45. Jacquemont to Venceslas Jacquemont, 10 January 1831 and 22 April 1831, in Jacquemont, *Correspondance pendant son voyage*, 1:353–54, 2:57; Jacquemont to Destutt de Tracy, 27 May 1831, in Jacquemont, *Correspondance inédite*, 2:86. Jacquemont's nineteenth-century belief in the progressive, modernizing effects of European colonial policies in India expressed the kind of universalizing, historical ideology that postcolonial theorists and historians have vehemently challenged by emphasizing the *plural* cultural and political paths toward modernity. See, for example, the influential argument in Chakrabarty, *Provincializing Europe*, 3–26.

46. Pratt, *Imperial Eyes*, 38.

47. Jacquemont, *Voyage dans l'Inde*, 1:448, 3:325–26.

48. Jacquemont to Destutt de Tracy, 25 April 1832, in Jacquemont, *Correspondance inédite*, 2:199.

49. Jacquemont to Destutt de Tracy, 27 May 1831, in Jacquemont, *Correspondance inédite*, 2:87–88.

50. Jacquemont to Joseph de Hezeta, 14 January 1830, in Jacquemont, *Correspondance inédite*, 1:347; Jacquemont to Porphyre Jacquemont, 14 May 1831, in *Correspondance pendant son voyage*, 2:71.

51. Jacquemont to Venceslas Jacquemont, 6 April 1831, in Jacquemont, *Correspondance pendant son voyage*, 2:7. Jacquemont's letters from India show how imperial "contact zones" became notable locations for the fusion of knowledge and power that Michel Foucault famously described in his analysis of post-Enlightenment European institutions and intellectual experts. See, for example, the essays in Foucault, *Power/Knowledge*, 109–45. For a summary of Victor Cousin's ideas and cultural status, see Goldstein, *Post-Revolutionary Self*, 139–232.

52. Jacquemont to Joseph de Hezeta, 11 May 1831, in Jacquemont, *Correspondance inédite*, 2:314; see also Jacquemont to Alexander Johnson, 6 July 1831, in this same volume, 2:320–22; and Jacquemont to Venceslas Jacquemont, 14 March [1831], in Jacquemont, *Correspandance pendant son voyage*, 1:414.

53. Jacquemont to Victor de Tracy, 1 September 1829, in Jacquemont, *Correspondance pendant son voyage*, 1:104–5.

54. Jacquemont to Victor de Tracy, 7 October 1830, in Jacquemont, *Correspondance pendant son voyage*, 1:325.

55. Jacquemont to Victor de Tracy, 11 April 1831, in Jacquemont, *Correspondance pendant son voyage*, 2:24.

56. Jacquemont to Porphyre Jacquemont, 10 May 1832, in Jacquemont, *Correspondance pendant son voyage*, 2:239. Jacquemont's remains were eventually returned to Paris in 1881 and buried at the Jardin des Plantes in 1893.

Chapter Two

1. Tristan has attracted more historical attention than Jacquemont, in part because of her contributions to both feminism and the early socialist movement among French workers. Important studies of Tristan include Puech, *La vie et l'oeuvre de Flora Tristan*; Baelen, *La vie de Flora Tristan*; Strumingher, *Odyssey of Flora Tristan*; Grogan, *Flora Tristan*; and the essays in Michaud, *Un fabuleux destin*. Other interesting accounts of Tristan's life and writings appear in Desanti, *Flora Tristan*; Hart, *Revolution and Women's Autobiography*; Pérez-Mejía, *Geography of Hard Times*; and Moses and Rabine, *Feminism, Socialism, and French Romanticism*. See also the additional perspectives in Michaud, "Flora Tristan Américaine" and in McCall, "Still Life and Fetal Exploits." My biographical summary draws from several of these sources but particularly from Strumingher and Grogan.

2. Tristan to Pío de Tristán, [1829], in Michaud, *Flora Tristan*, 45–47. Pío de Tristán y Moscoso had served like his brother Mariano in the Spanish army in Europe. He later held important positions in the Spanish colonial army and administration in Peru, but after national independence he would become minister of war and then minister of finance in the new Peruvian state before moving into other government positions in the late 1830s. Tristan's influential Peruvian family was thus prominent in both colonial and postcolonial Peruvian society.

3. For scholarly accounts of this transition, see the introduction in Michaud, *Flora Tristan*, 23; and the analysis in Cuche, "Le Perou de Flora." See also the discussions of Tristan's hybrid, transnational experiences in Nuñez, "Between France and the World"; Law-Sullivan, "Liberté, Égalité, Sororité"; and Vergereau-Dewey, "*Pérégrinations d'une paria* de Flora Tristan." These articles all offer good insights into the tensions and "plural identities" that emerged in Tristan's writings as she tried to fuse universal ideas about human rights with stories about the privileged social status of her Peruvian family and with her belief in the superiority of French national culture.

4. Tristan's campaigns on behalf of French workers included publication of a controversial (utopian) book, *The Workers' Union* (1843), and participation in workers' meetings wherever she could travel. This phase of her life is discussed in all the previously cited biographies and in a detailed study by Cross, *Flora Tristan's Politics*.

5. Tristan, *Peregrinations*, 171–73. This English edition cuts some passages from the original, 900-page French edition, but it includes the most important sections of the book (except for the preface) in a lively, reliable translation. Although I have changed some words from English to American spelling, I have used this edition for most quotations. The first French edition of *Pérégrinations d'une paria* was published in Paris in 1838. An English translation of short excerpts from this book and from Tristan's later writings about England, French workers, and travels within France is available in a helpful edited collection Tristan, *Flora Tristan, Utopian Feminist*, which was compiled by D. Beik and P. Beik.

6. See the two excellent introductory chapters in Moses and Rabine, *Feminism, Socialism, and French Romanticism*, 17–144. Moses emphasizes the possible influence of Saint-Simonian

ideas on what might be called Tristan's "inflated sense of self-importance" (77–78), whereas Rabine refers to Tristan's self-portrayal "in the various guises of a romantic heroine" (126). Their book also provides a valuable English translation of Tristan's foreword and preface from the 1838 French edition of *Peregrinations of a Pariah*, which does not appear in the otherwise reliable English translation by Jean Hawkes.

7. For analysis of the self-defined roles and theatrical identities that Tristan "played" in her writings and life, see Grogan, *Flora Tristan*; and Grogan's insightful essay "'Playing the Princess.'"

8. Tristan, preface to *Peregrinations*, in Moses and Rabine, *Feminism, Socialism, and French Romanticism*, 205.

9. Tristan, preface to *Peregrinations*, in Moses and Rabine, *Feminism, Socialism, and French Romanticism*, 205.

10. Tristan, preface to *Peregrinations*, in Moses and Rabine, *Feminism, Socialism, and French Romanticism*, 206–7, quotations on 207.

11. Tristan, preface to *Peregrinations*, in Moses and Rabine, *Feminism, Socialism, and French Romanticism*, 210.

12. Tristan, preface to *Peregrinations*, in Moses and Rabine, *Feminism, Socialism, and French Romanticism*, 208.

13. Tristan, preface to *Peregrinations*, in Moses and Rabine, *Feminism, Socialism, and French Romanticism*, 209. Tristan's autobiographical linkage of her own life to a broader social context or vision of social reform is discussed with helpful insights and comparisons in Hart, *Revolution and Women's Autobiography*, 44, 47–69. Hart argues that women's more politicized autobiographies separated this female genre from most memoirs by the era's Romantic male authors.

14. Tristan, preface to *Peregrinations*, in Moses and Rabine, *Feminism, Socialism, and French Romanticism*, 207–8.

15. Tristan, preface to *Peregrinations*, in Moses and Rabine, *Feminism, Socialism, and French Romanticism*, 211–12.

16. Tristan, preface to *Peregrinations*, in Moses and Rabine, *Feminism, Socialism, and French Romanticism*, 215.

17. This attack is discussed in all of the previously cited Tristan biographies. For more on the gendered themes of Chazal's self-justification and the legal arguments at his trial, see Grogan, *Flora Tristan*, 37–43.

18. The similarities between Tristan's travel narrative and the classic themes of a religious pilgrimage (or testing) are discussed, for example, in Hart, *Revolution and Women's Autobiography*, 72–73; and Gabaude, "*Les Pérégrinations*."

19. Tristan, *Peregrinations*, 172–73.

20. Tristan, *Peregrinations*, 33, 84–87, 89–91, 119–20, quotations on 84, 87.

21. Tristan, *Peregrinations*, 85.

22. Tristan, *Peregrinations*, 82, 87, 128.

23. Tristan, *Peregrinations*, 127.

24. Tristan, preface to *Peregrinations*, in Moses and Rabine, *Feminism, Socialism, and French Romanticism*, 215.

25. Tristan, *Peregrinations*, 17–18, 29, 111, 286.

26. Tristan, *Peregrinations*, 180.

27. Tristan, *Peregrinations*, 271–72.

28. Tristan, *Peregrinations*, 122–23, 279.

29. Tristan, *Peregrinations*, 102, 109.

30. Tristan, *Peregrinations*, 12.

31. Tristan, *Peregrinations*, 162, 175.

32. Tristan, *Peregrinations*, 29, 282–84. Tristan's comments on race and work appeared in her summary of a conversation with an enslaver (282). Tristan herself proposed a gradual emancipation of enslaved people, which would allow for education and vocational training during the transition to freedom. Ironically, however, as Vergereau-Dewey notes in a perceptive discussion of contradictions, Tristan was seeking Peruvian family wealth that was derived from a slave economy. See Vergereau-Dewey, "*Pérégrinations d'une paria* de Flora Tristan," 89. Slavery was not legally abolished in Peru until 1854. The paradoxical position of nineteenth-century French feminist travelers has also been noted in Eichner's important recent book, *Feminism's Empire*, 212. Eichner notes that such travelers "bore the cachet of white skin, Europeanness, and Frenchness. This bestowed a rarefied status that allowed immediate entrée to elite realms and a privileged social passport."

33. Tristan, *Peregrinations*, 101, 106.

34. Tristan, *Peregrinations*, 186–204, 239–41, quotation on 186.

35. Tristan, *Peregrinations*, 269, 273–74.

36. Tristan, *Peregrinations*, 230–32, 276, 292–305, quotations on 276, 230.

37. Tristan, *Peregrinations*, 275.

38. Tristan, *Peregrinations*, 180. Tristan's interest in the marginal *rabonas* shows her fascination with the social position of the "pariah," but Tristan's favorite, self-defining term came from the culture of southern India rather than from Peru. "Pariah" is a Tamil word for a member of a low caste, so the prominence of this word in Tristan's writing conveyed her identification with the marginal social groups that remained alien to Jacquemont as he traveled across India; but the references to both pariahs and *rabonas* helped Tristan describe her own position in modern French society.

39. Tristan, *Peregrinations*, 107–8.

40. Tristan, *Peregrinations*, 111, 126, 277.

41. Tristan, *Peregrinations*, 111.

42. Tristan, *Peregrinations*, 168.

43. Tristan, *Peregrinations*, 169–70, 220, 233.

44. Tristan, *Peregrinations*, 169.

45. Tristan stressed this political theme in her first publication, written shortly after her return to Paris. See Tristan, *Nécessité de faire un bon accueil*, 68.

46. Tristan to Louis Denoyers [1 December 1838], in Tristan, *Lettres*, 87–88.

47. See Pratt's discussion of Tristan's alternative narrative in *Imperial Eyes*, 152–57, where she refers to Tristan as a "social exploratress" (157).

48. Tristan, *Peregrinations*, 112, 289.

49. Tristan, *Peregrinations*, 124, 264, 266, 268.

50. Tristan, *Peregrinations*, 273.

51. Tristan, *Peregrinations*, 265–66.

Epilogue to Part I

1. Tristan, *Peregrinations*, 108; Jacquemont to Achille Chaper, 16 December 1831, in Jacquemont, *Letters to Achille Chaper*, 254.

2. This pattern of French self-discovery in non-European cultures would reappear in Tristan's famous grandson Paul Gauguin (1848–1903), the French artist whose flight to Tahiti and paintings of Tahitian subjects would become notable events and controversial influences in European art history.

Introduction to Part II

1. Cooper's travel writings in the early 1830s included *Gleanings in Europe: The Rhine* (1836) and *Gleanings in Europe: France* (1837). Twain's best-known travel book, *The Innocents Abroad* (1869), described a trip through Europe and the Middle East. James drew on his wide-ranging travel experiences in books such as *English Hours* (1905) and *A Little Tour of France* (1900). These books and the travel narratives of more than sixty other nineteenth-century American authors are discussed in two helpful volumes about early literary travelers. See Schramer and Ross, *American Travel Writers, 1776–1864*; and Ross and Schramer, *American Travel Writers, 1850–1915*. For interpretations of Twain and James as travel writers, see Ziff, *Return Passages*, 170–282; and for a comprehensive, annotated bibliography of roughly 1,800 American travel books published before 1900, see H. Smith, *American Travelers Abroad.*

2. The class and gender identities of American travelers between 1800 and 1850 (as well as the growing number of transatlantic passengers) are discussed in Kilbride, *Being American in Europe*, 2, 81–166. Many Americans went to England, but the specific American fascination with France is examined with engaging examples and stories in Levenstein, *Seductive Journey*; and in McCullough, *Greater Journey*. See also the wide-ranging analysis of American travelers in Sauvigny, *La France et les Français vus par les voyageurs américains*, which uses French travel records to confirm that about 30,000 Americans visited France between 1816 and 1848 (1:18–19), but the countrywide numbers were probably higher because Sauvigny focused mainly on Paris.

Chapter Three

1. Fuller has received far more scholarly attention than any other traveler who is discussed in this book. For information on Fuller's youth and education, see the excellent biography by Capper, *Margaret Fuller: An American Romantic Life*, vol. 1, *The Private Years* (hereafter *Fuller, Private Years*), especially 3–62. Other useful introductions to Fuller's early life include Kornfeld, *Margaret Fuller*, 6–50; Mehren, *Minerva and the Muse*; and Murray, *Margaret Fuller*, which develops a provocative psychological analysis of Fuller's relationship with her father and other men. See also the sections on her early years in biographies by Matteson, *Lives of Margaret Fuller*; and Marshall, *Margaret Fuller*. To separate Fuller from her father, I refer to her as Margaret in the years before his death.

2. Capper, *Fuller, Private Years*, 290–306. Fuller's view of intellectual life as an ongoing "conversation" continued to influence her writing when she traveled in Europe. See the interesting analysis of Fuller's dialogical approach to cross-cultural interpretations in Eckel, *Atlantic Citizens*, 46–70.

3. Fuller, *Woman in the Nineteenth Century*; this edition includes lengthy excerpts from *Summer on the Lakes*, but there is also a complete modern edition of *Summer on the Lakes* with a helpful introduction by Susan Belasco Smith. Kornfeld provides an insightful summary of the key themes in both books in *Margaret Fuller*, 38–50. Fuller's early travel writing also included a gendered critique of American materialism, as Healey explains in "'Mighty Meaning of the Scene.'"

4. Kornfeld, *Margaret Fuller*, 51–53. Fuller's widening, multicultural perspectives are examined in an informative essay on her New York journalism by Capper, "Getting from Here to There." Many of her *Tribune* articles have been collected in *Margaret Fuller, Critic.*

5. Fuller's relationship with James Nathan is described in the editor's introduction to volume 4 of Hudspeth, *Letters*, 4:7–11; see also Capper, *Margaret Fuller: An American Romantic Life*, vol. 2, *The Public Years* (hereafter *Fuller, Public Years*), 220–28. Murray analyzes Fuller's

emotional interest in Nathan as a psychological transference of her unconscious desire to recover the "pure" affection she had lost when her father died; see Murray, *Margaret Fuller*, 244–81.

6. Fuller sought financial assistance from her friend Samuel Ward; see Fuller to Samuel G. and Anna B. Ward, 3 March 1846, in Hudspeth, *Letters*, 4:193. For more details on the personal and professional arrangements that preceded Fuller's trip, see the editors' introduction in Fuller, *"These Sad but Glorious Days,"* 7–10. One of Fuller's immediate successors as a "European Correspondent" for the *Tribune* would be Karl Marx, who submitted articles from London between 1852 and 1862. See Marx, *Dispatches for the "New York Tribune."*

7. Fuller to James Nathan, [4? May? 1845], in Hudspeth, *Letters*, 4:95.

8. Fuller to Samuel G. and Anna B. Ward, 3 March 1846, in Hudspeth, *Letters*, 4:192–93.

9. This summary of Fuller's European travels and her experiences in Italy draws on the outstanding second volume of Capper's biographical study, *Fuller, Public Years*, 279–497. More information on Fuller's European experiences is available in Kornfeld, *Margaret Fuller*, 57–65; in the introduction by Reynolds and Smith in Fuller, *"These Sad but Glorious Days,"* 12–35; and in Reynolds, *European Revolutions*, 54–78. See also the chapter on Fuller in Stowe, *Going Abroad*, 102–24. Other valuable perspectives on Fuller's European transitions appear in Capper and Giorcelli, *Fuller: Transatlantic Crossings*, especially chapters 3–9, which focus on her life in Italy; and in Roberson, *Antebellum American Women Writers*, 150–67. Additional discussion of Fuller's engagement with European political conflicts and ideas can be found in the well-researched, cross-cultural study by Roberts, *Distant Revolutions*, 96–103; Schriber, *Writing Home*, 137–44; and Nerio, "Transcendentalist Abroad."

10. The evidence for Fuller's marriage to Ossoli (probably in April 1848) is described in Capper, *Fuller, Public Years*, 363–69; and in Mehren, "Fuller and the Marriage Question."

11. There are brief, well-informed accounts of Fuller's (likely) marriage, young child, literary plans, financial problems, and tragic final voyage in the editor's introductions to the later volumes of Hudspeth, *Letters*, 5:6–14 and 6:5–7. See also the discussion of these events in the introduction to Fuller, *"These Sad but Glorious Days,"* 18–35; and Capper describes Fuller's last days, her death in the shipwreck, and various public responses to these events in the vivid concluding chapter of *Fuller, Public Years*, 503–20.

12. Fuller, [Dispatch 34], from Rome, 6 July 1849, in *"These Sad but Glorious Days,"* 311.

13. Fuller to James Nathan, 31 August [with additions on 5 September] 1845, and Fuller to Nathan, [ca. 28 February 1846], in Hudspeth, *Letters*, 4:156, 190. Fuller's advice on putting "yourself" into travel narratives expressed Romantic views of the traveler's quest for self-knowledge. The "inner journey" became more important than empirical observations in most Romantic and post-Romantic accounts of other cultures. See the helpful analysis of these themes in Thompson, "Nineteenth-Century Travel Writing," 108–18; and in Youngs, *Cambridge Introduction to Travel Writing*, 53–55, 87–114.

14. Fuller, [Dispatch 9, undated, published in *Tribune*, 19 February 1847], in *"These Sad but Glorious Days,"* 94.

15. Fuller to Richard F. Fuller, 27 September 1846, in Hudspeth, *Letters*, 4:228.

16. Fuller, [Dispatch 4], from Edinburgh, 22 September 1846, in *"These Sad but Glorious Days,"* 67.

17. Fuller to Caroline Sturgis, [16? November 1846], in Hudspeth, *Letters*, 4:239.

18. Fuller to Margarett C. Fuller, 26 December 1846, and Fuller to Caroline Sturgis, 28 November [1846], in Hudspeth, *Letters*, 4:250, 253.

19. Fuller, [Dispatch 10], from Paris [undated, published in *Tribune*, 3 March 1847], in *"These Sad but Glorious Days,"* 105–6.

20. Fuller, [Dispatch 10], from Paris [undated, published in *Tribune*, 3 March 1847] and [Dispatch 13, undated, published in *Tribune*, 29 May 1847], in *"These Sad but Glorious Days,"* 104, 126–27.

21. Fuller, [Dispatch 15], from Milan, 9 August 1847, in *"These Sad but Glorious Days,"* 140.

22. Fuller, [Dispatch 14], from Rome, May 1847, in *"These Sad but Glorious Days,"* 132, 134–35. Fuller's themes confirm the scholarly argument that literary travelers have long wanted to define their own experiences as "authentic" by asserting their difference from the superficiality of "tourist visits." See the analysis of the traveler/tourist distinction in the previously cited studies by MacCannell, *Tourist*, 101–4; Culler, "Semiotics of Tourism"; Thompson, "Nineteenth-Century Travel Writing," 122–24; and Youngs, *Cambridge Introduction to Travel Writing*, 58–60.

23. Fuller, [Dispatch 19], from Rome, 17 December 1847, in *"These Sad but Glorious Days,"* 168.

24. Fuller, [Dispatch 19], from Rome, 17 December 1847, in *"These Sad but Glorious Days,"* 168.

25. Fuller to Richard F. Fuller, [ca. 16 November 1846]; Fuller to Caroline Sturgis, 28 November [1846]; and Fuller to Ralph Waldo Emerson, 18 January 1847, in Hudspeth, *Letters*, 4:243, 250, 259.

26. Fuller to Ralph Waldo Emerson, 20 June 1847, in Hudspeth, *Letters*, 4:276. The reference to "advantages for observation and enjoyment" may be an early, vague allusion to her new friendship with Ossoli.

27. Fuller to Sarah Ann Clarke, 18 January 1849, in Hudspeth, *Letters*, 5:172.

28. Fuller, [Dispatch 9, undated, published in *Tribune*, 19 February 1847], in *"These Sad but Glorious Days,"* 101. This article described Carlyle; her visit with Wordsworth was noted in an earlier article, [Dispatch 2], from Ambleside, Westmoreland, 27 August 1846, in *"These Sad but Glorious Days,"* 53.

29. Fuller, [Dispatch 10], from Paris [undated, published in *Tribune*, 3 March 1847], in *"These Sad but Glorious Days,"* 111.

30. Fuller to Ralph Waldo Emerson, 15 March 1847, in Hudspeth, *Letters*, 4:261–62. I have examined Mickiewicz's mystical, poetic identity as a nationalist leader among Polish exiles in Kramer, *Threshold of a New World*, 176–228.

31. Fuller to Marcus and Rebecca Spring, 10 April [1847], in Hudspeth, *Letters*, 4:263.

32. Adam Mickiewicz to Fuller, February 1847, in Hudspeth, *Letters*, 5:176. Hudspeth includes this letter in a footnote to a letter that Fuller sent early in 1849 to her American friend James Clarke (in which she included the message from Mickiewicz). The quoted passages are from Hudspeth's translation of the French text.

33. Fuller, [Dispatch 23], from Rome, 29 March 1848, and [Dispatch 24], from Rome, 19 April 1848, in *"These Sad but Glorious Days,"* 212, 223.

34. Phillips, "Apocalyptic Feminism," 31. Phillips emphasizes that Mickiewicz wanted Fuller to recognize that she did not need to "remain virgin" to play a leading role in the "deliverance" of modern women (a theme of Mickiewicz's letter of February 1847, cited in note 32). Capper also stresses that Mickiewicz advised Fuller to be open to physical relationships in letters he sent to her after she moved to Italy; see Capper, *Fuller, Public Years*, 333–35.

35. Fuller, [Dispatch 14], from Rome, May 1847; [Dispatch 19], from Rome, 17 December 1847; and [Dispatch 22], from Rome, January 1848, in *"These Sad but Glorious Days,"* 136, 172, 205.

36. Fuller, [Dispatch 12, undated, published in *Tribune*, 15 May 1847], in *"These Sad but Glorious Days,"* 119–20. This praise for Fourier became part of a wider defense of Fourier's ideas in Greeley's newspaper. For more discussion of Fuller's response to socialism and Fourier, see Tuchinsky, "American Socialism and Margaret Fuller's 1848."

37. Fuller, [Dispatch 6], from Paris, November 1846 (she apparently wrote at least part of this

article in Scotland, though it was sent from Paris); [Dispatch 5], from Birmingham, [England], 30 September 1846; and [Dispatch 13, undated, published in *Tribune*, 29 May 1847], all in *"These Sad but Glorious Days,"* 72, 79–80, and 128.

38. Fuller, [Dispatch 10], from Paris [undated, published in *Tribune*, 3 March 1847], and [Dispatch 15], from Milan, 9 August 1847, in *"These Sad but Glorious Days,"* 108–9, 143.

39. Fuller, [Dispatch 20], from Rome, 30 December 1847, in *"These Sad but Glorious Days,"* 179.

40. The quoted passages are from letters and journal excerpts that Fuller sent to Elizabeth Hoar early in 1847; they appeared in Fuller's *Memoirs* that Emerson, William Channing, and James Clarke organized for publication in 1852, and they have been republished in Chevigny, *Woman and the Myth*, 361–62.

41. Chevigny, *Woman and the Myth*, 362–63. Fuller's views of Sand have attracted increasing scholarly attention, even though the two writers had little direct contact. See, for example, Avallone, "Circles around George Sand."

42. Fuller, [Dispatch 15], from Milan, 9 August 1847, and [Dispatch 16], from Rome, October 1847, *"These Sad but Glorious Days,"* 146, 153.

43. Fuller, [Dispatch 17], from Rome, 18 October 1847, in *"These Sad but Glorious Days,"* 156–57, 160.

44. Fuller, [Dispatch 23], from Rome, 29 March 1848; [Dispatch 24], from Rome, 19 April 1848; and Fuller described the pope's flight from Paris at the end of the year, [Dispatch 26], from Rome, 2 December 1848, in *"These Sad but Glorious Days,"* 211–12, 222, 225–26, 240–44.

45. Fuller, [Dispatch 25], from Rome, 2 December 1848, in *"These Sad but Glorious Days,"* 234. Two different articles were dated 2 December 1848.

46. Fuller, [Dispatch 27], from Rome, 20 February 1849, in *"These Sad but Glorious Days,"* 250.

47. Fuller, [Dispatch 33], from Rome, 21 June 1849, in *"These Sad but Glorious Days,"* 300.

48. [Dispatch 34], from Rome, 6 July 1849, in *"These Sad but Glorious Days,"* 305, 308–9.

49. Fuller, [Dispatch 9, undated, published in *Tribune*, 19 February 1847], in *"These Sad but Glorious Days,"* 99. For more discussion of Mazzini's nationalism and its similarities with Mickiewicz's messianic nationalism, see Kramer, *Nationalism in Europe and America*, 59, 85–89, 106–13; and see the discussion of Fuller's engagement with the Romantic nationalism of Mazzini, Mickiewicz, and the Roman Republic in Eckel, *Atlantic Citizens*, 58–64, and "Radical Innocence."

50. Fuller, [Dispatch 28], from Rome, 20 February 1849; [Dispatch 29], from Rome, 20 March 1849; and [Dispatch 32], from Rome, 10 June 1849, in *"These Sad but Glorious Days,"* 257–58, 264, 294.

51. Fuller to Caroline Sturgis Tappan, 16 March 1849, in Hudspeth, *Letters*, 5:210.

52. Fuller to Ralph Waldo Emerson, 16 November 1846, in Hudspeth, *Letters*, 4:245.

53. Fuller to Margarett C. Fuller, 16 October 1847, in Hudspeth, *Letters*, 4:299–300, 302.

54. Fuller to Ralph Waldo Emerson, 19 May 1848, in Hudspeth, *Letters*, 5:66.

55. Fuller to Ralph Waldo Emerson, 11 July 1848, in Hudspeth, *Letters*, 5:86.

56. Fuller to Margarett C. Fuller, 16 November 1848, in Hudspeth, *Letters*, 5:149–50.

57. Fuller to James F. Clarke, 19 January 1849, in Hudspeth, *Letters*, 5:174.

58. Fuller to Anna Barker Ward, 18 March 1849, in Hudspeth, *Letters*, 5:217.

59. Fuller to Ellen Fuller Channing, 11 December 1849, in Hudspeth, *Letters*, 5:292.

60. Hudspeth summarizes the evolution of Fuller's relationship with Ossoli and her epistolary revelation of the marriage (and baby) in his introduction to *Letters*, 5:6–15. Other historical accounts of the marriage have been cited in this chapter's note 10.

61. Fuller to Margarett C. Fuller, [31 August 1849], in Hudspeth, *Letters*, 5:261. The surviving correspondence between Fuller and Ossoli suggests they were married on 4 April 1848; see

Fuller to Giovanni Angelo Ossoli, 4 April 1849, in Hudspeth, *Letters*, 5:223; and the detailed discussion of other documents in Mehren, "Fuller and the Marriage Question."

62. Fuller to Margarett C. Fuller, [31 August 1849], in Hudspeth, *Letters*, 5:261.

63. Fuller to William H. Channing, 17 December 1849, in Hudspeth, *Letters*, 5:300.

64. Fuller to Marcus and Rebecca Spring, 5 February 1850; Fuller to Lewis Cass Jr., 2 May 1850; and for an example of Fuller's anxiety about the voyage to America, see her letter to Constanza Arconati Visconti, 6 April 1850, all in Hudspeth, *Letters*, 6:53, 74, 83.

65. Fuller, [Dispatch 31], from Rome, 27 May 1849; Fuller discussed the arrival of the republican French forces in a previous article, [Dispatch 30], from Rome, 6 May 1849, in *"These Sad but Glorious Days,"* 275–76, 278.

66. Fuller, [Dispatch 37], from Florence, 6 January 1850, in *"These Sad but Glorious Days,"* 322.

67. Fuller to Richard F. Fuller, 27 September 1846; and Fuller to Margarett C. Fuller, 26 December 1846, in Hudspeth, *Letters*, 4:228, 253.

68. Fuller, [Dispatch 1], from Ambleside, Westmoreland, 23 August 1846, and [Dispatch 7], from Paris [November ?] 1846, in *"These Sad but Glorious Days,"* 42–43, 86.

69. Fuller, [Dispatch 18, undated, published in *Tribune*, 1 January 1848], in *"These Sad but Glorious Days,"* 161–62.

70. Fuller, [Dispatch 18, undated, published in *Tribune*, 1 January 1848], in *"These Sad but Glorious Days,"* 162.

71. Fuller, [Dispatch 18, undated, published in *Tribune*, 1 January 1848], and [Dispatch 28], from Rome, 20 February 1849, in *"These Sad but Glorious Days,"* 162, 257–58.

72. Fuller, [Dispatch 18, undated, published in *Tribune*, 1 January 1848], in *"These Sad but Glorious Days,"* 162.

73. Fuller, [Dispatch 16], from Rome, October 1847, and [Dispatch 18, undated, first published in *Tribune*, 1 January 1848], in *"These Sad but Glorious Days,"* 154, 165–66. For discussion of Fuller's evolving views of slavery, abolitionism, and women's rights, see Frank, "Margaret Fuller and Antislavery."

74. Fuller, [Dispatch 18, undated, published in *Tribune*, 1 January 1848], in *"These Sad but Glorious Days,"* 165–66.

75. Fuller, [Dispatch 17], from Rome, 18 October 1847, in *"These Sad but Glorious Days,"* 160–61.

76. Fuller, [Dispatch 26], from Rome, 2 December 1848; [Dispatch 28], from Rome, 20 February 1849; [Dispatch 30], from Rome, 6 May 1849; [Dispatch 31], from Rome, 27 May 1849; and [Dispatch 32], from Rome, 10 June 1849, in *"These Sad but Glorious Days,"* 245, 257–58, 277, 283–84, 294.

77. Fuller, [Dispatch 24], from Rome, 19 April 1848, in *"These Sad but Glorious Days,"* 230; this quoted passage was added to the dispatch on 7 May.

78. Fuller, [Dispatch 34], from Rome, 6 July 1849, in *"These Sad but Glorious Days,"* 311; this quoted passage was added to the dispatch on 10 July.

79. Fuller, [Dispatch 30], from Rome, 6 May 1849, and [Dispatch 36], from Florence, 15 November 1849, in *"These Sad but Glorious Days,"* 276–77, 316.

Chapter Four

1. There is no comprehensive biographical study of McGavock, but Herschel Gower has written an informative account of his life in an introduction to the published edition of McGavock's journals. My summary of McGavock's life draws on this biographical narrative in McGavock, *Pen and Sword*, 26–88. This collection of McGavock's writings is a valuable

source of information about his life and ideas because it includes the surviving journals from his time at Harvard, his travels in Europe (the journals for 1852 were lost), and his later career as a lawyer, political leader, and Confederate officer. Additional perspectives on McGavock's European travels can be found in Gower, "Tennessee Writers Abroad."

2. For examples of McGavock's discussion of his intellectual, political, and personal concerns at Harvard, see the following journal entries for 1848: 3 and 17 March, 6 April, 1 and 4 June, 18 July, 10 August, 2 September, and 26 October, in *Pen and Sword*, 111, 114, 118, 129–30, 137, 142, 149, 158.

3. McGavock described his visits to the White House in journal entries for 19, 27, and 28 January 1848 and wrote about his travel across upstate New York and Canada in a daily series of journal entries during August 1848. See *Pen and Sword*, 102, 104, 142–45.

4. McGavock, journal entry for 30 July 1848, in *Pen and Sword*, 140.

5. For more information on McGavock's life in Cambridge, his early legal career, and his relationship with Fanny Jane Crutcher, see Gower's biographical introduction in *Pen and Sword*, 37–50. Edwin Ewing was a former congressman whose precise connections with Frank Parrish were not explained by McGavock or by the editors of his journal (nobody referred to Parrish as an enslaved man). Gower describes him as a "mulatto barber" who had his own shop in Nashville. Other friends on McGavock's eastbound ship included an Episcopal bishop named James Harvey Otey, an aunt named Felicia Grundy Eakin, two cousins, and several other Nashville friends. McGavock separated from most of these people soon after he arrived in Europe, though he traveled across Italy and the Middle East with Ewing and Parrish; and he later traveled with a South Carolinian named William Johnstone, whom he met in Belgium. On the visit with President Fillmore and the list of traveling companions, see McGavock, journal entries for 2 and 10 April 1851, in *Pen and Sword*, 176, 179.

6. McGavock, journal entry for 20 March 1851, in *Pen and Sword*, 171.

7. McGavock, Letter 1, from the ship *Waterloo*, in *Tennessean Abroad*, 11; the more obscure personal reasons for the trip are suggested in the book's preface. McGavock reported in Letter 3, from Liverpool, that the transatlantic voyage on the *Waterloo* (powered by sails rather than steam) was a twenty-six-day trip. See *Tennessean Abroad*, v, 23.

8. McGavock, Letter 1, from the ship *Waterloo*, in *Tennessean Abroad*, 11.

9. McGavock, journal entry for 1 May 1851, in *Pen and Sword*, 187.

10. McGavock, journal entries for 1 June and 1 July 1851, in *Pen and Sword*, 199, 211.

11. McGavock, journal entries for 25 and 28 May 1851, in *Pen and Sword*, 196–97.

12. Gower discusses these events in the biographical introduction to McGavock's journals, and McGavock also described his return to the United States in a concise (undated) summary of his post-travel transitions. See McGavock, *Pen and Sword*, 50–58, 301–3.

13. McGavock, undated journal entry [after 1852], in *Pen and Sword*, 303.

14. McGavock described his failed efforts to secure diplomatic appointments from Presidents Franklin Pierce and James Buchanan (as well as his renunciation of office seeking) in an undated journal entry (after 1852) and in numerous journal entries during March 1857, when he traveled again to Washington after Buchanan's inauguration; see *Pen and Sword*, 304, 401–4.

15. McGavock wrote about his daily activities and career in regular journal entries until October 1862; Gower's introduction provides a concise summary of later-life events in *Pen and Sword*, 59–88. McGavock and Seraphine Deery married in 1855 and never had children.

16. McGavock, "Conclusion," *Tennessean Abroad*, 398.

17. McGavock, journal entries throughout 1848 for 7 and 8 April; 4, 11, and 17 June; 18 and 20 July; 15 October; and 19 November, in *Pen and Sword*, 118, 130–32, 137–38, 156, 162, quotations on 130, 132, 138.

18. McGavock, Letter 4, from Hucknall, near Newstead Abbey, England; Letter 26, from Geneva, Switzerland; Letter 29, from Venice, Italy; and Letter 56, from Trieste, in *Tennessean Abroad*, 32–33, 156, 168–69, 330. McGavock relied on John Murray's *Handbook for Travellers* for advice on the sights he should see in Europe. Updated versions of the *Handbook* were published throughout the 1840s and 1850s, and there were different editions for Germany, Italy, and other regions. McGavock's responses to "authentic" tourist sights thus reflected the influence of both guidebooks and literary texts, thereby exemplifying patterns that Jonathan Culler has analyzed in his excellent essay "Semiotics of Tourism," 164. Culler's key theme suggests why McGavock's literary references were important: "To be truly satisfying the sight needs to be certified, marked as authentic. . . . The paradox . . . is that to be experienced as authentic it must be marked as authentic, but when it is marked as authentic it is mediated . . . and hence lacks the authenticity of what is truly unspoiled, untouched by mediating codes."

19. McGavock, Letter 25, from the Falls of the Rhine, in *Tennessean Abroad*, 147.

20. McGavock, Letters 32, 33, and 34, all from Rome, in *Tennessean Abroad*, 181–82, 192.

21. For examples of the typical visits to British historic sites, see McGavock, Letter 5, from Stratford-on-Avon; Letter 6, from Oxford; and Letter 20, from Edinburgh; discussion of the Crystal Palace appears in Letter 7, from London, in *Tennessean Abroad*, 36, 38, 41–43, 112.

22. McGavock, Letter Seven, from London, in *Tennessean Abroad*, 41, 46; McGavock, journal entry for 22 May 1851, in *Pen and Sword*, 195.

23. For examples of his numerous visits to cultural sites and art museums, see McGavock, journal entries for 11 July and 10 November 1851, in *Pen and Sword*, 215, 262; and McGavock, Letter 23, from Amsterdam; Letter 30, from Florence; Letter 60, from Munich; Letter 61, from Dresden; and Letter 62, from Berlin, in *Tennessean Abroad*, 131–32, 171, 350–51, 354, 360.

24. McGavock, journal entry for 3 November 1851, in *Pen and Sword*, 258; McGavock, Letter 49, from Smyrna, Asia Minor, in *Tennessean Abroad*, 295.

25. McGavock, Letter 34, from Rome, in *Tennessean Abroad*, 194.

26. McGavock, Letters 41 and 42, from Jerusalem, in *Tennessean Abroad*, 237–58, quotations on 254, 257.

27. McGavock, Letters 42 and 44, from Jerusalem, and Letter 45, from Bethlehem, in *Tennessean Abroad*, 258, 265, 268.

28. McGavock, Letter 43, from Jerusalem, in *Tennessean Abroad*, 261–62.

29. McGavock, Letter 37, from Alexandria, and Letter 39, from Cairo, in *Tennessean Abroad*, 214, 221.

30. McGavock, journal entry for 21 December 1851, in *Pen and Sword*, 287–88.

31. McGavock, Letter 41e, from Jerusalem, in *Tennessean Abroad*, 245.

32. McGavock, journal entry for 31 December 1851, in *Pen and Sword*, 293; the quoted passage is the final statement in his travel journal because journal entries for the remainder of his trip were all lost.

33. McGavock, Letter 3, from Liverpool, England, and Letter 26, from Geneva, in *Tennessean Abroad*, 27, 149; McGavock, journal entry for 29 October 1851, in *Pen and Sword*, 255.

34. McGavock, Letter 35, from Naples, in *Tennessean Abroad*, 197.

35. McGavock, journal entries for 11, 24, 27, 29, and 30 December 1851, in *Pen and Sword*, 282, 288–93, quotation on 282; McGavock, Letter 38, from Cairo, in *Tennessean Abroad*, 218–19, quotation on 219. In a later report (Letter 41, from Jerusalem, in *Tennessean Abroad*, 238), McGavock noted that nine of the Arab fighters who had participated in the "battle of the Nile" were sent into exile as punishment for their assault on the Americans, and his detailed account of both the conflict and the legal proceedings conveyed his anti-Arab racism as well as his cultural identification with European imperialism.

36. McGavock, Letter 49, from Smyrna, Asia Minor, and Letter 65, from St. Petersburg, in *Tennessean Abroad*, 296–97, 373.

37. McGavock, Letter 59, from Vienna, and Letter 60, from Munich, in *Tennessean Abroad*, 345, 347; McGavock, journal entry for 14 July 1851, in *Pen and Sword*, 217.

38. McGavock, Letter 12, from London, and Letter 25, from the Falls of the Rhine, in *Tennessean Abroad*, 66–67, 143–44. For examples of McGavock's contacts with American diplomats and European social elites, see Letter 21, from Paris; Letter 53, from Constantinople; and Letter 64, from St. Petersburg, in *Tennessean Abroad*, 118, 315, 366–67.

39. McGavock, Letter 4r, from Hucknall, near Newstead Abbey, England, in *Tennessean Abroad*, 28.

40. McGavock, Letter 15, from Lakes of Killarney, Ireland, in *Tennessean Abroad*, 84.

41. McGavock, Letter 15, from Lakes of Killarney, Ireland, in *Tennessean Abroad*, 85.

42. McGavock, Letter 35, from Naples, in *Tennessean Abroad*, 197.

43. McGavock, Letter 37, from Alexandria, in *Tennessean Abroad*, 213.

44. McGavock, Letter 37, from Alexandria, in *Tennessean Abroad*, 214.

45. McGavock, Letter 11, from London, in *Tennessean Abroad*, 63. McGavock's defense of the "humane" American slave system's superiority to the social conditions of European factory workers expressed a common (but not universal) view of southern white Americans who visited Europe. Such travelers typically claimed to see no contradiction between slavery and the American belief in human freedom because they carried the racist assumption that *only* white people could be equal, rights-bearing citizens. Despite the era's intensifying conflicts over slavery, most American travelers from the North and the South therefore continued to see the United States as a union of people with shared political beliefs. See the discussion of these issues in Kilbride, *Being American in Europe*, 145–47, 151–53. Ignoring the systemic racism of the slave-based economy and political institutions, McGavock later wrote in his journal that southern whites "had always preserved the principles embodied in the Declaration, whereas they [northern Americans] had set at naught every principle contained in it." See McGavock, journal entry for 4 July 1862, in *Pen and Sword*, 647.

46. McGavock, Letter 38, from Cairo, in *Tennessean Abroad*, 217.

47. McGavock, Letter 37, from Alexandria, in *Tennessean Abroad*, 213–14.

48. McGavock, Letter 52, from Constantinople, in *Tennessean Abroad*, 307. McGavock's pervasive racism blinded him to the anger and resentments of enslaved people in his own household. When the Union army moved into Tennessee in 1862, McGavock was surprised and enraged to learn that a Black man named Martin, whom he called his "servant," had "left Nashville and—gone with the Fed army. He is not a valuable or reliable servant—and certainly an ungrateful dog." McGavock's racism enabled him to ignore why and how a Black man would have the will and independent spirit to flee from enslavement. See McGavock, journal entry for 9 June 1862, in *Pen and Sword*, 636.

49. For examples of McGavock's discussion of women in Europe, see Letter 23, from Amsterdam; Letter 50, from Smyrna, Asia Minor; Letter 54, from Athens; and Letter 67, from Stockholm, in *Tennessean Abroad*, 131, 299–300, 325–26, 387; see also (for the description of Swiss women) McGavock, journal entry for 15 September 1851, in *Pen and Sword*, 239.

50. McGavock, journal entry for 6 July 1851, in *Pen and Sword*, 213.

51. McGavock, journal entries for 12 and 13 July 1851, in *Pen and Sword*, 216.

52. McGavock, journal entries for 26 and 31 July 1851, in *Pen and Sword*, 220–21. It is somewhat surprising to find that McGavock wrote only one letter from Paris for the *Nashville Union*, though he was in the French capital for more than a month. He had written twenty letters for the *Union* during his previous two months in Britain and Ireland. Why, then, did

he fall relatively silent from Paris? Did his journey become more private or less cultural? The American male interest in "pleasure tourism" had become very common by the early 1850s. See the discussion of this divergence from "cultural tourism" in Levenstein, *Seductive Journey*, 70–81.

53. McGavock, journal entries for 11, 12, 17, 20, 22 and 23 October 1851, in *Pen and Sword*, 249–53.

54. McGavock, journal entries for 2 and 4 October 1851, in *Pen and Sword*, 247; McGavock, Letter 28, from Milan, in *Tennessean Abroad*, 162. He also complained about "passport" inspections, though he did not describe the kind of travel documents he carried on his trip.

55. McGavock, Letters 64 and 65, from St. Petersburg, in *Tennessean Abroad*, 366, 368. Such comments about his home-country right to move and "act freely" show again his unwillingness to recognize the obvious contradictions of racism and the American slave system.

56. McGavock, Letter 9, from London, in *Tennessean Abroad*, 54.

57. McGavock, journal entry for 25 July 1851, in *Pen and Sword*, 220.

58. McGavock, journal entry for 9 November 1851, in *Pen and Sword*, 262; McGavock, Letter 33, from Rome, and Letter 54, from Athens, in *Tennessean Abroad*, 188, 324.

59. McGavock, Letter 26, from Geneva, and Letter 28, from Milan, in *Tennessean Abroad*, 147–48, 163.

60. McGavock, journal entries for 14, 20, and 26 July, and 3 and 12 September 1851, in *Pen and Sword*, 216, 218, 220, 234, 238.

61. McGavock, Letter 58, from Vienna, in *Tennessean Abroad*, 339.

62. McGavock, Letter 64, from St. Petersburg, in *Tennessean Abroad*, 367.

63. McGavock, Letter 66, from Moscow, in *Tennessean Abroad*, 381–82.

64. McGavock, Letter 37, from Alexandria, and Letter 66, from Moscow, in *Tennessean Abroad*, 209, 374; McGavock, journal entry for 19 August 1851, in *Pen and Sword*, 228.

65. McGavock, Letter 7, from London, and Letter 50, from Smyrna, Asia Minor, in *Tennessean Abroad*, 46, 300.

66. McGavock, Letter 35, from Naples, in *Tennessean Abroad*, 195.

67. McGavock, Letter 2, from Irish Channel, below Liverpool, in *Tennessean Abroad*, 18.

68. McGavock, Letter 70, from Aix-La-Chapelle, in *Tennessean Abroad*, 393.

69. McGavock, "Conclusion," *Tennessean Abroad*, 397–98.

Introduction to Part III

1. For analysis of the complex cultural history of nineteenth-century African American travelers, see Gilroy, *Black Atlantic*, which includes a helpful commentary (pp. 19–29) on the travels of Martin Delany (1812–85). Delany was born the free child of a free African American woman in what is now West Virginia, but his mother moved with him to Pittsburgh, where he could be educated. His later experiences in Canada, Africa, and England before the Civil War influenced his ideas and identity, as Levine notes in the introduction to Delany, *Documentary Reader*, 1–22. A concise introduction to William Wells Brown (1814–84) and his European travel is available in Greenspan's introduction to Brown, *A Reader*, ix–xxvi. Like David Dorr, Brown was born into slavery (in Kentucky), but in contrast to Dorr he traveled after escaping from enslavement, and he wrote about his foreign journeys in *The American Fugitive in Europe. Sketches of Places and People Abroad* (1855). Phillis Wheatley (1753?–84) was born in Africa and transported to America as an enslaved child. Like Nancy Prince, she grew up in Massachusetts and worked in domestic service, though (unlike Prince) she was enslaved until she was

twenty. Educated by the family in which she was enslaved, Wheatley began to write poetry and then traveled to England, where she gained her freedom before returning to Boston. See the account of her difficult, impoverished life in Carretta's introduction to Wheatley, *Complete Writings*, xiii–xxxvii. Frederick Douglass (1818–95) was born into slavery in Maryland and escaped to freedom in 1838. He became active in the abolitionist movement and traveled in 1845–47 through England and Ireland, where he spoke about the struggle against slavery and gained a new sense of what it meant to live as a free man—as he explained in *My Bondage and My Freedom* (1855). For discussion of how Douglass interpreted his travels, see Blight, *Frederick Douglass*, 142–77. The lives and texts of these pre–Civil War Black writers suggest how Prince and Dorr should be placed in a transnational context of "Black Atlantic" travel.

2. Miller, "Historical Appreciation for the Biographical Turn," 44.

3. For Gilroy's interpretation of the "double consciousness" among transatlantic Black writers, see the first chapter in *Black Atlantic*, 1–40. For discussion of the narrative conventions that shaped African American autobiographies, see the insightful analysis in Andrews, *To Tell a Free Story*, 1–31; and for diverse examples of African American travel writing since the early nineteenth century, see Griffin and Fish, *Stranger in the Village*.

Chapter Five

1. Prince, *Life and Travels*, 5. All my citations for Prince's book refer to the second edition, which was published in 1853. A third edition was published in 1856, but the second edition is more readily accessible in an online edition. The quoted passages use Prince's spelling, syntax, and grammar, without corrections. Prince's autobiographical narrative is the main source of information about her life, but scholars have recently discovered a few additional historical details. See, for example, Walters, "Introduction," which appears in a modern print edition, and the insightful analysis of Prince's life and work in Fish, *Women's Travel Narratives*, 24–64. For other perspectives on Prince's life, see Gunning, "Prince and the Politics of Mobility," which uses Prince's narrative to challenge some of Gilroy's views of the Black diaspora; Peterson, *African American Women Speakers and Writers*, 90–98; and Gerzina, "Mobility in Chains." The biographical summary in the following paragraphs expands on Prince's own narrative by drawing especially on valuable information in the works by Fish and Gunning. Other views of Prince's self-reliance and distinctive writing style can be found in diverse analytical studies by Moody, *Sentimental Confessions*, 77–81, 86–102; Brusky, "Prince and Her Gothic Odyssey"; Steadman, *Traveling Economies*, 36–39, 48–54; and Foster, "Prince's Utopias."

2. Prince, *Life and Travels*, 5–8, 12.

3. Prince, *Life and Travels*, 11–18, quotations on 11, 14, 16, 17. The men in Prince's family often worked on ships that sailed out of Massachusetts on long ocean voyages. For a history of Black sailors in America's early maritime trade, see Bolster, *Black Jacks*. Bolster shows (235–39) that African American sailors made up roughly 15–20 percent of the crews on antebellum American trading ships.

4. Prince, *Life and Travels*, 17, 19–20, 22.

5. Prince, *Life and Travels*, 20–22. For more on Nero Prince's earlier life in Massachusetts, his links with the Masons, and his work in Russia, see Blakely, *Russia and the Negro*, 16–18.

6. Prince, *Life and Travels*, 21, 40–41.

7. Prince, *Life and Travels*, 42. Fish discusses the abolitionist/religious/gender debates in *Women's Travel Narratives*, 49–51; and additional analysis of Prince's response to problematic issues in Boston can be found in Gunning, "Prince and the Politics of Mobility," 47–49.

8. Prince, *Life and Travels*, 43–44.

9. Prince, *Life and Travels*, 85. Prince drew the biblical language in this passage directly from the final verses in chapter 8 of Paul's Letter to the Romans. Historians have noted how themes from traditional narratives about religious pilgrimages reappear in the stories of modern travelers who overcome obstacles on journeys toward new knowledge and virtue (themes that emerge in the travel stories of both Nancy Prince and Flora Tristan). See, for example, Stowe, *Going Abroad*, 20–22; and Leed, *Mind of the Traveler*, 7–14, 141–48, 242–46.

10. Prince, *Life and Travels*, 77–78. Prince's challenge to the religious hypocrisy of white southern Christians resembled her earlier critique of the abusive Christian family for whom she had worked in Massachusetts. Her religious faith provided a verbal sword she could use against anyone whose actions contradicted their professed beliefs in Christianity.

11. The comments about financial self-support appear in the unnumbered preface page of Prince, *Life and Travels*. For brief accounts of Prince's participation in the women's rights convention and her obscure later life, see Peterson, *African American Women Speakers and Writers*, 98; and Fish, *Women's Travel Narratives*, 35, 131, 143.

12. It may be ahistorical to link Prince to Aretha Franklin, but scholars have often noted how Franklin's version of the song "Respect" (written and first recorded by Otis Redding) asserted Black liberation and independent selfhood. See, for example, Awkward, *Soul Covers*, 75–77. For the song's lyrics, see the website SongMeanings (accessed 7 August 2023), https://songmeanings.com/songs/view/73556/.

13. Prince, *Life and Travels*, 11, 15–16.

14. Prince, *Life and Travels*, 23. Tsar Alexander I was a key leader of the European coalition that defeated Napoleon Bonaparte and then defended Europe's monarchical state system during the 1820s. For a good overview of his life and public actions, see Hartley, *Alexander I*.

15. Prince, *Life and Travels*, 34–35. For a well-informed account of the tsar and his court, see Lincoln, *Nicholas I*, which includes a good explanation of the Decembrist revolt (17–47).

16. Prince, *Life and Travels*, 35, 38–40.

17. Prince, *Life and Travels*, 41–42.

18. Prince, *Life and Travels*, 43, 45. Women writers often emphasized that they traveled to provide *female* service to people in need; see Fish, *Women's Travel Narratives*, 131–32. For detailed, insightful accounts of the slave system that deeply affected everyone whom Prince met in Jamaica, see V. Brown, *Reaper's Garden*; and Higman, *Slave Population and Economy in Jamaica*. On the struggle to abolish slavery in Jamaica and other colonies, see the excellent books by Drescher, *Mighty Experiment*, 121–57, and *Abolition*, 245–66.

19. Prince, *Life and Travels*, 47.

20. Prince, *Life and Travels*, 55.

21. Prince, *Life and Travels*, 60–62, quotation on 62.

22. Prince, *Life and Travels*, 63.

23. First-person descriptions of foreign holidays, social customs, and natural spaces appear, for example, in Prince, *Life and Travels*, 24–26, 28–29, 30.

24. Prince, *Life and Travels*, 30.

25. Prince, *Life and Travels*, 30, 38.

26. Prince, *Life and Travels*, 39.

27. Prince, *Life and Travels*, 53.

28. Prince, *Life and Travels*, 67–68.

29. Prince, *Life and Travels*, 27–28, 40.

30. Prince, *Life and Travels*, 56–57.

31. Prince, *Life and Travels*, 46–47, 50, 60, 62–63.

32. Prince, *Life and Travels*, 75.
33. Prince, *Life and Travels*, 86.
34. Prince, *Life and Travels*, 5.
35. Prince, *Life and Travels*, 6–7.
36. Prince, *Life and Travels*, 38. Prince may have downplayed the family separations among Russian serfs, but historians have confirmed the contrasts she observed in the 1820s. See, for example, Kolchin, *Unfree Labor*, 117, 119. Kolchin notes here some key differences in the two systems: "Although forced separations of bondsmen occurred in Russia, they were less common than in the United States. . . . American slave marriages had no standing before the law, but marriages of serfs received full legal recognition. . . . Russian custom, unlike American, acted to minimize the number of family separations. . . . American slavery was rooted in family separations: Africans brought to America were invariably torn . . . from their loved ones. . . . The enserfment of Russian peasants in their own land, by contrast, did not involve their wholesale separation from homes, culture, or families."
37. The economic challenges and conflicts that accompanied the transitions from slave labor to free labor are discussed in Drescher, *Mighty Experiment*, 158–78; and Holt, *Problem of Freedom*, 55–114. Scholnick also notes the economic legacies of Jamaica's slave system in his introduction to a book by the nineteenth-century abolitionist John Bigelow, *Jamaica in 1850*, xiv–xxii. Prince was especially concerned about formerly enslaved women who had faced the challenges of childbearing as well as agricultural labor. For a well-researched analysis of these issues, see Turner, *Contested Bodies*. When slavery was abolished in 1834, about 312,000 enslaved people lived in Jamaica (within an overall population of over 370,000). For more on the population numbers, agricultural labor, and geographical distribution of Jamaica's enslaved workers in the early 1830s, see Higman, *Slave Population and Economy in Jamaica*, 16, 38, 53.
38. Prince, *Life and Travels*, 59–60.
39. Prince, *Life and Travels*, 53.
40. Prince, *Life and Travels*, 51, 58.
41. Prince, *Life and Travels*, 49–50, 54.
42. Prince, *Life and Travels*, 72.
43. McGavock, "Conclusion," *Tennessean Abroad*, 397.
44. Prince, *Life and Travels*, 76–77.
45. Prince, *Life and Travels*, 77.
46. Prince, *Life and Travels*, 78–79.
47. Prince, *Life and Travels*, 79–80.
48. Prince, *Life and Travels*, 82–83.
49. Prince, *Life and Travels*, 31–32.
50. Prince, *Life and Travels*, 31–33. The tsar's government convicted 289 people for involvement in the Decembrist plot. Most were sent to prison or into exile, but five were hanged in a public square. See Lincoln, *Nicholas I*, 80–82. Prince reported that four were also burned to death. Her memory of the "appalling sight" may have been slightly inaccurate, but the story of severe punishments confirmed her status as a firsthand observer and resembled her later descriptions of mistreated, enslaved people in the Americas.
51. Prince, *Life and Travels*, 61–62.
52. Prince, *Life and Travels*, 46. Prince did not identify the misguided instructor's race, but the nature of the conflict suggested that she may have been white.
53. Prince, *Live and Travels*, 62–63. The "deluded" grandmother's race was not identified, but Prince clearly described her as a victim of religious misinformation.
54. Prince, *Life and Travels*, 87–88.

Chapter Six

1. Dorr, *Colored Man round the World*, 7, 12, 61. This is a modern reprint of the first edition, which was published in Cleveland by the author in 1858. All my quotations from this book use Dorr's spelling and grammar, without corrections. The author was identified as a "Quadroon." Schueller's excellent introduction to this reprinted edition discusses the complexity of the multiracial "quadroon" identity in antebellum New Orleans (xv–xvii). Racial boundaries became more rigid in Louisiana during the 1850s, and in 1857 the legislature made the manumission of enslaved people illegal. See the discussion of Louisiana's racial boundaries in R. Scott, *Degrees of Freedom*, 14–16; and the excellent historical analysis of how light-skinned enslaved women were described and controlled during this era in Clark, *Strange History of the American Quadroon*, 1–70.

2. Dorr, *Colored Man round the World*, 12. For examples of the allusions to Byron and Shakespeare, see the references on 27, 47, 140. Dorr's interest in Byron resembled McGavock's fascination with the same poet and confirms Buzard's argument that nineteenth-century male travelers drew on the "Byronic precedent" to affirm their "unfettered" independence from home. See Buzard, *Beaten Track*, 130.

3. Dorr, *Colored Man round the World*, xiii. The entire anonymous review from the *Cleveland Plain Dealer* (20 September 1858) is reproduced in Schueller's introduction.

4. This biographical information comes from Schueller's introduction to Dorr, *Colored Man round the World*, xi–xv. Few scholars have written about Dorr's life or writings. In addition to Schueller's well-researched account, there are brief discussions of Dorr's work in Schmeller, *Perceptions of Race*, 55–59; Stowe, *Going Abroad*, 61–67; and Bendixen, "American Travel Books," 121.

5. Schueller summarizes Dorr's military career in the introduction to Dorr, *Colored Man round the World*, xii–xv. Information about the Civil War campaigns of the Seventh Ohio Volunteer Infantry Regiment can be found at the website Civil War in the East, https://civilwarintheeast.com/us-regiments-batteries/ohio/7th-ohio-infantry/ (accessed 9 August 2023).

6. Schueller, introduction to Dorr, *Colored Man round the World*, xii, xv, xxxix.

7. Dorr, *Colored Man round the World*, 14.

8. Dorr, *Colored Man round the World*, 16–17.

9. Dorr, *Colored Man round the World*, 17–18. John Murray III was the previously noted British writer and book publisher who began producing widely used travel guidebooks in the 1830s. McGavock also carried *Murray's Hand-Book for Travellers*, and American tourists continued to use "Murray" throughout the nineteenth century. See Youngs, *Cambridge Introduction to Travel Writing*, 61.

10. Dorr, *Colored Man round the World*, 30–31.

11. Dorr, *Colored Man round the World*, 60, 72, 177, 184–85, 188.

12. Dorr, *Colored Man round the World*, 190. Charles W. March had published a memoir, *Reminiscences of Congress*, shortly before his trip to Europe. George W. Kendall had published articles about Mexico in the *New Orleans Picayune* and written two books about his Mexican journeys and his observations of the war between the United States and Mexico: *Narrative of the Texan Santa Fe Expedition* and *The War between the United States and Mexico*. Kendall's reports on the war have been republished in *Dispatches from the Mexican War*. Dorr's conversations with such authors may have encouraged his ambition to write a travel memoir.

13. Dorr, *Colored Man round the World*, 22, 35, 98, 126–28, 141, 156.

14. Dorr, *Colored Man round the World*, 98.

15. Dorr, *Colored Man round the World*, 125–27. Sultan Abdülmecid I (reigned 1839–1861) was known for introducing reforms to the Ottoman Empire and for his alliance with Britain

and France during the Crimean War against Russia (1853–56). He died at age thirty-nine from tuberculosis, so Dorr's report on the sultan's physical contrasts with Queen Victoria suggested what foreign observers might have noted during even brief or distant encounters with each monarch.

16. Dorr, *Colored Man round the World*, 40.

17. Dorr, *Colored Man round the World*, 52.

18. Dorr, *Colored Man round the World*, 155–56.

19. Dorr, *Colored Man round the World*, 39–40. For more on the views of race in nineteenth-century New Orleans, see Nystrom, *New Orleans after the Civil War*, 18–21, 140–59.

20. Dorr, *Colored Man round the World*, 118–19. Parrish's actions in Egypt have been noted in the discussion of McGavock's Middle Eastern journey; see chapter 4. Dorr mentioned these actions (which defended the Tennesseans from an assault along the banks of the Nile) in a passage about Parrish's wounds, cited below in note 21; and McGavock described the same events in Letter 38, from Cairo, in *Tennessean Abroad*, 218–19, and in his journal entry for 24 December 1851, in *Pen and Sword*, 288–89. Parrish was accompanying Edwin Ewing, but Parrish was a free man who worked as a barber in Nashville. See the summary of the American consul's report from Alexandria and the description of Parrish's serious wounds in Gower's introduction to McGavock, *Pen and Sword*, 52–53. Gower also briefly summarizes Parrish's post-travel career in Nashville in this same book, 179.

21. Dorr, *Colored Man round the World*, 126–27.

22. Dorr, *Colored Man round the World*, 126–27. Dorr used only one *r* in spelling Parrish's name.

23. Dorr, *Colored Man round the World*, 141. King Otho I became king of Greece as part of the international agreement that confirmed Greek independence from the Ottoman Empire in 1832 (a settlement reached among European diplomats in London). Otho was a son of the king of Bavaria (his German name was Otto), and he became an unpopular outsider in Greek society. He reigned from 1833 until he was forced to give up the throne to a brother in 1862.

24. Dorr, *Colored Man round the World*, 138–40. The lines Parrish quoted were the opening words in Byron's "Maid of Athens"—a poem that Byron wrote for a young Greek girl he met during a brief visit to Greece in 1810. McGavock also visited the Athenian "fertility stone" in this same week, so he might have encountered Dorr. See McGavock, Letter 54, from Athens, in *Tennessean Abroad*, 322.

25. Dorr, *Colored Man round the World*, 126, 140.

26. Dorr, *Colored Man round the World*, 15–17. William Stowe uses this early scene in Dorr's narrative to show how the self-flattering sexism in Dorr's book is problematic for modern readers. Stowe finds that Dorr's entire literary persona is "often repugnant," though he recognizes Dorr's complex desire to define himself as a free man. Stowe's understandable dislike for the attitudes and behavior of nineteenth-century Louisiana "gentlemen" thus leads him to emphasize Dorr's sexism and to downplay the recurring affirmations of African American autonomy (for example, in Dorr's portrait of Frank Parrish). See Stowe, *Going Abroad*, 62–67.

27. Dorr, *Colored Man round the World*, 29–32.

28. Dorr, *Colored Man round the World*, 36–38, 94. As noted in chapter 4, Randal McGavock also discussed visits to the garden balls in his journal entries for 26 and 31 July 1851, in McGavock, *Pen and Sword*, 220–21. Dorr did not give precise dates for his first visit to Paris, but he was in the French capital at roughly the same time. On the foreign fascination with nineteenth-century Parisian social life, see Kramer, *Threshold of a New World*, 15–36.

29. Dorr, *Colored Man round the World*, 94–95. The German literary critic Walter Benjamin famously described the pleasures that male *flâneurs* such as Dorr found in their

nineteenth-century strolls through the Parisian streets and crowds. See the discussion of "The Flâneur" in Benjamin, *Writer of Modern Life*, 66–96.

30. Dorr, *Colored Man round the World*, 95.

31. Dorr, *Colored Man round the World*, 87. The word "surrealism" was not used before Parisian writers and artists invented the term in the 1920s to emphasize the creative significance of dreams and dreamlike juxtapositions. For a perceptive, well-informed account of the movement, see Caws, *Surrealism*.

32. Dorr, *Colored Man round the World*, 89.

33. Dorr, *Colored Man round the World*, 90.

34. Dorr, *Colored Man round the World*, 91. The reference to "the Dutch" suggests that Dorr dreamed his surrealistic Parisian vision during his second extended stay in Paris, which came after he had visited the Netherlands.

35. Later sections of Dorr's book included, for example, sexually charged descriptions of adulterous women in Naples, harems in Ottoman Turkey, and female dancers in Egypt. See Dorr, *Colored Man round the World*, 107, 128–29, 177–78.

36. Dorr, *Colored Man round the World*, 122–24.

37. Dorr, *Colored Man round the World*, 12.

38. Dorr, *Colored Man round the World*, 20.

39. Dorr, *Colored Man round the World*, 141.

40. Dorr, *Colored Man round the World*, 162.

41. Reclus, *Voyage to New Orleans*, 52. The quoted passage comes from an article Reclus published in 1860 after his return to France. For more information about Reclus in Louisiana, see Sancton, *Sweet Land of Liberty*, 35–37.

42. Dorr, *Colored Man round the World*, 61. For additional discussion of how Louisiana enslavers described and analyzed the bodies of enslaved men, women, and children, see Follett, *Sugar Masters*, 49–64.

43. Dorr, *Colored Man round the World*, 61.

44. Dorr, *Colored Man round the World*, 62.

45. Dorr, *Colored Man round the World*, 68–69.

46. Dorr, *Colored Man round the World*, 70.

47. Dorr, *Colored Man round the World*, 11.

48. Dorr, *Colored Man round the World*, 11–12.

49. Dorr, *Colored Man round the World*, 19–20.

50. For examples of Dorr's descriptions of historic sites and literary figures, see *Colored Man round the World*, 43, 55, 101, 137, 142, 168–69, 184–85.

51. Dorr, *Colored Man round the World*, 93.

52. For a concise summary of Louis-Napoleon's ambitions and actions in this era, see Price, *French Second Empire*, 9–37; and the national resistance to his coup d'état is discussed in Margadant, *French Peasants in Revolt*.

53. Dorr, *Colored Man round the World*, 82–84. Most reports place the number of deaths somewhere between 150 and 350, so Dorr exaggerated when he suggested that "thousands" were "moving on to eternity."

54. Dorr, *Colored Man round the World*, 86.

55. Dorr, *Colored Man round the World*, 181, 186. Some historians have noted how Dorr's view of sacred sites differed from traditional pious narratives about the Holy Land. His irreverent attitudes suggest why parts of his narrative might be compared to Mark Twain's bemused perspectives in his famous travel book, *Innocents Abroad*. For brief discussions of Dorr's travel

in Palestine, see Obenzinger, *American Palestine*, 228–29; and Yothers, *Romance of the Holy Land*, 91–94.

56. Dorr, *Colored Man round the World*, 168.

57. Dorr, *Colored Man round the World*, 134, 169. For discussion of the nineteenth-century views of Egyptian and North African civilization that influenced Dorr, see Schueller, *U.S. Orientalisms*, 33–38, 105–7.

58. Dorr, *Colored Man round the World*, 191.

59. Nietzsche, *Beyond Good and Evil*, 236–37.

60. Dorr, *Colored Man round the World*, 191.

61. Dorr, *Colored Man round the World*, 191–92.

62. Dorr, *Colored Man round the World*, 192.

Epilogue to Part III

1. Prince, *Life and Travels*, 85.

Introduction to Part IV

1. For classic and more recent examples of the literature on French travelers in America, see Jones, *America and French Culture*; Echeverria, *Mirage*; Mathy, *Extrême-Occident*, especially 1–51; and Sancton, *Sweet Land of Liberty*, especially 31–47. On Chateaubriand's American travels, see Bazin, *Chateaubriand en Amérique*; and the introduction in Chateaubriand, *Travels in America*. Jacquemont's travel in the United States has been discussed in chapter 1; and the American journeys of Lafayette and Tocqueville are compared in Kramer, *Lafayette in Two Worlds*, 185–226.

2. Neither of these authors has attracted much interest from modern historians, but Audouard has recently received more scholarly attention than Point. There is a detailed account of Point's life in Buckley, *Nicolas Point*, 1–242, 405–39. This biographical information precedes and follows Buckley's translated edition of Point's letters on his missionary work in the 1840s. Other biographical summaries appear in Donnelly's introduction to Point, *Wilderness Kingdom*, 1–9; and in Garraghan, *Chapters in Frontier History*, 136–57. Point's artistic interests and methods are analyzed in a valuable article by Rochford, "Father Nicolas Point." An introduction to Audouard's life and writing can be found in Monicat, "Ecritures du voyage et féminismes," and in Monicat's book *Itinéraires de l'écriture au féminin*, 37–38, 89–93; and there is a brief summary of Audouard's political ideas in Moses, *French Feminism*, 178–79, 195. More recent analysis of Audouard's life and writing appears in a critical assessment by Eichner, *Feminism's Empire*, 4–6, 34–36, 41–50, 57–65, 178–91, 214–16; in Nuñez, "Rethinking Universalism"; and in the somewhat sprawling study by Schiffer, *Olympe*.

3. On the evolving French views of America, see Echeverria, *Mirage*, 39–78, 175–224; Mathy, *Extrême-Occident*, 22–51; the two volumes by Rémond, *Les États-Unis devant l'opinion française*; Roger, *American Enemy*, 1–63; and Sancton, *Sweet Land of Liberty*, 1–47.

Chapter Seven

1. This summary of Point's early life draws on biographical information in Buckley, *Nicolas Point*, 3–43; and Donnelly's introduction to Point, *Wilderness Kingdom*, 1–3. On the repression of the Jesuits in 1828, see Sauvigny, *Bourbon Restoration*, 410–13. Although the Jesuit Society

remained an illegal order in France, the Jesuits were allowed to resume many of their activities during the 1820s.

2. Accounts of Point's religious career during this period appear in Buckley, *Nicolas Point*, 43–84; and in Donnelly's introduction to Point, *Wilderness Kingdom*, 3–4. Point's early interest in American Indians is noted in Garraghan, *Chapters in Frontier History*, 138. The declining status of Europe's traditional aristocracy and Catholicism led some European conservatives to look for other noble traditions or values in Native American cultures. Point was not an aristocrat, but he may have carried similar interests into his religious mission in the American West. For discussion of these European projections, see Liebersohn, *Aristocratic Encounters*.

3. Point, "De Saint-Acheul à Saint-Marie," from his journal "Souvenirs et mémoires illustrés," quoted in Buckley, *Nicolas Point*, 86. The journal manuscript is at the Archives of the Society of Jesus, Saint-Jerome, Quebec.

4. Buckley tells the full story of Point's early American travels, early educational work, and early conflicts at American Jesuit schools in Buckley, *Nicolas Point*, 87–176. Among other issues at St. Charles College in Louisiana, local white people believed the Jesuits were too sympathetic to enslaved Black workers; and Buckley suggests that Point may have angered local white people by shaking hands with an enslaved man (176, 472). Additional information about Point's work in Louisiana can be found in Garraghan, *Jesuits*, 3:135–45.

5. Buckley, *Nicolas Point*, 164.

6. The name "Flatheads" had been given to the Salish Indians by earlier European visitors who thought they were describing a distinctive "cranial flattening," but the Salish never engaged in such practices and never used the name for themselves. The modern "Flathead Reservation" in Montana includes people in the tribal communities of the Bitterroot Salish, Upper Pend d'Oreille, and the Kootenai. For more on the history and current activities of these tribal groups, see "History and Culture" on the website of Confederated Salish and Kootenai Tribes (accessed 11 August 2023), https://csktribes.org/index.php/history-culture. Chateaubriand's influence on Point is noted in Buckley, *Nicolas Point*, 204, 208.

7. The quoted comment on Point's psychology appeared in a letter from the Jesuit priest Gregory Mengarini to his superior, Jan Roothaan, 10 March 1842, quoted in Garraghan, *The Jesuits*, 2:455. Garraghan provides a concise summary of the Jesuit mission to the Northwest Indian tribes and Point's role in the project (2:442–57). The leader of the mission, Peter de Smet, wrote an early account of the expedition in *Letters and Sketches* (1843), which was republished in Thwaites, *Early Western Travels*. Point's critic Mengarini also wrote a memoir about these events, *Recollections of the Flathead Mission*. Buckley provides the most recent history of the mission in *Nicolas Point*, 177–242.

8. These tribal nations continue to be based on reservations in northwestern Montana and northwestern Idaho and identify themselves with the names that Point used. For an overview of their history as well as their current political and cultural activities, see the websites of the Blackfeet Nation, https://blackfeetnation.com/, and the Coeur d'Alene Tribe, https://www.cdatribe-nsn.gov/ (both accessed 11 August 2023).

9. The quotation is from Pierre Point's manuscript memoir "Vie du Père Nicolas Point, S.J.," which is in the Archives of the Society of Jesus, Saint-Jerome, Quebec, cited in Donnelly's editorial appendix in Point, *Wilderness Kingdom*, 264. Donnelly carefully translated Point's memoir for this English version of the book and added this appendix to explain how Point worked on his *Recollections of the Rocky Mountains* and how the manuscript was preserved in the archives of the Collège Sainte-Marie in Montreal. Point's artwork is thoughtfully analyzed in the previously cited article by Rochford, "Father Nicolas Point."

10. Passages from Point's *Recollections of the Rocky Mountains* were first printed in a journal

called *Woodstock Letters* between 1882 and 1884, but Donnelly published the first modern translation as well as a large collection of Point's illustrations in *Wilderness Kingdom*. Point's letters about the Blackfeet tribe (which were "reports" rather than personal letters to a correspondent) were long preserved at the archives of the Paris Province of the Society of Jesus in Chantilly, France, but a private collector purchased them in 1962 and gave them on permanent loan to the Gleeson Library at the University of San Francisco (Buckley, *Nicolas Point*, ix). Some of the material in these letters overlaps with passages in *Recollections*. Buckley's translation and publication of the "letters" provided the first printed edition of these texts.

11. Nicolas Point, "Saint-Marie du Kentuky" [*sic*], in Point's unpublished "Souvenirs et mémoires illustrés," manuscript at the Archives of the Society of Jesus, Saint-Jerome, Quebec, quoted in Buckley, *Nicolas Point*, 103–4.

12. Point, "Journey on a Barge down the Missouri," in Point, *Wilderness Kingdom*, 225. This journal, which is an addendum to the main narrative of *Recollections*, describes the barge trip that Point took from Fort Lewis back to Missouri after leaving the Northern Rockies in 1847. There is a copy of this manuscript in the archives at St. Louis University.

13. Point, *Wilderness Kingdom*, 162–63.

14. Point, *Wilderness Kingdom*, 14.

15. Point, *Wilderness Kingdom*, 14.

16. Point, "Saint-Marie du Kentuky," quoted in Buckley, *Nicolas Point*, 109.

17. Buckley, *Nicolas Point*, 109–10.

18. Point, *Wilderness Kingdom*, 27. Point used the then-common term "Kansa" (the origin for the state name of Kansas) to describe Indigenous people who refer to themselves as the Kaw Nation. They were the first Native Americans whom Point encountered after he left Missouri on his western journey. The tribal population was devastated in the nineteenth century by diseases and forced removals from ancestral lands, but some Kaw survived and finally settled in Oklahoma. For more on history of this tribal displacement, see the "The Kanza People" on the website of the Kaw Nation (accessed 11 August 2023), https://www.kawnation.gov/the-kanza-people/.

19. Point, *Wilderness Kingdom*, 23–24. Point's criticism of the Osage tribe was one of his harshest Eurocentric judgments of non-Christian people who faced the usual racist displacements as European Americans settled in their ancestral territories. They were later forced to move to lands in present-day Oklahoma. For more on the history of the Osage people, see "Osage Cultural History" on the website of the Osage Nation (accessed 11 August 2023), https://www.osagenation-nsn.gov/who-we-are/historic-preservation/osage-cultural-history.

20. Point, *Wilderness Kingdom*, 30–35, quotation on 34.

21. Point, *Wilderness Kingdom*, 174; Point, "Fourth Excursion," in Buckley, *Nicolas Point*, 362. The Latin words *Quis ut Deus* mean "Who [is] like God," and they are a translation of the Hebrew name Michael. French Catholics have long viewed Saint Michael as a guardian archangel who protected their Catholic nation against its most dangerous enemies—a transcendent mission that Point wanted to honor.

22. Point, "Fourth Excursion," in Buckley, *Nicolas Point*, 363.

23. Point, *Wilderness Kingdom*, 12, 14. The Blackfeet were also known as the Siksika, and a branch of the tribe carrying this name is currently in western Canada. For more information about the history of Siksika people, see "About Siksika Nation" on the website of the Siksika Nation (accessed 11 August 2023), https://siksikanation.com/about/. The French gave the name Gros Ventres ("large stomachs") to people who called themselves the A'aninin, which means "People of the White Clay." They were closely allied with the Blackfeet but remained a separate tribe.

24. Point, *Wilderness Kingdom*, 14.

25. Point, "Fifth Excursion," in Buckley, *Nicolas Point*, 369. He was referring to the A'aninin, which was the Blackfeet-affiliated tribal branch whom the French called the Gros Ventres.

26. Point, *Wilderness Kingdom*, 50.

27. Point, *Wilderness Kingdom*, 120, 145.

28. Point, *Wilderness Kingdom*, 150. Members of the Nez Perce tribe are also known as the Nimiipuu people. For more on their cultural history, see "History" on the website of the Nez Perce Tribe (accessed 11 August 2023), https://nezperce.org/about/history/. For another example of Point's contacts with influential leaders, see his description of a Blackfeet chief named Panarkuinimaki in Point, "First Excursion," in Buckley, *Nicolas Point*, 347–51.

29. Point, *Wilderness Kingdom*, 147.

30. Point, "Fourth Letter," in Buckley, *Nicolas Point*, 284–85. Point arrived at the Salish camp on the day after the battle, so he heard about the events from numerous participants.

31. Point, "Eleventh Letter," in Buckley, *Nicolas Point*, 323.

32. Point, "Tenth Letter," in Buckley, *Nicolas Point*, 316; Point, *Wilderness Kingdom*, 70. For other examples of how Christian missionaries long struggled to alter marriage practices in Native American communities, see Pearsall, *Polygamy*, 37–38, 215–17, 226–27.

33. Point, "Seventh Letter," in Buckley, *Nicolas Point*, 298–99.

34. Point, "Sixth Letter," in Buckley, *Nicolas Point*, 294; Point, *Wilderness Kingdom*, 166.

35. Point, "Fifth Letter," in Buckley, *Nicolas Point*, 288–90, quotation on 290.

36. Point, "Thirteenth Letter," in Buckley, *Nicolas Point*, 336.

37. Point, *Wilderness Kingdom*, 120–21.

38. Point, *Wilderness Kingdom*, 15.

39. Point, "Tenth Letter," in Buckley, *Nicolas Point*, 313.

40. Point, "Eleventh Letter," in Buckley, *Nicolas Point*, 325.

41. Point, *Wilderness Kingdom*, 82.

42. Point, "An Overall View of the Blackfeet," in Buckley, *Nicolas Point*, 247.

43. Point, "First Letter" and "Third Letter," in Buckley, *Nicolas Point*, 253, 270–71.

44. Point, "Fourth Letter," in Buckley, *Nicolas Point*, 285.

45. Point, "Third Letter," "Sixth Letter," and "Sixth Excursion," in Buckley, *Nicolas Point*, 274, 295–96, 374–75, quotations on 274, 375.

46. Point, *Wilderness Kingdom*, 19–20, 99.

47. Point, *Wilderness Kingdom*, 15–17, quotation on 16.

48. Point, *Wilderness Kingdom*, 16; Point, "Tenth Letter," in Buckley, *Nicolas Point*, 316–18.

49. Point, *Wilderness Kingdom*, 67.

50. Point, *Wilderness Kingdom*, 74–75.

51. Point, "Ninth Letter" and "Tenth Letter," in Buckley, *Nicolas Point*, 309, 319.

52. Point, "First Letter" and "Eleventh Letter," in Buckley, *Nicolas Point*, 259, 322, quotation on 259.

53. Point, "Ninth Letter," in Buckley, *Nicolas Point*, 309; Point, *Wilderness Kingdom*, 210.

54. Point, *Wilderness Kingdom*, 13. For an example of Point's advice on communicating with tribal communities, see his suggestions for speaking the language of the Gros Ventres in Point, "Fifth Excursion," in Buckley, *Nicolas Point*, 370.

55. Point, *Wilderness Kingdom*, 39.

Chapter Eight

1. Audouard, *Voyage a travers mes souvenirs* (hereafter *Mes souvenirs*), 3–4. This memoir was published in 1884, when Audouard was about fifty-two years old; she never completed

a planned second volume. The main scholarly sources for information about Audouard's life are cited above in note 2 of the Introduction to Part IV. Important recent discussions of Audouard's ideas can be found in the previously cited books by Schiffer, *Olympe*; and Eichner, *Feminism's Empire*, 4–6, 34–36, 41–50, 57–65, 178–91, 214–16. Schiffer confirms that Audouard was born in 1832, whereas other sources place her birthdate in 1830. Eichner describes Audouard as a liberal Catholic advocate for women's legal equality and the right to divorce who opposed French imperialism, but she also emphasizes the racism and anti-Semitism in Audouard's travel writings.

2. Audouard, *Mes souvenirs*, 10, 19, 24–27, quotation on 26.

3. Audouard, *Mes souvenirs*, 45.

4. Audouard, *Mes souvenirs*, 46.

5. Audouard, *Mes souvenirs*, 46, 73–75.

6. Audouard described her evolving friendship with Gautier and other writers who supported Le *Papillon* in *Mes souvenirs*, 78–79, 122–28. All issues of the journal can be viewed through the online Gallica collection at the Bibliothèque nationale de France. More than ninety issues appeared between January 1861 and December 1863, but publication ceased after the death of Audouard's son. On the early deaths of Audouard's sons, see Schiffer, *Olympe*, 40.

7. Audouard, *Mes souvenirs*, 76, 79. She discussed the beginning of her career as a travel writer in her book about Turkey, *Mystères du sérail*, 4, 12. Her father apparently paid for this first foreign trip, but her publisher, Édouard Dentu, must have provided some money or loans for her later travels. Most of her travel books were published by Dentu, and Audouard conveyed her respect for him in a collection of "literary portraits" she published in 1883. Stressing his love for eating, reading, and good conversations, she described Dentu as "very Parisian, very literary, and very sympathetic." Audouard, *Silhouettes Parisiennes*, 143.

8. Audouard noted the date of her departure for America in her book À *travers l'Amérique: North-America, États-Unis* (hereafter *États-Unis*), 102. She reported the August departure from New York in her other American travel book, *À travers l'Amérique: Le Far-West* (hereafter *Le Far-West*), 53. The precise length of her American journey is unclear; her account in *États-Unis*, 10, refers to a thirteen-month trip, and *Le Far-West*, 13, refers to a ten-month trip, but this may simply refer to the months after she left New York.

9. Audouard, *Mes souvenirs*, 24, 27. As noted earlier, this memoir is the best source for Audouard's own views of her life, but the narrative is often more anecdotal than factual or chronological.

10. Audouard, *Mes souvenirs*, 24, 27. Audouard's works on eastern Europe included *Les nuits russes* and *Voyage au pays des Boyards*. Eichner discusses anti-Semitism and class consciousness in these books in *Feminism's Empire*, 178–91. On Audouard's lectures and problems with the police, see Moses, *French Feminism*, 179, 195. The French government's suppression of Audouard's attempts to publish a new political journal, *La Revue cosmopolite* (1867), probably became one of the reasons for her trip to America in 1868.

11. Audouard, *Mes souvenirs*, 348.

12. Audouard, *États-Unis*, 42–43.

13. Audouard, *États-Unis*, 54. For Voltaire's influential example of cross-cultural analysis, see Voltaire, *Letters on England*.

14. Audouard, *États-Unis*, 43–45, 55–56, 59–60, 90. For information on enrollments in nineteenth-century public schools, see the Center on Education Policy's informative "History and Evolution of Public Education in the US" at the website of the George Washington University Graduate School of Education and Human Development (accessed 12 August 2023), https://files.eric.ed.gov/fulltext/ED606970.pdf.

15. Audouard, *États-Unis*, 66; Audouard, *Le Far-West*, 30–33, quotation on 30–31.

16. Audouard, *États-Unis*, 119, 144–47, quotation on 147.

17. Audouard, *États-Unis*, 327; Audouard, *Le Far-West*, 40, 56, 68–69, 126, 130, quotation on 68–69.

18. Audouard, *Le Far-West*, 255–56.

19. Audouard, *Le Far-West*, 259.

20. Audouard, *États-Unis*, 333.

21. Audouard, *États-Unis*, 7, 18–20. She went on to describe all the ways in which France might emulate the American political system, 28–42.

22. Audouard, *États-Unis*, 16–18.

23. Audouard, *Le Far-West*, 138. Pensions for Union army veterans were granted during and after the Civil War only to those who were discharged with disabilities.

24. Audouard, *Le Far-West*, 11, 104, 130–34, 280, 283–88.

25. Audouard, *Le Far-West*, 140; Audouard, *États-Unis*, 162–65.

26. Audouard, *Le Far-West*, 232–33, 237.

27. Audouard, *Le Far-West*, 87–88; Audouard, *États-Unis*, 132–33, 300–309, 327–29, quotation on 133.

28. Audouard, *Le Far-West*, 12–13, 51, 228–30; Audouard, *États-Unis*, 141, 176–78.

29. Audouard, *États-Unis*, 172–79, quotations on 176–77.

30. Audouard, *États-Unis*, 180–81.

31. Audouard, *États-Unis*, 150–56.

32. Audouard, *Le Far-West*, 77–78, 84–85.

33. Audouard, *Le Far-West*, 9–10. She had also condemned the Confederacy's pro-slavery actions during the Civil War. See, for example, her journal Le *Papillon*, 18 January 1863, 34.

34. Audouard, *Le Far-West*, 224–26.

35. Audouard, *Le Far-West*, 149–50, 170–71, 197, quotation on 170.

36. Audouard, *Le Far-West*, 146–47, 172, 176, 183–85, quotation on 185. The vehement racism in Audouard's critique of American Indians is striking, but its dehumanizing themes may have reflected her strong desire to identify with "modernity" and the idea of progress. She could define her own advanced social position through her opposition to Native Americans as well as her opposition to the gendered social system in France. Audouard's otherwise sympathetic recent analysts have criticized her racist ideas and noted the recurring European feminist tendency to repeat the racism of colonizing European men while denouncing their sexism. See, for example, the critiques in Nuñez, "Rethinking Universalism," 38–39; Monicat, "Ecritures du voyage et féminismes," 27–29; Schiffer, *Olympe*, 164–65, 226–27; and Eichner, *Feminism's Empire*, 34–36.

37. Audouard, *Le Far-West*, 173–75, 194–95, 198, quotation on 198.

38. Audouard, *Le Far-West*, 186, 202.

39. Audouard, *États-Unis*, 366–69, quotations on 366 and 368.

40. Audouard, *États-Unis*, 344–45, 347–48, quotations on 344 and 348.

41. Audouard, *États-Unis*, 347–48.

42. Audouard, *États-Unis*, 334–38, 355.

43. Audouard, *États-Unis*, 349–50, 355, quotation on 355. Audouard may have met graduates of the New England Female Medical College, where hundreds of women received medical training between the late 1840s and 1870s; but there were also medical colleges for women in New York and Pennsylvania by the time of Audouard's visit to the United States in 1868.

44. Audouard, *États-Unis*, 336.

45. Audouard, *États-Unis*, 352, 357–58, quotation on 352.

46. Audouard, *Mystères du Sérail*, 26, 31, 70, 138, 142–43, quotation on 70.

47. Audouard, *Mystères du Sérail*, 87, 95–99, 112, 188–89. Rachel Nuñez provides an interesting analysis of how Audouard "undermined the logic of Orientalism" by arguing that Muslim customs for both marriage and divorce "better embodied the liberal ideals that the French took to be their own." See Nuñez, "Rethinking Universalism," 27–28, 30–31. As Nuñez also notes, however, Audouard continued to believe in the superiority of French cultural achievements.

48. Audouard, *Le Far-West*, 320–22, 325–26, 334–37.

49. Audouard, *Le Far-West*, 340–41, 352–54. Recent scholarship supports Audouard's claim that most nineteenth-century Mormon women found opportunities and happiness in polygamous marriages. As Laurel Thatcher Ulrich explains in a carefully researched account, "nothing outraged Mormon women more than the notion that they were simply the pawns of patriarchy," and Ulrich concludes that "there could have been no such thing as plural marriage if hundreds of women had not accepted 'the principle' and passed it on to new generations." See Ulrich, *House Full of Females*, 385, 387. See also the discussion of Mormon women who defended "plural marriage" in Pearsall, *Polygamy*, 267–88. Modern research shows that Audouard's report on Brigham Young's marriages was not entirely accurate because he had fifty-five "sealed" wives, including twenty-three who were part of his households and sixteen who were mothers of his fifty-seven children. See Johnson, "Determining and Defining 'Wife.'"

50. Audouard, *Le Far-West*, 345–46, 348–49, quotations on 345, 348.

51. Audouard, *Le Far-West*, 368; the quoted passage follows the discussion of European "Mormonism" on 366–67.

52. Audouard, *Le Far-West*, 370.

53. Audouard, *Le Far-West*, 60; Audouard, *États-Unis*, 205.

54. Audouard, *Le Far-West*, 116–18.

55. Audouard, *Le Far-West*, 119–20.

56. Audouard, *Le Far-West*, 121–22. Monicat discusses Audouard's strategic defense of "feminine" writing and suggests that the "marginal" woman's voice could have a "subversive power" in travel literature; see Monicat, "Ecritures du voyage et féminismes," 32–34.

Conclusion

1. Seigel, *Idea of the Self*, 5.

2. The expanding critical literature on the social, economic, environmental, and cultural impact of travel and tourism includes a wide range of scholarly and journalistic assessments. See, for example, the recent essays in Stoffelen and Ioannides, *Handbook of Tourism Impacts*; and in Honey and Frenkiel, *Overtourism*. For a helpful newspaper summary of some typical books on travel and environmental issues, see Williams, "Must-Read Books"; and for a rejection of the whole idea that travel can be a transformative experience, see the vehement anti-travel argument in Callard, "Case against Travel."

3. Dorr, *Colored Man round the World*, 192.

BIBLIOGRAPHY

This bibliography lists the sources and scholarly works that have been most important for my study of specific nineteenth-century French and American travelers. There is a vast literature on travel in all historical eras and regions of the world that cannot be included here. The bibliography provides information about printed sources, but many of these books, journals, and articles are also available online through libraries and publishers. Most nineteenth-century French texts are now accessible via the website of the outstanding Gallica collection at the Bibliothèque nationale de France, https://gallica.bnf.fr/accueil/en/content/accueil-en?mode=desktop.

Works by Nineteenth-Century Travelers

Audouard, Olympe. *À travers l'Amérique: Le Far-West.* Paris: E. Dentu, 1869.

———. *À travers l'Amérique: North America, États-Unis: Constitution, moeurs, usages, lois, institutions, sectes religeuses.* Paris: E. Dentu, 1871.

———. *Les mystères de l'Égypte dévoilés.* Paris: E. Dentu, 1866.

———. *Les mystères du sérail et des harems turcs.* 3rd ed. Paris: E. Dentu, 1866. First published 1863.

———. *Les nuits russes.* Paris: E. Dentu, 1876.

———. *Silhouettes parisiennes.* Paris: C. Marpon and E. Flammarion, 1883.

———. *Voyage à travers mes souvenirs: Ce que j'ai connus, ce que j'ai vu.* Paris: E. Dentu, 1884.

———. *Voyage au pays des Boyards.* Paris: E. Dentu, 1880.

———, ed. *Le Papillon* [journal]. Paris: 1861–1863. Gallica collection at the Bibliothèque Nationale de France. Accessed 12 August 2023. https://gallica.bnf.fr/ark:/12148/cb32831916r/date1861.liste.

Bigelow, John. *Jamaica in 1850 or, The Effects of Sixteen Years of Freedom on a Slave Colony.* Edited by Robert J. Scholnick. Urbana: University of Illinois Press, 2006.

Brown, William Wells. *William Wells Brown: A Reader.* Edited by Ezra Greenspan. Athens: University of Georgia Press, 2008.

Buckley, Cornelius M. *Nicolas Point, S.J.: His Life and Northwest Indian Chronicles.* Chicago: Loyola University Press, 1989. [The second section is a collection of Point's translated reports and letters about his missionary work.]

Chateaubriand, René de. *Travels in America.* Translated by Richard Switzer. Lexington: University of Kentucky Press, 1969.

Cooper, James Fenimore. *Gleanings in Europe: France.* Edited by Thomas Philbrick and Constance Ayers Denne. Albany: State University of New York Press, 1983.

———. *Gleanings in Europe: The Rhine.* Edited by Ernest Redekop, Maurice Geracht, and Thomas Philbrick. Albany: State University of New York Press, 1986.

Delany, Martin R. *Martin R. Delany: A Documentary Reader.* Edited by Robert S. Levine. Chapel Hill: University of North Carolina Press, 2003.

Dorr, David F. *A Colored Man round the World*. Edited by Malini Johar Schueller. Ann Arbor: University of Michigan Press, 1999.

Fuller, Margaret. *Margaret Fuller, Critic: Writings from the "New York Tribune," 1844–46*. Edited by Judith Mattson Bean and Joel Myerson. New York: Columbia University Press, 2000.

———. *Memoirs of Margaret Fuller Ossoli*. Boston: Philipps, Sampson, and Co., 1852.

———. *Summer on the Lakes in 1843*. Introduction by Susan Belasco Smith. Urbana: University of Illinois Press, 1991.

———. *"These Sad but Glorious Days": Dispatches from Europe, 1846–1850*. Edited by Larry J. Reynolds and Susan Belasco Smith. New Haven: Yale University Press, 1991.

———. *Woman in the Nineteenth Century and Other Writings*. Edited and with an introduction by Donna Dickensen. Oxford: Oxford University Press, 1994.

Hudspeth, Robert N., ed. *The Letters of Margaret Fuller*. 6 vols. Ithaca: Cornell University Press, 1983–94.

Jacquemont, Victor. *Correspondance de Victor Jacquemont avec sa famille et plusieurs de ses amis pendant son voyage dans l'Inde (1828–1832)*. 5th ed. 2 vols. Paris: Garnier Frères, 1861.

———. *Correspondance inédite de Victor Jacquemont avec sa famille et ses amis, 1824–1832*. Introduction by Prosper Mérimée and biographical note by V. Jacquemont [nephew]. 2 vols. Paris: Michel Lévy Frères, 1867.

———. *Letters to Achille Chaper: Intimate Sketches of Life among Stendhal's Coterie*. Edited by J. F. Marshall. Philadelphia: American Philosophical Society, 1960.

———. *Lettres à Stendhal*. Edited by Pierre Maes. Paris: A. Poursin & Cie, 1933.

———. *Voyage dans l'Inde pendant les années 1828 à 1832* [journals]. 4 vols. Paris: Firmin Didot Frères, 1841–44.

James, Henry. *English Hours*. Introduction by Leon Edel. Oxford: Oxford University Press, 1981.

———. *A Little Tour of France*. Introduction by Leon Edel. New York: Farrar, Straus and Giroux, 1983.

Kendall, Geo. Wilkins. *Dispatches from the Mexican War*. Edited and with an introduction by Lawrence Delbart Cress. Norman: University of Oklahoma Press, 1999.

———. *Narrative of the Texan Santa Fe Expedition*. 2 vols. New York: Harper and Bros., 1844.

———. *The War between the United States and Mexico, Illustrated*. New York: D. Appleton and Company, 1851.

March, Charles W. *Reminiscences of Congress*. New York: Baker and Scribner, 1850.

Marx, Karl. *Dispatches for the "New York Tribune": Selected Journalism of Karl Marx*. Selected and with an introduction by James Ledbetter, foreword by Francis Wheen. New York: Penguin, 2007.

McGavock, Randal W. *Pen and Sword: The Life and Journals of Randal W. McGavock*. Edited by Herschel Gower and Jack Allen. Nashville: Tennessee Historical Commission, 1959.

———. *A Tennessean Abroad, or Letters from Europe, Africa, and Asia*. New York: Redfield, 1854.

Mengarini, Gregory. *Recollections of the Flathead Mission*. Translated and edited by Gloria Ricci Lothrop. Glendale, CA: Arthur H. Clark Co., 1977.

Michaud, Stéphane, ed. *Flora Tristan: La Paria et son rêve. Correspondance établie par Stéphane Michaud*. Preface by Mario Vargas Llosa. 2nd ed. Paris: Presses Sorbonne nouvelle, 2003.

Nietzsche, Friedrich. *Beyond Good and Evil: Prelude to a Philosophy of the Future.* Translated by Walter Kaufmann. New York: Vintage Books, 1966.

Point, Nicolas. *Wilderness Kingdom: Indian Life in the Rocky Mountains, 1840–1847; The Journals and Paintings of Nicolas Point, S.J.* Translated and introduced by Joseph P. Donnelly, S.J. Chicago: Loyola University Press, 1967.

Prince, Nancy. *A Narrative of the Life and Travels of Mrs. Nancy Prince: Written by Herself.* 2nd ed. Boston: Published by the author, 1853. Accessed 11 November 2022. https://ia800903.us.archive.org/28/items/narrativeoflifet1853prin/narrativeoflifet1853prin.pdf.

Reclus, Elisée. *A Voyage to New Orleans: Anarchist Impressions of the Old South.* Translated and edited by John Clark and Camille Martin. Thetford, VT: Glad Day Books, 2004.

Smet, Peter de. *Letters and Sketches: With a Narrative of a Year's Residence among the Indian Tribes of the Rocky Mountains.* Philadelphia: M. Fithian, 1843. Republished in Reuben Gold Thwaites, ed. *Early Western Travels, 1748–1846.* Vol. 27. Cleveland: Arthur H. Clark Company, 1906.

Stendhal. *The Red and the Black: A Chronicle of 1830.* Translated by Burton Raffel, introduction by Diane Johnson. New York: Modern Library, 2004.

Tristan, Flora. *Flora Tristan, Utopian Feminist: Her Travel Diaries and Personal Crusade.* Selected, translated, and with an introduction to her life by Doris Beik and Paul Beik. Bloomington: Indiana University Press, 1993.

———. *Lettres.* Edited by Stéphane Michaud. Paris: Seuil, 1980.

———. *Nécessité de faire un bon accueil aux femmes étrangères.* Edited by Denys Cuche. Paris: L'Harmattan, 1988.

———. *Pérégrinations d'une paria (1833–1834).* 2 vols. Paris: Arthus Bertrand, 1838.

———. *Peregrinations of a Pariah.* Edited and translated by Jean Hawkes. London: Virago, 1986.

Twain, Mark. *The Innocents Abroad, or The New Pilgrims' Progress.* Introduction by Jane Jacobs. New York: Modern Library, 2003.

Wheatley, Phillis. *Phillis Wheatley: Complete Writings.* Edited and with an introduction by Vincent Carretta. New York: Penguin Books, 2001.

Books on Travel, Travel Writing, Transnational Experiences, Identities, and Nineteenth-Century Atlantic Cultures

Andrews, William L. *To Tell a Free Story: The First Century of Afro-American Autobiography, 1760–1865.* Urbana: University of Illinois Press, 1986.

Awkward, Michael. *Soul Covers: Rhythm and Blues Remakes and the Struggle for Artistic Identity (Aretha Franklin, Al Green, Phoebe Snow).* Durham, NC: Duke University Press, 2007.

Baelen, Jean. *La vie de Flora Tristan: Socialism et feminism au XIXe siècle.* Paris: Seuil, 1972.

Bayly, C. A. *Empire and Information: Intelligence Gathering and Social Communication in India, 1780–1870.* Cambridge: Cambridge University Press, 1996.

Bazin, Christian. *Chateaubriand en Amérique.* Paris: La Table Rond, 1969.

Benjamin, Walter. *The Writer of Modern Life: Essays on Charles Baudelaire.* Edited by Michael W. Jennings and translated by Howard Eiland . . . [et al.]. Cambridge, MA: Harvard University Press, 2006.

Blakely, Allison. *Russia and the Negro: Blacks in Russian History and Thought.* Washington: Howard University Press, 1986.

Blanton, Casey. *Travel Writing: The Self and the World.* New York: Twayne Publishers, 1997.

Blight, David W. *Frederick Douglass: Prophet of Freedom.* New York: Simon & Schuster, 2018.

Bolster, W. Jeffrey. *Black Jacks: African American Seamen in the Age of Sail.* Cambridge, MA: Harvard University Press, 1997.

Botton, Alain de. *The Art of Travel.* New York: Vintage Books, 2002.

Bouglé, Célestin. *Essays on the Caste System.* Translated by D. F. Pocock. Cambridge: Cambridge University Press, 1971.

Bouvier, Pierre. *De Dakar à Tokyo.* Paris: Galilée, 2014.

Bronner, François. *La Schiassetti: Jacquemont, Rossini, Stendhal . . . Une saison parisienne au Théâtre-Italien, 1824–1826.* Paris: Hermann, 2011.

Brown, Vincent. *The Reaper's Garden: Death and Power in the World of Atlantic Slavery.* Cambridge, MA: Harvard University Press, 2008.

Buzard, James. *The Beaten Track: European Tourism, Literature, and the Ways to Culture, 1800–1918.* Oxford: Oxford University Press, 1993.

Caplan, Jane, and John Torpey, eds. *Documenting Individual Identity: The Development of State Practices in the Modern World.* Princeton: Princeton University Press, 2001.

Capper, Charles. *Margaret Fuller: An American Romantic Life.* Vol. 1, *The Private Years.* Oxford: Oxford University Press, 1992.

———. *Margaret Fuller: An American Romantic Life.* Vol. 2, *The Public Years.* Oxford: Oxford University Press, 2007.

Capper, Charles, and Cristina Giorcelli, eds. *Margaret Fuller: Transatlantic Crossings in a Revolutionary Age.* Madison: University of Wisconsin Press, 2007.

Caws, Mary Ann. *Surrealism.* New York: Phaidon, 2004.

Chakrabarty, Dipesh. *Provincializing Europe: Postcolonial Thought and Historical Difference.* With a new preface by the author. Princeton: Princeton University Press, 2008.

Chaucer, Geoffrey. *The Canterbury Tales.* Verse translation with an introduction and notes by David Wright. Oxford: Oxford University Press, 2008.

Chevigny, Bell Gale. *The Woman and the Myth: Margaret Fuller's Life and Writings.* Revised and expanded ed. Boston: Northeastern University Press, 1994.

Clark, Emily. *The Strange History of the American Quadroon: Free Women of Color in the Revolutionary Atlantic World.* Chapel Hill: University of North Carolina Press, 2013.

Clifford, James. *Routes: Travel and Translation in the Late Twentieth Century.* Cambridge, MA: Harvard University Press, 1997.

Coulmas, Florian. *Identity: A Very Short Introduction.* Oxford: Oxford University Press, 2019.

Cross, Máire Fedelma. *The Letter in Flora Tristan's Politics, 1835–1844.* New York: Palgrave Macmillan, 2004.

Darwin, Charles. *The Voyage of the* Beagle. Edited by Janet Browne and Michael Neve. London: Penguin Books, 1989.

Derrida, Jacques. *Of Grammatology.* Translated by Gayatri Chakravorty Spivak. Baltimore: Johns Hopkins University Press, 1974.

Desanti, Dominique. *Flora Tristan.* Paris: Hachette, 2001.

Drescher, Seymour. *Abolition: A History of Slavery and Antislavery.* Cambridge: Cambridge University Press, 2009.

———. *The Mighty Experiment: Free Labor versus Slavery in British Emancipation.* Oxford: Oxford University Press, 2002.

Dumont, Louis. *Homo Hierarchicus: An Essay on the Caste System.* Translated by Mark Sainsbury. Chicago: University of Chicago Press, 1970.
Echeverria, Durand. *Mirage in the West: A History of the French Image of American Society to 1815.* Princeton: Princeton University Press, 1957.
Eckel, Leslie. *Atlantic Citizens: Nineteenth-Century American Writers at Work in the World.* Edinburgh: Edinburgh University Press, 2013.
Eichner, Carolyn J. *Feminism's Empire.* Ithaca: Cornell University Press, 2022.
Fish, Cheryl J. *Black and White Women's Travel Narratives: Antebellum Explorations.* Gainesville: University Press of Florida, 2004.
Follett, Richard. *The Sugar Masters: Planters and Slaves in Louisiana's Cane World, 1820–1860.* Baton Rouge: Louisiana State University Press, 2005.
Foucault, Michel. *The Order of Things: An Archeology of the Human Sciences.* New York: Vintage Books, 1973.
———. *Power/Knowledge: Selected Interviews and Other Writings, 1972–1977.* Edited by Colin Gordon, translated by Colin Gordon, Leo Marshall, John Mepham, and Kate Sopur. New York: Pantheon Books, 1980.
Fritzsche, Peter. *Stranded in the Present: Modern Times and the Melancholy of History.* Cambridge, MA: Harvard University Press, 2004.
Garraghan, Gilbert J. *Chapters in Frontier History: Research Studies in the Making of the West.* Milwaukee: Bruce Pub. Co., 1934.
———. *The Jesuits of the Middle United States.* 3 vols. New York: America Press, 1938.
Gilroy, Paul. *The Black Atlantic: Modernity and Double Consciousness.* Cambridge, MA: Harvard University Press, 1993.
Goldstein, Jan. *The Post-Revolutionary Self: Politics and Psyche in France, 1750–1850.* Cambridge, MA: Harvard University Press, 2005.
Graham, Sarah, ed. *A History of the Bildungsroman.* Cambridge: Cambridge University Press, 2019.
Green, Nancy L. *The Limits of Transnationalism.* Chicago: University of Chicago Press, 2019.
Griffin, Farah J., and Cheryl J. Fish, eds. *A Stranger in the Village: Two Centuries of African American Travel Writing.* Boston: Beacon Press, 1998.
Grogan, Susan. *Flora Tristan: Life Stories.* New York: Routledge, 1998.
Hart, Kathleen. *Revolution and Women's Autobiography in Nineteenth-Century France.* Amsterdam: Rodopi, 2004.
Hartley, Janet M. *Alexander I.* New York: Longman, 1994.
Herodotus. *The Histories.* Translated by Robin Waterfield. Edited with introduction and notes by Carolyn Dewald. Oxford: Oxford University Press, 2008.
Higman, B. W. *Slave Population and Economy in Jamaica, 1807–1833.* Cambridge: Cambridge University Press, 1976.
Holt, Thomas C. *The Problem of Freedom: Race, Labor, and Politics in Jamaica and Britain, 1832–1938.* Baltimore: Johns Hopkins University Press, 1992.
Honey, Martha, and Kelsey Frenkiel, eds. *Overtourism: Lessons for a Better Future.* Washington, DC: Island Press, 2021.
Hulme, Peter, and Tim Youngs, eds. *The Cambridge Companion to Travel Writing.* Cambridge: Cambridge University Press, 2002.
Izenberg, Gerald N. *Identity: The Necessity of a Modern Idea.* Philadelphia: University of Pennsylvania Press, 2016.

———. *Impossible Individuality: Romanticism, Revolution, and the Origins of Modern Selfhood, 1787–1802*. Princeton: Princeton University Press, 1992.
Jacquemont. Edited by the Muséum national d'histoire naturelle. Paris: Muséum national d'histoire naturelle, 1959.
Jaume, Lucien. *Tocqueville: The Aristocratic Sources of Liberty*. Translated by Arthur Goldhammer. Princeton: Princeton University Press, 2013.
Jay, Martin. *Songs of Experience: Modern American and European Variations on a Universal Theme*. Berkeley: University of California Press, 2005.
Jones, Howard Mumford. *America and French Culture, 1750–1848*. Chapel Hill: University of North Carolina Press, 1927.
Kaplan, Caren. *Questions of Travel: Postmodern Discourses of Displacement*. Durham, NC: Duke University Press, 1996.
Kempe, Margery. *The Book of Margery Kempe*. Translated with an introduction by Anthony Bale. Oxford: Oxford University Press, 2015.
Kilbride, Daniel. *Being American in Europe, 1750–1860*. Baltimore: Johns Hopkins University Press, 2013.
Kolchin, Peter. *Unfree Labor: American Slavery and Russian Serfdom*. Cambridge, MA: Harvard University Press, 1987.
Kornfeld, Eve. *Margaret Fuller: A Brief Biography with Documents*. Boston: Bedford Books, 1997.
Kramer, Lloyd. *Lafayette in Two Worlds: Public Cultures and Personal Identities in an Age of Revolutions*. Chapel Hill: University of North Carolina Press, 1996.
———. *Nationalism in Europe and America: Politics, Cultures, and Identities since 1775*. Chapel Hill: University of North Carolina Press, 2011.
———. *Threshold of a New World: Intellectuals and the Exile Experience in Paris, 1830–1848*. Ithaca: Cornell University Press, 1988.
LaCapra, Dominick. *Understanding Others: People, Animals, Pasts*. Ithaca: Cornell University Press, 2018.
Leed, Eric J. *The Mind of the Traveler: From Gilgamesh to Global Tourism*. New York: Basic Books, 1991.
Levenstein, Harvey. *Seductive Journey: American Tourists in France from Jefferson to the Jazz Age*. Chicago: University of Chicago Press, 1998.
Levine, Robert S. *Martin Delany, Frederick Douglass, and the Politics of Representative Identity*. Chapel Hill: University of North Carolina Press, 1997.
Lévi-Strauss, Claude. *Structural Anthropology*. Translated by Claire Jacobson and Brooke Grundfest Schoepf. New York: Basic Books, 1963.
———. *Tristes Tropiques*. Translated by John Russell. New York: Atheneum, 1964.
Liebersohn, Harry. *Aristocratic Encounters: European Travelers and North American Indians*. Cambridge: Cambridge University Press, 1998.
Lincoln, Bruce. *Nicholas I: Emperor and Autocrat of All the Russias*. Bloomington: Indiana University Press, 1978.
Longino, Michèle. *French Travel Writing in the Ottoman Empire: Marseilles to Constantinople, 1650–1700*. New York: Routledge, 2015.
Lowenthal, David. *The Past Is a Foreign Country—Revisited*. Cambridge: Cambridge University Press, 2015.
MacCannell, Dean. *The Tourist: A New Theory of the Leisure Class*. With a new foreword by Lucy R. Lippart and a new epilogue by the author. Berkeley: University of California Press, 1999.

Maes, Pierre. *Un ami de Stenhdal, Victor Jacquemont*. Paris: Desclée de Brouwer, 1934.
Margadant, Ted W. *French Peasants in Revolt: The Insurrection of 1851*. Princeton: Princeton University Press, 1979.
Marshall, Megan. *Margaret Fuller: A New American Life*. Boston: Houghton Mifflin Harcourt, 2013.
Mathy, Jean-Philippe. *Extrême-Occident: French Intellectuals and America*. Chicago: University of Chicago Press, 1993.
Matteson, John. *The Lives of Margaret Fuller*. New York: W. W. Norton, 2012.
McCullough, David. *The Greater Journey: Americans in Paris*. New York: Simon and Schuster, 2011.
Mehren, Joan von. *Minerva and the Muse: A Life of Margaret Fuller*. Amherst: University of Massachusetts Press, 1994.
Michaud, Stéphane, ed. *Un fabuleux destin: Flora Tristan*. Dijon: Editions universitaires de Dijon, 1985.
Monaghan, Frank. *French Travellers in the United States, 1765–1932: A Bibliography*. New York: New York Public Library, 1933.
Monicat, Bénédicte. *Itinéraires de l'écriture au féminin: Voyageuses du 19e siècle*. Amsterdam: Rodopi, 1996.
Moody, Joycelyn. *Sentimental Confessions: Spiritual Narratives of Nineteenth-Century African American Women*. Athens: University of Georgia Press, 2001.
Moses, Claire Goldberg. *French Feminism in the 19th Century*. Albany: State University of New York Press, 1984.
Moses, Claire Goldberg, and Leslie Wahl Rabine. *Feminism, Socialism, and French Romanticism*. Bloomington: Indiana University Press, 1993.
Murray, Meg McGavran. *Margaret Fuller: Wandering Pilgrim*. Athens: University of Georgia Press, 2008.
Nisbet, Robert. *History of the Idea of Progress*. With a new introduction by the author. New Brunswick, NJ: Transaction Publishers, 1994.
Nystrom, Justin A. *New Orleans after the Civil War: Race, Politics, and a New Birth of Freedom*. Baltimore: Johns Hopkins University Press, 2010.
Obenzinger, Hilton. *American Palestine: Melville, Twain, and the Holy Land Mania*. Princeton: Princeton University Press, 1999.
Oldfield, J. R. *Transatlantic Abolitionism in the Age of Revolution: An International History, c. 1787–1820*. Cambridge: Cambridge University Press, 2013.
Pearsall, Sarah M. S. *Polygamy: An Early American History*. New Haven: Yale University Press, 2019.
Pérez-Mejía, Angela. *A Geography of Hard Times: Narratives about Travel to South America, 1780–1849*. Translated by Dick Cluster. Albany: State University of New York Press, 2004.
Peterson, Carla L. *"Doers of the Word": African American Women Speakers and Writers in the North (1830–1880)*. New Brunswick, NJ: Rutgers University Press, 1998.
Polo, Marco. *The Travels*. Translated and with an introduction by Nigel Cliff. London: Penguin Books, 2015.
Porter, Dennis. *Haunted Journeys: Desire and Transgression in European Travel Writing*. Princeton: Princeton University Press, 1991.
Pratt, Mary Louise. *Imperial Eyes: Travel Writing and Transculturation*. 2nd ed. London: Routledge, 2007.
Price, Roger. *The French Second Empire: An Anatomy of Political Power*. Cambridge: Cambridge University Press, 2001.

Puech, Jules-L. *La vie et l'oeuvre de Flora Tristan, 1803–1844*. Paris: Librairie Marcel Riviére, 1925.

Rémond, René. *Les États-Unis devant l'opinion française 1815–1852*. 2 vols. Paris: A. Colin, 1962.

Reynolds, Larry J. *European Revolutions and the American Literary Renaissance*. New Haven: Yale University Press, 1988.

Roberson, Susan L. *Antebellum American Women Writers and the Road: American Mobilities*. New York: Routledge, 2011.

Roberts, Timothy Mason. *Distant Revolutions: 1848 and the Challenge to American Exceptionalism*. Charlottesville: University of Virginia Press, 2009.

Robertson, Craig. *The Passport in America: The History of a Document*. New York: Oxford University Press, 2012.

Roger, Philippe. *The American Enemy: A Story of French Anti-Americanism*. Translated by Sharon Bowman. Chicago: University of Chicago Press, 2005.

Rosenblatt, Helena. *Liberal Values: Benjamin Constant and the Politics of Religion*. Cambridge: Cambridge University Press, 2008.

Ross, Donald, and James Schramer, eds. *American Travel Writers, 1850–1915*. Vol. 189 in *Dictionary of Literary Biography*. Detroit: Gale Research, 1998.

Said, Edward. *Culture and Imperialism*. New York: Knopf, distributed by Random House, 1993.

———. *Orientalism*. New York: Vintage Books, 1978.

Sancton, Tom. *Sweet Land of Liberty: America in the Mind of the French Left, 1848–1871*. Baton Rouge: Louisiana State University Press, 2020.

Saussure, Ferdinand. *Writings in General Linguistics*. Translated by Carol Sanders and Matthew Pires. Oxford: Oxford University Press, 2006.

Sauvigny, Guillaume de Bertier de. *The Bourbon Restoration*. Translated by Lynn M. Case. Philadelphia: University of Pennsylvania Press, 1966.

———. *La France et les Français vus par les voyageurs américains, 1814–1848*. 2 vols. Paris: Flammarion, 1982.

Schiffer, Liesel. *Olympe: Être femme et féministe au temps de Napoleon III*. Paris: Vendémiaire, 2021.

Schmeller, Erik S. *Perceptions of Race and Nation in English and American Travel Writers, 1833–1914*. New York: Peter Lang, 2004.

Schramer, James, and Donald Ross, eds. *American Travel Writers, 1776–1864*. Vol. 183 in *Dictionary of Literary Biography*. Detroit: Gale Research, 1997.

Schriber, Mary Suzanne. *Writing Home: American Women Abroad, 1830–1920*. Charlottesville: University Press of Virginia, 1997.

Schueller, Malini Johar. *U.S. Orientalisms: Race, Nation, and Gender in Literature, 1790–1890*. Ann Arbor: University of Michigan Press, 1998.

Scott, Rebecca J. *Degrees of Freedom: Louisiana and Cuba after Slavery*. Cambridge, MA: Harvard University Press, 2005.

Segalen, Victor. *Essay on Exoticism: An Aesthetics of Diversity*. Translated and edited by Yaël Rachel Schlick, foreword by Harry Harootunian. Durham, NC: Duke University Press, 2002.

Seigel, Jerrold. *Between Cultures: Europe and Its Others in Five Exemplary Lives*. Philadelphia: University of Pennsylvania Press, 2016.

———. *The Idea of the Self: Thought and Experience in Western Europe since the Seventeenth Century*. Cambridge: Cambridge University Press, 2005.

Siegel, Kristi, ed. *Gender, Genre, and Identity in Women's Travel Writing.* New York: Peter Lang, 2004.
Sklar, Kathryn Kish, and James Stewart, eds. *Women's Rights and Transatlantic Antislavery in the Era of Emancipation.* New Haven: Yale University Press, 2007.
Smith, Harold F. *American Travelers Abroad: A Bibliography of Accounts Published before 1900.* 2nd ed. Lanham, MD: Scarecrow Press, 1999.
Spitzer, Alan B. *The French Generation of 1820.* Princeton: Princeton University Press, 1987.
Steadman, Jennifer Bernhardt. *Traveling Economies: American Women's Travel Writing.* Columbus: Ohio State University Press, 2007.
Stoffelen, Arie, and Dimitri Ioannides, eds. *Handbook of Tourism Impacts: Social and Environmental Perspectives.* Northampton, MA: Edward Elgar Publishers, 2022.
Stowe, William W. *Going Abroad: European Travel in Nineteenth-Century American Culture.* Princeton: Princeton University Press, 1994.
Strumingher, Laura S. *The Odyssey of Flora Tristan.* New York: P. Lang, 1988.
Subrahmanyam, Sanjay. *Three Ways to Be Alien: Travails and Encounters in the Early Modern World.* Waltham, MA: Brandeis University Press, 2011.
Taylor, Charles. *Sources of the Self: The Making of the Modern Identity.* Cambridge, MA: Harvard University Press, 1989.
Torpey, John. *The Invention of the Passport: Surveillance, Citizenship and the State.* 2nd ed. Cambridge: Cambridge University Press, 2018.
Turner, Sasha. *Contested Bodies: Pregnancy, Childrearing, and Slavery in Jamaica.* Philadelphia: University of Pennsylvania Press, 2017.
Ulrich, Laurel Thatcher. *A House Full of Females: Plural Marriages and Women's Rights in Early Mormonism, 1835–1870.* New York: Alfred A. Knopf, 2017.
Urry, John. *The Tourist Gaze.* 2nd ed. Thousand Oaks, CA: Sage, 2002.
Vespucci, Amerigo. *Letters from a New World: Amerigo Vespucci's Discovery of America.* Edited and with an introduction by Luciano Formisano and foreword by Garry Wills. Translated by David Jacobson. New York: Marsilio, 1992.
Voltaire. *Letters on England.* Translated by Leonard Tancock. London: Penguin Press, 2005.
Yothers, Brian. *The Romance of the Holy Land in American Travel Writing, 1790–1876.* Burlington, VT: Ashgate, 2007.
Youngs, Tim. *The Cambridge Introduction to Travel Writing.* Cambridge: Cambridge University Press, 2013.
Ziff, Larzer. *Return Passages: Great American Travel Writing, 1780–1910.* New Haven: Yale University Press, 2000.

Articles and Book Chapters on Travel, Travel Writing, Transnational Experiences, Identities, and Nineteenth-Century Atlantic Cultures

"AHR Conversation: On Transnational History." *American Historical Review* 111, no. 5 (2006): 1440–64.
Avallone, Charlene. "Circles around George Sand: Margaret Fuller and the Dynamics of Transnational Reception." In *Margaret Fuller and Her Circles,* edited by Brigitte Bailey, Katherine P. Viens, and Conrad Edick Wright, 206–28. Durham: University of New Hampshire Press, 2013.
Bendixen, Alfred. "American Travel Books about Europe before the Civil War." In *The*

Cambridge Companion to American Travel Writing, edited by Alfred Bendixen and Judith Hamera, 103–26. Cambridge: Cambridge University Press, 2009.

Brown, A. W. "Jacquemont et l'Inde anglaise." In *Jacquemont*, edited by the Muséum national d'histoire naturelle, 365–428. Paris: Muséum national d'histoire naturelle, 1959.

Brusky, Sarah. "Nancy Prince and Her Gothic Odyssey: A Veiled Lady." In *Gender, Genre, and Identity in Women's Travel Writing*, edited by Kristi Siegel, 167–180. New York: P. Lang, 2004.

Callard, Agnes. "The Case against Travel." *New Yorker*, 24 June 2023. https://www.newyorker.com/culture/the-weekend-essay/the-case-against-travel

Caplan, Jane. "'This or That Particular Person': Protocols of Identification in Nineteenth-Century Europe." In *Documenting Individual Identity: The Development of State Practices in the Modern World*, edited by Jane Caplan and John Torpey, 49–66. Princeton: Princeton University Press, 2001.

Capper, Charles. "Getting from Here to There: Margaret Fuller's American Transnational Odyssey." In *Transatlantic Crossings in a Revolutionary Age*, edited by Charles Capper and Cristina Giorcelli, 3–26. Madison: University of Wisconsin Press, 2007.

Chinard, Gilbert. "Les expériences américaines de Victor Jacquemont." In *Jacquemont*, edited by the Muséum national d'histoire naturelle, 139–98. Paris: Muséum national d'histoire naturelle, 1959.

Collins, Jacob. "French Liberalism's 'Indian Detour': Louis Dumont, the Individual, and Liberal Political Thought in Post-1968 France." *Modern Intellectual History* 12, no. 3 (2015): 685–710.

Craiutu, Aurelian. "A Precursor of Tocqueville: Victor Jacquemont's Reflections on America." In *America through European Eyes: British and French Reflections on the New World from the Eighteenth Century to the Present*, edited by Aurelian Craiutu and Jeffrey C. Isaac, 117–41. University Park: Pennsylvania State University Press, 2009.

Cuche, Denys. "Le Perou de Flora: Du rêve à la réalité." In *Un fabuleux destin: Flora Tristan*, edited by Stéphane Michaud, 19–37. Dijon: Editions universitaires de Dijon, 1985.

Culler, Jonathan. "The Semiotics of Tourism." In *Framing the Sign: Criticism and Its Institutions*, 153–67. Norman: University of Oklahoma Press, 1988.

Derrida, Jacques. "White Mythology: Metaphor in the Text of Philosophy." In *Margins of Philosophy*, 207–72. Translated with additional notes by Alan Bass. Chicago: University of Chicago Press, 1982.

Eckel, Leslie Elizabeth. "Radical Innocence: Margaret Fuller's Utopian Rome." *Transatlantica, Revue d'études américaines* 2 (2015). Accessed 19 August 2023. https://journals.openedition.org/transatlantica/7754.

Forsdick, Charles. "Travel Writing in French." In *The Cambridge History of Travel Writing*, edited by Nandini Das and Tim Youngs, 236–51. Cambridge: Cambridge University Press, 2019.

Foster, Amber. "Nancy Prince's Utopias: Reimagining the African American Utopian Tradition." *Utopian Studies* 24, no. 2 (2013): 329–48.

Frank, Albert J. von. "Margaret Fuller and Antislavery: 'A Cause Identical.'" In *Margaret Fuller and Her Circles*, edited by Brigitte Bailey, Katherine P. Viens, and Conrad Edick Wright, 128–147. Durham: University of New Hampshire Press, 2013.

Gabaude, Florence. "*Les Pérégrinations d'une paria*: initiation, observation, révélation." *French Review* 71, no. 5 (1998): 809–19.

Gerzina, Gretchen Holbrook. "Mobility in Chains: Freedom of Movement in the Early Black Atlantic." *South Atlantic Quarterly* 100, no. 1 (Winter 2001): 41–59.

Gower, Herschel. "Tennessee Writers Abroad, 1851: Henry Maney and Randal W. McGavock." *Tennessee Historical Quarterly* 26 (1967): 396–403.

Green, Nancy L. "The Comparative Gaze: Travelers in France before the Era of Mass Tourism." *French Historical Studies* 25, no. 3 (2002): 423–40.

Grogan, Susan. "'Playing the Princess': Flora Tristan, Performance, and Female Moral Authority during the July Monarchy." In *The New Biography: Performing Femininity in Nineteenth-Century France*, edited by Jo Burr Margadant, 72–98. Berkeley: University of California Press, 2000.

Guentner, Wendelin. "Nineteenth-Century Travel Writing." In *The Cambridge History of French Literature*, edited by William Burgwinkle, Nicholas Hammond, and Emma Wilson, 504–12. Cambridge: Cambridge University Press, 2011.

Gunning, Sandra. "Nancy Prince and the Politics of Mobility, Home and Diasporic (Mis) Identification." *American Quarterly* 53, no. 1 (March 2001): 32–69.

Healey, Kathleen. "'The Mighty Meaning of the Scene': Feminine Landscapes and the Future of America in Margaret Fuller's *Summer on the Lakes in 1843*." *Humanities* 8 (2019): 31. https://www.mdpi.com/2076-0787/8/1/31.

Jennings, Jeremy. "French Visions of America: From Tocqueville to the Civil War." In *America through European Eyes: British and French Reflections on the New World from the Eighteenth Century to the Present*, edited by Aurelian Craiutu and Jeffrey C. Isaac, 161–84. University Park: Pennsylvania State University Press, 2009.

Johnson, Jeffrey Ogden. "Determining and Defining 'Wife': The Brigham Young Households." *Dialogue: A Journal of Mormon Thought* 20, no. 3 (1987): 57–70.

Kramer, Lloyd. "Historical Narratives and the Meaning of Nationalism." *Journal of the History of Ideas* 58 (1997): 525–45.

Law-Sullivan, Jennifer. "Liberté, Égalité, Sororité: Flora Tristan and the Contact Zone between Race and Gender." *Nineteenth-Century French Studies* 39, no. 1–2 (2010–11): 62–76.

McCall, Anne E. "Still Life and Fetal Exploits in Flora Tristan's *Pérégrinations d'une paria*." *Romantic Review* 98, no. 1 (2007): 83–101.

Mehren, Joan von. "Margaret Fuller, the Marchese Giovanni Ossoli, and the Marriage Question: Considering the Research of Dr. Roberto Colzi." *Resources for American Literary Study* 30 (2005): 104–43.

Michaud, Stéphane. "Flora Tristan Américaine." *Romantic Review* 98, no. 1 (2007): 7–21.

Miller, Joseph C. "A Historical Appreciation for the Biographical Turn." In *Biography and the Black Atlantic*, edited by Lisa A. Lindsay and John Wood Sweet, 19–47. Philadelphia: University of Pennsylvania Press, 2014.

Monicat, Bénédicte. "Ecritures du voyage et féminismes: Olympe Audouard ou le féminin en question." *French Review* 69, no. 1 (1995): 24–36.

Moyn, Samuel, and Andrew Sartori. "Approaches to Global Intellectual History." In *Global Intellectual History*, edited by Samuel Moyn and Andrew Sartori, 3–30. New York: Columbia University Press, 2013.

Nerio, Magdelana. "A Transcendentalist Abroad: Margaret Fuller's European Correspondence." *Prose Studies* 33, no. 2 (2011): 102–116.

Nuñez, Rachel. "Between France and the World: Cosmopolitanism and Nationalism in the Work of Flora Tristan." *Proceedings of the Western Society for French History* [now the *Journal of the Western Society for French History*] 34 (2006): 162–76.

———. "Rethinking Universalism: Olympe Audouard, Hubertine Auclert, and the Gender Politics of the Civilizing Mission." *French Politics, Culture and Society* 30, no. 1 (2012): 23–45.

Obenzinger, Hilton. "Americans in the Holy Land, Israel, and Palestine." In *The Cambridge Companion to American Travel Writing*, edited by Alfred Bendixen and Judith Hamera, 145–64. Cambridge: Cambridge University Press, 2009.

Parfit, Derek. "Personal Identity." *Philosophical Review* 80, no. 1 (1971): 3–27.

Phillips, Ursula. "Apocalyptic Feminism: Adam Mickiewicz and Margaret Fuller." *Slavonic and East European Review* 87, no. 1 (2009): 1–38.

Roberson, Susan L. "American Women and Travel Writing." In *The Cambridge Companion to American Travel Writing*, edited by Alfred Bendixen and Judith Hamera, 214–27. Cambridge: Cambridge University Press, 2009.

Rochford, Thomas M. "Father Nicolas Point: Missionary and Artist." *Oregon Historical Quarterly* 97, no 1 (1996): 46–69.

Scott, Joan W. "The Evidence of Experience." *Critical Inquiry* 17, no. 4 (1991): 773–97.

Smith, Virginia Whatley. "African American Travel Literature." In *The Cambridge Companion to American Travel Writing*, edited by Alfred Bendixen and Judith Hamera, 197–213. Cambridge: Cambridge University Press, 2009.

Steele, Jeffrey. "Margaret Fuller." In *American Travel Writers, 1776–1864*, edited by James Schramer and Donald Ross, 126–138. Detroit: Gale Research, 1997.

Stowe, William W. "'Property in the Horizon': Landscape and American Travel Writing." In *The Cambridge Companion to American Travel Writing*, edited by Alfred Bendixen and Judith Hamera, 26–45. Cambridge: Cambridge University Press, 2009.

Thompson, Carl. "Nineteenth-Century Travel Writing." In *The Cambridge History of Travel Writing*, edited by Nandini Das and Tim Youngs, 108–24. Cambridge: Cambridge University Press, 2019.

Torpey, John. "The Great War and the Birth of the Modern Passport System." In *Documenting Individual Identity: The Development of State Practices in the Modern World*, edited by Jane Caplan and John Torpey, 256–70. Princeton: Princeton University Press, 2001.

Tuchinsky, Adam-Max. "'More Anon': American Socialism and Margaret Fuller's 1848." In *Margaret Fuller and Her Circles*, edited by Brigitte Bailey, Katherine P. Viens, and Conrad Edick Wright, 100–27. Durham: University of New Hampshire Press, 2013.

UN World Tourism Organization. *UNWTO World Tourism Barometer* 18, no. 1 (January 2020) (excerpt). https://www.e-unwto.org/doi/abs/10.18111/wtobarometereng.2020.18.1.1.

Vergereau-Dewey, S. Pascale. "*Pérégrinations d'une paria* de Flora Tristan: Novelogue d'une rebelle visionnaire et militante." In *Rebelles et criminelles chez les écrivains d'expression française*, edited by Fréderique Chevillot and Colette Trout, 75–94. Amsterdam: Rodopi, 2013.

Walters, Ronald G. "Introduction." In *A Black Woman's Odyssey through Russia and Jamaica: The Narrative of Nancy Prince*, ix–xxiii. New York: Markus Wiener, 2009.

Williams, Erin E. "These Must-Read Books Will Make Your Travel Greener." *Washington Post*, July 14, 2022.

INDEX